Multiculturalism and The Welfare State

Multiculturalism and The Welfare State: Recognition and redistribution in contemporary democracies

Edited by
Keith Banting and Will Kymlicka

OXFORD
UNIVERSITY PRESS

OXFORD
UNIVERSITY PRESS

Great Clarendon Street, Oxford OX2 6DP

Oxford University Press is a department of the University of Oxford.
It furthers the University's objective of excellence in research, scholarship,
and education by publishing worldwide in

Oxford New York

Auckland Cape Town Dar es Salaam Hong Kong Karachi
Kuala Lumpur Madrid Melbourne Mexico City Nairobi
New Delhi Shanghai Taipei Toronto

With offices in

Argentina Austria Brazil Chile Czech Republic France Greece
Guatemala Hungary Italy Japan Poland Portugal Singapore
South Korea Switzerland Thailand Turkey Ukraine Vietnam

Oxford is a registered trade mark of Oxford University Press
in the UK and in certain other countries

Published in the United States
by Oxford University Press Inc., New York

British Library Cataloguing in Publication Data
Data available

Library of Congress Cataloging in Publication Data
Data available

Typeset by SPi Publisher Services, Pondicherry, India
Printed in Great Britain
on acid-free paper by
Biddles Ltd., King's Lynn

ISBN 0–19–928917–4   978–0–19–928917–2 (hbk)
ISBN 0–19–928918–2   978–0–19–928918–9 (pbk)

1 3 5 7 9 10 8 6 4 2

Acknowledgements

The origins of this volume date back to a paper we presented in Brussels at a conference on Cultural Diversity versus Economic Solidarity, organized in honour of Philippe van Parijs. The rich debates at that conference confirmed our sense that the questions swirling around the relationship between multicultural diversity and redistribution represented a compelling research agenda and we invited a distinguished group of scholars to pursue the issues in this book. We are grateful they agreed to join us.

We have accumulated many debts along the way. For helpful comments and suggestions regarding our index of multicultural policies and categorization of countries, we would like to thank James Anaya, Rainer Bauböck, Meyer Burstein, Joseph Carens, Stephen Castles, Adrian Favell, Augie Fleras, Donald Forbes, Montserrat Guibernau, Duncan Ivison, Christian Joppke, Michael Keating, Jacob Levy, Ruth Rubio, and Neus Torbisco. For assistance with data on redistribution from the Luxembourg Income Study, we thank David Jesuit and Vince Mahler. For thoughtful questions and comments on our initial paper at a number of conferences and colloquia, we are grateful to Peter Evans, Alexander Hicks, Justine Lacroix, David Laitin, David Miller, John Myles, Neus Torbisco, Philippe Van Parijs, and Jonathan Wolff. Thanks are also due to Heather Andersen, Erich Hartmann, Patti Lenard, and Lisa Vanhala for research assistance.

First drafts of the papers in this book were presented at a workshop held at Queen's University. For perceptive comments on the papers, we thank Catherine Conaghan, Thomas Faist, John McGarry, and Melissa Williams. Valerie Jarus helped prepare the manuscript, meticulously integrating the idiosyncratic styles of authors from many countries and disciplines. At Oxford University Press, we are indebted to Dominic Byatt for his enthusiasm for the project, and to Edwin Pritchard for his careful copy-editing.

Acknowledgements

We also wish to acknowledge funding support from a number of organizations. Keith Banting thanks the Social Sciences and Humanities Research Council of Canada and the Research Chairs Program of Queen's University. Will Kymlicka thanks the Canadian Institute for Advanced Research.

Our final thanks are to Marilyn Banting and Sue Donaldson. For everything.

KB
WK

Queen's University
Kingston Ontario

Contents

Contents

Part III. Theoretical reflections

Notes on contributors

Willem Assies is an anthropologist and senior researcher at the Van Vollenhoven Institute of the Faculty of Law of Leiden University in the Netherlands. He is currently coordinator of a research project on the socio-legal aspects of land tenure security in various countries in Africa, Asia, and Latin America. He has published extensively in both Spanish and English on indigenous and other issues in Latin America. He is co-editor of *The Challenge of Diversity: Indigenous Peoples and Reform of the State in Latin America* (Thela, 2000), and of *Citizenship, Political Culture and State Transformation in Latin America* (Dutch University Press, 2005). His most recent monograph is *Crisis in Bolivia: The Elections of 2002 and their Aftermath* (Institute of Latin American Studies, 2003).

Keith Banting is Queen's Research Professor in Public Policy in the School of Policy Studies and the Department of Political Studies at Queen's University. His research interests focus on the politics of public policy, especially social policy. He is the author of *Poverty, Politics and Policy: Britain in the 1960s* (Macmillan, 1979), and *The Welfare State and Canadian Federalism* (McGill-Queen's University Press, 1987). He is also the editor or co-editor of another fourteen books dealing with politics, political institutions, and social policy. Among these edited books are *The Politics of Constitutional Change in Industrial Nations* (Macmillan, 1985); The *State and Economic Interests* (University of Toronto Press, 1986); *Degrees of Freedom: Canada and the United States in a Changing World* (McGill-Queen's University Press, 1997), and *Health Policy and Federalism: A Comparative Perspective on Multi-Level Governance* (McGill-Queen's University Press, 2002).

Markus Crepaz is Associate Professor in the School of Public and International Affairs at the University of Georgia, and Associate Director of GLOBIS (Center for the Study of Global Issues). He finished his Ph.D. in political science at the University of California, San Diego, in 1992, and since 1993 has been a faculty member at the University of Georgia. His research focus is comparative politics, particularly comparative political economy and institutions, West European Politics, research methods, and social theory. He is the author of *Trust without Borders: Immigration, the Welfare State and Identity in Modern Societies*, forthcoming from University of Michigan Press, co-author with Jurg Steiner of *European Democracies*, 5th edition, forthcoming from Longman-Pearson; and co-editor *of Democracy and Institutions: The Life Work of Arend Lijphart* (University of Michigan Press, 2000).

Han Entzinger is Professor of Migration and Integration Studies and Head of the Department of Sociology at Erasmus University Rotterdam. His research interests include international migration, social and economic integration, multiculturalism, and comparative policy evaluation. He is past president (1994–2002) of the Research Committee on Migration of the International Sociological Association. Over many years his publications have been influential in shaping integration policy in the Netherlands. He is also an adviser to the European Union and the Council of Europe. His latest book in English is *Migration between States and Markets* (Ashgate, 2004; with Marco Martiniello and Catherine Wihtol de Wenden, eds.). Other English-language publications include chapters on Dutch integration and citizenship policy in Christian Joppke and Ewa Morawska (eds.), *Toward Assimilation and Citizenship: Immigrants in Liberal Nation-States* (Palgrave, 2004); Paul Statham and Ruud Koopmans (eds.), *Challenging Immigration and Ethnic Relations Politics: Comparative European Perspectives* (Oxford University Press, 2001); Robin Cohen (ed.), *Cambridge Survey of World Migration* (Cambridge University Press, 1995), and Bernard Lewis and Dominique Schnapper (eds.), *Muslims in Europe* (Pinter, 1994).

Geoffrey Evans is Official Fellow in Politics, Nuffield College, and Professor of the Sociology of Politics and Director of the Centre for Research Methods in the Social Sciences, University of Oxford. His research interests include the analysis of electoral behaviour and political attitudes, democratization and party system formation in transition democracies, and the relation between social structure and politics. He is the editor of *The End of Class Politics?* (Oxford University Press, 1999), editor (with Pippa Norris) of *Critical Elections* (Sage, 1999), and editor (with Harold Clarke) of the journal *Electoral Studies*. He publishes widely in professional journals including the *Annual Review of Political Science, Annual Review of Sociology, British Journal of Political Science, British Journal of Sociology, Comparative Political Studies, Electoral Studies, European Sociological Review, Journal of Politics, Parliamentary Affairs, Political Studies, Social Science*

Research, Sociology, and many others, as well as in numerous edited collections.

Rodney E. Hero is the Packey J. Dee Professor of American Democracy in the Department of Political Science at the University of Notre Dame. He specializes in US politics, with particular attention to Latino and ethnic/minority politics, state/urban politics, and federalism. His book, *Latinos and the U.S. Political System* (Temple University Press, 1992), received the American Political Science Association's Ralph J. Bunche Award ('best scholarly work in political science published in the previous year which explores the phenomenon of ethnic and cultural pluralism'). He also authored *Faces of Inequality: Social Diversity in American Politics* (Oxford University Press, 2000), which was selected for the American Political Science Association's Woodrow Wilson Foundation Award ('best book published on government, politics, or international affairs'). He has served on the editorial boards of such political science journals as the *American Political Science Review, American Journal of Political Science, Journal of Politics, Political Research Quarterly, Urban Affairs Review,* and *Political Behavior.* He is also Chair of the Political Science Department at Notre Dame.

Matt James received his BA from Queen's University at Kingston and his MA and Ph.D. from the University of British Columbia. He is currently Assistant Professor in the Department of Political Science at the University of Victoria. A student of social movements, constitutionalism, and citizenship, he is presently conducting a multi-year research project that studies reparations movements as a window on Canadian social movements and citizenship in an era of neo-liberalization. Results of this research have already been published in the *Canadian Journal of Political Science* and a number of edited collections. His book, *Misrecognized Materialists: Social Movements in Canadian Constitutional Politics, 1938–1992,* is forthcoming in 2006 from University of British Columbia Press.

Richard Johnston is Professor of Political Science and Research Director of the National Annenberg Election Study of the University of Pennsylvania. He is author or co-author of *Public Opinion and Public Policy in Canada* (University of Toronto Press, 1986); *Letting the People Decide* (McGill-Queen's University Press and Stanford University Press, 1992); *The Challenge of Direct Democracy* (McGill-Queen's University Press, 1996); *The 2000 Presidential Election and the Foundations of Party Politics* (Cambridge University Press, 2004); and *The End of Southern Exceptionalism: Class, Race,* *and Partisan Change in the Postwar South* (Harvard University Press, 2006). He has also published articles in the *Canadian Journal of Political Science, American Journal of Political Science, British Journal of Political Science, Journal of Politics, Electoral Studies,* and other journals; and chapters in numerous edited volumes. *Letting the People Decide* won the Harold Adams Innis Prize as the best Canadian book published in English in the social sciences in 1992. He has also won four APSA organized-section best paper prizes. His primary research focus has been on elections and public opinion, recently with a special emphasis on media effects in campaigns. He also has a long-standing interest in the connections among social capital, civil society, and support for the welfare state.

Peter A. Kraus is a professor based at CEREN (Centre for Research on Ethnic Relations and Nationalism), Swedish School of Social Science, University of Helsinki. He has previously been an associate professor of political science at Humboldt University in Berlin, a Kennedy Fellow at the Center for European Studies at Harvard University, and a Heuss Visiting Lecturer at the New School in New York. He has written exten-sively on cultural pluralism, nationalism, and democracy in the European context. This includes two monographs published in German: *National-ismus und Demokratie: Politik im spanischen Staat der Autonomen Gemein-schaften* (Nationalism and Democracy: Politics in the Spanish State of the Autonomous Communities, DUV, 1996) and *Europäische Öffentlichkeit und Sprachpolitik* (The European Public Sphere and Language Policy, Campus, 2004); an updated English version of the latter is in preparation for Cam-bridge University Press. Among his English-language articles are: 'Political Unity and Linguistic Diversity in Europe', *Archives Européennes de Sociologie* (2000) and 'Cultural Pluralism and European Polity-Building', *Journal of Common Market Studies* (2003).

Will Kymlicka is the author of five books published by Oxford University Press: *Liberalism, Community, and Culture* (1989), *Contemporary Political Philosophy* (1990; second edition 2002), *Multicultural Citizenship* (1995), which was awarded the Macpherson Prize by the Canadian Political Sci-ence Association, and the Bunche Award by the American Political Science Association, *Finding our Way: Rethinking Ethnocultural Relations in Canada* (1998); and *Politics in the Vernacular* (2001). He is also the editor of *Justice in Political Philosophy* (Elgar, 1992), *The Rights of Minority Cultures* (OUP, 1995), and co-editor of *Ethnicity and Group Rights* (NYU Press, 1997), *Citi-zenship in Diverse Societies* (OUP, 2000), *Can Liberal Pluralism Be Exported?* (OUP, 2001), and *Language Rights and Political Theory* (OUP, 2003). He is currently the Canada Research Chair in Political Philosophy at Queen's University.

Nicola McEwen is Lecturer in Politics in the School of Social and Political Studies at the University of Edinburgh. Her main research interests include comparative nationalism and territorial politics, and the politics of devolution in the UK, and she has published widely in these fields. Recent publications include *Nationalism and the State: Welfare and Identity in Scotland and Quebec* (Regionalism and Federalism Book Series, IEP/Peter Lang, 2006), and an edited collection (with Luis Moreno), *The Territorial Politics of Welfare* (Routledge, 2006). She is an Associate Director of the Institute of Governance, and Co-Convenor of the PSA specialist group on British and Comparative Territorial Politics.

David Miller is Professor of Political Theory at Nuffield College, Oxford. His most recent books include *On Nationality* (Oxford University Press, 1995); *Principles of Social Justice* (Harvard University Press, 1999), and *Citizenship and National Identity* (Polity Press, 2000). He is a Fellow of the British Academy, and co-editor of the Oxford Political Theory series. He is currently completing a book on national responsibility and global justice, and continues to work on problems of social justice in multicultural societies.

John Myles holds a Canada Research Chair in the Department of Sociology, University of Toronto. His research interests focus on the political economy of the welfare state in Western nations. He is the author or co-author of *Old Age in the Welfare State* (Little, Brown, 1984); *Relations of Ruling: Class and Gender in Postindustrial Societies* (McGill-Queens University Press, 1994); and *Why We Need a New Welfare State* (Oxford University Press, 2002); and he is co-editor of *States, Labour Markets and the Future of Old Age Policy* (Temple University Press, 1991). He has served on the editorial boards of the *American Journal of Sociology*, *Contemporary Sociology*, *Canadian Journal of Sociology*, and *Journal of Ageing Studies*. He is the recipient of the 1991 Distinguished Scholar Award of the American Sociological Association, Section on Ageing, and the Harold Adam Innis Award (Best Book in Canadian Social Sciences) from the Social Science Federation of Canada.

Robert R. Preuhs is an instructor in the Department of Political Science at the University of Colorado at Boulder. His research interests focus on racial and ethnic diversification and the ability of formal democratic institutions to incorporate, and respond to, the interests of racial and ethnic minority groups in the United States. His work on these and other topics has been published in the *Journal of Politics*, *Political Research Quarterly*, *Social Science Quarterly*, *Electoral Studies*, and *State Politics and Policy Quarterly*, among others.

Karen Schönwälder is a political scientist and currently head of the Programme on Intercultural Conflicts and Societal Integration at the Social Science Research Centre Berlin. Her research interests include migration policy and more generally the migratory experience in Germany and Britain, the ideology and practice of New Labour, and the history of German universities and academia. She is a co-editor of two books in English: *European Encounters: Migrants, Migration and European Societies since 1945* (Ashgate, 2003), with Rainer Ohliger and Triadafilos Triadafilopoulos; and *The German Lands and Eastern Europe: Essays on the History of their Social, Cultural and Political Relations* (Macmillan, 1999), with Roger Bartlett. In addition, she has published an extensive series of papers and chapters on related issues in both English and German, including most recently 'Why Germany's Guestworkers were largely European: The Selective Principles of Post-war Labour Recruitment Policy', *Ethnic and Racial Studies*, 27(2) (2004).

Stuart Soroka is an Associate Professor and William Dawson Scholar in the Department of Political Science at McGill University. He is the author of *Agenda-Setting Dynamics in Canada* (University of British Columbia Press, 2002), and has articles appearing in the *Journal of Politics*, the *British Journal of Political Science*, and the *Canadian Journal of Political Science*. His research interests include policy responsiveness in democratic systems, and the relationships between ethnicity, trust, and support for the welfare state. In this second area, he is the co-author of papers with Keith Banting and Richard Johnston on 'Ethnicity, Trust and the Welfare State' and 'Immigration and Redistribution in the Global Era', both appearing in edited collections.

Sébastien St-Arnaud is a Ph.D. candidate in sociology at the University of Toronto. His primary research interests include welfare regimes and production regimes, and in particular differences between regions at the subnational level. He is also currently researching whether institutional characteristics of advanced democracies can account for national variation in welfare attitudes.

Donna Lee Van Cott is an Associate Professor of Political Science at Tulane University. She is the author of *From Movements to Parties: The Evolution of*

Ethnic Politics in Latin America (Cambridge University Press, 2005), *The Friendly Liquidation of the Past: The Politics of Diversity in Latin America* (University of Pittsburgh Press, 2000), and editor of *Indigenous Peoples and Democracy in Latin America* (St Martin's, 1994). Her articles on ethnic politics and democratization have been published in journals that include *Comparative Political Studies, Democratization, Journal of Latin American Studies,* and *Studies in Comparative International Development.* She is writing a book on radical democracy in the Andes, which examines experiments by indigenous political parties in designing innovative local institutions.

1

Introduction
Multiculturalism and the welfare state: Setting the context

Keith Banting and Will Kymlicka

The past thirty years have witnessed a dramatic change in the way many Western democracies deal with issues of ethnocultural diversity. In the past, ethnocultural diversity was often seen as a threat to political stability, and hence as something to be discouraged by public policies. Immigrants, national minorities, and indigenous peoples were all subject to a range of policies intended to either assimilate or marginalize them.

During the last decades of the twentieth century, however, many Western democracies abandoned these earlier policies, and shifted towards a more accommodating approach to diversity. This is reflected, for example, in the widespread adoption of multiculturalism policies for immigrant groups, the acceptance of territorial autonomy and language rights for national minorities, and the recognition of land claims and self-government rights for indigenous peoples.

We will refer to all such policies as 'multiculturalism policies' or MCPs. This term covers a very wide range of policies, and we will discuss some of the important differences between them in Chapter 2. But what they all have in common is that they go beyond the protection of the basic civil and political rights guaranteed to all individuals in a liberal-democratic state, to also extend some level of public recognition and support for ethnocultural minorities to maintain and express their distinct identities and practices.

The adoption of MCPs has been and remains controversial, for a variety of reasons. One line of critique has been philosophical. Critics argue that

MCPs are inherently inconsistent with basic liberal-democratic principles. MCPs are said to contradict principles of individual freedom (because they privilege 'group rights' over 'individual rights') and/or principles of equality (because they treat people differently on the basis of race or ethnicity). Defenders of MCPs respond that these policies often enhance the choice of individuals, by making available options that would not otherwise be available, and promote the equality of citizens, by removing barriers and contesting stigmas that disadvantage members of ethnic and racial minorities.

This philosophical debate about the moral foundations of multiculturalism dominated the academic literature in the 1980s and early 1990s, and remains a source of ongoing controversy. However, it has recently been supplemented, and to some extent supplanted, by a range of more sociological concerns about the unintended effects of MCPs. In this volume, we examine one such set of concerns: namely, that adopting MCPs makes it more difficult to sustain a robust welfare state. On this view, there is a trade-off in practice between a commitment to MCPs and a commitment to the welfare state. Critics generally acknowledge that defenders of MCPs do not *intend* to weaken the welfare state. On the contrary, most defenders of MCPs are also strong defenders of the welfare state, and view both as flowing from the same underlying principle of justice. The conflict between MCPs and the welfare state, therefore, is not so much a matter of competing ideals or principles, but of unintended sociological dynamics. MCPs, critics worry, gradually erode the interpersonal trust, social solidarity, and political coalitions that sustain the welfare state.[1]

This is not of course the only sort of concern that has been raised about the effects of MCPs. Some have expressed concern that they slow the incorporation of immigrant minorities into the economic and social mainstream, and lead to their isolation or segregation. In recent years, several European states, including the Netherlands and Britain, have concluded that older models of multiculturalism did not do enough to ensure the economic and political integration of immigrants, and that new pro-integration policies are required. However, there is disagreement about whether these new policies should be seen as *alternatives* to MCPs or

---

[1] These complaints often go together. People who view MCPs as rooted in an illiberal philosophy are also likely to assert that MCPs have a corrosive effect on the welfare state. But the two critiques are logically separate. There are some people who argue that MCPs are consistent with basic liberal-democratic values, yet who share the fear that they are eroding the welfare state (e.g. Phillips 1999). Conversely, there are some authors who dispute the philosophical arguments for many MCPs, yet who deny that they negatively impact the welfare state (e.g. Galston 2001).

as necessary *supplements* to them. The current British approach operates primarily on the latter assumption, and the Netherlands on the former (Hansen, forthcoming; Joppke, forthcoming).

More alarming, particularly since 9/11, is the prospect that multiculturalism policies may have unintentionally created spaces for radical religious and political movements to operate, creating a threat to the safety of citizens and the security of the state. In the name of promoting inclusion and tolerance, multiculturalism policies may have created institutional structures within minority communities (like schools, media, community organizations) that have been captured by fundamentalist groups committed to attacking the liberal-democratic order. In contrast, some experts argue that multiculturalism policies make it less likely that such fundamentalist groups will take root, since the state is better able to monitor and influence minority institutions that have been set up under the aegis of multiculturalist public policies. On this view, terrorist cells are more likely to arise in countries where the state takes a hands-off attitude to the religious and cultural organizations of minority groups (Keeble 2005).

These debates about the link between MCPs, economic and political integration, and national security are sometimes more dramatic than concerns about the gradual erosion of the welfare state. However, the latter is arguably of wider significance. To date, for example, security concerns in the West have largely focused on Muslim immigrants. The welfare state concern, by contrast, has been raised more widely, in relation to MCPs for a broad range of ethnic and racial minorities.

Indeed, part of the reason why the link between MCPs and the welfare state has become such a lively topic of debate is that it fits into a broader debate about the impact of ethnic and racial diversity as such on social solidarity and on the welfare state. Concerns about MCPs are often interwoven with concerns about the effects of ethnic and racial diversity on the redistributive role of the state.

These two concerns—about the impact of racial and ethnic diversity as such, and about the impact of multiculturalism policies—are often lumped together, but it is important to keep them distinct. A growing chorus of researchers and commentators argue that ethnic/racial diversity makes it more difficult to sustain redistributive policies, regardless of the types of policies that governments adopt to manage that diversity. Such arguments assume that it is inherently difficult to generate feelings of national solidarity and trust across ethnic/racial lines, and that the very presence of sizeable ethnic/racial diversity erodes the welfare state. We will call this the 'heterogeneity/redistribution trade-off' hypothesis.

Such fears are often reinforced by concerns that the 'multiculturalism' policies adopted to recognize or accommodate ethnic groups tend to further undermine national solidarity and trust. The underlying hypothesis here is that there is a trade-off between recognition and redistribution; the more a country embraces the 'politics of (ethnic) recognition', the harder it is to sustain the 'politics of (economic) redistribution'. We will call this the 'recognition/redistribution trade-off' hypothesis.

In effect, the first hypothesis argues that the very presence of sizeable ethnic/racial diversity erodes the welfare state, regardless of what sorts of policies governments adopt to manage that diversity. The second hypothesis argues that the typical way in which many Western governments today attempt to manage diversity—namely, by attempting to accommodate it through multiculturalism policies, rather than ignoring or suppressing it—worsens the problem.

If these hypotheses are true, we face a serious and growing problem, because there is no reason to expect either that ethnic/racial minorities will diminish as a percentage of the overall population in most Western countries, or that these groups will abandon their claims for multicultural accommodations. On the contrary, there is every reason to expect that minorities will continue to grow as a percentage of the overall population. For example, indigenous peoples are the fastest-growing segment of the population in countries like Canada, the USA, and Australia, with a higher birth rate than the non-indigenous population. Also, immigration into the Western democracies will continue to grow, partly to offset the declining birth rate and ageing population, and partly because there are limits on the state's ability to stop would-be migrants from entering the country. Similarly, there is every reason to expect that minorities, whether they are historically rooted or newer migrants, will continue to press demands for recognition, which grow out of deep forces of contemporary societies.[2]

So if there is a tendency for either ethnic/racial heterogeneity and/or multiculturalism policies to erode the welfare state, the problem is likely to get worse. If either of these hypotheses were true, the very idea of a 'multicultural welfare state'—a welfare state that respects and accommodates diversity—would be almost a contradiction in terms. The redistributive state has been under pressure in recent decades from a number of economic changes: globalization, technological change, demographic

---

[2] For a discussion of these forces, including the post-war human rights revolution, the desecuritization of state-minority relations, and democratization, see Kymlicka (2004).

trends and the ageing of society, shifting ideologies. Should we add growing ethnic diversity, and claims for its accommodation, to this already lengthy list?

This worry has been labelled as the 'progressive's dilemma' (Goodhart 2004; Pearce 2004). Social democrats, it is said, are faced with a tragic trade-off between sustaining their traditional agenda of economic redistribution and embracing ethnocultural diversity and multiculturalism. The belief in such a trade-off is creating a major political realignment on these issues. In the past, most resistance to immigration and multiculturalism came from the right, who viewed them as a threat to cherished national traditions or values. Today, however, opposition to immigration and multiculturalism is also emerging within the left, as a perceived threat to the welfare state.[3]

But is the 'progressive's dilemma' real? Our main goal in this volume is to examine the belief that there is a trade-off between policies of multicultural recognition and policies of economic redistribution. As we shall see below, there is remarkably little evidence in the existing research literature to support such an argument. There is a growing research literature on the impact of ethnic heterogeneity as such, although even here the evidence is very mixed. But there is virtually no systematic research on the impact of MCPs on the welfare state. This volume seeks to help fill this yawning gap.

In the rest of this introduction, we provide an overview of the debate on MCPs and redistribution, outlining the views of the critics who contend that such a policy approach erodes the welfare state. We then go on to survey the evidence that has been developed to date. As we will see, there are many unanswered questions about the conditions under which the heterogeneity/redistribution and recognition/redistribution trade-offs may exist, about the causal mechanisms that underpin them, and about the possible strategies for reducing them. Finally, we describe how the chapters in this volume attempt to fill in some of the important gaps in our knowledge, and identify some critical directions for future research.

The various chapters do not point to a single, simple answer to the question of how multiculturalism policies affect the welfare state. However, they do suggest that concerns about the corrosive effect of MCPs have

---

[3] For an overview of the debates within European social democratic parties on these issues, see Cuperus, Duffek, and Kandel (2003).

been significantly overstated, and that there may indeed be some circumstances where MCPs actually help to strengthen the welfare state.

1. Multiculturalism and the politics of recognition

Despite the various philosophical and sociological concerns that have been raised about the theory and practice of multiculturalism, it remains a powerful force in modern societies. Some critics have expressed the hope that it simply represents a passing fad or fashion (Barry 2001), and others have pointed to evidence of a 'retreat from multiculturalism', and a return to more traditional ideas of homogeneous and unitary republican citizenship, in which ethnocultural diversity is banished from the public realm and relegated to the private sphere (Joppke 2004; Brubaker 2001; Entzinger 2003). In reality, however, multiculturalism has become deeply embedded in the legislation, jurisprudence, and institutions of many Western countries, and indeed in their very self-image. While there has indeed been a retreat from some multiculturalism policies for some types of ethnocultural groups in some countries, these high-profile cases of 'backlash' can blind us to more general trends regarding the accommodation of ethnocultural diversity in the West.

Consider, for example, the case of national minorities. As we will see in Chapters 2 and 9, there has been a clear trend towards greater recognition of non-immigrant substate national groups, often in the form of regional autonomy and official language status. That trend remains untouched: there has been no backlash against the rights of national minorities within the Western democracies. There is no case in the West of a country retreating from any of the accommodations it has accorded to its substate national groups. On the contrary, this trend has been reaffirmed and strengthened by the development of international norms, such as the Framework Convention for the Protection of National Minorities, adopted by the Council of Europe, and comparable declarations by the Organization for Security and Cooperation in Europe.[4]

Or consider the case of indigenous peoples. As we will see in several chapters (2, 8, 10, and 11), there has been a clear trend towards greater recognition of indigenous rights, often in the form of land claims, recognition of customary law, and self-government rights. That trend remains

---

[4] The Convention was adopted in 1995, but the monitoring bodies have adopted a norm of 'progressive implementation' which means that the threshold countries are expected to meet continually rises (Weller 2004).

fully in place, without any measurable backlash or retreat, and it too has been reaffirmed and strengthened by the development of international norms, such as the UN's Draft Declaration on the Rights of Indigenous Peoples, or comparable declarations of indigenous rights by the Organization of American States, the International Labour Organization, or the World Bank.

So there is no across-the-board retreat from multiculturalism. For both substate national groups and indigenous peoples, the trend towards the public recognition and accommodation of ethnocultural diversity remains intact, and indeed is now more firmly entrenched, rooted not only in domestic accommodations and negotiations, but also ratified and protected by international norms.

The retreat from multiculturalism, therefore, is largely restricted to one domain of ethnocultural diversity—namely, immigration. Here, as we will see in Chapters 4–7, there has been a backlash and retreat from multiculturalism policies relating to post-war migrants in some Western democracies. And, unlike the case of national minorities and indigenous peoples, there has been no serious attempt to codify cultural rights for immigrants at the international level. It is an important question why immigrant multiculturalism in particular has come under such attack, to which we will return below. But we can begin by dismissing one popular explanation. As we noted earlier, various commentators have suggested that the retreat from immigrant multiculturalism reflects a return to the traditional liberal belief that ethnicity belongs in the private sphere, that the public sphere should be neutral, and that citizenship should be undifferentiated. On this view, the retreat from immigrant multiculturalism reflects a rejection of the whole idea of a liberal-democratic conception of multiculturalism.

But this cannot be the explanation. If Western democracies were rejecting the very idea of liberal multiculturalism, they would have rejected the claims of substate national groups and indigenous peoples as well as immigrants. After all, the claims of national groups and indigenous peoples typically involve a much more dramatic insertion of ethnocultural diversity into the public sphere, and a more dramatic degree of differentiated citizenship, than is demanded by immigrant groups. Whereas immigrants typically seek modest variations or exemptions in the operation of mainstream institutions, historic national minorities and indigenous peoples typically seek a much wider level of recognition and accommodation, including such things as land claims, self-government powers, language rights, separate educational systems, and even separate legal systems. These claims involve a much more serious challenge to ideas of undifferentiated citizenship and the privatization of ethnicity than is involved in accommodating immigrant groups. Yet Western democracies have not retreated at all from their commitment to accommodating these historic minorities.

Western democracies are, in fact, increasingly comfortable with claims to differentiated citizenship and the public recognition of difference, when these claims are advanced by historic minorities. So it is not the very idea of liberal multiculturalism per se that has come under attack.[5] The backlash, rather, is largely restricted to immigration. And even within the sphere of immigration, the retreat from multiculturalism is far from uniform across countries: it is more pronounced in the Netherlands than Canada, for example. And in many countries, the shift has been greater at the level of rhetoric than actual policies.[6]

Even within a single country, there are important variations in the attitude towards the claims of different immigrant groups. Public debates in many countries distinguish 'good' immigrant groups, who are seen as hard-working and law-abiding and hence deserving of reasonable multicultural accommodations, from 'bad' immigrant groups, who may be seen as illegal or lazy, or as prone to crime, religious fanaticism, or political extremism. When the latter are seen as the prime beneficiaries of multiculturalism, public support for MCPs can dramatically diminish, leading to high-profile cases of 'retreat'.[7]

But even as states seek to curtail the perceived 'excesses' of multiculturalism, they typically emphasize that they are not reverting to older homogenizing and assimilationist models of immigration, and accept the need for public institutions like the schools, media, health care, and police to adapt to deal better with the realities of ethnic diversity. Immigrant groups are no longer expected to hide their ethnic identity in public life, and can expect reasonable forms of recognition and accommodation in public institutions (e.g. in the common school curriculum). In short, talk about a 'retreat from (immigrant) multiculturalism' typically obscures a more complex story in which a few MCPs are curtailed while others become more deeply institutionalized. As with national minorities and

---

[5] Commentators who argue that Western democracies are rejecting liberal culturalism per se typically simply ignore the obvious counter-examples of national minorities and indigenous peoples (see e.g. Joppke 2004; Barry 2001).

[6] For examples of rhetorical shifts that obscure the persistence of MCPs in practice, see Hansen (forthcoming); Schain (1999); and Entzinger's chapter below.

[7] For the importance of these perceptions in explaining public support for immigrant MCPs, see Kymlicka (2004).

indigenous peoples, a baseline level of 'recognition' and 'accommodation' for immigrants has increasingly been accepted as an inevitable and legitimate aspect of life in a liberal democracy.

So there is no single story of 'advance' or 'retreat' of multiculturalism. There are different types of ethnocultural diversity, each raising its own distinctive sorts of multicultural claims, and each with its own trajectories of resistance, acceptance, and backlash. It is important to keep these distinct trajectories in mind, since, as we will see throughout this volume, there is a distressing tendency in the literature to make claims about the negative impact of 'heterogeneity' as such, or of 'multiculturalism' as such, based on the experiences of a single type of group or a single country.

If we think about the impact of these different patterns, multiculturalism is one of the most important social and political trends of the past forty years, remaking states and societies around the world. There are many different explanations for the enduring and pervasive nature of claims for multiculturalism, and many different theories of their normative underpinnings. Some suggest that the aim of multiculturalism should be to create the conditions for a Habermasian ethic of intercultural dialogue (Benhabib 2002) or an inclusive democratic contestation (Williams 1998); others argue that multiculturalism should be founded on the idea of a 'right to culture' (Tamir 1993; Margalit and Halbertal 1994); yet others argue that multiculturalism should be premissed on the Shklarian idea of the avoidance of cruelty (Levy 2000); or on the need of individuals for the recognition of their authentic identities (Taylor 1994); as a precondition for individual autonomy (Kymlicka 1995); or on the idea of tolerance (Kukathas 2003). The philosophical literature contains many sophisticated discussions of these various arguments, all of which attempt to ground ideas of multiculturalism in deeper principles of freedom and democracy. But for our purposes, we can perhaps step back from the details of these arguments, and simply note that on all of these views, the rise of multiculturalism is related to, and an extension of, the modern human rights revolution. The same human rights ideals that inspired the struggle against colonialism, racial segregation, and caste discrimination have also inspired the struggle by other historically disadvantaged ethnocultural groups to contest the lingering manifestations of ethnic and racial hierarchy. Indeed, the modern rhetoric of multiculturalism draws explicitly on the discourses (and strategies) developed during the anticolonial national liberation movements and the African-American civil rights movements, adapting them to the specific needs of different types of groups in different countries. This link between MCPs and human rights norms is often explicitly invoked by legislators and courts in explaining the rationale for various multicultural policies and laws, and is found in international law documents on minority and indigenous rights as well.[8]

This helps explain why multiculturalism should not be dismissed as a passing fad or fashion. While its outer limits are deeply contested, its inner core is inextricably linked to widely accepted norms of freedom, equality, human rights, and democracy. In short, claims for multiculturalism are grounded in some of the most basic principles of justice in contemporary societies. The question for our volume is whether the pursuit of social justice for ethnocultural minorities through MCPs is, unintentionally, weakening society's capacity to pursue the more traditional aspect of social justice relating to economic inequality and disadvantage.

2. The case for a recognition/redistribution trade-off

Why have so many observers argued that there is a trade-off between recognition and redistribution? Critics have speculated about a range of mechanisms by which the adoption of MCPs could inadvertently erode the welfare state.[9] We can summarize these mechanisms under three headings.

The crowding-out effect

According to one line of argument, MCPs weaken pro-redistribution coalitions by diverting time, energy, and money from redistribution to recognition. People who would otherwise be actively involved in fighting to enhance economic redistribution, or at least to protect the welfare state from right-wing retrenchment, are instead spending their time on issues of multiculturalism.

Todd Gitlin gives an example of this. He discusses how left-wing students at his university (UCLA) fought obsessively for what they deemed a more 'inclusive' educational environment, through greater representation

---

[8] For a more detailed defence of this link, see Kymlicka (forthcoming *b*).

[9] In identifying these complaints, we have drawn in particular on the writings of a set of critics whose works have become widely cited in the literature: Brian Barry (2001), Todd Gitlin (1995), Richard Rorty (1998, 2000), and Alan Wolfe and Jyette Klausen (1997, 2000). When referring to 'the critics', we have these authors in mind, as well as the many commentators who have endorsed their arguments.

of minorities in the faculty and curricula. At the same time, however, they largely ignored huge budget cuts to the state educational system that were making it more difficult for minority students to even get to UCLA. As he puts it, 'much of the popular energy and commitment it would have taken to fight for the preservation—let alone the improvement—of public education was channelled into acrimony amongst potential allies' (Gitlin 1995: 31). This 'channelling' of energy is captured nicely in one of his chapter titles: 'Marching on the English Department while the Right Took the White House' (Gitlin 1995: 126).[10]

The corroding effect

Another line of argument suggests that MCPs weaken redistribution by eroding trust and solidarity amongst citizens, and hence eroding popular support for redistribution. MCPs are said to erode solidarity because they emphasize differences between citizens, rather than commonalities. Citizens have historically supported the welfare state, and been willing to make sacrifices to support their disadvantaged co-citizens, because they viewed these co-citizens as 'one of us', bound together by a common identity and common sense of belonging. However, MCPs are said to corrode this overarching common identity. MCPs tell citizens that what divides them into separate ethnocultural groups is more important than what they have in common, and that co-citizens from other groups are therefore not really 'one of us'.

According to Wolfe and Klausen, for example, in the early days of the British welfare state in the 1940s and 1950s, 'people believed they were paying the social welfare part of their taxes to people who were like themselves'. But with the adoption of MCPs, and the resulting abandonment of the 'long process of national homogenization', the outcome has been growing 'tax resistance', for 'if the ties that bind you to increasingly diverse fellow citizens are loosened, you are likely to be less inclined to share your resources with them' (Wolfe and Klausen 2000: 28).

For some critics, this corroding of solidarity by MCPs is almost a logical necessity. Wolfe and Klausen, for example, assert that 'if groups within the nation state receive greater recognition, it *must* follow that conceptions of overarching national solidarity *must* receive less' (2000: 29, emphasis added). But other critics of MCPs offer a more nuanced explanation.

---

[10] See also Barry's complaint that MCPs involve 'dissipating' energies that 'might have gone into' redistributive politics (Barry 2001: 197).

According to one version, the problem with 'greater recognition' of sub-groups is, at least in part, that this recognition almost inevitably has a backward-looking remedial aspect to it. 'Recognizing' a group, in the context of MCPs, often involves acknowledging its sense of historic grievance, and acknowledging that it has historically been stigmatized and excluded, and mistreated in a paternalistic and condescending way by the dominant society. Recognizing a group then involves including the story of the historic injustices it has suffered within the school curriculum, or within the media, or within the national narratives more generally. In short, MCPs nurture a 'politics of grievance' that results in increased distrust between members of different groups, and makes it more difficult for cross-ethnic coalitions of the poor or disadvantaged to coalesce. Indeed, Gitlin argues that MCPs encourage a 'go-it-alone mood' that views attempts at building winning coalitions as 'as a sign of accommodation' (Gitlin 1995: 230–1).

Another version suggests that the corrosion of solidarity is most likely when MCPs involve some degree of institutional separateness. As Barry puts it, 'a situation where groups live in parallel universes is not one well calculated to advance mutual understanding or encourage the cultivation of habits of co-operation or sentiments of trust' (Barry 2001: 88). On this basis, he distinguishes two conceptions of 'multicultural education': the first involves ensuring that all children have a common curriculum that includes information about all the groups that coexist within the state; the second involves creating separate schools with separate curricula for distinct groups (Barry 2001: 237–8). The latter, he says, would be particularly corrosive of trust and solidarity.[11]

So the corrosion argument suggests that MCPs undermine trust and solidarity, either intrinsically, and/or when they are linked to a politics of grievance, and/or when they are linked to institutional separateness.

The misdiagnosis effect

A third line of argument suggests that MCPs lead people to misdiagnose the problems that minorities face. It encourages people to think that the problems facing minority groups are rooted primarily in cultural 'misrecognition', and hence to think that the solution lies in greater state

---

[11] Another version of this argument has been made by Dominique Schnapper, who argues that multiculturalism erodes the common public space needed to sustain relations of solidarity amongst equal citizens (Schnapper 1998).

recognition of ethnic identities and cultural practices. In reality, however, these 'culturalist' solutions will be of little or no benefit, since the real problems lie elsewhere.

This argument comes in two different forms. One version claims that the focus on cultural difference has displaced attention to *race*, and thereby ignored the distinctive problems facing groups like African-Americans. Barry, for example, argues that 'one of the most serious mistakes by multiculturalists is to misunderstand the plight of American blacks'. He goes on to quote Kwame Anthony Appiah's observation that

> it is not black culture that the racist disdains, but blacks. There is no conflict of visions between black and white cultures that is the source of racial discord. No amount of knowledge of the architectural achievements of Nubia or Kush guarantees respect for African-Americans . . . Culture is not the problem, and it is not the solution. (Appiah 1997: 36, quoted in Barry 2001: 306)

Since the problem of racism in the United States is not primarily one of cultural misrecognition, it cannot be resolved by making 'Martin Luther King Day' a national holiday, or celebrating Kwanza in schools, or teaching about the accomplishments of pre-colonial African societies. According to critics, the problem here is not just that such changes are insufficient, but rather that they blind people to the real problem. The rhetoric of MCPs lumps all ethnic groups together, as equal victims of cultural misrecognition, while obscuring the distinctive problems faced by those racial groups which suffer the consequences of segregation, slavery, racism, and discrimination (cf. Favell 2001).

A second version of the misdiagnosis argument claims that the focus on ethnic or racial difference has displaced attention to *class*, and thereby made pan-ethnic alliances on class issues less likely. On this view, the real problem is economic marginalization, not cultural misrecognition, and the solution is not to adopt MCPs but rather to improve people's standing in the labour market, through better access to jobs, education and training, and so on. The multiculturalist approach encourages people to think that what low-income Pakistani immigrants in Britain need most is to have their distinctive history, religion, or dress given greater public status or accommodation, when in fact their real need is for improved access to decent housing, education and training, and gainful employment—a need they share with the disadvantaged members of the larger society or other ethnic groups, and a need which can only be met through a pan-ethnic class alliance.

Both versions of the misdiagnosis argument claim that MCPs do not simply divert energy from more pressing issues of race and class (that is the 'crowding out' effect), but that they distort people's understanding of the causes of disadvantage, by denying or failing to acknowledge the reality of racism and class inequality. A Machiavellian version of this argument suggests that right-wing political and economic elites have in fact promoted MCPs precisely in order to obscure the reality of racism and economic marginalization. On this view, the tendency to misdiagnose the plight of African-Americans as one of cultural misrecognition is not an unintended by-product of MCPs, but rather was their intended purpose.

At first glance, all three of these critiques have some plausibility. Their plausibility is strengthened by the indisputable fact that the rise of MCPs has largely coincided with the period of retrenchment in many social programmes. The question naturally arises whether there is some connection between these two trends. Perhaps the rise of MCPs has somehow played a role in supporting, or obscuring, the retreat from redistribution. The crowding-out, corroding, and misdiagnosing effects could all help to explain why the rise of MCPs might have intentionally or inadvertently contributed to the retrenchment of the welfare state. The plausibility of this concern has even led some defenders of MCPs to rethink their approach. Anne Phillips, for example, who ardently defended a strongly multiculturalist conception of democracy in her 1995 book (Phillips 1995), subsequently wrote 'I cannot avoid troubled thoughts about the way developments I otherwise support have contributed (however inadvertently) to a declining interest in economic equality' (Phillips 1999: 13).

However, there are also important reasons for questioning the suggested linkage between the rise of MCPs and retrenchment in many social programmes. After all, the welfare state has been under pressure throughout the Western democracies, including in countries that strongly resist MCPs, like Germany, as well as pro-MCP countries, like Canada. It is not at all clear that the presence or absence of MCPs had any bearing on whether or how the welfare state was restructured. Indeed, as Chapter 2 will show, some pro-MCP countries resisted the retrenchment of the welfare state better than some anti-MCP countries. So the existence of a general link between MCPs and the welfare state is not self-evident.

Moreover, once we think about it, the three more specific critiques of MCP listed above are not self-evident either. Let's take them one by one:

14

Crowding-out: The counter-claim

The claim that MCPs 'crowd out' welfare state issues rests on the implicit assumption that there would have been a sizeable coalition of politically engaged citizens willing to act to defend the welfare state, were they not distracted by MCP issues. This is explicit in the Gitlin quote we cited earlier. Yet Gitlin himself concedes that this was not true. As he notes, the vast majority of students at UCLA, and indeed the vast majority of American citizens generally, had lost faith in their capacity to influence the structure of economic inequality. As he notes in explaining why students did not protest budget cuts to education:

The national political scene is forbidding. The public at large has little confidence that problems can be solved by government actions. Even Americans unpersuaded by Ronald Reagan that 'government is not the solution, government is the problem', lack the faith that anyone knows what to do about cities, jobs, education, or race relations. (Gitlin 1995: 159)

Similarly, Anne Phillips acknowledges that the main reason why issues of economic inequality have been occluded in Britain is that most people, including most on the left, have become 'astonishingly fatalistic about economic inequalities':

Everyone now knows that nationalized industries become stultified and inefficient, that initiatives to end poverty can end up condemning people to a poverty trap, that when public authorities set out to protect employees' wages and conditions from the harsher realities of the market they often do this at the expense of good service provision. We have even discovered, to our dismay, that the free health and education that was the great achievement of the welfare state can end up redistributing wealth from the poor to the middle classes. With the best will in the world, programmes for redistributive justice often backfire. Since we can no longer pretend to confidence about what makes people economically equal, it is hardly surprising that so many have turned their attention elsewhere. (Phillips 1999: 11, 34)

In other words, the rise of MCPs did not lead people on the left to abandon issues of economic inequality. Many people had already abandoned issues of economic inequality out of a sense of hopelessness. On Gitlin's and Phillips's own analysis, the presence of MCPs made no difference to the left's passivity towards economic issues.[12]

Barry too acknowledges that the left's passivity on economic issues is due to 'despair at the prospects of getting broad-based egalitarian policies

---

[12] See Caputo (2001) for a similar analysis.

adopted', and that this despair pre-dated the rise of MCPs, rather than being caused by MCPs (Barry 2001: 326). However, he worries that this economic fatalism will become a 'self-fulfilling prophecy' if people's energies are 'dissipated' in struggles over MCPs (Barry 2001: 197). Perhaps, but one could also speculate that the emergence of MCPs may actually have helped to reinvigorate the left. It provided a context for the left to get involved in politics again, by providing an issue on which progressives felt it was possible to make a difference. Getting involved and making a difference helped revive confidence in the possibility of challenging economic inequalities. Indeed, this is what happened in Gitlin's own story. Having successfully achieved various MCP reforms, the UCLA students who previously had been fatalistic about economic issues started to lobby regarding the budget cuts. Gitlin's official story is that MCPs drained the energy that would have otherwise gone into fighting economic inequality. His own anecdote, however, suggests that there was no energy to fight those battles, until the successful struggle for MCPs inspired confidence in tackling the economic issues. Donna Lee Van Cott's chapter below tells a similar story about the way struggles for multiculturalism have fed into struggles for redistribution in Latin America.[13]

The 'crowding-out' argument is a common one that has been used historically by traditional leftists to condemn political mobilization around the environment, or gay rights, or animal rights. All of these were said to channel energy away from issues of economic inequality. This argument rests on the assumption that there is a fixed and static amount of time, energy, and money that will be spent on political mobilization, such that any effort spent on one issue necessarily detracts from another. However, there is an alternative view about political mobilization that is not zero-sum. On this view, the real challenge is to get people involved in politics at all, on any issue—i.e. to believe that their activity can make a difference on any issue worth fighting about. Once they are involved, and have this sense of political efficacy, they are likely to support other progressive issues as well.

It is thus unclear how successful political mobilizations around new issues of justice affect older issues of justice. The former may crowd out the latter, as critics of MCPs fear; but they may also help to sustain a public culture in which issues of justice matter, to reinforce the belief that citizens have effective political agency, and to relegitimate the state as an

---

[13] More generally, one could speculate whether the success of the politics of recognition has helped to inspire some of the protest around globalization.

institution that is capable of achieving public interests. At any rate, the latter possibility is at least as plausible as the idea that MCPs crowd out issues of economic justice.

The corroding effect: The counter-claim

The argument that MCPs corrode the interethnic trust and solidarity needed to sustain the welfare state is also debatable. For one thing, it assumes that prior to the adoption of MCPs there were high levels of interethnic trust and solidarity, which are slowly (or quickly) being eaten away. However, historically, Western states often adopted exclusionary and assimilationist policies precisely because there was little trust or solidarity across ethnic and racial lines. Dominant groups felt threatened by minorities, and/or superior to them, and/or simply indifferent to their well-being, and so attempted to assimilate, exclude, exploit, or disempower them. This, in turn, led minorities to distrust the dominant group. In these situations, MCPs were not the original cause of this distrust or hostility, and in many cases the adoption of MCPs was a response to this pre-existing lack of trust/solidarity. By adopting MCPs, the state can be seen as trying both to encourage dominant groups not to fear or despise minorities, and also to encourage minorities to trust the larger society. By acknowledging the reality of historic injustices against minorities, the state acknowledges the existence of these feelings of prejudice and contempt against minorities, and affirms a public duty to fight against them and their consequences. Many defenders of MCPs argue that, by tackling these feelings, MCPs will actually help to strengthen the trust and solidarity needed for a strong welfare state.

Of course, there is no guarantee that MCPs will succeed in this regard. However, when reflecting on this question, it is important to keep the historical context in mind. For example, Barry's main empirical evidence for the corrosion effect is the famous 'robber's cave' experiment conducted in 1961 in which 'a party of eleven year old children in a summer camp were divided into two competing groups, which "produced in-group friendships and hostility toward the other group"', a result he describes as unsurprising (Barry 2001: 88–9, citing Sherif et al. 1961). Indeed, the result is unsurprising, but it is not clear how it is analogous to the role of MCPs in countries where there has been a history of mistrust and antipathy between groups, embodied in (and reinforced by) official state policies that excluded, segregated, exploited, and disempowered minority groups. In contexts where people have had no prior history of mistrust or mistreatment, arbitrarily dividing them into competing groups may well reduce pre-existing levels of trust and solidarity. But this is not the only or even the normal context in ethnic relations. Often, the more apt analogy would be to consider a summer camp that had historically excluded Asians and Arabs, and admitted African-Americans only as slaves or servants, and which was now considering how to deal with the resulting legacy of mistrust and antipathy. Or consider a school, or hospital, or police force, or public media or public museum, all of which have the same history. In these contexts, adoption of MCPs can be seen as reflecting a particular view about how best to overcome the pre-existing forms of interethnic mistrust and antipathy, to reduce the majority's antipathy towards minorities and the minority's feelings of distrust in institutions and processes of the larger society. Defenders of MCPs would argue that without these efforts to contest both the causes and consequences of the history of exclusion, distrust and antipathy are likely to remain, even in institutions that no longer formally discriminate.

These hopes of strengthening trust and solidarity through MCPs may be misplaced, but it seems at least as plausible as the complaint that MCPs corrode trust and solidarity.[14] Matt James's chapter below discusses the complex dynamics put in play by the linking of multiculturalism with 'redress politics'.

The misdiagnosis effect: The counter-claim

Finally, consider the misdiagnosis argument, which argues that adopting MCPs blinds people to the salience of non-cultural factors in explaining group disadvantage. The paradigm case of this, according to both Barry and Gitlin, is the misdiagnosis of the situation of African-Americans, for

[14] It should be noted, moreover, that the 'Robber's Cave' argument, applied consistently, threatens the critics' preferred alternative to MCPs. According to many critics, the alternative to MCPs is a more rigorous enforcement of anti-discrimination law, so as to ensure the equal enjoyment of common citizenship rights. But anti-discrimination law, as much as MCPs, requires categorizing people into different ethnic and racial categories on the basis of their historic mistreatment and their vulnerability to social stigmatization. To make a claim under anti-discrimination law, people must identify themselves as a member of a protected group, and these claims are tested in part by assessing how other members of the group have fared within a particular organization or company. The more rigorously anti-discrimination law is monitored and enforced, the more salient these categorizations become, and this can generate the same corroding 'in-group, out-group' dynamic that critics ascribe to MCPs. And indeed some left-wing commentators have argued that anti-discrimination laws involve their own 'recognition versus redistribution' trade-off (Choudhry 2000). Whether the sort of group recognition required by anti-discrimination law or MCPs does indeed have this polarizing effect—or whether it instead helps to increase solidarity by reducing inherited forms of prejudice and distrust—must, in both cases, be examined empirically.

whom issues of race and class are much more salient than cultural recognition. This is just one example, they argue, of a more general tendency for MCPs to generate misdiagnoses of the causes of disadvantage or injustice, relevant to other groups as well.

The critics acknowledge that the relative salience of these various factors differs for different groups. In some cases, issues of class are comparatively insignificant. For example, Jews in North America, or Hong Kong immigrants, have higher-than-average levels of income and education, yet have faced difficulties regarding the accommodation of religious and cultural practices, stereotyping in the media, greater vulnerability to violence, and so on. Similarly, some national minorities, like the Québécois or Catalans, are as well off economically as the dominant society, yet feel their language and culture has been systematically marginalized in public institutions (such as the courts, civil service, or national media) in relation to the dominant language and culture.

So there are various dimensions on which ethnic groups can face injustice—including race, class, and culture—and groups are often located at different places on these different dimensions. For example, a group may be privileged in terms of race yet disadvantaged in terms of class (e.g. Portuguese in North America), or it may be privileged in terms of class and race but disadvantaged in terms of cultural recognition and accommodation (e.g. Catalans), and so on.

The misdiagnosis argument, then, as we understand it, claims that the presence of MCPs leads people to ignore (or minimize) the salience of the race and class dimensions of inequality, and to exaggerate the salience of the cultural dimension. It leads people to assume that racial and class inequalities are either unimportant or derivative of cultural inequalities.

Why would MCPs lead people to believe this? One possible explanation is that people's sense of justice is zero-sum: enhanced sensitivity to one form of injustice inevitably entails reduced sensitivity to other forms of injustice. On this view, people who are keenly sensitive to issues of racism or sexism, for example, are inevitably less sensitive to issues of class inequality or cultural accommodation, and vice versa. But is this true? Is it not possible that the different dimensions of our sense of justice are mutually reinforcing—i.e. that people who have the awareness and motivation to look out for one form of injustice are also likely to be more open to considerations of other types of injustice? Conversely, perhaps those people who have a stunted sense of justice regarding race, say, are also likely to have a stunted sense of justice regarding gender or class.

To be sure, there are circumstances where a fixation on one form of injustice can blind people to other forms. The paradigm case, historically, is Marxism, which was ideologically committed to the view that class inequality was the only 'real' inequality, and that all other forms of inequality including sexism and racism were epiphenomenal, and would disappear with the abolition of classes. In this case, it was an explicit and foundational part of the Marxist ideology that one dimension of inequality had primacy over the others. Marxism systematically misdiagnosed a range of inequalities because it dogmatically assumed class was the primary inequality, without looking at the evidence in particular cases.

In order to avoid misdiagnosis, we need to avoid these sorts of dogmatic presumptions. Since the salience of different kinds of disadvantage differs between groups, and over time, it is important for people to be open-minded about this, and to be willing to consider the claims and the evidence as they are raised by various groups. The issue then becomes whether MCPs encourage or discourage this sort of open-minded approach to the salience of different forms of inequality. Does multiculturalism have a foundational ideological commitment to the primacy of cultural inequalities over other inequalities, comparable to the Marxist commitment to the primary of economic inequalities? Does it encourage people to assume that cultural inequalities are the real problem, without examining the evidence in particular cases? Or do MCPs instead make space for an open debate about their relative salience?

Defenders of MCPs would argue that multiculturalism, in both theory and practice, has helped to open up this debate. After all, multiculturalism emerged as part of the New Left's rejection of the Marxist dogmatic assertion of the primacy of class. Multiculturalists were not suggesting that we should replace class inequality with cultural inequality as the monocausal motor of history, but rather contesting the very idea of a monocausal motor of history. It was contesting the idea that all inequalities can be reduced to one 'real' inequality, and insisting instead that culture, race, class, and sex are all real loci of inequality, of varying salience, not reducible to each other.

This seems clear enough in the case of multiculturalist theorists. It is a central claim of most multiculturalist theorists that the relative salience of inequalities relating to race, class, and culture varies greatly across different groups in society. Paradoxically, this is particularly clear in the case Barry and Gitlin cite, of African-Americans. All of the major multicultural theorists who have written on African-Americans have emphasized that what distinguishes this case from that of some other minority groups

in the United States or other Western democracies is precisely the overwhelming salience of race and class in comparison with cultural difference (see Spinner 1994; Young 1995; Fraser 1998; Kymlicka 1998: ch. 5).
None of the multiculturalist theorists asserts that the accommodation of
cultural difference is the main problem facing African-Americans. Indeed,
African-Americans are often discussed precisely to illustrate the point that
there is no one model or formula for determining the relative salience of
these different forms of injustice.

One might respond that even if theorists do not assert the primacy of
cultural inequalities over other dimensions of inequality, the actual implementation of MCPs encourages a kind of false consciousness amongst the
members of minority groups, leading them to blame their fate on cultural
misrecognition rather than other factors of race and class. But is it likely
that the presence of MCPs blinds group members to the salience of race
and class in their lives?[15]

To say that some groups face cultural inequalities that warrant remedy-
ing through MCPs is not to say that these are the only inequalities they
face, or that they are the most important ones. Nor is it to assert that all
groups face such inequalities. It simply says that cultural inequalities are
one 'real' form of injustice that we must be sensitive to, alongside others,
when evaluating the situation of different groups, and that provides a
legitimate basis for potential claims. The task of arriving at a correct
diagnosis of the causes of a particular group's disadvantage is not always
an easy one. Even in the case of African-Americans, there is a long-
standing and still-unresolved dispute about the relative significance of
race and class (e.g. Wilson 1980). Arriving at an informed judgement on
these issues requires that we have a conceptual vocabulary to describe all
of the different dimensions of inequality, and also political space in which
to discuss them freely and evaluate their relative salience. One could argue
that the theory and practice of multiculturalism is intended precisely
to supplement and enrich our conceptual tools and political spaces for

[15] Indeed, Barry himself says that most people (unlike the elites) are unaware of the
presence of MCPs, and so presumably their self-understandings are unaffected by them (Barry
2001: 295). This raises a puzzle about who exactly is supposed to be making the misdiagnoses.
Is it academic political theorists who write on multiculturalism, or policy makers, or minority
members themselves? Barry's main focus is on the former, but even if it is true that a handful
of academic political theorists misdiagnose the situation of various groups, how could this
affect the broader decision-making processes regarding the welfare state? Barry himself claims
that these academic theories are 'esoteric' and are 'virtually unknown to the wider public'
(Barry 2001: 365–6, quoting Pascal Zachary). But if the broader public is blissfully unaware of
both academic multiculturalism theories and actual multiculturalism policies, how then does
the misdiagnosis argument work?

arriving at a more adequate diagnosis of the full range of injustices faced by different groups in our society.

In short, none of the arguments for the alleged harmful impact of MCPs on the welfare state are self-evident. They may seem to have some initial plausibility, but there are equally plausible arguments why MCPs would strengthen the welfare state. Many of the these critiques blame MCPs for problems that in fact pre-date the adoption of MCPs (e.g. interethnic mistrust; fatalism about economic structures); others assume political energies and moral sensitivities are zero-sum (i.e. that concern for cultural inequality inevitably reduces concern for other struggles).

It should be clear, we hope, that this debate cannot be resolved by more armchair theorizing, or by trading anecdotes. We need to look more closely and systematically at the evidence.

3. The available evidence

What then is the evidence that MCPs erode the welfare state? As we noted earlier, the critics themselves do not provide systematic evidence to support their claims. Nor do they cite any empirical studies showing a correlation between the adoption of MCPs and the erosion of the welfare state. This is perhaps not surprising because, so far as we can tell, there are no empirical studies for critics (or defenders) to cite. No one has even attempted to test the recognition/redistribution trade-off hypothesis.

This is an important gap in what is otherwise an enormous and impressive comparative literature on the factors that shape the welfare state. One stream within this literature seeks to explain variations in the level of social spending across OECD countries by reference to a wide range of factors, such as the level of economic development, the openness of the economy, the size of the elderly population, the strength of organized labour, the historic dominance of parties of the left or right, and the structure of political institutions and the electoral system (see, for example, Huber and Stephens 2001; Swank 2002; Castles 2004; Hicks 1999). However, none of these studies has integrated MCPs into the analysis.

The same gap exists in the related literature on 'welfare state regimes'. Drawing on Esping-Andersen's ground-breaking work (1990, 1996), several scholars have examined why countries differ, not only in their level of social spending, but also in the way welfare benefits are structured, focusing on the balance between income transfers and social services, and the role of universal versus targeted programmes. Studies of these different welfare state 'regimes' have also not yet integrated MCPs into their analysis (e.g. Castles 1989, 1998; Ferrera 1996).

In short, discussions of the recognition/redistribution trade-off to date are unsupported by any systematic empirical research. In Chapter 2, we list twenty-three multiculturalism policies that have been adopted by various Western democracies, and so far as we know, no one has attempted to test the impact of any of these MCPs on the welfare state.

The only partial exception concerns recent work on the relationship between federalism and the welfare state. As we discuss in Chapter 2, federalism is one way in which countries can seek to accommodate the aspiration for self-government by national minorities, and so the adoption of federalism can be seen, in some contexts, as a form of 'MCP'. Several cross-national studies of the welfare state have concluded that, all other things being equal, federal states tend to have lower levels of social spending (Swank 2002; Huber and Stephens 2001; Huber, Ragin, and Stephens 1993; Hicks and Misra 1993; Hicks and Swank 1992; and Crepaz 1998). This might be seen as preliminary evidence that at least one form of MCP erodes the welfare state. However, such studies do not distinguish between 'multi-nation' countries such as Canada, Belgium, Spain, and the United Kingdom, where federal or quasi-federal institutions were adopted at least in part to accommodate substate nationalism, from countries such as Australia, Germany, and the United States, where federalism owes its roots to other considerations. Federalism counts as an MCP in the former, but not in the latter. For our purposes, the question is not how federal states compare to unitary states in general, but rather whether states that adopt federalism to accommodate national minorities fare worse in social spending compared to states that do not accord territorial autonomy to their national minorities. And that question, like all questions about the relationship between MCPs and the welfare state, has not yet been empirically tested.

In contrast to this virtual silence on the impact of MCPs on the welfare state, there is a recent and growing literature on the related hypothesis discussed earlier that ethnic/racial diversity itself weakens economic redistribution (what we called the 'heterogeneity/redistribution trade-off' hypothesis). Given the importance of distinguishing between the impact of heterogeneity and the impact of MCPs, it is worth reviewing this literature here.

In one sense, the idea that ethnic/racial heterogeneity can weaken the pursuit of a robust welfare state is an old one. Karl Marx argued that racial divisions within the working class in the USA would undermine its capacity to demand progressive reforms, and this has been a recurring theme in American politics.[16] Hints that ethnic diversity was potentially important occasionally emerged in the literature on the development of the welfare state in the post-war era (Wilensky and Lebeaux 1965; Wilensky 1975). For example, in his early cross-national study of the emergence of the welfare state, John Stephens found that ethnic and linguistic diversity was strongly and negatively correlated with the level of labour organization, a key variable in analysis of the determinants of social spending across OECD countries (Stephens 1979). The implication would seem to be that heterogeneity weakens the mobilization of the working class by dividing organized labour along ethnic and linguistic lines, making it more difficult to focus on an agenda of economic inequality. Unfortunately, subsequent generations of this research did not follow up on this lead, and ethnic, racial, and linguistic diversity has not been included as a variable in several of the most influential cross-national studies of welfare state spending (e.g. Swank 2002; Hicks 1999).[17]

Including ethnic/racial heterogeneity as an explanatory variable in comparative studies of social spending is therefore a recent trend, which initially emerged in two discrete geographical contexts. First, development economists, including some associated with the World Bank, pointed to ethnic and tribal diversity in attempting to explain the poor economic and social performance of countries in sub-Saharan Africa. The focus here was initially on the impact of ethnic heterogeneity on economic growth, rather than social policy. The primary concern was that ethnic tensions lead to communal rent-seeking in government, poor macroeconomic policies, and in some cases high levels of violent conflict, all of which retard the rate of economic growth in developing countries. However, subsequent research has extended the focus to examine the negative impact of heterogeneity on the provision of public goods, such as public education. Studies suggest that while the association between ethnic diversity and the size of the state is weak, spending on private as opposed to public education tends to be higher in developing countries with more religious and linguistic diversity, and transfer payments tend to be lower in countries with high levels of ethnic diversity (Collier 2000, 2001; Collier and Gunning 1999; Easterly and Levine 1997; Easterly 2001a, 2001b; Montalvo and Reynal-Querol 2005; Nettle 2000;

---

[16] For a discussion of the history of this argument, see Lipset and Marks (2000).

[17] Interestingly, this observation also applies to Stephens' own recent work, which does not incorporate ethno-linguistic diversity. See Huber and Stephens (2001).

James 1987, 1993; Grafton, Knowles, and Owen 2002; Miguel 2004; Miguel and Gugarty 2005).[18] In a similar vein, La Ferrara has demonstrated the importance of ethnicity in conditioning access to informal credit and group loans in Africa (La Ferrara 2002, 2003).

The second context concerns the United States. Race has played a central role in the history of US social programmes from their earliest origins (Skocpol 1992). During the passage of the Social Security Act in 1935, resistance from southern congressmen and other conservatives led to the exclusion of agricultural and domestic labourers, denying coverage to three-fifths of black workers; and southern congressmen led a successful campaign in the name of 'states' rights' against national standards in public assistance, leaving southern blacks at the mercy of local authorities (Quadagno 1988; Orloff 1988). In the 1960s, racial politics swirled around Aid to Families with Dependent Children (AFDC) and the Great Society programmes. As welfare rolls expanded and new poverty programmes were put in place, the profile of the poor became racially charged. Black families represented close to half of the AFDC caseload and Hispanic groups were increasingly over-represented. Resentment against these programmes helped fracture the New Deal coalition and the base of the Democratic Party. White union members, white ethnics, and southerners deserted their traditional political home, especially in presidential elections, in part because of its image on race and welfare issues. The effect was so powerful that the Democratic Party sought to insulate itself in the 1990s by embracing hard-edged welfare reforms, including the 1995 reforms signed by President Clinton.

Given this history, it is not surprising that scholars interested in the US experience increasingly add ethnic and racial heterogeneity to models that seek to explain differences in social spending, both within the USA and between the USA and other countries. The size of racial minorities helps explain differences in social expenditures across cities and states in the USA (Alesina, Baqir, and Easterly 2001; Hero 1998; Hero and Tolbert 1996; Plotnick and Winters 1985; Johnson 2001, 2003; Soss et al. 2001; Soss, Schram, and Fording 2003; Fellowes and Rowe 2004; Luttmer 2001). These studies consistently show, for example, that the higher the proportion of African-Americans or Hispanics within a state, the more restrictive state-level welfare programmes such as Medicaid are.[19] More recently,

---

[18] One of the few exceptions is Posner (2005), who did not discover the expected correlation between ethnic diversity and public goods provision in Uganda.

[19] See the overview of this research in Chapter 4 below. This correlation is backed up by survey evidence showing that the best predictor of people's support for welfare in the USA is

Alesina and Glaeser have extended this analysis to the cross-national level, arguing that differences in racial diversity are a significant part of the explanation of why the United States did not develop a European-style welfare state (Alesina and Glaeser 2004).

Such results have led several scholars to conclude that there is a universal tendency for people to resist interethnic redistribution. Explanations differ as to why this tendency exists.[20] Some simply view it as a brute preference or 'taste' (Luttmer 2001). Others argue that ethnocentrism is a genetically determined disposition, since evolution would select for 'ethnic nepotism' (Salter 2004).[21] Others offer a more nuanced account for this tendency. Even if people are willing in principle to make sacrifices for co-citizens who are not co-ethnics—perhaps motivated by some sense of common citizenship or shared patriotism—they are only likely to do so if they trust the would-be recipient to reciprocate. However, this sort of trust is difficult to generate across ethnic lines. For one thing, it is easier to sanction 'defectors' within one's own ethnic group than to sanction members of other ethnic groups (Miguel and Gugarty 2005). Also, trust can be seen as a component of social capital that develops in associational life, and Putnam argues that the sort of associational life that generates social capital is lower in ethnically heterogeneous neighbourhoods.[22] Yet other explanations focus on the impact of ethnic and racial diversity on the political coalitions and parties that normally support the welfare state. Ethnic cleavages may pose particular challenges for the formation of a united and powerful labour movement (Alesina and Glaeser 2004; Stephens 1979), and offer particular openings for right-wing populist

not whether they self-identify as right or left, or liberal or conservative, or even whether they believe that the poor are lazy. Rather, the most powerful predictor is the belief that *blacks* are lazy (Gilens 1999).

[20] For a more extensive discussion of these competing explanations, and the objections to each, see Kymlicka (forthcoming *a*). It is important here to distinguish episodic 'humanitarian' charity in response to disasters from ongoing institutionally compelled redistribution. The debate concerns resistance to the latter.

[21] The expression of this universal tendency may be influenced by the presence of racialist ideologies that have been developed to provide intellectual justification for privileging co-ethnics. However, for those who endorse the evolutionary account, the tendency to privilege co-ethnics is prior to, and more widespread than, any particular ideology of racialism or ethnocentrism, and is found as much in African or Asian societies as in European societies.

[22] Putnam argues that social capital, in the form of trust and engagement in social networks, is critical to a wider sense of public purpose and a capacity for collective action through the public sector. But social capital, he has recently concluded, is weakened by ethnic diversity. Early findings based on his Social Capital Benchmark Study suggest that individuals in ethnically diverse regions and neighbourhoods in the United States are much less engaged in their community and wider social networks than individuals living in more homogeneous parts of the country (Putnam 2004; also Goodhart 2004).

parties that combine anti-immigrant nativism with attacks on the welfare state (Kitschelt 1995).

Whatever the explanation—whether seen as an inherent genetic disposition or as a predictable by-product of social capital deficits, weakened pro-welfare coalitions or electoral processes—there is an increasing tendency to assume that ethnic/racial heterogeneity erodes redistribution. Although the main evidence for this assumption comes from two specific contexts—namely, sub-Saharan Africa and the United States—it is increasingly treated as a universal tendency. The strongly racialized dimension of US welfare politics is no longer seen as an anomaly—a pernicious legacy of the peculiar American history of slavery and segregation—but rather as a normal, even inevitable, reaction to the simple fact of ethnic/racial heterogeneity. Indeed, the United States has come to represent the leading international example of the proposition that heterogeneity as such erodes redistribution. Its story has emerged as a sort of 'master narrative', the quintessential model of the (inherently weak) heterogeneous welfare state.

Based on this assumption, scholars have drawn rather dire predictions about the future of the welfare state across the Western democracies. If it is the mere presence of ethnic and racial minorities that has weakened the welfare state in the United States, then increasing immigration threatens to do the same in Europe. In 1986, Gary Freeman predicted that immigration would lead to 'the Americanization of European welfare politics' (Freeman 1986: 62), and more recent commentators have reiterated this prediction (Glazer 1998; Faist 1995; Goodhart 2004). In their comparison of the US and European welfare states, Alesina and Glaeser conclude with a caution about current directions in European politics: 'As Europe has become more diverse, Europeans have increasingly been susceptible to exactly the same form of racist, anti-welfare demagoguery that worked so well in the United States. We shall see whether the generous welfare state can really survive in a heterogeneous society' (Alesina and Glaeser 2004: 180–1).

However, there are important reasons for being careful about assertions of a general tendency for ethnic heterogeneity to erode the welfare state. The empirical evidence is drawn from two contexts that are arguably atypical. In the sub-Saharan context, the artificiality of state boundaries, combined with the weakness of state institutions at the time of independence, meant that states had no usable traditions or institutional capacity for dealing with diversity. In the American context, racial animosity had been sedimented by centuries of slavery and segregation, whose maintenance depended on state-sponsored ideologies and practices that dehumanized Blacks. One could argue that neither of these contexts provides a reliable basis for predicting the impact of, say, increasing Turkish immigration on the German welfare state, or increasing Philippine immigration on the Canadian welfare state. Where minorities are newcomers rather than historically enslaved groups, and where state institutions are strong rather than weak, the impact of increasing heterogeneity may be quite different.

Indeed, recent attempts to test the heterogeneity/redistribution hypothesis beyond the USA and Africa have a number of limitations. Alesina and Glaeser (2004: 141) report a negative relationship between racial diversity and social spending across a wide range of countries at very different levels of economic development. While the relationship holds when the level of development is controlled, the strength of the correlation in the case of developed countries is influenced strongly by the USA, which is an outlier in terms of both racial diversity and levels of social spending (Hvinden 2006). Moreover, Alesina and Glaeser adopt the unusual assumption that several factors which normally figure prominently in comparative analyses of the welfare state, especially the strength of the political left, are simply a reflection of the level of racial diversity, and therefore do not include them in this phase of their analysis. Other researchers, however, have challenged this assumption. For example, when Taylor-Gooby (2005) includes the strength of the political left among the controls, racial diversity has no statistically significant effect on social spending in Western Europe. He concludes that there is, as yet, no evidence that immigration will have the same effect on European welfare states that race has historically had on the American welfare state. Similarly, after a comprehensive analysis of cross-national data on public attitudes, Crepaz warns against extrapolating from the American experience. The challenge posed by immigration in Europe unfolds in a context in which the welfare state has reached maturity and is embedded deeply in public expectations, unlike the American experience in which the politics of race hampered movement towards a more comprehensive welfare state from the outset. As a result, he concludes, 'there is little evidence that immigration-induced diversity will lead to an "Americanization" of the European welfare state' (Crepaz forthcoming).

An additional problem concerns the ways in which different forms of multicultural diversity are integrated into analyses of the politics of redistribution. The literature tends to be concerned primarily with immigrant minorities, and treats national minorities and indigenous peoples in a very inconsistent manner—sometimes they are included, sometimes not. This can be seen in the Index of Ethno-linguistic Fractionalization developed by Alesina and his colleagues, which is used increasingly in studies of these issues (Alesina et al. 2003). The UK data on ethno-linguistic fractionalization, for example, ignores national minorities in Scotland and Wales, as well as white immigrants such as the Irish. As a result, the Index is only measuring 'racial' differences in the UK: white 93.7 per cent; Indian 1.8 per cent; other UK 1.6 per cent; Pakistani 1.4 per cent; Black 1.4 per cent. In Canada, however, the Index subdivides the white majority into a range of different ethnic and linguistic subgroups, including French 22.8 per cent; British 20.8 per cent; German 3.4 per cent; Italian 2.8 per cent; Dutch 1.3 per cent and so on.[23] As a result, the Index is not a consistent measure of either the diversity of the ethnic origins of a population or its politically salient ethnic identities. As we will see in Chapter 2, when we test on a more consistent basis the impact of national minorities and indigenous peoples on the welfare state in Western democracies, no significant relationship emerges.

In the end, John Myles and Sébastian St-Arnaud conclude that existing research on the relationship between ethnic diversity and the welfare state is 'simply too thin and contradictory to draw strong conclusions' (Myles and St-Arnaud, this volume). Claims about an inherent trade-off between heterogeneity and redistribution should therefore be treated with caution.

It is not clear how widespread the phenomenon is, or what mechanisms underlie it. Although a growing literature suggests that such an effect exists in particular times and places—and of course we can see evidence of that every day in countries suffering from ethnic conflict and racist violence—we cannot assume that it is a universal tendency. Much more research is required before any definitive judgement can be made.

Our focus here is on the link between ethnic diversity and redistribution, but it should be noted that this was just one part of a larger debate swirling in the late 1990s around the potentially negative political and economic implications of ethnic diversity. For example, there were preliminary studies suggesting that countries with high levels of ethnic diversity were more prone to civil war, and were less likely to develop into democracies. However, more recent research, using more rigorous methods, suggests that ethnically diverse societies are not in

---

[23] The full listing for Canada (in per cent) is: French 22.8; other Canadian 43.5; British 20.8; German 3.4; Italian 2.8; Chinese 2.2; Amerindian 1.5; Dutch 1.3.

fact more prone to civil war (Fearon and Laitin 2003; Young 2002), or less likely to be democracies (Fish and Brooks 2004). Similarly, early assertions that ethnic diversity has negative effects on economic growth have been qualified by more recent research demonstrating, among other things, that the negative relationship fades away at higher levels of development and in democratic countries (Alesina and La Ferrara 2005; Collier 2000; Lian and Oneal 1997). Thus earlier assumptions about the inherently negative impact of ethnic diversity on peace, democracy, and economic development are now widely seen as overstated. In the same way, the evidence about the relationship between diversity and social spending summarized here points to the need for caution about assumptions that there is a universal trade-off between heterogeneity and redistribution.

The need for more research applies even more forcefully to the issue of primary concern in this volume, the alleged trade-off between multicultural recognition and economic redistribution. As we have seen, this is much less explored territory. Yet it is also critical in policy terms. From the perspective of public policy debates, studies of the link between levels of ethnic/racial heterogeneity and the welfare state represent a rather academic discussion. For most practical purposes, the level of ethnic/racial heterogeneity is a given. A country simply finds itself with certain ethnic/racial minorities, and unless it is willing to contemplate genocide or ethnic cleansing, this must be accepted as a reality. The size of ethnic/racial minorities can be affected at the margins, by increasing or decreasing immigration, but this only has a significant effect on overall levels of diversity over the long term.

For most policy makers, therefore, the crucial issue is not 'what level of ethnic heterogeneity is desirable', but rather 'how should we respond to the ethnic heterogeneity that already exists in our society'. As we noted earlier, during the last two decades of the twentieth century, many Western democracies shifted towards a more accommodating approach to diversity, reflected in the adoption of MCPs for immigrant groups, national minorities, and indigenous peoples. This shift has generated widespread controversy, including anxiety over its implications for the welfare state. Whether these fears are justified is one of the compelling issues in contemporary policy debates.

We believe that the research reported in the following chapters, while perhaps not definitive, provides a crucial first step in exploring issues that will be of fundamental importance for the future of the welfare state in the twenty-first century.

4. Overview of the volume

This volume adopts a number of methodological approaches to increase our understanding of the relationship between MCPs and the welfare state. In part, we rely on cross-national statistical analysis. This approach is well suited to testing the extent to which there is a systematic relationship between MCPs and the welfare state, as implied by the critics of such policies. Statistical techniques are also helpful in attempting to distinguish between the impact of ethnic diversity on one hand and MCPs on the other, as well as to taking account of a wide range of other factors that are known to influence the strength of the welfare state. These are important advantages. However, statistical methods also face important constraints in this context. First, cross-national data sets on our issues are less than ideal at the best of times, and the limited number of Western democracies for which any data are available limits how far multivariate analysis can take us. Second, while statistical analysis can reveal whether or not there is a systematic relationship between MCPs and the welfare state, it does not answer questions about the range of causal mechanisms that might be at work. Moreover, cross-national analysis is inevitably silent on the nature of the relationship in particular cases. As we will see, while the cross-national analysis in Chapter 2 finds no statistically significant negative relationship between MCPs and the welfare state, this does not preclude the possibility that such tensions exist in particular countries or periods, or that some particular forms of MCPs do have corrosive potential.

To explore the dynamics in particular cases, the volume includes a number of case studies that examine in depth particular countries or sets of countries. We include some countries that have adopted multicultural policies, where a tension between recognition and redistribution has been widely predicted or assumed. But we also include studies of countries which have resisted multicultural approaches, in part to understand whether a fear that MCPs might weaken the welfare state and other dimensions of solidarity help explain why they have not followed that path.

The volume is organized in three parts. Part I reports the findings of two cross-national statistical tests of the linkage between the levels of MCPs and the strength of the welfare state across the OECD countries. Part II contains the case studies examining the link between MCPs and the welfare state in particular countries, or in relation to particular types of diversity, trying to identify some of the underlying trends and mechanisms at work. Finally, Part III provides two concluding reflections on the relevance of our findings for broader debates in political theory and social science.

Part I: Cross-national studies

We begin with two chapters that explore the relationship between MCPs and the welfare state on a broad cross-national comparative basis among OECD countries. In Chapter 2, Banting, Johnston, Kymlicka, and Soroka introduce a new framework for testing the recognition/redistribution hypothesis. First, they develop an index of twenty-three different types of MCPs that have been adopted for three different types of minority groups (immigrants, national minorities, and indigenous peoples); second they categorize Western countries in terms of their level of MCPs; and third, they test whether countries with higher levels of MCPs have faced an erosion of the welfare state as compared to countries with lower levels of MCPs. Their findings show no negative correlation between the strength of a country's commitment to MCPs and its ability to sustain welfare spending or economic redistribution. As part of the multivariate analysis, this chapter also examines the heterogeneity/redistribution hypothesis, and shows that this too is overstated. In general, the size of immigrant groups, national minorities, and indigenous peoples in Western countries does not affect a country's ability to sustain its welfare commitments, although a rapid change in the size of immigrant groups does seem to have an effect. Yet even here, the authors argue, there are hints that adopting MCPs can help to mitigate whatever negative effect a rapidly increasing immigrant population may have.

These results provide some preliminary reassurance that the conflicts between multicultural recognition and economic redistribution are not as severe as many people believe. However, it is possible that the negative effects of MCPs simply take a long time to show up. Welfare states evolve slowly, as complex policy changes in some programmes, such as pensions, can take considerable time to come fully into effect. For this reason, it is useful to look, not only at welfare spending levels, but also at public support for the welfare state. This is the focus of Chapter 3, by Markus Crepaz. As he notes, we can view public attitudes as the 'canary in the mine'. If the politics of multicultural recognition are going to have a corroding impact on the politics of redistribution, this will likely show up first in a drop in public support for the welfare state, before it shows up in actual changes in spending levels. Drawing on public opinion data from a variety of surveys across the Western democracies, Crepaz asks whether states with higher levels of MCPs have seen an erosion in public support for redistribution, in comparison with countries with lower levels of MCPs. Here again, the results are encouraging: he finds no evidence that adopting MCPs erodes trust, solidarity, or support for redistribution.

Part II: Case studies

While cross-national studies provide fairly strong evidence that there is no *general* or systematic tendency for multicultural recognition to erode economic redistribution, they leave a number of questions unanswered, many of which can only be addressed through more detailed case studies.

We begin Part II with a study of the American context, which has driven much of the debate. The impact of racial diversity on welfare policy in the United States has been well studied, and indeed has often served as the paradigm case for the heterogeneity/redistribution trade-off. In Chapter 4, Rodney Hero and Robert Preuhs summarize the clear evidence that support for welfare programmes diminishes in American states that have higher levels of Blacks and Hispanics. The main question they address, however, is how the presence of MCPs, such as bilingual education for Hispanics, affects this familiar dynamic. They develop an index of state-level MCPs, including the interesting category of 'anti-MCPs'—that is, policies adopted precisely to prevent the future adoption of MCPs (such as 'Official English' laws). Drawing on cross-state statistical analysis, they show that there is no tendency for states that have adopted stronger MCPs to suffer more serious erosion in their welfare programmes compared to other states.

Another context where a recognition/redistribution trade-off has been widely predicted concerns immigrants in Europe, particularly the recent growth in non-white immigration. We have included three case studies of this phenomenon, focusing on three countries that have been at the epicentre of these trends: the Netherlands, Germany, and the United Kingdom. In each case, we are interested, not only in whether we can find empirical evidence for this predicted trade-off, but also in exploring why so many political actors believe that such a trade-off exists. In all three countries, we can observe the political realignment we mentioned at the start of this introduction—namely, a growing tendency within the social-democratic left to question its previous support for immigration and multiculturalism, in part on grounds of their impact on the welfare state. Many people in these three countries believe that they face the 'progressive's dilemma' of choosing between diversity and redistribution, and this is affecting political alliances and strategies. So we are interested in political attitudes and public discourse, as well as actual impacts on the welfare state.

In Chapter 5, Geoffrey Evans examines the case of Britain, focusing on the nature of public attitudes towards ethnic diversity, MCPs and the welfare state in that country, and their implications for party politics. Evans focuses on two predictions implicit in the critics' worries about multiculturalism: that public opposition to increasing ethnic diversity and MCPs will lead to an erosion in social trust and a decline in support for the welfare state; and that the politics of diversity will crowd out the politics of recognition, increasing the salience of cultural over redistributive issues in shaping voters' choices of which party to support, with negative consequences for left parties. Evans concludes the predictions fail on several fronts. First, there has been no backlash against ethnic diversity and MCPs in Britain. Public attitudes towards minorities have become more tolerant over time, and public opposition to MCPs has softened. Second, although there has been some weakening in public support for redistribution, this trend has much more to do with changing economic conditions than with immigration or MCPs. Finally, although there is some evidence that immigration may sometimes crowd out redistributive concerns in determining people's voting behaviour, there is no evidence that MCPs for already settled minorities have had this effect. In short, Evans concludes, 'we must cast doubt on the prognosis of a trade-off between multiculturalism policies and commitment to the welfare state.'

In Chapter 6, Han Entzinger examines the case of the Netherlands. If Britain has witnessed a mild pulling back from multiculturalism on the left, the Netherlands is often seen as the paradigm case of a wholesale retreat. During the post-war years, the Dutch built one of the most generous welfare states in Europe and adopted a strongly multiculturalist Minorities Policy, which reflected an extension of their approach to historic diversities, known as pillarization. During the 1990s, however, the Netherlands reduced the scope of its welfare state and shifted away from multiculturalism. Were these two trends related? Did the allegedly corrosive effects of MCPs contribute to the decline of the Dutch welfare state? Entzinger argues no. The two policy currents were driven by different concerns. On one side, restructuring the welfare state reflected economic and ideological trends common to Western democracies, and there is little evidence that issues of immigration or multiculturalism played a role in the political shift. On the other side, the shift away from the traditional approach to multiculturalism was driven by concern that the approach was contributing to the exclusion of minorities from the economic and social mainstream of Dutch society, and not by concerns about the impact of multiculturalism on the welfare state. While the Dutch experience of the 1990s does not correspond to the political dynamics anticipated by the critics of MCPs, Entzinger nonetheless predicts that the retreat from MCPs in the Netherlands is likely to endure, and that government policies to enhance the solidarity that underpins the welfare state will not, and perhaps should not, include a revival of multiculturalism.

In Chapter 7, Peter Kraus and Karen Schönwälder examine the case of Germany. Whereas the left in both Britain and the Netherlands had embraced multiculturalism in the 1980s, the left in Germany had always felt much more conflicted. Kraus and Schönwälder describe the historical factors that explain this resistance to multiculturalism, which are partly rooted in the nature of the German welfare state and labour relations. They also examine the more recent cautious opening towards ideas of multiculturalism. In this sense, the German case represents a slightly different trajectory from the Britain and the Netherlands. In the past decade, the German left (particularly the Social Democratic Party) has had an intense internal debate about whether to embrace MCPs, and how such a shift towards multiculturalism would affect its electoral chances and its traditional social policy goals. This chapter examines the different positions adopted in this debate, the basis for fears that MCPs might jeopardize welfare state goals, and the factors shaping the resulting political strategies. While the authors find no evidence that MCPs have weakened the welfare state, the German case suggests that fears of such an impact can weaken the political alliances necessary to introduce or sustain MCPs.

Chapter 8 focuses on another specific context where MCPs have been predicted to have corroding effects—namely, when they are linked to issues of historical redress. As we noted earlier, some commentators have suggested that MCPs are most likely to corrode solidarity and trust when they involve highlighting issues of historical injustice, generating a form of 'grievance politics'. This backward-looking focus on past wrongs against particular groups is said to inhibit forward-looking campaigns to achieve justice for all. In this chapter, Matt James examines this issue in the particular context of three redress campaigns in Canada: redress for the harms of residential schooling for aboriginals; redress for the wartime internment of Japanese- and Ukrainian-Canadians; and redress for the demolition of Africville, a black neighbourhood in Halifax. He argues that while redress campaigns can indeed promote attitudes that render cross-ethnic cooperation more difficult, they also help create the conditions under which such coalitions are possible.

While much of the literature on the recognition/redistribution trade-off has focused on the case of immigrant multiculturalism, there are other forms of ethnic diversity that also raise potential recognition/redistribution issues. In Chapter 9, Nicola McEwen focuses on the case of national minorities, particularly the Scots, Flemish, and Québécois. In a sense, it is surprising that more attention has not been paid to this issue, since minority nationalism has arguably had a much greater impact on the development of the welfare state than immigration. Most Western states with sizeable national minorities have accommodated minority nationalist aspirations through some form of federal or quasi-federal territorial autonomy. This sort of political restructuring of the state can have a dramatic impact on the evolution of the welfare state, and many commentators have argued that it is typically a detrimental impact, making it more difficult to sustain or build comprehensive welfare programmes. McEwen examines the impact of this sort of devolution/regionalization on the welfare state in the UK, Belgium, and Canada. She argues that the institutional reforms intended to enable national self-government for these minorities have had complex effects on social policy, both at the central level and in the self-governing regions. It has set in play political dynamics that sometimes work to strengthen social policy, as a tool of nation building, and sometimes serve to inhibit new redistributive policies. As a result, no simple, general pattern leaps out.

We conclude Part II with two chapters that move beyond OECD countries and focus on the case of indigenous peoples in Latin America. Many of the issues being raised in the recognition/redistribution debate in the West had already been extensively debated in the Latin American context, where the trend towards greater recognition of indigenous rights has occurred at roughly the same time as the trend towards neoliberal reforms that have cut back on social spending. There are several contending theories about how these two trends are related, many of which are actually more developed versions of the arguments that have been advanced in the West. In Chapter 10, Donna Lee Van Cott outlines these theories, and examines the empirical evidence for and against them, drawing on both case studies and cross-national statistics regarding structural reform in the region. While some commentators have argued that the trend towards indigenous rights has unintentionally reinforced neoliberal restructuring,

Van Cott argues, on the contrary, that the mobilization for indigenous rights has often served as an effective vehicle for building new left-wing coalitions that challenge neoliberalism.

In Chapter 11, Willem Assies examines in detail one of the most controversial cases in Latin America regarding the link between indigenous rights and neoliberal retrenchment. Bolivia is a central case because some indigenous leaders have entered into alliances with neoliberal parties, gaining modest indigenous MCPs in return for not opposing structural reforms. Yet this alliance did not last, and many indigenous leaders insist that neoliberalism and indigenous rights are inherently in conflict. This chapter explores what the Bolivian case tells us about the potential for alliances between MCPs and neoliberalism, and their limits.

As we said earlier, the picture that emerges from these various chapters about the relationship between MCPs and the welfare state is not a simple or straightforward one. Most of the chapters acknowledge that potential tensions could emerge under particular conditions or scenarios. Yet, overall, the research described here provides grounds for cautious optimism. None of the chapters has found clear evidence that MCPs have seriously weakened the welfare state, even in countries or contexts where commentators have predicted such trade-offs to exist. In that sense, the case studies support the main conclusion of the cross-national studies in Part I.

Part III: Theoretical reflections

We finish with reflections from leading scholars in two fields at the heart of the controversies examined in this book, political theory and the study of the welfare state. David Miller and John Myles and Sébastien St-Arnaud review the contributions in the volume and reflect on the implications for theoretical debates and future research in their respective fields. Both Miller and Myles/St-Arnaud conclude that the critics' original complaints against MCPs were overstated, but that there are still potential tensions here that require further analysis and careful managing.

David Miller accepts that the adoption of MCPs, taken by itself, cannot be held responsible for the weakening of the redistributive impact of the welfare state in Western democracies. Nevertheless, he sees dangers, particularly in the case of immigration. Miller distinguishes between multiculturalism as *policy* and multiculturalism as *ideology*, arguing that problems can emerge if the 'discourse' or 'ideology' of multiculturalism seems to imply that immigrants can claim rights to accommodation of their difference without accepting any corresponding civic responsibilities to adapt and integrate. Such a view, he argues, is deeply unpopular among Western electorates. It is therefore critical, in his view, to pay careful attention to whether MCPs conform or not to citizens' everyday sense of fairness. In particular, MCPs are likely to corrode solidarity when they are seen as providing 'free-rider' benefits to immigrants who are unwilling (or indeed discouraged) from making a good-faith effort to integrate. Clearly, this is a narrower claim than earlier critiques of MCPs, which, as we have seen, anticipated a general pattern of crowding out, corrosion, and misdiagnosis. Moreover, the solution, according to Miller, does not lie in abandoning multiculturalism. Supplementing MCPs with robust nation-building policies that expect and encourage immigrants to make an effort to integrate can help prevent the potentially corrosive possibilities of multiculturalism. The task is to think hard 'about how integration policies can work *alongside* multiculturalism policies' (Miller, this volume).

Myles and St-Arnaud reach a similar emphasis on integration through a very different route. They note that ethnic diversity has been largely absent in conventional welfare state theories, and conclude that the evidence in this volume confirms that ethno-racial heterogeneity and MCPs have not played a significant role in the development of contemporary welfare states, outside the well-documented US case. However, in their view, evidence from the past, even the recent past, does not settle the issue for the future. There is still a danger, especially in Europe, that rising ethno-racial diversity due to immigration might be transformed into ethno-racial political cleavages, which can be manipulated by right-wing populist political parties, with corrosive effects for the welfare state. Forestalling this danger requires the successful economic and political integration of immigrants, which in turn depends on a complex range of factors, including the immigrant selection process, labour market institutions and policies, and the electoral strength of minority groups themselves. MCPs can contribute to this integration, especially if they conform to popular perceptions of just desert and fair competition, but only as part of a much larger package.

Thus both Miller and Myles/St-Arnaud agree that the initial critiques of MCPs have proven unfounded to date, but that it is premature to dismiss the concerns that motivated the critics in the first place, at least in relation to the case of immigrant ethnic diversity.[24]

---

[24] Neither attempts to revive the critics' worry in relation to MCPs of national minorities and indigenous peoples, even though, as we noted earlier, these MCPs arguably involve a

5. Future directions

The chapters in this volume, while covering a wide range of groups and countries, can only be seen as a starting point for further research. As the commentaries by Miller and Myles/St-Arnaud make clear, there are many unanswered questions about the relationship between heterogeneity, multiculturalism policies, and the welfare state. In particular, both commentaries emphasize the importance of situating debates within a broader framework that examines how MCPs interact with other public policies relating to citizenship, national cohesion, and socio-economic integration. Taken on their own, MCPs are unlikely to have any 'inherent' or 'natural' tendency to undermine (or strengthen) the welfare state. However, in conjunction with other policies, and when operating under particular socio-economic and political conditions, MCPs may turn out to be important components in a larger constellation of factors that can strongly affect social solidarity and the welfare state. It is these constellations of factors, not MCPs in isolation, which we need to study.

Based on the analyses provided in the various chapters of this volume, we see at least two broad areas for future research: (*a*) the role of MCPs within a broader process of *political* integration that can sustain the forms of solidarity and citizenship upon which the welfare state depends; and (*b*) the role of MCPs within a broader process of *socio-economic* integration that can prevent the rise of 'welfare chauvinism' and other forms of populist backlash against the inclusion of minorities in the welfare state.

Regarding the first, many critics such as Gitlin, Wolfe, and Barry assumed that MCPs inherently corrode any sense of common national identity, or any sense of a common civic relationship between citizens and the state. It is clear from the various case studies in this volume that this fear is overstated. There are real-world examples of 'multicultural citizenship', or what we might even call 'multicultural nationhood', in which MCPs coexist with a strong sense of shared nationhood and citizenship. However, much work remains to be done in analysing how precisely MCPs relate to ideas of nation building and citizenship.

One way to proceed, following David Miller's earlier work, would be to distinguish 'moderate' from 'radical' conceptions of multiculturalism. In the former, but not the latter, MCPs are supplemented with policies that

much more dramatic reconfiguration of our inherited ideas of statehood, citizenship, and nationhood.

nurture an overarching political identity. A 'moderate' conception of multiculturalism in Britain, for example, would tell citizens there are many different and legitimate ways of 'being British', and that being British is consistent with the public expression and accommodation of other identities, including 'being Muslim' or 'being Scottish'. However, such MCPs recognizing and accommodating minority identities would also be accompanied by policies that actively promote the sense of 'being British'. By contrast, a 'radical' philosophy of multiculturalism would suggest that minorities should be absolved or discouraged from adopting such a pan-ethnic superordinate political identity (Miller 1995: ch. 5; Miller 2000: 105–6). The radical conception, he argues, is corrosive of solidarity and the welfare state. In the absence of appropriate nation-building policies, MCPs will reduce solidarity and trust, by focusing exclusively on the minority's difference. But in the presence of such nation-building policies, the same MCPs may in fact enhance solidarity and trust, by reassuring members of the minority group that the larger identity promoted by nation-building policies is an inclusive one that will fairly accommodate them.

The case studies in this volume suggest that such a simple dichotomy does not capture the complexity of the relationship between MCPs and national citizenship. So far as we can tell, no country in the West has adopted radical multiculturalism. All Western countries adopt a range of policies to inculcate overarching national identities and loyalties, including the mandatory teaching of the nation's language, history, and institutions in schools, language tests for citizenship, the funding of national media and museums, and the diffusion of national symbols, flags, anthems and holidays, to name just a few. Even in those Western countries that have strongly moved in the direction of MCPs, the resulting approach is best described as 'robust forms of nation-building combined and constrained by robust forms of minority rights' (Kymlicka 2001: 3).[25] So all of the countries that we describe in Chapter 2 as having 'strong' or 'modest' levels of MCPs fall into the moderate category on Miller's terminology. We do not believe there is any Western democracy that has adopted 'radical' multiculturalism in Miller's sense.

However, it is certainly true that countries vary in the strength and effectiveness of their nation-building policies, and that countries periodically need to reassess whether to strengthen their policies in this

---

[25] For a more detailed discussion of the enduring centrality of nation-building policies, even in pro-MCP countries like Canada or Australia, see Kymlicka (1998, 2001). On the way MCPs interact with pro-citizenship policies in Canada, see Bloemraad (2006).

area—e.g. by providing greater funding for immigrants to learn the official language, or by providing citizenship education classes, or establishing citizenship oaths and ceremonies for immigrants who naturalize. This indeed is part of what we see in the last few years in some Western European countries, such as the Netherlands or Britain. The Netherlands has decided that more effort must be spent on encouraging and enabling immigrants to learn the official language (Fermin 2001; Baubock 2003; Entzinger 2003). So too has Britain, which has also adopted a national policy of promoting citizenship education in the schools, and creating citizenship ceremonies and oaths (White Paper 2002).

These shifts in Britain and the Netherlands have been described as a 'retreat from multiculturalism' by Christian Joppke (Joppke 2004; cf. Brubaker 2001). But in the British case the 'retreat from multiculturalism' is primarily at the level of rhetoric, and few MCPs have been replaced or abolished (Hansen, forthcoming).[26] Even in the Netherlands—which has certainly undergone a wrenching national debate around these issues, and a marked growth in public anxiety about immigrant integration—a number of MCPs remain in place.[27] The primary change has been to strengthen the nation-building policies that accompany those MCPs.

Joppke is surely right that these policy shifts are often *perceived* by the general public as a wholesale 'retreat from multiculturalism'. This is due, at least in part, to the fact that political leaders in many countries have shifted away from the discourse or rhetoric of multiculturalism, which has become less fashionable. Fewer politicians extol its virtues or identify themselves as 'multiculturalists', although nor do they propose to abolish or retrench all existing MCPs.[28] In this context, decisions to supplement MCPs with nation-building policies are nonetheless perceived by many citizens (and academic commentators) as a 'retreat' from MCPs. If Miller is correct that multicultural ideology can be as significant as multicultural

[26] It is particularly puzzling to describe the new British policy as a retreat from multiculturalism, since it is explicitly modelled on Canadian policies. For example, the new citizenship oaths and citizenship ceremonies, as well as the language tests for citizenship, are drawn in part on similar Canadian policies, and are defended in part by emphasizing their role in the success of the Canadian approach to immigrant integration. Indeed, with the adoption of these enhanced nation-building policies, Britain has become closer to, not farther from, the Canadian model of immigrant integration, with its 'robust nation-building combined and constrained by robust minority rights'.

[27] As Entzinger notes in Chapter 6 below, 'Today's assimilative rhetoric, particularly at the national level, disguises the perpetuation of certain multicultural practices.' Dutch MCPs that remain wholly or partially in place include consultative bodies, funding for minority religious schools, and provisions for multiculturalism in the media.

[28] For speculation on the decline of the rhetoric of multiculturalism, despite the persistence of MCPs, see Kymlicka (2003).

policy, then this change may be important.[29] But unfortunately, it has often obscured rather than clarified the range of existing and potential relationships between multicultural policies and nation-building policies.

In short, we need to be careful not to prejudge the connection between MCPs and nation-building, or the connection between rhetoric and policy. There are substantial variations between countries, or over time within countries, in the rhetorical significance attached to ideas of 'nationhood', 'citizenship', and 'multiculturalism'. In some times and places, a resurgent rhetoric of nationhood and citizenship crowds out any talk of multiculturalism; in other cases, the opposite seems to hold. But these highly visible shifts in rhetoric may obscure an ongoing, and less visible, process by which countries try to build policy frameworks that combine MCPs with nation-building and citizenship-promoting policies in a mutually supporting way. The viability of a multicultural welfare state may depend on a more nuanced understanding of the nature and functioning of such frameworks.

Equally important is the economic and social integration of minorities. Much of the current tension in Europe is rooted in economic and social exclusion of immigrants. Unemployment haunts non-EU immigrants throughout Europe. Even in the countries with the best records, the unemployment rate of non-EU foreigners is twice that of the population as a whole, whereas in other countries, the rate can range as high as five times that for the population as a whole (Koopmans 2005, as summarized in Hansen, forthcoming). The economic exclusion implicit in unemployment is often compounded by social separateness, reflecting parallel societies with few links bridging across cultural divides. More worryingly, the seeds of exclusion are being sown in the second generation. The 2000 Programme for International Student Assessment (PISA) revealed a stunning gap between migrant children and other children in reading, mathematics, and science knowledge in a diverse set of countries, including the Netherlands, Germany, Switzerland, France, and Sweden (ibid.).

Here the interaction between integration and the welfare state is more direct and obvious. Minority groups with persistently high levels of unemployment are likely to be disproportionately dependent on social assistance and other welfare programmes, creating dry tinder for political firestorms. Two forms of backlash have emerged in different countries.

---

[29] We consider the claim that focusing on ideology would generate different results than our focus on policies in Chapter 2, n. 3.

First, many governments have resorted to 'welfare chauvinism', which supports the welfare state but seeks to deny newcomers access to its benefits (Banting 1999; Kitschelt 1995; Andersen 1992; Andersen and Bjørklund 1990). A long list of countries have introduced or lengthened minimum residency periods for social programmes, limiting immigrants access to benefits. Second, a political backlash against minority dependency on welfare might help fuel a broader neoliberal attack on the welfare state, strengthening radical right-wing parties and/or leading mainstream parties to quietly withdraw their support for social redistribution. The impact might be felt primarily by programmes which support the poor generally but on which minorities have been particularly dependent. The classic example here is welfare reform in the USA in the mid-1990s, which eliminated Aid to Families with Dependent Children (AFDC) and replaced it with the term-limited Temporary Aid to Needy Families (TANF). However, the impact might be a more pervasive weakening of the redistributive aspects (as opposed to the social insurance aspects) of the welfare state, as anticipated by David Miller in his reflections (this volume). These two forms of backlash—welfare chauvinism and a broader neoliberalism—obviously distribute the burdens of retrenchment differently. But both represent an erosion of the universalistic conception of the welfare state.

Overcoming the economic and social exclusion of immigrant minorities is clearly one of the great policy challenges confronting European countries.[30] A wide range of policy instruments are relevant, including immigration policies, settlement programmes, language acquisition programmes, anti-discrimination laws, education and training, labour market institutions and policies, to name a few. Some critics have assumed that MCPs crowd out or displace such policies, but here again our case studies show that this is not true. Countries can combine strong MCPs with strong policies to improve the access of immigrants to education and the labour market. Indeed, one immigrant MCP—namely, affirmative action—is exclusively focused on this issue. But as Myles and St-Arnaud emphasize, MCPs are likely to be only one part of a larger incorporation regime, and questions remain about what exactly is the link between MCPs and labour market integration. For example, how do different

---

[30] As Schierup et al. (2006) argue, Europeans confront this challenge at the same time as they face powerful pressures to restructure the welfare state. The restructuring and integration agendas are driven by separate forces, with the pressures on the welfare state flowing primarily from globalization, economic restructuring, technological change, and neoliberal ideologies. However, while the two agendas are propelled by different forces, their resolution is clearly interrelated.

kinds of multicultural education, mother-tongue services, and culturally sensitive settlement programmes interact with different kinds of labour market policies?

Thus one promising field for future research is to develop a more subtle conceptualization of the possible links between MCPs and political and economic integration of minorities, and then to test which packages or combinations of these policies have been most successful in sustaining the welfare state. In effect, we need to develop a typology of incorporation regimes, analogous to the typologies of welfare state regimes which proved so productive in comparative welfare state research. We make some tentative suggestions along this line at the end of Chapter 2.

6. Conclusions

How to maintain and strengthen the bonds of community in ethnically diverse societies is one of the most compelling questions confronting Western democracies. The growing diversity of Western societies has generated pressures for the construction of new and more inclusive forms of citizenship and national identity. Finding our way forward requires much more knowledge about the underlying relationships between ethnic diversity, multiculturalism, and solidarity than we have today.

We therefore close with a caution. Given the limited nature of our hard information in this area, there is a danger that the experiences of one country will emerge as a sort of master narrative, a story that is seen as capturing the essence of the issues in play. For many Europeans, the United States has become the quintessential multicultural country, and the key test case of the relations between diversity, recognition, and redistribution. In the United Kingdom, for example, analysts such as David Goodhart (2004) depict the American experience as clear evidence that ethnic heterogeneity and multicultural approaches erode redistribution, and as providing a warning about the future of their country. The corrosive aspects of US welfare politics are no longer seen as a reflection of a particular history of slavery and segregation, but rather as a normal, even inevitable, reaction to the simple fact of diversity and its recognition in public policy.

This is a field in which simple narratives are as likely to mislead as inform. Distinctive histories and traditions matter here, and it is important not to project the experience of one country onto the rest of the world. Rather, the priority is to uncover diverse narratives, a variety of stories that point to different possible relationships between diversity, multiculturalism, and redistribution. The evidence in this book stands as an antidote to fatalistic assertions that multiculturalism policies necessarily weaken support for social programmes. The complex patterns across countries are hopeful signs, which suggest that there is no inevitability at work and that wise policy choices matter.

Part I
Cross-national studies

2

Do multiculturalism policies erode the welfare state? An empirical analysis

Keith Banting, Richard Johnston, Will Kymlicka, and Stuart Soroka

There is a growing debate about the impact of diversity on the welfare state. As discussed in Chapter 1, there are in fact two separate debates here. Some people fear that ethno-linguistic or racial diversity by itself weakens the welfare state, because it is difficult to generate feelings of trust and solidarity across ethnic and racial lines. We call this the 'heterogeneity/ redistribution trade-off' hypothesis: the larger the size of ethnic/racial minorities as a percentage of the population, the more difficult it is to build or sustain a robust welfare state. Others fear that the adoption of multiculturalism policies (MCPs) to recognize and accommodate ethnic groups generates political dynamics that inadvertently undermine the welfare state in Western democracies. We call this the 'recognition/ redistribution trade-off' hypothesis: the more a country embraces the multicultural 'politics of (ethnic) recognition' through MCPs, the more difficult it is to sustain a 'politics of (economic) redistribution' through the welfare state. This is the heart of the critics' case against MCPs discussed in Chapter 1.

These two debates are obviously connected. Many people who believe that ethnic/racial heterogeneity erodes the welfare state assume that MCPs must do so as well. After all, if the presence of sizeable ethnic and racial minorities tends to weaken the welfare state, presumably our goal should be to reduce the public visibility and political salience of these ethnic/racial differences, rather than emphasizing and celebrating them, as is done by MCPs.

However, as far as we can tell, no one has actually empirically tested the relationship between MCPs and social redistribution. As we saw in Chapter 1, there is a growing literature on the first hypothesis, which suggests that, in at least some contexts, increasing ethnic and racial diversity is correlated with weaker welfare states. But all of these studies focus on ethnic diversity as a demographic phenomenon, and are silent on the implications of the adoption of MCPs. Such studies tell us nothing about whether MCPs increase any tension that may exist between ethnic diversity and social redistribution, as the critics suggest, or potentially mitigate it, as the defenders reply. We are therefore left with the need to find a way of illuminating this issue more directly.

The purpose of this chapter is to provide an initial answer to this question, by focusing on the experience of Western democracies and utilizing the tools of empirical analysis. Is it true that countries that adopt multiculturalism policies for immigrant minorities have greater difficulty in sustaining and developing their welfare state? Do countries that recognize and support national minorities and indigenous peoples pay a price in terms of their wider social commitments? Is the very idea of a multicultural welfare state a contradiction in terms?

To examine this question, the chapter proceeds in three stages. Section 1 takes the first step by providing a more rigorous definition of MCPs and measuring differences in the strength of such policies in Western democracies, grouping the countries into three broad categories, those with strong MCPs, those with modest MCPs, and those with weak MCPs. Section 2 then introduces a set of indicators of the strength of the welfare state, and examines whether the group of countries with strong MCPs fared worse in terms of the evolution of their welfare states when compared with countries with modest or weak MCPs. As we shall see, this section finds no evidence of a systematic relationship between the adoption of MCPs and the erosion of the welfare state over the last two decades of the twentieth century. Section 3 takes the final step, conducting a multivariate analysis that also takes account of other factors that influence the welfare state. Given the debate about whether ethnic diversity itself weakens social redistribution, we seek to disentangle empirically the effects of ethnic diversity and the effects of MCPs. In addition, we incorporate a number of other factors that previous studies have identified as powerful drivers of social spending in OECD countries. This multivariate analysis confirms that fears of the impact of MCPs on the welfare state are overstated. Indeed, there are some suggestive hints in the data that adopting MCPs might in fact, under some circumstances, strengthen the welfare state. Finally, Section 4 pulls together the threads of the argument and reflects on their implications for the larger debates.

1. The nature and strength of multiculturalism policies

Determining whether there is a correlation between MCPs and changes in social redistribution requires a clear definition of MCPs and a classification of countries in terms of the extent to which they have adopted such policies. Unfortunately, there is no consensus in the literature on how to define the term 'multicultural policies'. The term has quite different connotations in different countries. Many writers employ the term without ever defining it, and those who do make an effort to define it offer very different accounts of the necessary or sufficient conditions for a policy to qualify as a 'multicultural' policy. Given this lack of consensus, any account that we provide will inevitably be contestable, and to some extent stipulative. Some commentators will find our definition unduly narrow, others will find it unduly broad. We will discuss some of these objections as we go. However, for reasons we explain below, we think it unlikely that expanding or narrowing the definition of MCPs would change the basic empirical findings we present in sections 2 and 3.

What then do we mean by MCPs? To begin with, we are focusing on the treatment of ethnocultural groups. This is already to narrow the field compared to some other accounts of MCPs. In some contexts, the term multiculturalism is used to cover a broader range of forms of diversity, including gender/sexual orientation/disability and so on. On this broader view, 'multiculturalism' is virtually coextensive with 'the politics of recognition'. In this study, however, we are restricting the term multiculturalism to the context of ethnocultural diversity.

Even if we limit our focus to ethnocultural groups, there is still plenty of scope for disagreement about what counts as a 'multicultural' policy towards such groups. In the account we give below, we have tried as much as possible to follow what we take to be the most common usages of the term, in both public as well as scholarly debate. However, we have also tried to ensure that our account reflects the issues raised by the critics of MCPs. For this reason, we have excluded from our account of MCPs any policies that simply involve the non-discriminatory access to, or non-discriminatory enforcement of, the traditional civil and political rights of citizenship for the individual members of ethnic groups. In some countries, the rhetoric of multiculturalism is advanced to defend such non-discriminatory protection of the common rights of liberal-democratic citizenship. For example, some German politicians have invoked multicultural rhetoric to eliminate legal provisions that made it more difficult for ethnic Turks than for ethnic Germans to become citizens, and to extend the scope of anti-discrimination laws to cover the Turks. While described by some politicians as a form of 'multiculturalism', and defended as 'recognizing' or 'accommodating' Germany's ethnic diversity, these are not the sorts of policies that our critics view as a threat to the welfare state. Respecting the common individual rights of citizenship is indeed one essential form of accommodating the members of minority groups, but the critics are not objecting to 'recognizing' immigrants in this sense—i.e. as equal individual citizens. They are only concerned with policies that go beyond the protection of traditional individual rights of citizenship to provide some additional form of public recognition or support or accommodation of ethnic groups, identities, and practices. Since this is the concern of critics, we will limit our definition of MCPs to such policies of public recognition, support, and accommodation.

But what does it mean to provide public 'recognition', 'support', or 'accommodation' to ethnic groups? It is difficult to answer this question in the abstract, since different groups seek quite different forms of recognition, support, and accommodation. To help identify these policies more precisely, it is useful to distinguish different categories of ethnic groups, and to see how Western states have accommodated them (or not). For the purposes of this chapter, we will focus on three types of ethnic groups: immigrants, national minorities, and indigenous peoples.

Before turning to an examination of specific policies for these three groups, however, two further clarifications are important. First, our focus in this chapter is on multiculturalism *policies*, and we are not addressing the impact of multiculturalist *discourse*. In many cases, policies and discourse go together. Countries with strong MCPs are likely to be characterized by the rhetoric of multiculturalism. But the relationship between multiculturalist policies and multiculturalist rhetoric is complicated. One can have multiculturalist rhetoric without MCPs. For example, as we noted earlier, in Germany today the rhetoric of multiculturalism is invoked to defend policies of the non-discriminatory enforcement of traditional individual civil and political rights. Conversely, one can have multiculturalist policies without multiculturalist rhetoric. This is the case in Britain, where senior government officials explicitly express their dislike for the term 'multiculturalism'. It is also true, to a lesser extent, in Australia, where the word multiculturalism is less common than ten or fifteen years ago.[1]

We emphasize this point in part to avoid potential misunderstandings about our categorization of countries below. When we describe Germany as 'minimally' MCP, we are referring to the relative absence of multiculturalist policies, not the absence of multiculturalist rhetoric. Conversely, when we describe Australia as strongly MCP, we are referring to the wide range of MCPs that are present, not to the varying level of multiculturalist rhetoric. But we also emphasize this point because it raises an interesting issue about the empirical critique of multiculturalism. All of the critics we have cited claim that multiculturalism policies erode the welfare state. But, as David Miller notes in Chapter 12 below, it is possible that what some of them are really concerned about is the rhetoric or discourse of multiculturalism (see also Brubaker 2004: 125 n. 15). For example, it is not clear that either the misdiagnosis effect or the corroding effect described in Chapter 1 really depends on the presence of MCPs, rather than simply multiculturalist discourse. It is not clear how one would measure the level of multiculturalist discourse cross-nationally, to see whether it is correlated with erosion of the welfare state, but it is a hypothesis that might be worth investigating.[2] In this chapter, however, we are focused exclusively on multicultural policies.

Second, because some of the critical data on welfare state redistribution are available on a cross-national basis only for the period up to 2000, we examine the relationship between MCPs and the welfare state in the period from 1980 to 2000. As a result, we categorize the strength of MCPs in different countries based on the policies they had in place for a substantial portion of those years. This two-decade period saw intense debates over MCPs, and several countries adopted or significantly extended MCPs in these years. Our aim is therefore to assess the impact of these policy

---

[1] Conversely, countries that have dogmatically rejected the discourse of multiculturalism may contain a (minimal) number of MCPs. This is true, for example, of France (Schain 1999). As Schain argues, the anti-multiculturalist government rhetoric in France obscures as much as it reveals about France's actual policies.

[2] We suspect that the results of such a test would not significantly differ from our results in this chapter, since the adoption of MCPs is both the result of political mobilization employing multiculturalist rhetoric, and typically encourages further utilization of that rhetoric by non-state actors seeking access to public institutions. So, while multicultural policies and multicultural political rhetoric are not the same, they are likely to be highly correlated, and testing the former is arguably a good proxy for testing the latter.

choices on the welfare state. As a result, our rankings may not reflect the most recent changes in some countries. For example, with the legislation adopted in Britain in 1998 to devolve powers to Scotland and Wales, one could argue that Britain should now fall into the strong-MCP category in its approach to sizeable national minorities. However, this change is too recent to have affected the evolution of the welfare state from 1980 to 2000. If devolution has an eroding effect on social redistribution, it will only show up in later years. Similarly, some commentators have argued that the Netherlands and Britain have recently 'retreated' from multiculturalism in their treatment of immigrant groups. As we discuss more fully in section 4, the nature of these policy shifts is complicated, but in any event, this shift is too recent to have affected social programmes in the period we are studying. We categorize a country as 'strongly' or 'modestly' MCP if it had in place strong or modest MCPs for a significant portion of the period between 1980 and 2000, and we are interested in the relationship between these policies and the welfare state in those years.

With those qualifications in mind, it is time to develop our classification of specific MCPs and to rank Western countries in terms of the strength of the MCPs adopted in response to the concerns of three ethnic minorities: immigrants, national minorities, and indigenous minorities.

Immigrants

Historically, the most important countries of immigration (i.e. Australia, Canada, New Zealand, and the USA) had an assimilationist approach to immigration. Immigrants were encouraged and expected to assimilate to the pre-existing society, with the hope that over time they would become indistinguishable from native-born citizens in their speech, dress, recreation, and way of life generally. Any groups that were seen as incapable of this sort of cultural assimilation were prohibited from immigrating in the first place, or from becoming citizens. This was reflected in laws that excluded Africans and Asians from entering these countries of immigration for much of the twentieth century, or from naturalizing.

Beginning in the late 1960s, however, we saw a dramatic change in this approach. There were two related changes: first, the adoption of race-neutral admissions criteria, so that immigrants to these countries are increasingly from non-European (and often non-Christian) societies; and second, the adoption of a more 'multicultural' conception of integration, one which expects that many immigrants will visibly and proudly express their ethnic identity, and which accepts an obligation on the part of public institutions (like the police, schools, media, museums, etc.) to accommodate these ethnic identities.

These twofold changes occurred, to varying degrees, in all of the traditional countries of immigration. All of them shifted from discriminatory to race-neutral admissions and naturalization policies. And all of them shifted from an assimilationist to a more multicultural conception of integration. Of course, there were important differences in how official or formal this shift to multiculturalism has been. In Canada, as in Australia and New Zealand, this shift was formally and officially marked by the declaration of a multicultural policy by the central government. But even in the United States, we saw similar changes on the ground. The USA does not have an official policy of multiculturalism at the federal level, but if we look at lower levels of government, such as states or cities, we often find a broad range of multiculturalism policies. If we look at state-level policies regarding the education curriculum, for example, or city-level policies regarding policing or hospitals, we often find that they are indistinguishable from the way provinces and cities in Canada or Australia deal with issues of immigrant ethnocultural diversity. As in Canada, they have their own diversity programmes and/or equity officers. As Nathan Glazer (1977) puts it, 'we are all multiculturalists now', although this perhaps understates the considerable variation across cities and states in the USA in their commitment to MCPs.[3]

Similarly, in Britain, while there is no nationwide multiculturalism policy, many of the same basic ideas and principles are pursued through their race relations policy.[4] All of these countries have accepted the same twofold change—adopting race-neutral admissions and naturalization policies, and imposing on public institutions a duty to accommodate immigrant ethno-cultural diversity—although the degree and formal recognition of the latter change varies from country to country.

This trend applies primarily to countries of immigration—i.e. countries which legally admit immigrants as permanent residents and future citizens. Amongst such countries, the main exception to this trend is France, which retains an assimilationist conception of French republican citizenship. It is a different story, however, in those countries that do not

---

[3] Experts in immigration and integration issues have repeatedly demolished the mythical contrast between the American 'melting pot' and the Canadian 'mosaic', yet the myth endures in the popular imagination. For more on MCPs in the American context, see Chapter 4 below.

[4] For the British model of multiculturalism through race relations, see Favell (2001), Hansen (forthcoming).

legally admit immigrants, such as most countries of northern Europe. These countries may well contain large numbers of 'foreigners', in the form of illegal economic migrants, asylum seekers, or 'guest-workers', but these groups are not admitted as part of an immigration policy. As it happens, even some of these countries adopted aspects of a 'multicultural' approach in the period we are studying (e.g. Sweden and the Netherlands). But in general, the trend from assimilation to multiculturalism is one that has taken place most strongly within countries of immigration.

What then are the specific MCPs that reflect this shift in approach? For the purposes of this chapter, we will take the following eight policies as the most common or emblematic forms of immigrant MCPs:

(1) Constitutional, legislative or parliamentary affirmation of multiculturalism, at the central and/or regional and municipal levels;
(2) the adoption of multiculturalism in the school curriculum;[5]
(3) the inclusion of ethnic representation/sensitivity in the mandate of public media or media licensing;
(4) exemptions from dress codes, Sunday closing legislation etc. (either by statute or by court cases);
(5) allowing dual citizenship;[6]
(6) the funding of ethnic group organizations to support cultural activities;[7]

---

[5] Not all forms of education that teach about immigrant cultures qualify as 'multicultural education'. In Germany, for example, special education arrangements were set up for the children of Turkish guest-workers with the goal of preparing them to return to their 'home' (even if they were in fact born in Germany), on the assumption that they did not really belong in Germany. This sort of 'preparationist education' clearly differs from what is typically understood as 'multicultural education', and does not count as an MCP on our account. As discussed earlier, MCPs on our view are policies that seek to recognize and accommodate ethnic diversity as a fact of society, not policies that seek to encourage ethnic groups to leave.

[6] As noted earlier, we do not consider non-discriminatory access to citizenship as itself a form of MCP, in part because it would not be contested by most critics of MCPs. Naturalization policy only qualifies as an MCP where it has been modified in order to accommodate immigrant ethnic identities, most obviously by recognizing and accommodating the desire of immigrants to maintain a link with their country of origin through dual citizenship. As with many of these criteria, questions can be raised about the motive for these policy shifts. In some cases, dual citizenship has been allowed, not in order to accommodate the desires of immigrants within the country to maintain their previous nationality, but rather to enable emigrants or expatriates who live outside the country to retain a link with the country. But this is not the standard case in countries of immigration.

[7] In many countries, ethnic organizations are eligible to receive public funding to provide social services, alongside other non-governmental organizations. To qualify as an MCP, however, public funding must also be available to support the cultural life of the minority.

(7) the funding of bilingual education or mother-tongue instruction;

(8) affirmative action for disadvantaged immigrant groups.[8]

Some commentators have suggested including a ninth policy—namely, a policy of admitting large numbers of immigrants as permanent residents and future citizens. Some people view a pro-immigration policy as itself a form of MCP, on the assumption that only a country that is willing to accommodate diversity would voluntarily admit immigrants as future citizens. However, the link between immigration policy and MCPs is complex. Many critics of MCPs are in fact defenders of more open borders: they are happy with the idea of greater ethnic and racial diversity in the population, but simply oppose any government recognition or accommodation of this diversity through MCPs. This is a long-standing view amongst libertarians. Conversely, in some countries, support for MCPs is dependent on sharply limiting the number of new immigrants who can take advantage of these policies. This is often said to be the case in Britain. The quasi-multiculturalism policies adopted in the 1970s (under the heading of race relations) were part of a package in which the government said to Britons: 'we will close the door to new immigrants; but we expect you to accept and accommodate the immigrants from the Caribbean and South Asia who have already arrived'. Reopening the door to immigration was seen as undermining the tenuous support for MCPs.[9] So for our purposes, we limit immigrant MCPs to policies that concern

[8] Including affirmative action as an MCP is potentially controversial, since it need not involve any recognition or affirmation of cultural difference. Indeed, some of its defenders have defended it precisely as a tool of assimilation. By 'artificially' fostering integration into common institutions, it discourages the formation of distinct 'ethnic economies' in which members of particular groups specialize in a particular economic niche and reproduce the cultural traditions associated with that niche. So this is a case of a policy that 'recognizes' distinct groups, for the purposes of making various admission or employment decisions, but which need not be centrally concerned with 'accommodating' ethno-cultural diversity. However, in many cases, the adoption of affirmative action policies has gone hand-in-hand with a commitment to reform the institution to make it more accommodating of members of minority groups (e.g. the adoption of multiculturalism in school curricula, or changes to the work schedule or work uniforms to accommodate minority groups). Affirmative action to recruit more teachers or police officers from minority communities is also often defended as a way of making these institutions better able to accommodate the needs of the ethnic groups in their clientele. So affirmative action is often, though not always, part of a larger package of MCPs.

[9] A similar comment applies to refugee policy. While there is a clear trend for pro-MCP countries to have more generous policies on the admission of refugees (Kate 2005), this is not always the case, as witnessed by the harsh treatment of refugees in Australia, compared with the (formerly) generous openness to refugees in Germany, even though the former is pro-MCP and the latter not. Policies about whether to admit people as immigrants or refugees, and policies about how to accommodate them once admitted, raise quite distinct issues.

the treatment of immigrant groups that already reside on the territory of the state, such as the eight policies listed above.

For each of the MCPs in our list, we gave each country a score of 1.0 if it had explicitly adopted and implemented the policy for much of the period we are examining (1980 to 2000), 0.5 if it adopted the policy in an implicit, incomplete, or token manner, and 0 if it did not have the policy. This generates a total possible score of 8.0, and the detailed scoring for each county is reported in Appendix 2.1. If a country scored at least 6.0 out of a possible 8.0, we have categorized it as 'strong'. If it scored between 3.0 and 5.5, we have categorized it as 'modest'. If it scored under 3.0, we have categorized it as 'weak'. On this basis, we have categorized countries this way:

STRONG: Australia, Canada
MODEST: Belgium, Netherlands, New Zealand, Sweden, UK, US
WEAK: Austria, Denmark, Finland, France, Germany, Greece, Ireland, Italy, Japan, Norway, Portugal, Spain, Switzerland

Sizeable national minorities

A second trend concerns the treatment of substate/minority nationalisms, such as the Québécois in Canada, the Scots and Welsh in Britain, the Catalans and Basques in Spain, the Flemish in Belgium, the German-speaking minority in South Tyrol in Italy, and the Hispanics in Puerto Rico in the United States.[10] In all of these cases, we find a regionally concentrated group that conceives of itself as a nation within a larger state, and mobilizes behind nationalist political parties to achieve recognition of its nationhood, either in the form of an independent state or through territorial autonomy within the larger state.

In the past, most if not all of these countries have attempted to assimilate or suppress these forms of substate nationalism. To have a regional group with a sense of distinct nationhood was seen as a threat to the state. Various efforts were made to erode this sense of distinct nationhood, including restricting minority-language rights, abolishing traditional forms of regional self-government, and encouraging members of the dominant group to settle in the minority group's homeland so that the minority becomes outnumbered even in its traditional territory.

[10] We could also include the French- and Italian-speaking minorities in Switzerland, although some people dispute whether they manifest a 'national' consciousness.

However, there has been a dramatic change in the way most Western countries deal with substate nationalisms. Today, all of the countries we have just mentioned have accepted the principle that these substate national identities will endure into the indefinite future, and that their sense of nationhood and nationalist aspirations must be accommodated in some way or other. This accommodation has typically taken the form of what we can call 'multination federalism': that is, creating a federal or quasi-federal subunit in which the minority group forms a local majority, and so can exercise meaningful forms of self-government. Moreover, where the group has a distinct language, this language is typically recognized as an official state language, at least within their federal subunit, and perhaps throughout the country as a whole.

At the beginning of the twentieth century, only Switzerland and Canada had adopted this combination of territorial autonomy and official language status for substate national groups. Since then, however, most Western democracies that contain sizeable substate nationalist movements have moved in this direction. The list includes the adoption of autonomy for the Swedish-speaking Aland Islands in Finland after the First World War, autonomy for South Tyrol and Puerto Rico after the Second World War, federal autonomy for Catalonia and the Basque Country in Spain in the 1970s, for Flanders in Belgium in the 1980s, and most recently devolution for Scotland and Wales in the UK in the 1990s.

This shift from suppressing substate nationalisms to accommodating them through regional autonomy and official language rights is now widespread. Amongst the Western democracies with a sizeable national minority, the most obvious exception to this trend is France, in its refusal to grant autonomy to its main substate nationalist group in Corsica. However, legislation was recently adopted to accord autonomy to Corsica, and while a ruling of the Constitutional Court prevented its implementation, France too may join the bandwagon soon.

There are some other potential exceptions. Northern Ireland is difficult to categorize, since Catholics are clearly a national minority, but are not territorially concentrated, and so the model of multination federalism is not available. Even here, however, we see clear movement in the direction of greater recognition of minority nationalism. Northern Ireland has recently adopted a peace agreement that explicitly accords Catholics a number of guarantees in terms of representation, and acknowledges their identification with co-nationals in Ireland.

Another complicated case is the Netherlands, where the sizeable Frisian minority lacks territorial autonomy or significant language rights, although this is largely because (virtually alone amongst such sizeable national minorities in the West) the group has not in fact mobilized along nationalist lines to acquire such rights. It is not clear that the Netherlands would reject such claims if clearly supported by most Frisians, but we do not include the country in our analysis.

Amongst Western countries, perhaps the only country that remains strongly and ideologically opposed to the official recognition of substate national groups is Greece, where the once sizeable Macedonian minority has now been swamped in its traditional homeland.

We can call this a shift towards a 'multicultural' approach to substate national groups, although this terminology is rarely used by these groups themselves, who prefer the language of nationhood, self-determination, federalism, and power sharing. What then are the specific policies that are indicative of this shift? We consider the following six policies as emblematic of a multicultural approach to substate national groups:

(1) federal or quasi-federal territorial autonomy;
(2) official language status, either in the region or nationally;
(3) guarantees of representation in the central government or on Constitutional Courts;
(4) public funding of minority-language universities/schools/media;
(5) constitutional or parliamentary affirmation of 'multinationalism';
(6) according international personality (e.g. allowing the substate region to sit on international bodies, or sign treaties, or have their own Olympic team).

It is important to emphasize that this category only refers to 'sizeable' national minorities. There are many much smaller national groups within the Western democracies who lack the numbers or territorial concentration to be able to exercise territorial autonomy or to support separate institutions such as mother-tongue universities. This would include, for example, the Slovenians in Austria, the Sorbs in Germany, the Germans in Denmark, the Tornedal-Finns in Sweden, and so on. We have, somewhat arbitrarily, set the dividing line between 'small' and 'sizeable' national minorities at 100,000 people, although all of the smaller groups just mentioned are in fact under 50,000 people. The treatment of such small national minorities raises a different set of issues, and deserves a separate category, which we have not been able to cover in this chapter.

Once again we gave each country a score of 1.0, 0.5, or 0 for each of the MCPs, and the total scores for each country can be found in Appendix 2.1. If a country scored 4.0 or more out of a possible 6.0, we have categorized it as 'strong'; if it scored between 2.0 and 3.5, we have categorized it as 'modest'; and if it scored under 2.0, we have categorized it as 'weak'. Based on these criteria, we have categorized those Western democracies that contain sizeable national minorities this way:

STRONG: Belgium, Canada, Finland, Spain, Switzerland
MODEST: Italy, UK, US (with respect to Puerto Rico)
WEAK: France, Greece, Japan

Indigenous peoples

A third trend concerns the treatment of indigenous peoples, such as the Indians and Inuit in Canada, the Aboriginal peoples of Australia, the Maori of New Zealand, the Sami of Scandinavia, the Inuit of Greenland, and Indian tribes in the United States. In the past, all of these countries had the same goal and expectation that indigenous peoples would eventually disappear as distinct communities, as a result of dying out, or intermarriage, or assimilation. Various policies were adopted to speed up this process, such as stripping indigenous peoples of their lands, restricting the practice of their traditional cultures, languages, and religions, and undermining their institutions of self-government.

However, there has been a dramatic change in these policies, starting in the early 1970s. Today, all of the countries we have just mentioned accept, at least in principle, the idea that indigenous peoples will exist into the indefinite future as distinct societies within the larger country, and that they must have the land claims, cultural rights (often including recognition of customary law), and self-government rights needed to sustain themselves as distinct societies.

We see this pattern in all of the Western democracies. Consider the constitutional affirmation of Aboriginal rights in the 1982 Canadian constitution, along with the land claims commission and the signing of new treaties; the revival of treaty rights through the Treaty of Waitangi in New Zealand; the recognition of land rights for Aboriginal Australians in the Mabo decision; the creation of the Sami Parliament in Scandinavia, the evolution of 'Home Rule' for the Inuit of Greenland; and the laws and court cases upholding self-determination rights for American Indian tribes (not to mention the flood of legal and constitutional changes recognizing indigenous rights in Latin America). In all of these countries there is a gradual but real process of decolonization taking place, as indigenous peoples regain their lands, customary law, and self-government.

Here again, we will call this a shift towards a more 'multicultural' approach, although this term is not typically used by indigenous peoples themselves, who prefer the terminology of self-determination, treaty rights, and aboriginality or indigeneity. What are the specific policies that are indicative of the shift to a more multicultural approach? We consider the following nine policies as emblematic of the new approach:

(1) recognition of land rights/title;
(2) recognition of self-government rights;
(3) upholding historic treaties and/or signing new treaties;
(4) recognition of cultural rights (language; hunting/fishing);
(5) recognition of customary law;
(6) guarantees of representation/consultation in the central government;
(7) constitutional or legislative affirmation of the distinct status of indigenous peoples;
(8) support/ratification for international instruments on indigenous rights;
(9) affirmative action.

The total score for each country is again to be found in Appendix 2.1. We have categorized countries as 'strong' if they scored at least 6.0 out of a possible 9.0; 'modest' if they scored between 3.0 and 5.5, and 'weak' if they scored 2.5 or under. On this basis, we have categorized those Western countries containing indigenous peoples as:

STRONG: Canada, Denmark, New Zealand, USA[11]
MODEST: Australia, Finland, Norway
WEAK: Japan, Sweden

Given the limited resources at our disposal, this classification must obviously be considered preliminary along several dimensions. Our list of

---

[11] There is some dispute amongst experts about whether to list the USA as 'strong' or 'modest' in its approach to indigenous peoples. On the one hand, the 'domestic dependent nations' status recognized by the US Supreme Court in the nineteenth century has provided American Indian tribes with a legal status throughout much of the nineteenth and twentieth centuries that most indigenous peoples around the world could only dream of. On the other hand, that status has recently been whittled away by the increasing assertion of state jurisdiction over Indian reservations, and there has been no dramatic reaffirmation of indigenous rights in the USA to match the Treaty of Waitangi Commission in New Zealand, the 'reconciliation' process in Australia, or the constitutional entrenchment of indigenous rights in Canada. We have decided to leave the USA in the 'strong' category, in part to avoid any suggestions of biasing the analysis. If the USA were included in the 'modest' category, as some experts suggested, the numbers would even more strongly refute the argument advanced by the critics of MCPs.

MCPs is inevitably partial; one could quickly think of other possible policies to include, if one wanted to expand the list. Others might want to adopt a more restrictive list, applying the term MCPs only to policies that 'recognize' and 'accommodate' minorities in a very specific way (e.g. through legal exemptions to common laws). We discuss some of these issues in Appendix 2.1, which considers alternative ways of defining MCPs.[12] However, we believe that our list is a fair representation of the sorts of policies that have been adopted or debated by various countries, defended by advocates of multiculturalism, and attacked by their critics. While there is undoubtedly room for refinement, we believe that our classification scheme and ranking represent a reasonable starting point for our discussion.

There are of course other kinds of ethno-cultural groups, often tied to the unique circumstances of particular countries. An important case is that of the African-Americans. Indeed, some of the critics who argue that MCPs harm the welfare state are primarily concerned with this particular case. Although they state their critique in a very general form that condemns MCPs across the board, their real concern is with this one group in particular. Our focus here, however, is to test the critique in its general form. And so we have focused on three types of groups that are sufficiently common across a range of Western countries that we can make cross-national comparisons.

2. MCPs and the welfare state: A first look

Having categorized Western democracies in terms of the strength of MCPs, the next step is to examine the implications for the evolution of the welfare state. Do countries with stronger MCPs show signs of a weakened welfare state? Is there any evidence for a 'recognition/redistribution' trade-off?

In making this assessment, we look at the relationship between the strength of MCPs and two types of measures: changes in the strength of the welfare state; and changes in social outcomes. For evidence of changes in the strength of the welfare state, we rely primarily on two types of indicators: social spending as a proportion of GDP; and the

---

[12] Brian Barry, for example, sometimes restricts the term multiculturalism to policies that involve granting minority groups a legal exemption from common laws; and/or that involve granting groups separate and parallel institutions. See our discussion of Barry's definition in Appendix 2.1.

redistributive impact of government taxes and transfers. These indicators capture two dimensions of the strength of the welfare state. Social spending as a proportion of GDP measures the proportion of the nation's resources directed by government to social purposes. On its own, however, this indicator says little about the extent of redistribution that emerges from these expenditures. We therefore also present two measures of the redistributive impact of government: we compare the level of poverty before and after government taxes and transfers are taken into account; and we compare the level of inequality in market incomes and inequality in disposable incomes (after taxes and transfers are taken into account). These are probably the measures that go most directly to the heart of the questions raised by the critics of MCPs.

Unfortunately, however, data on redistribution are only available for twelve of our countries. We therefore also provide two measures of social outcomes, for which data are available for a larger set of countries: the level of child poverty; and the level of income inequality. These measures are not direct measures of the strength of social programmes, since trends in child poverty and income inequality are also influenced powerfully by other factors, including economic cycles and unemployment levels, change in family formation, and so on. However, the two measures add useful supplementary information. The level of child poverty measures the extent to which one vulnerable section of the community is protected; and the level of inequality measures the overall distribution of well-being in the country.

In sum, we have five distinct measures of changes in the welfare state:

- social spending as a proportion of GDP;
- the effect of redistribution in reducing poverty;
- the effect of redistribution in reducing inequality;
- the level of child poverty;
- the level of inequality.

The first three directly measure social policy; the latter two measure social outcomes that are influenced by social policy. Appendix 2.2 provides details on the ways in which these measures are calculated, as well as descriptions of the data sets on which we draw.[13]

---

[13] Because of lack of data on key variables, Greece, Japan, New Zealand, Portugal, and Switzerland are excluded from the analysis. See Appendix 2.2 for details.

It is important to emphasize that our focus is on *change* in measures of the welfare state from the early 1980s to 2000, not on the *level* of social spending and redistribution in different countries. When critics argue that there is a correlation between MCPs and a weakened welfare state, they are not arguing that only weak welfare states adopt MCPs. Their claim is that even if countries with strong welfare states adopt MCPs, they will have more difficulty sustaining the strength of their welfare states over time than countries with only weak MCPs. So their argument is not that countries with strong MCPs will necessarily have lower absolute levels of spending and redistribution than countries with weak MCPs. Rather, their claim is that countries adopting strong MCPs are likely to have witnessed relative decline in levels of spending and redistribution as compared to countries with weak MCPs. Their claim is not about differences in absolute levels, but about changes in levels over time. Hence our test, too, focuses on the size and direction of changes in redistribution in the 1980s and 1990s.

To illustrate this point, we do not ask why Australia, Canada, and the United States failed to develop European-style welfare states during the post-war years. Rather, we are interested in changes in levels of social redistribution in these countries since their adoption of stronger MCPs in recent decades in comparison with changes in social redistribution in countries that did not. If social redistribution faded in such countries relative to other countries, then the critics' case gains considerable support. But if there is no systematic relationship between the adoption of MCPs and changes in redistribution, the critics' case is considerably weakened.

At this stage, we are simply comparing the strength of MCPs and the evolution of the welfare state over a twenty-year period. No effort is made to control for other factors influencing social spending, including the possibility that ethnic diversity on its own may constrain the redistributive role of the state. We address those issues in the next section.

The results of our examination of measures of change in social spending and redistribution are clear: there is no consistent relationship between the adoption of MCPs and the erosion of the welfare state. Tables 2.1, 2.2, and 2.3 present our MCP groupings and our measures of change in the welfare state, as well as the background information on social outcomes.[14] We discuss the results for each type of minority group separately.

[14] The detailed data on levels, from which the measures of change were calculated, can be found in Appendix 2.2. The data presented here have been updated to the year 2000, and therefore differ marginally from those presented in earlier versions of this analysis (Banting and Kymlicka 2003, 2004*a*).

Immigrants

Table 2.1 summarizes our five indicators in the case of immigrant minorities. Some readers may be surprised that, despite decades of cuts in many countries, social spending continued to rise as a proportion of GDP. Demographic and cost pressures in major programmes such as pensions and health care have more than counterbalanced retrenchment efforts. In our context, however, what is striking is that countries with strong MCPs saw the largest rise in social spending and the greatest strengthening of their redistributive effort. It is true that countries with modest MCPs did less well than the two other groups on both dimensions. But the overall pattern does not support the critics' case.

While overall social spending is up across the Western democracies, the two measures of social outcomes help to explain the widespread belief that the welfare state is not fulfilling its post-war aspirations. Average measures of child poverty and inequality show a drift upwards in our period, reflecting the impact of all of the forces debated in the literature on the welfare state: globalization, technological change, political conservatism, social policy retrenchment, and so on. Our focus, however, is whether MCPs exacerbate these trends. And here the two outcome measures point in different directions. Child poverty grew less in countries with strong and modest MCPs than in those with weak MCPs, whereas the pattern in overall inequality is the opposite. Clearly, there is no evidence of a systematic relationship between the adoption of MCPs and the erosion of the welfare state here.

National minorities

Table 2.2 provides the same data for the case of national minorities. While the details are different, the overall conclusion points in the same direction. In this case, the strong-MCP counties outperformed the modest group on every indicator except child poverty, which was a dead heat. The weak-MCP category had a stronger performance on most of the indicators, but the evidence here has limitations. There is only one country in the category, France, and the available data for France on four of the five indicators is particularly limited, as it ends in 1994.[15] Once again, there appears to be no consistent relationship between MCPs and the performance of the welfare state.[16]

[15] It is clear the politics of retrenchment continued in France throughout the 1990s as in many countries. For an excellent analysis, see Smith (2004).

[16] There is a complication here that should be noted. As we have seen, one feature of a strong MCP approach towards sizeable national minorities is the adoption of a federal

Table 2.1 MCPs and immigrant minorities: change in social spending, redistribution, and social outcomes, 1980–2000 or near year

MCP category	Country	Social spending Proportion of GDP %Δ		Redistribution Reduction in poverty %Δ		Redistribution Reduction in inequality %Δ		Social outcomes Child poverty Δ in percentage points		Social outcomes Inequality %Δ	
		Country	Average	Country	Average	Country	Average	Country	Average	Country	Average
Strong	Australia	64.6	42.8	1.0	10.5	7.6	11.8	2.0	1.1	10.7	8.5
	Canada	21.0		20.0		15.9		0.1		6.3	
Modest	Belgium	10.8	3.8	−5.9	−5.1	−8.4	−9.2	2.7	1.8	22.0	13.8
	Netherlands	−19.0		−14.5		−2.5		7.1		−4.6	
	Sweden	−0.7		−3.5		−16.3		−0.6		27.9	
	UK	21.2		−7.1		−14.6		2.8		13.9	
	USA	6.8		5.5		−4.4		−3.1		9.9	
Weak	Austria	15.6	18.3		4.8	23.2	10.6	3.0	2.3	14.5	6.7
	Demark	−0.7		13.1		−9.0		0.3		−7.1	
	Finland	32.4		2.0		11.2		0.0		18.2	
	France	34.1		4.9		14.8		1.0		0.0	
	Germany	18.3		−3.8		13.0		6.2		8.2	
	Ireland	−20.0						3.4		−1.5	
	Italy	31.0						5.2		8.8	
	Norway	28.5		7.7				−1.4		12.6	
	Spain	25.2						3.4		6.9	
Average Δ All		16.8		1.6		2.5		2.0		9.2	

Notes: See Appendix 2.2 for data sources and details of calculations, and Appendix 2.3 for the data upon which the calculations are based.

Zeros indicate no change; blank cells indicate insufficient data to complete calculation.

Table 2.2 MCPs and national minorities: change in social spending, redistribution, and social outcomes, 1980–2000 or near year

MCP category	Country	Social spending Proportion of GDP %Δ		Redistribution Reduction in poverty %Δ		Reduction in inequality %Δ		Social outcomes Child poverty Δ in percentage points		Inequality %Δ	
		Country	Average	Country	Average	Country	Average	Country	Average	Country	Average
Strong	Canada	21.0		20.0		15.9		0.1		6.3	
	Belgium	10.8	22.4	–5.9	5.4	–8.4	–0.5	2.7	1.6	22.0	13.4
	Finland	32.4		2.0		–9.0		0.0		18.2	
	Spain	25.2						3.4		6.9	
Modest	Italy	31.0		–7.1		–14.6		5.2		8.8	
	UK	21.2	19.7	5.5	0.8	–4.4	–9.5	2.8	1.6	13.9	10.9
	USA	6.8						–3.1		9.9	
Weak	France	34.1	34.1	4.9	4.9	11.2	11.2	1.0	1.0	0.0	0.0
Average Δ All			22.8		3.2		1.6		1.5		10.8

Notes: See Appendix 2.2 for data sources and details of calculations, and Appendix 2.3 for the data on which calculations are based. Zeros indicate no change; blank cells indicate insufficient data to complete calculations.

Indigenous peoples

Table 2.3 completes the evidence by providing measures for the case of indigenous peoples. Because a smaller number of countries have indigenous peoples, the patterns are particularly vulnerable to the experience of individual countries. In particular, once again only one country (Sweden) has been classified as weak-MCP, although in contrast to France in the case of national minorities, the data on Sweden does cover the entire period from 1980 to 2000. For what it is worth, the strong-MCP countries lead on redistribution and child poverty; the modest-MCP countries perform best on social spending and overall inequality; and the weak-MCP country performs least well on every measure.

In short, we see no consistent relationship between adopting MCPs and changes in social spending, redistribution, or social outcomes. We can make the same point more simply. The last two decades have been turbulent times for the welfare state in all Western countries. On average, for example, across the Western world:

- social spending increased by 16.8 per cent;
- the redistributive reduction of poverty increased by 1.6 per cent;
- the redistributive reduction in inequality increased by 2.5 per cent;
- child poverty increased by 2 per cent;
- inequality grew by 9.2 per cent.

These numbers represent the norm for how Western welfare states responded to the challenges of last twenty years of the twentieth century. If the critics were correct, we would expect countries with strong MCPs to have fared worse than average. Focusing on the case of immigrant minorities, however, the result is exactly the opposite for four of our five measures. Countries with strong MCPs have done better than average on changes in social spending, reduction in poverty, reduction in inequality, and overall child poverty.

---

or quasi-federal regime that devolves substantial powers of self-government to a region dominated by a national minority. These powers of self-government often include jurisdiction over issues that affect both MCPs and the welfare state. As a result, many of the questions we have been addressing in this chapter at the national level also arise at the substate level. For example, the Québécois, Scots, Flemish, and Catalans have all been engaged in their own debate about how adopting substate-level MCPs would affect substate-level welfare state policies. A full investigation of the relationship between MCPs and welfares state would need to examine their relationship at this substate level as well. It would be interesting to see, for example, whether substate governments with strong MCPs (like Quebec) have fared worse, in terms of changing levels of welfare state spending, than substate governments with weaker MCPs (like Flanders).

Table 2.3 MCPs and indigenous peoples: change in social spending, redistribution, and social outcomes, 1980–2000 or near year

MCP category	Country	Social spending		Redistribution				Social outcomes			
		Proportion of GDP %Δ		Reduction in poverty %Δ		Reduction in inequality %Δ		Child poverty Δ in percentage points		Inequality %Δ	
		Country	Average	Country	Average	Country	Average	Country	Average	Country	Average
Strong	Canada	21.0	9.0	20.0	12.9	15.9	11.6	0.1	-0.9	6.3	3.0
	Denmark	-0.7		13.1		23.2		0.3		-7.1	
	USA	6.8		5.5		-4.4		-3.1		9.9	
Modest	Australia	64.6	41.8	1.0	3.6	7.6	3.9	2.0	0.2	10.7	13.8
	Finland	32.4		2.0		-9.0		0.0		18.2	
	Norway	28.5		7.7		13.0		-1.4		12.6	
Weak	Sweden	-0.7		-3.5		-16.3		-0.6		27.9	
Average Δ All		21.7		6.5		4.3		-0.4		11.2	

Notes: See Appendix 2.2 for data sources and details of calculations, and Appendix 2.3 for the data upon which calculations are based.
Zeros indicate no change; blank cells indicate insufficient data to complete calculation.

Narrowing the sample

So far, we have been looking across the broad sweep of the Western democracies. In fairness, however, it must be said that most of the critics are focused on a narrower set of countries, and it is possible that if we reduce the sample, a pattern may emerge that is obscured when the full set of Western democracies is included.

For some critics, the focus is quite narrow—namely, the 'Anglo' countries. In Brian Barry's book, for example, virtually all of his examples of MCPs (and virtually all of the multicultural theorists he criticizes) are drawn from the UK, USA, Canada, and Australia. He argues that MCPs have had deleterious effects at least in these four countries. Narrowing our sample to these four countries should, therefore, provide another test of his theory. Although Barry does not provide a systematic ranking of countries in terms of their level of MCPs, he does say that Canada has 'gone farther down the path' of MCPs than the United Kingdom and the United States (Barry 2001: 294), and implies that Australia is closer to Canada in this regard (e.g. Barry 2001: 169). If his argument is correct, we should expect Canada and Australia to have fared worse on welfare state measures than the USA and the UK. In fact, the results are just the opposite. As Table 2.4 indicates, if we compare the performance of these four countries on social spending and redistribution, which reflects Barry's main concern, the strong-MCP pair has superior performance to that of the more modest pair, especially in the overall redistributive impact on inequality, which strengthened in Canada and Australia and weakened in the United Kingdom and the United States.

In short, the more we narrow our focus to the countries that are of most concern to the critics, the more problems their argument faces. The statistical evidence from across a large sample of Western democracies

Table 2.4 MCPs and immigrant minorities in Anglo-American countries: change in social redistribution, 1980–2000

MCP ranking	Social spending	Redistribution Reduction in poverty	Reduction in inequality
	%Δ	%Δ	%Δ
Canada	64.6	1.0	7.6
Australia	21.0	20.0	15.9
UK	21.2	−7.1	−14.6
USA	6.8	5.5	−4.4

provides no support for the critics, but if we narrow our focus to the Anglo countries, the evidence actually contradicts the charge.

Summary

The cumulative weight of the evidence is clear. While indicators for specific groups occasionally move in the direction predicted by critics of MCPs, there are at least as many indicators moving in precisely the opposite direction. Moreover, the most comprehensive indicator of the social role of the state, change in redistribution, favours the strong-MCP group. Strong-MCP countries outperform modest-MCP countries in redistribution in all three minority group contexts. Strong-MCP countries also perform better than weak-MCP countries on both measures of redistribution in the case of immigrants and indigenous peoples, and on one of the measures in the case of national minorities. So far, the bottom line is that there is no evidence of a consistent pattern of the adoption of MCPs leading to the erosion of the welfare state.

3. Diversity, multiculturalism policies, and the welfare state: A multivariate analysis

We believe that the data described in the previous section provide strong evidence against the critics of MCPs. However, the results would be more conclusive if the analysis was extended to incorporate a wider range of factors that influence social spending. The large literature on the welfare state has identified a number of powerful drivers of social spending in advanced democracies (see for example Hicks 1999; Huber and Stephens 2001; Swank 2002; Castles 2004). For example, we know that social spending tends to increase alongside both the proportion of the population over 65 years of age and the proportion of women in the workforce. In this section, we build on existing models of social spending that include such factors, to see what impact (if any) MCPs have once these other factors are controlled for.

There are at least two important reasons for engaging in this more complicated multivariate analysis. First, it is theoretically possible that once the impact of these other factors is held constant, a negative relationship will emerge between MCPs and social spending. We know from the previous section that strong-MCP countries have not had more difficulty sustaining social programmes compared to the OECD average. However, perhaps that is because strong-MCP countries happen to have higher-than-average numbers of elderly or higher-than-average percentages of women in the labour market. If so, then one would have expected these factors to have pushed social spending well above the OECD average; that is, these other factors may mask a negative impact of strong MCPs. We can only rule out such a possibility if we control for these other factors that influence social spending.

There is a second, more specific, reason for engaging in multivariate analysis. Chapter 1 refers to the recent literature examining the link between the size of ethno-racial minorities and the welfare state. According to a number of scholars, welfare states are easier to build and maintain in countries that are ethnically/racially homogeneous, but become harder to build or to sustain as ethnic/racial minorities increase in size. This effect has been measured in several contexts based solely on the size of the minorities, without attention to whether government policies seek to manage this diversity through the adoption of MCPs. If it is true that there is a tension between ethnic/racial diversity and redistribution, this has important consequences for our test. For as we will see below, countries with strong MCPs also tend to be countries with higher-than-average levels of ethnic and racial diversity. Not surprisingly, countries where minorities are demographically stronger are more likely to adopt MCP policies that recognize and accommodate them.

This means that many of the strong-MCP countries would be predicted to face special difficulties in supporting the welfare state, given their above-average levels of ethnic and racial diversity. Yet, as we have seen, strong-MCP countries have not fared below average, at least in terms of changes in social spending over the twenty-year period in question. This suggests the intriguing possibility that MCPs may in fact have a positive impact on social spending, in the sense that they help mitigate the negative impact that ethnic and racial diversity as such is predicted to have. Perhaps strong-MCP states will turn out to have higher-than-expected levels of social spending, given their levels of ethnic and racial diversity.

In order to evaluate these hypotheses, we need a model that both incorporates other principal drivers of social spending and allows for the effect of diversity to be mediated (augmented or diminished) by the scope of MCPs. We develop this model below. First, however, we explore the relationship between the size of minorities and the level of MCPs, as an initial step towards disentangling the effects of the level of ethnic diversity on one hand and the adoption of MCPs on the other.

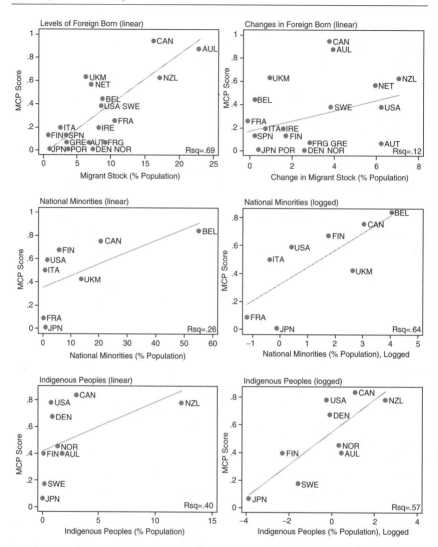

Figure 2.1 Minority population and minority policy

Minority demography and MCPs

Multicultural politics do not exist in a vacuum. Not surprisingly, there is a strong relationship between the size of the various minorities and the strength of MCPs in response to their concerns, as Figure 2.1 shows. The figure contains six panels, two for each of the three types of minorities. The horizontal axis in each panel displays the average 1980–2000 share of the population for the indicated minority, by country, except for the second panel for immigrant minorities, which captures the extent of change in the immigrant share of the population between 1980 and 2000. (We draw on this particular panel in the next section.) The vertical axis of all of the panels represents the country's MCP score for the relevant minority. In each domain the regression line linking policy outcome to population share is also plotted.[17]

As the first panel confirms, the commitment to immigrant MCPs is powerfully related to the immigrant share of the total population. Australia and Canada have the strongest immigrant MCPs, and both also have large percentages of foreign born. Several other countries cluster at the low end on both dimensions. It is the middle of the range that is most interesting. Here one finds the United Kingdom and the Netherlands with relatively strong MCPs relative to the proportionate size of their foreign-born populations, as well as Germany and France with the least supportive MCPs relative to the size of their foreign-born communities. The pattern is highly suggestive of the underlying political dynamics. The political base for MCPs is strong in countries with large immigrant populations; and the issue simply does not break through in countries with small numbers of foreign born. It is in countries in the middle where the politics of multiculturalism are most uncertain and the policy outcomes most varied.

The relationship between national minorities and MCPs is illustrated in the third and fourth panels. The third panel shows the normal, linear relationship between the two variables, and suggests a clear link. However, the slope here is driven in large part by a striking outlier, Belgium, which fittingly has the highest multicultural score. It also has by quite a margin the largest national minority, since our characterization of national minority politics requires labelling the Flemish majority as the leading minority.[18] A better sense of the relationship can be had

[17] To facilitate comparison among domains, scores are scaled to a 0.1 interval, even though the number of potential MCPs varies from scale to scale. For a given regression line only countries that can reasonably have a multicultural policy enter the calculation. In the case of indigenous peoples, nine countries are relevant. For national minorities, the number of relevant countries is eight. Switzerland does not appear in the latter group because data problems preclude its inclusion in the analysis of social spending. Including Switzerland, however, would not alter any conclusion about the link between population percentage and policy.

[18] To recall, we characterize 'national minorities' as historically disadvantaged homeland groups that mobilize against the central state for greater language rights, self-government, and institutional completeness. While the Flemish are now a demographic majority in Belgium, they have historically been subordinate to the francophone Walloons, and hence it is they, more than the numerically smaller Walloons, who have engaged in substate nationalist mobilization.

by using the natural log of the national minority population, which serves to stretch out the low end of that axis while at the same time compressing the high end. Results are shown in the fourth panel. Here, the relationship between population and MCPs emerges much more clearly. Canada and Belgium have large national minorities and strong MCPs. Japan and France have essentially no MCPs for their respective national minorities, which are small. Italy and the USA have relatively supportive policies given the size of their minorities, whereas the United Kingdom (for the pre-devolution era) lies below the line, although not outstandingly so.

The story is similar for indigenous minorities, in the fifth and sixth panels. Once again, the normal, linear relationship suggests a link between the size of the minority population and the strength of related MCPs. But again, the slope is driven by an outlier, in this case New Zealand, which is tied with the USA as having the second strongest MCPs. However, the Maori share of the New Zealand total is so much larger than the indigenous share for any other country (four times as large as the share in second-place Canada, for instance) that even were New Zealand to have the world's highest indigenous multicultural policy score, the relationship in this figure would still appear deceptively weak. The relationship therefore emerges much more clearly when we use the natural log of the indigenous population, which appears in the final panel: marginal increases in indigenous population at the low end of the scale are associated with relatively large increases in MCPs; at the high end of the scale, the effect of marginal increases is considerably lower. The fact that a log transformation provides a better fit raises interesting questions about the nature of the relationship. Perhaps after a certain point, MCPs are relatively well developed, and further increases in the indigenous population will have little effect. Alternatively, as Donna Lee Van Cott suggests in her discussion of experience in Latin America (this volume), it may be easier to gain acceptance for indigenous rights when the groups are smaller.

In short, for all three types of MCPs, there is a tendency for the level of MCPs in any given country to be correlated with the size of its minority. That said, there are enough exceptions and outliers that we can try to examine the independent effects of both on social spending in our multivariate analysis. As we will see, results confirm findings in previous sections—namely, there is no systematic tendency for MCPs to erode social spending.

Minorities, MCPs, and the determinants of social spending

We now model the effect of minority populations and MCPs on social welfare spending. To do so, we use a model of the determinants of social spending in OECD countries which has been adapted from standard models developed in the literature on the welfare state, and which is more fully described in Soroka, Banting, and Johnston (2006). Our dependent variable is growth in social spending over the period 1980–2000.[19] As noted above, social spending grew in all of the countries in our sample, so the issue is the relative rate of growth. Our independent variables include the following set of controls:

- The level of social spending in 1980, as a percentage of GDP. This appears as the first factor accounting for 1980–2000 change, as much spending growth may be 'catch-up' by initially low-spending states. If it is, the coefficient should be negative; low initial levels of spending should lead to higher growth.

- The strength of the political left in government, as measured by the percentage of the parliamentary seats of the governing coalition that are held by left parties. This reflects the finding in the welfare state literature that the strength of the left is a key factor in spending growth (Huber and Stephens 2001; Swank 2002).

- The percentage of females in the labour force. According to Huber and Stephens (2001), this a major driver of child-care costs.

- The percentage of the population over 64, the most powerful single driver of social spending growth.

These variables serve two general purposes. To the extent that they covary with the size of minorities or the strength of MCPs, controlling for them is necessary to address the possibility that the findings of our initial test are spurious, that is, to reveal whether or not MCPs have a negative impact that was obscured by our earlier test. At the same time, any factor that contributes to the overall explanation of spending growth should make the impact estimated for MCPs more precise.

For each type of minority group, the sequence of our regression models is essentially the same. We start with the control variables above, along with the population percentage for the group in question—immigrant

---

[19] As in the analysis in section 2, data on social spending are from the OECD Social Expenditures database, which is described in Appendix 2.2. Social spending is measured as a percentage of GDP, and values are percentage-point gains.

minorities, national minorities, or indigenous minorities. We then add the MCP score as a 'main effect'. This indicates if the strength of policy has an effect, positive or negative, over and above that from the mere size of the group itself. In this second model, then, both the minority group and MCPs can have direct, independent effects on changes in social spending. However, it is likely that these two variables interact; as discussed in the preceding section, the effect of minority groups may be mediated by the existence of MCPs. This possibility is explored in a third model, which includes an interaction between the strength of policy and the minority population.

Note that in these models we represent minority populations differently. For national minorities and indigenous peoples, we use these groups' share of the population. But in the case of immigrant minorities, two dimensions seem potentially relevant: their share of the total population, and the extent of change in that share. In contrast to the cases of national minorities and indigenous minorities, the immigrant share of the population in many Western nations—what the United Nations rather inelegantly calls 'migrant stock'—changed significantly in our period. For most countries, immigrant stocks were low in 1980, and the stocks that had accumulated by 2000 were mainly the result of inflows over the interim. This is the case for most European Union countries but also for the USA. Moreover, for all countries, even traditional countries of immigration, the 1980–2000 shift captures the change in origins, the shift from mainly European to mainly non-European sources. So percentage-point change in the foreign-born share is arguably the vital political indicator, for it captures more precisely than any alternative the growth in pressure for specifically cultural recognition, as opposed to other, structural elements in immigrant accommodation. Accordingly, we tested both the average level of migrant stock over the period and changes in migrant stock.

Results

Estimated models are shown in Tables 2.5 and 2.6. For the most part, factors other than the size of the minority or MCPs are critical elements in spending growth. As suspected, the level of spending in 1980 is important for 1980–2000 growth, as initially weaker spenders caught up with the early leaders. Also critical is the population share of persons over 64, actual or potential retirees. The left-party share in government and the female share of the labour force were also factors. The partisan

Table 2.5 Immigrant minorities, MCPs and social spending: 20-year change cross-sectional models (1980–2000)

	Dependent variable: Δ Social welfare spending (% GDP)					
	Immigrant minorities (levels)			Immigrant minorities (changes)		
Population	−.014	.004	.039	−.064*	−.064*	−.086
	(.102)	(.170)	(.168)	(.032)	(.033)	(.063)
MCPs	—	−.425	.456	—	.004	−.623
		(3.178)	(3.180)		(1.759)	(2.384)
Interaction	—	—	−.118	—	—	.064
			(.092)			(.156)
Spending	−.721***	−.719***	−.688***	−.672***	−.672***	−.674***
(1980)	(.104)	(.108)	(.108)	(.094)	(.098)	(.102)
Left parties in	.128***	.126**	.128**	.141***	.141***	.142***
govt.	(.040)	(.043)	(.042)	(.035)	(.036)	(.038)
Female labour	.087	.087	.122	.126*	.126*	.118
force	(.067)	(.069)	(.073)	(.060)	(.063)	(.068)
Population over	1.220***	1.214***	.983**	.991***	.991**	1.051**
64 yrs	(.359)	(.374)	(.408)	(.302)	(.342)	(.383)
Constant	−5.736	−5.651	−4.359	−4.531	−4.535	−4.946
	(4.866)	(5.085)	(5.069)	(4.007)	(4.475)	(4.735)
Observations	20	20	20	20	20	20
Adjusted R^2	.75	.73	.74	.85	.85	.86

$* p < .10;\ ** p < .05;\ *** p < .01$

Note: Cells contain coefficients from OLS regression with standard errors in parentheses.

indicator is consistently significant, the female labour force one intermittently so. These are the important drivers, as the welfare state literature suggests.

Our primary interest is of course in the effects of minority populations, MCPs, and the interaction between the two. For the most part, however, we find that these variables are much less important than the structural factors outlined above, and results confirm the findings in our initial tests in Section 2.

We start with immigrant minorities. We have previously reported that the relative size of the immigrant minority has no impact on social spending—it is the *change* in the size of the immigrant minority that matters (Soroka, Banting, and Johnston 2006). Table 2.5 supports this hypothesis. The first three columns show results from a model in which change in spending is regressed on the average *level* of the immigrant minority over the time period. The size of this minority has no significant impact on spending growth (column one); nor do MCPs (column two), or the interaction between MCPs and the size of the immigrant minority (column three).

Change in immigrants' share of the population does seem to influence welfare state growth, however, as the final three columns of Table 2.5 show. The first estimation (column four) indicates that the greater the growth in the foreign-born percentage, the slower is the growth in welfare spending, *ceteris paribus*.[20] The average level of increase in foreign-born lowers the predicted growth in welfare spending by 0.8 points, about 21 per cent of the average expenditure growth during the period. The pattern is thus interesting. As the first three columns in the table confirm, immigrants' actual share of the population did not matter—countries with large but stable immigration populations did not have greater difficulty in developing or sustaining their welfare states in this period than did other countries. But growth in immigrants' share of the population did matter. As often in social life, change in one's social setting may be more important than the nature of the setting itself. And, of course, more recent flows of immigrants have been the source of greater racial diversity in many countries.[21]

What about the effects of MCPs? Strictly speaking, the answer is that there are none. In column five, we introduce the MCP variable, and it has no negative impact on social spending (indeed, it has a positive sign, albeit very small and statistically insignificant). In column six, we then introduce the interaction variable (allowing the effects of migrant stock to vary with different levels of MCPs), with the same result—no negative effect.[22]

---

[20] Immigration growth appears as a quadratic term, consistent with the argument and evidence in Soroka, Banting, and Johnston (2006). The implication is that change in migrant stock becomes more important at the margin as the margin shifts upward. The USA and the Netherlands are critical to the story as countries with two of the three highest foreign-born gains (Austria is the third) and the two slowest rates of spending growth.

[21] The precise causal link between diversity and social welfare spending is of course difficult to tease out using aggregate data. That the effect is at least partly a product of individuals reacting to increasing diversity appears to be supported by work at the individual level, however. See Soroka, Johnston, and Banting (2006).

[22] The statistical techniques involved in estimating the 'interaction effect' in the third row of column six require changing the basis on which both the 'population change' and 'MCPs' effects (in the first two rows) are interpreted. To oversimplify, the first row now estimates the impact of maximal population change with minimal MCPs, whereas the second row now estimates the impact of maximal MCPs with minimal population change. Of course, most real-world cases fall in between these two extremes—they have both population change and MCPs—and results for these cases are captured through a combination of the 'direct' effect of 'population change' or 'MCPs', and the interaction coefficient in the third row. One result of this statistical technique is that the direct effect of MCPs seems to switch signs, from positive (in row 2, column 5) to negative (in row 2, column 6), although statistically insignificant in both cases. However, this apparent negative effect of MCPs in column six is misleading. As we can see in panel 2 of Figure 2.1, there are no real-world cases of countries with maximal MCPs and no increase in immigrant population, and so row two of column six is estimating a hypothetical scenario. The real issue is the impact of varying levels of MCPs under varying

We thus find no statistically significant effect of immigrant MCPs on social welfare spending. Having said that, there are hints of an interesting story in column six. Though statistically insignificant, the interaction term here is positive. The implication is that an accommodating policy may in fact mitigate the main effect of immigration, offsetting its tendency to reduce spending growth. More precisely, it may be true that, particularly under higher-migration conditions, adopting stronger MCPs is positively correlated with spending growth. Whereas some commentators worry that high levels of immigration will inevitably erode European welfare states (Freeman 1986; Alesina and Glaeser 2004: 180–1), then, our results point to the possibility that the depressive effect of immigration growth may be offset by robust MCPs.

Again, recall that these are statistically fragile results: the interaction coefficient is not even half as large as its standard error, not significantly different from zero by any reasonable criterion.[23] The trends shown here do remain in other specifications, however, which lends some more credibility to the results.[24] Nevertheless, the trend in the data is, at best, suggestive. It is not a statistically significant finding, although it is certainly an intriguing one that deserves further study.

The story for national and indigenous minorities is more straightforward. In contrast to indigenous peoples, the size of national minorities varies across a considerable range. But as Table 2.6 indicates, their demographic strength, the depth of MCP commitment, and the interaction between MCP commitment and population share are all simply irrelevant to growth in social spending.[25] The story for indigenous peoples is similar: no representation of indigenous presence or indigenous MCPs affects welfare spending for the country as a whole. The relative size of the indigenous population has no effect. This is not surprising, perhaps, as the actual variance, New Zealand aside, in the indigenous percentage is tiny. MCP commitment is similarly unrelated to spending growth, and this

levels of population change. And to assess this, the effect of the MCP coefficient here must be interpreted in conjunction with the effect of the interaction term. For all our cases, the interaction mitigates entirely the negative effect of MCPs apparent in column six.

[23] Note, moreover, that both the direct effect of change in migrant stock and the interaction coefficient are dogged by multicollinearity. Their standard errors are inflated by factors of 2.5 and 3.1 respectively.

[24] For example, the results remain with additional controls and using a yearly time-series cross-sectional set-up.

[25] If this finding seems to fly in the face of claims that US social spending levels are low because of anti-black prejudice, recall that in our terms African-Americans are not a *national* minority. They do not make (or they make few) claims that distinguish them as an internal nation, in contrast to Puerto Ricans and, for that matter, Native Americans.

Table 2.6 Indigenous peoples and national minorities, MCPs and social spending: 20-year change cross-sectional models (1980–2000)

	Dependent variable: Δ Social welfare spending (% GDP)					
	Indigenous peoples			National minorities		
Population	.045	.046	.059	.056	.043	−.352
	(.062)	(.064)	(.070)	(.097)	(.115)	(.409)
MCPs	—	−.767	−.406	—	.398	.194
		(2.305)	(2.446)		(1.764)	(1.774)
Interaction	—	—	−.191	—	—	.609
			(.330)			(.605)
Spending	−.739***	−.740***	−.745***	−.715***	−.717***	−.739***
(1970)	(.103)	(.106)	(.109)	(.102)	(.106)	(.108)
Left parties in	.127***	.125***	.129***	.134***	.134***	.130***
govt.	(.038)	(.040)	(.041)	(.041)	(.042)	(.042)
Female labour	.084	.103	.122	.076	.080	.080
force	(.063)	(.086)	(.095)	(.065)	(.069)	(.069)
Population over	1.269***	1.230***	1.176***	1.242***	1.243***	1.378***
64 yrs	(.309)	(.340)	(.361)	(.309)	(.320)	(.346)
Constant	−6.174	−6.142	−6.109	−6.100	−6.305	−7.577
	(4.403)	(4.551)	(4.671)	(4.431)	(4.678)	(4.843)
Observations	20	20	20	20	20	20
Adjusted R^2	.82	.82	.83	.82	.82	.83

$* p < .10; ** p < .05; *** p < .01$

Note: Cells contain coefficients from OLS regression with standard errors in parentheses.

commitment also does not interact in an interesting way with population share.[26]

In sum, our results show only marginal effects of the size of minority populations and the level of MCPs on social spending. The size of indigenous peoples and national minorities are irrelevant to growth in social spending, as are the level of MCPs in each of these domains. Post-1980 increases in immigration are a factor in inhibiting spending growth, but adopting MCPs for newcomers, if it has any effect at all, may mitigate the relationship, helping to sustain social spending from the potentially eroding effects of increased ethnic/racial diversity, particularly where there is medium to high growth in migrant stock. With these results in mind, strident claims about the impact of MCPs on the welfare state hardly seem justified.

[26] While we show results using just the linear version of national minorities and indigenous population here, no transformation of those variables (exponential or log, for instance) shows any relationship either. Also, if we substitute any representation of spending *level*, as opposed to change, the result is the same: no effects of any sort.

4. Summary and reflections

To return to our original question, do multiculturalism policies erode the welfare state? Is there a 'recognition/redistribution' trade-off? The evidence in this chapter is clear. There is no systematic pattern of countries that have adopted strong MCPs seeing erosion in their welfare states relative to countries that have resisted such programmes.

For students of the welfare state, this result is not surprising. Social policy analysts established long ago that the social role of the state is rooted in core features of the political economy of each country. As we have seen, the political strength of the political left, the participation of women in the paid labour force, and the age structure of the population are powerful drivers of social spending. Other analysts have turned to such factors as economic growth, the openness of the economy, unemployment levels, the strength of organized labour, the dominance of Christian Democratic parties, the structure of political institutions, and the nature of electoral systems. In comparison with such core features of Western democracies, it would be surprising if MCPs proved to be as powerful a factor as their critics have suggested.

Perhaps more surprising is the lack of evidence we have found for the 'heterogeneity/redistribution' trade-off. While many scholars have recently asserted that social spending is negatively related to the proportion of ethnic and racial minorities in the population, we found little evidence for this assumption. In the case of indigenous peoples and national minorities, changes in social spending in the period in question do not seem to vary at all with the size of the minority group. There is some evidence for a heterogeneity/redistribution trade-off in the case of immigration, although it is not the relative size of the foreign-born population per se that seems to affect social spending. Rather, it is the rate of growth in the foreign-born population that may exert downward pressure on social spending. (That is, countries with small but fast-growing foreign-born populations have had smaller increases in social spending than countries with larger but stable numbers of foreign-born.) Moreover, there is some preliminary evidence that even here, the adoption of MCPs can mitigate the negative effect of rapid growth in immigration-based heterogeneity on social spending.

If confirmed by further research—and Markus Crepaz finds similar evidence at the level of public attitudes in Chapter 3—this is an interesting finding that some people may find counter-intuitive. If growth in ethnic and racial diversity from immigration tends to depress social spending, then surely it is dangerous to highlight diversity, and render it more politically salient, through MCPs. If diversity is bad for social spending, surely it is better to ignore or downplay the existence of diversity, rather than to publicly acknowledge and affirm it. Yet it is possible that MCPs can acknowledge diversity in a way that makes it less threatening to members of the dominant group, and that reduces the 'otherness' of ethnic and racial minorities, enabling members of the dominant group to view minorities as 'one of us'. This, of course, is precisely what defenders of MCPs have long argued. As was discussed in Chapter 1, the ability of MCPs to achieve this goal may depend on how they fit into a larger package of public policies, including nation-building policies and policies designed to enhance the economic integration of newcomers.

In short, the evidence in this chapter suggests that both the heterogeneity/redistribution and the recognition/redistribution trade-off have been overstated. Of course, as we have repeatedly emphasized, this is just a first attempt at trying to develop a method for testing the critics' claims, and it is possible to raise a number of objections to our conclusions.

One objection, raised by Philippe Van Parijs in response to an earlier version of this research, is that the corrosive effects of MCPs take time to weaken the welfare state, and that the twenty-year period examined here is too short to draw definitive conclusions: 'time (is) required for these sociological processes to work themselves out and be politically exploited' (Van Parijs 2004: 382).[27] However, the multivariate analysis presented here renders this objection less plausible. The twenty-year period was long enough for other political factors, such as the role of left-wing parties, to emerge strongly in the multivariate analysis; more tellingly, perhaps, the effects of change in the proportion of the population born outside of the country also emerged clearly in the twenty-year analysis. The objection must assume that there is something special about the effects of MCPs, compared to immigration and other political factors, which slows the impact. It is difficult to see what that critical difference might be. In the final analysis, only time can finally answer this objection definitively. But as Van Parijs himself concedes, 'the longer the prophecies of doom fail to show up in the figures', the less plausible the basic critique of MCPs becomes (ibid.).

Others might object that our definition of MCPs is too broad, and that we need to distinguish different ways in which diversity can be

---

[27] John Myles and Sébastien St-Arnaud (this volume) raise a related objection.

'recognized' and 'accommodated'. For example, someone might argue that policies designed to accommodate diversity *within common institutions* are consistent with the welfare state, but that policies that establish 'parallel institutions' are more likely to erode redistribution. As we discuss in Appendix 2.1, Barry sometimes defines MCPs in this narrower way. Yet our earlier observations stand here as well. It is doubtful that narrowing the definition of the MCPs would alter the results. The rankings of different countries implicit in Barry's own analysis are fully consistent with our own, and it is unlikely that adopting his narrower definition would alter the rank order of countries or affect the empirical analysis of the relationship between MCPs and the welfare state.

A final objection is that conclusions flowing from cross-national analyses do not necessarily apply with equal force to individual countries. One can go further. The conclusion that there is no statistically significant relationship between MCPs and redistribution is consistent with two interpretations. The first is that MCPs have no effect. The second is that MCPs have potentially significant effects but these effects differ and may be in the opposite direction depending on other social and political conditions in the country. That is, in some contexts MCPs may indeed reinforce the politics of retrenchment in the welfare state, as the critics contend, whereas in other contexts MCPs may enhance a sense of social solidarity and reinforce redistribution, as the defenders reply. We acknowledge that there may well be tension between MCPs and the welfare state in particular places and in particular periods, just as there are undoubtedly contexts in which MCPs mitigate tensions between diversity and redistribution. Refining our analysis further will therefore depend on rich case studies of the experience of individual countries. Other chapters in this book take precisely this approach.

Nevertheless, the broad comparative approach in this chapter does have powerful implications. Chapter 1 summarized two vigorous debates: the heterogeneity/redistribution debate, which centres on arguments that ethnic diversity itself erodes the welfare state; and the recognition/redistribution debate, which centres on arguments that MCPs erode the welfare state. These are critical debates, which cannot be dismissed lightly. There is no question that there is a *potential* conflict between ethnic diversity and solidarity. We do not need social scientists to tell us that. There is far too much evidence of ethnic and racial intolerance on our television screens. But we need to avoid premature judgements about the universality—indeed, the inevitability—of trade-offs and tragic choices between economic redistribution and cultural recognition. The evidence presented in this chapter about the relationship between immigration and social spending on one hand, and the impact of multiculturalism policies on the welfare state on the other, point to the need for nuanced analyses. The findings also underscore the need to understand the factors that mediate between diversity, multiculturalism strategies, and redistribution. There is a compelling research agenda here.

Appendix 2.1. Measuring MCP levels

Table A 2.1 Country MCP scores

Country	Immigrant MCPs[a]	National minority MCPs[b]	Indigenous MCPs[c]
Australia	7.0	—	3.5
Austria	0.5	—	—
Belgium	3.5	5.0	—
Canada	7.5	4.5	7.5
Denmark	0.0	—	6.0
Finland	1.0	4.0	3.5
France	2.0	0.5	—
Germany	0.5	—	—
Greece	0.5	0.0	—
Ireland	1.5	—	—
Italy	1.5	3.0	—
Japan	0.0	0.0	0.5
Netherlands	4.5	—	
New Zealand	5.0	—	7.0
Norway	0.0	—	4.0
Portugal	0.0	—	—
Spain	1.0	4.5	—
Sweden	3.0	—	1.5
Switzerland	1.0	4.5	—
United Kingdom	5.0	2.5	—
United States	3.0	3.5	7.0

[a] Immigrant MCPs score is out of a possible 8.0.

[b] National Minorities MCPs score is out of a possible 6.0.

[c] Immigrant MCPs score is out of a possible 9.0.

Source: Lisa Vanhala, 'Multicultural Policies: Cross-Country Comparison (1980–2000)' (unpublished report, September 2004, on file with authors).

Note on Defining MCPs

As we noted earlier, our definition and list of MCPs is not necessarily equivalent to that of any particular critic (or defender) or MCPs. We think our view is broadly consistent with the implicit definition of MCPs used by two of the most influential critics—namely, Todd Gitlin (1995) and Alan Wolfe and Jyette Klausen (1997, 2000). However, it is important to note that our definition of MCPs is broader than that offered by Barry (2001). Since Barry's book has had an important influence on the debate, it may be useful to clarify how our account of MCPs differs from his, and how this might affect the empirical results.

Consider the issue of education. Barry specifically denies that the adoption of a multicultural curriculum within common public schools qualifies as a form of MCP. To qualify as an MCP, on his view, an educational policy must go beyond recognizing or accommodating diversity within a common curriculum in common schools. One way it can go beyond is to create institutional separateness—that is, separate publicly funded schools for distinct ethnic or religious groups. This is a lively issue in many Western countries, often debated as a form (or implication) of 'multiculturalism'. And as we noted in Chapter 1, Barry is particularly concerned about the impact of institutional separateness on trust and solidarity and hence the welfare state (Barry 2001: 88). Yet in places, Barry wants to narrow the definition of MCPs even further, to restrict it to policies that involve some form of group-specific legal right or exemption (Barry 2001: 294–5). A policy that granted all groups a right to public funding for separate schools would not qualify, on this very narrow definition, since there is no group-specific right or exemption. Educational policy would only qualify as an MCP if it allowed specific groups to be exempted from general educational laws (e.g. allowing fundamentalist Christians or Muslim girls to be exempted from sex education classes) or granted specific groups specific rights to educational facilities (e.g. granting one ethnic group the right to mother-tongue education, but not others).

We have obviously not restricted our account of MCPs in this way. Depending on how broadly or narrowly the idea of group-differentiated rights/exemptions is interpreted, it is possible that only two of the eight immigrant MCPs we identify would qualify as MCPs on Barry's definition (i.e. group-specific exemptions and affirmative action).[28] We have several reasons for not following Barry's narrow definition. First, as Barry himself notes, his definition is wildly at odds with everyday usage, since for many people the idea of a multicultural curriculum is the very paradigm of an MCP (Barry 2001: 234). Second, Barry's emphasis on the narrow set of group-specific rights/exemptions seems more relevant to his philosophical critique of MCPs than his empirical critique. Most of Barry's book is devoted to arguing that MCPs tend to violate liberal principles of freedom and equality, and for this philosophical purpose he argues that group-specific rights/exemptions are more likely to be illiberal or inegalitarian than policies that accommodate diversity within common rules in common institutions. However, it is not clear whether he thinks that the empirical critique advanced in the final chapter of his book only applies exclusively or even primarily to the narrower

---

[28] By contrast, virtually all of the nine MCPs we identify under indigenous people would, we assume, qualify under Barry's definition.

range of policies. After all, according to Barry, MCPs in this more narrow sense of group-specific rights and exemptions tend to be adopted without any public discussion, and are often completely unknown by the general public (Barry 2001: 295). The crowding, corroding, and misdiagnosing effects Barry attributes seem to require a significant level of public awareness, and on Barry's own account, this public awareness applies more to the broader issues such as multicultural education rather than to the narrow issues of group-specific exemptions. Moreover, Barry expresses sympathy with Gitlin's empirical critique, yet Gitlin (like Wolfe) argues that the crowding, corroding, and misdiagnosis effects apply to the broader range of MCPs, not just the narrow range Barry emphasizes. Indeed, the case Gitlin spends most time on in his book is precisely the struggles over multicultural textbooks in the public schools. So it is possible, although not certain, that Barry intends his empirical critique to apply to broader forms of MCPs.

Finally, and most importantly, we doubt that adopting the narrow definition of MCPs would affect the test results. It is possible, in principle, that countries which are categorized as 'strongly' MCP on our broad criteria might turn out to be 'weakly' MCP on Barry's narrow criteria (and vice versa). However, Barry himself suggests otherwise. While he does not offer a systematic categorization of countries as more or less multicultural in their public policies, he does observe that MCPs have primarily been adopted within the traditional countries of immigration, and that within this camp Canada has 'gone further along the path of multiculturalism than Britain or the United States' (Barry 2001: 294). This suggests a ranking in which Canada is more strongly MCP than the USA/Britain, which in turn are more strongly MCP than, say, Austria or Germany. This is entirely consistent with our own ranking. So we suspect that adopting Barry's narrow criteria would not significantly affect the country rankings, and hence would not affect the empirical findings about how the level of MCPs affects the welfare state. However, this conclusion must be provisional, until someone engages in a systematic attempt to categorize countries on Barry's narrower criteria.[29]

[29] One additional reason is that it is unclear (to us) what policies would qualify under this more narrow definition. In the case of national minorities or indigenous peoples, for example, does the decision to create a territorial subunit controlled by the minority group qualify as a group-specific right, given that the state would not create such a subunit for immigrant enclaves? Does according official language status to the language of a national minority qualify as a group-specific right when the languages of equally large immigrant groups are not given this status? (For example, German is an official language in Belgium, but German-speakers are outnumbered by Arab-speakers. So too with Romansch in Switzerland.) Barry expressed general support for the policy of according territorial autonomy and official language status to national minorities, and according land claims and self-government to indigenous peoples, so long as these groups exercise their self-governing powers in accordance with liberal constitutional values. Yet it is not clear whether he views these policies that recognize and empower particular groups and support their languages and separate institutions as exceptions to the rule that group-specific policies are illegitimate, or as somehow not involving group-specific rights. Since we are not sure how to apply Barry's narrow criteria, we have stuck instead with the more familiar broader definition.

Appendix 2.2. Data sources

Welfare state measures

This chapter employs two types of direct indicators of the strength of the welfare state and redistribution in countries: public social expenditures as a per cent of GDP; and two measures of the redistributive impact of government taxes and transfers. In addition, it uses two measures of social outcomes: the child poverty rate; and the level of income inequality.

Data for public social expenditures as a per cent of GDP are from the OECD Socx data set, and can be obtained from **www.oecd.org**. Data on the other measures are from the Luxembourg Income Study (LIS), a cooperative research project that has established a collection of household income surveys from countries around the world. The LIS team harmonizes and standardizes the micro-data from the different surveys to facilitate comparative research. Because the original country surveys were conducted in different years, LIS-based research normally compares countries in five-year periods (early 1980s, etc.), a practice followed here. The latest data available at the time of writing are for 2000 or near year. More information on the LIS database can be found at **www.listproject.org**.

The five specific measures employed in this chapter are calculated as follows:

Public social spending as a per cent of GDP. In general terms, public social expenditure includes expenditures on health, income transfers, and social services (but not education). In specific terms, the category includes: old age benefits, disability cash benefits, occupational injury/disease benefits, sickness benefits, services for elderly and disabled people, survivors, family cash benefits, family services, active labour market programmes, unemployment benefits, health, housing benefits, and other contingencies. Appendix 2.3 provides the basic levels of public social expenditures as a per cent of GDP for 1980 and 2000. The figures for 'change' in Tables 2.1–2.3 measure the change between 1980 and 2000 as a per cent of the 1980 level.

Redistribution measures. The two measures of redistribution capture the extent to which the levels of poverty and inequality implicit in market or private incomes are reduced by government taxes and transfers. Data for both measures are from Mahler and Jesuit (2005). We are grateful to the authors for their willingness to share their detailed data appendix with us, and for assistance in interpreting the results. Figures for specific periods in Appendix 2.3 (e.g. early 1980s) measure the extent to which poverty and inequality were reduced by government taxes and transfers, and are expressed in percentage terms. Figures for 'change' in Tables 2.1–2.3 are the change in these redistribution measures between the earliest and latest period available as a per cent of the earliest period.

Social outcomes. The measures of child poverty and inequality refer to patterns after government taxes and transfers are taken into account. Data are from the LIS website, as downloaded on 21 June 2005. In the LIS database, the poverty line is set at 50 per cent of median adjusted disposable income for all persons. Appendix 2.3 reports the child poverty rate, defined as the percentage of all children in poverty, for specific periods (e.g. the early 1980s). The figures for 'change' in Tables 2.1–2.3 are the change in the rate of child poverty between the earliest and latest data available for each country. In this calculation, a change from a child poverty rate of 6 per cent in the earliest period to 8 per cent in the latest period is a change of 2. Data on inequality are for disposable income for all households, the LIS aggregate income variable labelled DPI. Figures for specific periods in Appendix 2.3 (e.g. early 1980s) are gini coefficients, a measure of inequality in which the higher the number, the greater the level of inequality. Figures for 'change' in Tables 2.1–2.3 are the percentage change in the gini coefficient for the earliest and latest periods available for each country (i.e. the change between the earliest and the latest gini coefficients expressed as a per cent of the earliest gini coefficient).

Demographic data

Data on the size of immigrant minorities are based on United Nations estimates of 'foreign-born migrant stock'. Data on the size of national minorities and indigenous minorities are from Minority Rights Group 1997.

Other variables

The regressions in Tables 2.5 and 2.6 also include the following: (1) left parties in government, drawn from Duane Swank's *Comparative Parties* Dataset and updated to 2001 using recent electoral results; (2) female labour force participation, drawn from OECD *Labour Statistics*, and (3) population over 64 years, drawn from OECD *Health Data*.

The sample of countries

Countries included in the analysis are Western democracies, and had democratic political institutions throughout the period under study (1980 to 2000). The primary limitation on inclusion in the sample was availability of data. Data on redistribution were available for only twelve countries. However, other countries were included in the analysis of the evolution of the welfare state if data on both social spending and social outcomes measures were available. See Appendix 2.3 for details.

Appendix 2.3. Welfare state indicators: Social spending, redistribution, and social outcomes, 1980–2000 or near year

Country	Public social expenditures % GDP		Redistribution								Social outcomes							
			Reduction in poverty (%)				Reduction in inequality (%)				Child poverty rate (%)				Inequality gini coefficient			
	1980	2000	Early 80s	Late 80s	Early 90s	2000	Early 80s	Late 80s	Early 90s	2000	Early 80s	Late 80s	Early 90s	2000	Early 80s	Late 80s	Early 90s	2000
Australia	11.3	18.6	61.7	62.2	62.3		29.0	29.0	31.2		13.8	15.0	15.8	7.8	.281	.304	.311	.260
Austria	22.5	26.0			88.0	82.8			50.1	45.9		4.8	9.7	6.7		.227	.280	.277
Belgium	24.1	26.7			63.2	61.3			30.6	26.9		3.8	4.6		.227	.232	.224	.302
Canada	14.3	17.3	51.1	59.0	81.1		23.2	26.9	44.6		14.8	14.8	15.3	14.9	.284	.283	.281	.247
Denmark	29.1	28.9		71.7				36.2	48.4			4.7	5.0			.254	.236	
Finland	18.5	24.5		84.1	84.1	85.8		46.8		42.6		2.8	2.3	2.8		.209	.210	
France	21.1	28.3	77.1	75.0	80.9		36.5	39.5	40.6		6.9	8.3	7.9	9.0	.288	.287	.288	.264
Germany	23.0	27.2	82.2	80.3	77.7	79.1	37.1	39.0	41.0	42.6	2.8	4.1	9.5	17.2	.244	.257	.272	.323
Ireland	17.0	13.6										13.8	14.6	16.6		.328	.333	.333
Italy	18.4	24.1										11.4	14.0			.306	.290	
Netherlands	26.9	21.8	89.7	87.5	83.0	76.7	44.7	46.1	40.6	43.6	2.7	5.2	8.1	9.8	.260	.256	.266	.248
Norway	17.9	23.0		74.2	78.2	79.9		33.8	38.2	38.2	4.8	4.3	5.2	3.4	.223	.233	.231	.251
Spain	15.9	19.9									12.7		12.2	16.1	.318	.303	.353	.340
Sweden	28.8	28.6	85.7	80.3	83.9	82.7	52.1	49.1	50.3	43.6	4.8	3.5	3.0	4.2	.197	.218	.229	.252
UK	17.9	21.7		77.2	65.0	71.7		36.3	29.4	31.0		12.5	18.5	15.3		.303	.336	.345
USA	13.3	14.2		40.0	44.6	42.2		22.5	23.6	21.5		25.0	25.6	21.9		.335	.338	.368

Notes: See Appendix 2.2 for data sources and details of calculations.

3

'If you are my brother, I may give you a dime!' Public opinion on multiculturalism, trust, and the welfare state

Markus Crepaz

I am a part of all that I have met.

Lord Alfred Tennyson

Since the mid-1970s a veritable 'crisis literature' on the welfare state has developed, heralding its death in multitudinous ways: women joining the workforce, rising individualism, the 'greying' of societies, globalization, declining organizational capacity of unions, post-materialism, the decline of the family, deindustrialization, diminishing class identity, 'post-Fordist' production methods, and a whole host of other explanations. Recently, yet a new element has been identified that is argued to pierce the heart of the welfare state: rising diversity as a result of increased immigration is said to inject different religions, races, ethnic groups, and languages into the national polity. As a result, the foundation of citizenship which 'requires a direct sense of community membership based on loyalty to a civilization which is a common possession' (Marshall 1950: 25) can no longer be taken for granted.

The question of 'who belongs' becomes critical when distributional issues arise. Societal homogeneity, according to many observers, is crucial because the sacrifice involved in giving up part of your income is more easily made if the benefits go to someone who looks and behaves like

This chapter builds on my forthcoming book (Crepaz, forthcoming).

you, hence the title of this chapter. For the welfare state to function, so the argument goes, requires a certain amount of fellow feeling, a caring about other people's life chances and a sense of belonging to a community of fate. It is said that this is easier to come by if the person in need shares similar 'primordial' characteristics with you.[1]

Intriguingly, much of this literature highlights the American experience with diversity. Racial diversity combined with a mainstream media that 'racializes' images of poverty and of African-Americans as illegitimate receivers of welfare benefits are often cited as the main reasons why America has failed to develop a more complete welfare state (Gilens 1999; Alesina and Glaeser 2004). Those who apply the American experience to the European context typically end with dire proclamations such as the warning from one of the keenest observers of matters of race, ethnicity, and the American welfare state, Nathan Glazer (1998: 17): 'what will happen to European social benefits as they are seen to go disproportionately to immigrants...and to fellow citizens different in religion and race[?]...One may well see a withdrawal in European countries from the most advanced frontier of social policy...because these are seen as programs for "others"'.

This argument has raised its head not only in explanations for the relative meagreness of the American welfare state and of the impact of rapid immigration on European forms of social provision, but also in the context of multiculturalism policies (MCPs). MCPs not only recognize the ethnic, racial, and religious differences of newcomers but actively support them through state-sanctioned efforts designed to protect and further the interests of such groups. Assimilation, or perhaps more properly, integration, is an alternative strategy which calls for newcomers to adjust and ultimately to blend into the host society.[2]

The critiques of multiculturalism generally centre around the perceived loss of the majority identity, what Brian Barry called, 'losing our way'

---

[1] Such 'primordial' arguments are enjoying an unexpected comeback. For the general validity of these arguments and why they are arising now, see Crepaz (forthcoming). Brian Barry, who rarely left one guessing where he stood exactly, dealt with the 'primordial' argument as follows: 'The wiseacres who say that there is something "natural" or "primordial" about these forces merely reveal their historical and sociological illiteracy. It was said of the Bourbons when they were restored to the throne in France in 1815 that they had learned nothing and forgotten nothing. The same may be said of those who pursue policies of ethnocultural nationalism and particularism, and also of those who lend them intellectual support' (Barry 2001: 4).

[2] Nathan Glazer speaks of a school pageant in a Dearborn school in Michigan in the 1930s in which distinctly dressed immigrants enter a 'melting pot' on one side and exit it on the other side all dressed alike (Glazer 1997).

(Barry 2001: 1). In addition, critics of MCPs argue that by highlighting differences between different groups, the sense of common identity, which is necessary for the welfare state to command support, is undermined. Alan Wolfe and Jytte Klausen pinpoint 'a difficult dilemma for identity groups: they can choose to strengthen the group and in the process, to weaken the state (whose purpose, presumably, is to provide enhanced benefits back to the group) or they can choose to strengthen the state, thereby expanding benefits to members of the group, but only by weakening the formal political claims of the group as a group' (Wolfe and Klausen 1997: 247). They do believe that the modern welfare state is robust and can absorb 'mild forms of identity politics... as long as there are well-understood principles of assimilation and accommodation'. However, 'if claims for recognition on behalf of those groups weaken government, such groups may be accorded symbolic equality without government provisions to back them up—a Pyrrhic victory indeed' (Wolfe and Klausen 1997: 242). For Wolfe and Klausen, redistribution is prior to recognition; in fact, recognition of identity groups is ineffective without active government support. Focusing on identity politics, so the critics argue, directs attention away from the truly important issues such as rising inequality, and issues of economic redistribution. This critique was evocatively captured in one of Todd Gitlin's (1995: 126) chapter titles, 'Marching on the English Department while the Right Took the White House'.

Critics have been unsparing in the demolition of multiculturalism particularly the essential claim by multiculturalists that different groups must not only be recognized but their interests must be specifically supported by the state. A defender of nationality, David Miller, has argued that such a singling out of groups 'is liable to backfire, by exposing groups to outright rejections and rebuffs which they would not experience under a less politically charged regime of toleration' (Miller 2000: 75). Brian Barry (2001: 21) echoes that view by scolding that 'the politics of difference is a formula for manufacturing conflict, because it rewards those groups that can most effectively mobilize to make claims on the polity'. And Harold Wilensky (2002: 653), a long-time observer of welfare states, bluntly states that 'A country that makes a serious effort to... assimilate immigrants via inclusionary naturalization policies, job creation, training, and placement, and language training and citizenship education will minimize nativist violence.'

Keith Banting and Will Kymlicka (Chapter 1 of this volume) summarize one of the critiques against MCPs, the so-called 'corroding effect'. This thesis claims that 'multiculturalism policies erode solidarity because they emphasize differences between citizens, rather than commonalties. Citizens have historically supported the welfare state, and been willing to make sacrifices to support their disadvantaged co-citizens, because they viewed these co-citizens as "one of us", bound together by a common identity and common sense of belonging. However, multiculturalism policies are said to corrode this overarching common identity.'

While concisely summarizing the critics' arguments, multiculturalists such as Banting and Kymlicka, of course, take a very different view claiming that at least as far as Canada and Australia are concerned, evidence indicates that multiculturalism policies have not eroded social unity. If anything, Kymlicka (2001: 37) argues, such policies have enhanced social unity as evidenced by 'increases in the levels of interethnic friendships and intermarriage'. He claims that Canada and Australia 'do a better job integrating immigrants into common civic and political institutions than any other country in the world' (Kymlicka 2001: 37). If it is indeed the case that newcomers or minorities and natives engage in *each other's* traditions, history, and culture it seems apparent that more empathy for the respective conditions ensues. As Keith Banting and Will Kymlicka (p. 17 above) put it, 'By adopting multiculturalism policies, the state can be seen as trying both to encourage dominant groups not to fear or despise minorities, and also to encourage minorities to trust the larger society.'

These are radically opposing viewpoints that are more deeply examined by the theorists in later chapters of this volume. The purpose of this chapter is to examine empirically public reactions to MCPs using survey instruments. The central question that arises flows directly out of the brief theoretical overview just provided: do MCPs undermine the public's willingness to continue funding the welfare state? Two opposing reactions are theoretically plausible. The first holds that precisely because MCPs highlight differences between natives and newcomers, such policies should lead to adverse reactions by natives. As they see government policies favouring 'out-groups' they may 'detach' from the welfare state and no longer support a redistributive system that benefits 'others'.

Alternatively, as a result of official recognition by the state, both minorities and natives may develop a sense of belonging to an 'imagined community' that unites them through common citizenship and the sharing of basic liberal values that make such recognition possible in the first place. Thus, it is the very sharing of basic liberal values that not only allows a politics of difference to flourish but that ultimately makes up the cement of society upon which continued support for the welfare state may be built. Primordial differences often become salient when overlaid or reinforced by class, income, or education. It is rarely the case that primordial differences alone are responsible for social conflicts between newcomers and natives. A welfare state that includes newcomers combined with policies that recognize and support the cultural idiosyncrasies of minorities may help reduce the differences in life chances between natives and newcomers.

This chapter examines two central issues: first, how widespread are multiculturalist attitudes? This question is relevant because many critics of multiculturalism argue that it is a project driven by elites with very little support by the public. This charge raises serious issues of the democratic legitimacy of multiculturalism. Therefore, the first section will probe how widespread multiculturalist attitudes among the public are, relying on four major, large-scale, multinational public opinion surveys, the World Values Survey (WVS), the European Social Survey (ESS), the International Social Survey Programme (ISSP), and the Eurobarometer (EB) series.

The second major issue is the impact of MCPs on the welfare state. The central claim of the critics of MCPs is basically twofold: first, that MCPs undermine interpersonal trust and secondly, as a result of reduced trust a diminishing readiness by natives to fund the welfare state should ensue. If this is indeed the case, such sentiments should be observable in two crucial ways: first, interpersonal trust should decline over the time frame in which MCPs have been applied and secondly, declining public support for the redistributive state should be observable.

These issues are examined by analysing responses to questions about multiculturalism, support for the welfare state, and 'trust' across different publics and across time as much as possible. This should provide a dynamic picture in different countries as to how MCPs have been perceived and how they affect the publics' readiness to support the welfare state. Examining such attitudes can be done in basically two ways: by aggregating individual attitudes to the national level, and by using 'multilevel analysis' or 'hierarchical linear modelling'. Both methods will be employed and special emphasis will be placed on examining attitudes over time.

This contribution centres on public opinion for the following reason: public opinion is the first causal link in the chain between proposed policies and their estimated effects. Critics of MCPs claim that such policies lead to a fragmenting of community which will ultimately be visible in reduced aggregate welfare measures. However, welfare measures, even disaggregated to health policies, sickness benefits, or unemployment compensation are very complex policy outputs that reflect the vector sum of many different, often cross-cutting interests.

Consequently, before multiculturalism policies manifest themselves in concrete policy outputs they affect public opinion. Any adverse public reactions to MCPs and the welfare state should manifest itself in public sentiments long before aggregate data on public expenditures would show such a connection. In that sense, public opinion is like the proverbial canary in the coalmines giving warnings that the environment is becoming toxic, allowing coalminers and policy makers to extract themselves before the (social) explosion occurs. If there is any truth to the corroding effect of multiculturalism policies, i.e. that such policies corrode the 'fellow feeling' among natives, an undermining of the sense of 'that could be me in need of help', such changes should become visible in public opinion surveys long before they manifest themselves in aggregate statistics.

At the same time it is important to be cautious when examining public opinion. As in real life it is advisable not to always believe what people say. It is true that public opinion is temperamental, suffers from systematic measurement problems, and is oftentimes skilfully manipulated by political actors to such an extent that instead of public opinion being the final arbiter of public policy, debates about public policy shape public opinion. Despite all these caveats, one hopes that there is some connection between public opinion and policy.[3] At the end of the day, it is impossible to deny *vox populi* in a liberal democratic system.

1. For elites only? The expanse of multiculturalism attitudes across modern societies

Before delving into the connections between MCPs and attitudes on the welfare state, this section explores the public support and distribution of multiculturalism attitudes across modern societies. Many critics of

---

[3] Much of the literature that uses public opinion polls, takes public opinion as the 'popular will', in other words public opinion is prior to public policy which is supposed to reflect, ultimately, public opinion. However, 'Public opinion is not a genuine "will of the citizens", it only tells how people have responded to the questions asked' (Forma 1999: 90). One of the most contested issues is the degree to which public opinion actually impacts public policy. Some observers found that public opinion does impact public policy (Erikson 1976; Monroe 1979; Whiteley, 1981), while others such as Harold Wilensky (1981) and Murray Edelman (1977) believe that public opinion can be selectively created by politicians so that in fact it is public policy that drives public opinion rather than the other way round.

multiculturalism have highlighted how these policies are 'out of touch' with 'the people' and that they are driven by elites such as 'advocacy groups, judges and educational bureaucrats' (Barry 2001: 228) who impose these policies on the common man. According to Brian Barry, these 'behind the scenes manipulations' have 'strong[ly] anti-majoritarian implications' and, thus, are inconsistent with democratic principles. Barry (2001: 299) goes on to explain 'That multiculturalist policies continue to be pursued in the face of a high degree of public hostility is a remarkable tribute to the effectiveness of the elites who are committed to them.'

How widespread are multiculturalism attitudes? There are very few comparative surveys that have specifically tapped such attitudes. Among the 'big four' surveys, the ISSP, the WVS, the ESS, and the EB, only the last has specifically asked European publics about MCPs. Most surveys ask more general questions, e.g. whether ethnic and racial minorities should keep their customs or whether they should adapt to the larger society. For example, the WVS in 2000 asked the following question: 'Which statement is nearest to your opinion? Immigrants should 1) maintain distinct customs and traditions; 2) take over the customs of the country.' Most proponents of multiculturalism would take the answer option 'maintain customs and traditions' as the central goal of multiculturalism. On average, across eleven countries (Austria, Belgium, Denmark, Finland, France, Germany, Ireland, Italy, Netherlands, Sweden, and the United Kingdom), 33.7 per cent of the respondents indicated that immigrants should maintain customs and traditions and two-thirds thought that immigrants should take over the customs of the country. However, in Ireland and Italy there was a majority favouring multiculturalism of 56.8 per cent and 59.7 per cent respectively.

In 2002 the European Social Survey (ESS) asked a similarly worded question: 'Tell me how much you agree or disagree with each of these statements. It is better for a country if almost everyone shares the same customs and traditions.' On average across thirteen European countries (Austria, Germany, Belgium, Switzerland, Denmark, Finland, France, Great Britain, Ireland, Italy, Netherlands, Norway, and Sweden) around 58 per cent either agreed strongly or agreed with this statement while 42 per cent disagreed or disagreed strongly—the latter 42 per cent of course representing the multiculturalist option. Interestingly, across this sample there was only one country in which there was a majority that disagreed with the statement: Switzerland. Their reaction is not surprising since Switzerland has had a long tradition of giving political, linguistic, and ethnic autonomy to the people in its cantons.

In 1995 the International Social Survey Programme asked the following question: 'Some people say that it is better for a country if different racial and ethnic groups maintain their distinct customs and traditions. Others say that it is better if these groups adapt and blend into the larger society. Which of these views comes closer to your own?' Again, 'maintaining distinct customs and traditions' is closely related to the central idea of multiculturalism while 'adapting and blending into the larger society' denotes the integrationist or assimilationist option. Figure 3.1 shows results for two groups: a group of twelve liberal democracies and a second group of nine Eastern European transition countries.

The only country which passes the majority threshold is West Germany where slightly over 52 per cent of respondents believe that different ethnic and racial groups should maintain their distinct customs and traditions. The two countries with the strongest multiculturalism policies, Australia and Canada, score lower with only slightly over 17 per cent in Australia and over a third in Canada believing that minorities should maintain their distinct customs and traditions. The fieldwork for this survey was done in 1995, even before Pauline Hanson had made her maiden speech in the Australian House of Representatives and before her flash in the pan 'One Nation' party won an astonishing almost 25 per cent of the popular vote in Queensland in 1998. Since then, however, her party has fizzled out and today *The Economist* describes her and her party as 'merely a footnote of history' (*Economist* 2005). 'To the visitor', *The Economist* continues, 'Australia seems like a model of harmonious race relations. No matter where you come from, people assume you are a native, because in this melting pot of race you might very well be.'

One of the most intriguing aspects of Figure 3.1 is the observation that multiculturalism policies appear to be much more favoured in Eastern European countries which are transitioning from communist, authoritarian rule to capitalist democracy. Even between West and East Germany there is an almost 10 per cent difference. What could explain these differences between Eastern and Western Europe?

The difference between Eastern and Western Europe (in political terms) is most likely explained by the different types of minorities existing in the two parts of Europe. The lower support in Western Europe may be driven by the fact that these minorities are relatively new immigrant minorities. When publics in Eastern Europe are asked about whether 'groups' should maintain their customs and traditions, they think first and foremost of long-standing, historic minorities, not recent immigrant groups, of which there are few if any in these societies. For instance,

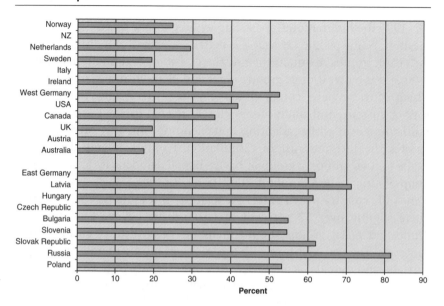

Figure 3.1 Multiculturalist attitudes in Eastern and Western Europe

Survey question: 'Some people say that it is better for a country if different racial and ethnic groups maintain their distinct customs and traditions. Others say that it is better if these groups adapt and blend into the larger society. Which of these views comes closer to your own?'

Note: Entries represent the percentage of those who believe that it is 'better for society if groups maintain their distinct customs and traditions' as opposed to that 'groups adapt and blend into the larger society'.

Source: ISSP (1998).

people in Bulgaria would be thinking about their historic Turkish minority; people in Slovakia would be thinking about their historic Hungarian minority. While oftentimes relationships with these minorities are tense, the basic legitimacy of their existence as culturally distinct 'groups' is largely unquestioned. These groups have been living side by side with the majority group for centuries and can plausibly claim that this is as much their homeland as it is the majority group's.[4]

In Western Europe, on the other hand, the minorities are 'new', i.e. immigrant minorities. Thus, most West Europeans will interpret the survey question as referring to the rights of newcomers who have no historic claim to practise their traditional culture in their new country of residence. After all, they have voluntarily left their homeland, and, as

---

[4] I thank Keith Banting and Will Kymlicka for their insights in the interpretation of the survey results in the Eastern European countries.

a result, may be thought of as having waived their right to practise their traditional culture (Kymlicka 1995). As a result, West European publics are more hesitant to allow immigrant minorities to practise their culture and customs which manifests itself in lower scores on that particular survey question.

Asking more specifically about public support for MCPs the Eurobarometer series in the year 2000 asked publics across Europe how much support there is for such policies (Eurobarometer 53, 2000). The precise question was as follows: 'What do you think ought to be done to improve the relationship between people of different races, religions or cultures in [your country]?' Respondents could either 'mention' or 'not mention' the respective policies. Entries in Figure 3.2 represent percentages of people who mentioned the following policies:

1. Do nothing.
2. Promote understanding of different cultures and lifestyles in [your country].
3. Promote equality of opportunity in all areas of social life.
4. Encourage the creation of organizations that bring people from different races, religions, or cultures together.
4. Promote the teaching of mutual acceptance and respect in schools.

Figure 3.2 reveals a rather intriguing picture. There is strong support across European publics for schools to teach 'mutual acceptance and respect' (on average over 55 per cent) and also for promoting policies that assist in understanding different cultures and lifestyles (on average 42 per cent). When it comes to promoting equality of opportunity European publics are becoming a bit more hesitant with only 38 per cent mentioning this option. Less than a third (31.5 per cent) encourage the creation of organizations to bring together people of different races, religions, and cultures. When asked whether nothing should be done to 'improve the relationship between people of different races, religions and cultures' only around 6 per cent of respondents mentioned this option.

Finally, using the same Eurobarometer survey the public's attitudes towards minorities and diversity in general is examined. Four items in particular are relevant in gauging support for multiculturalism across European publics. The lead statement is as follows: 'Now can we talk about the place of people belonging to minority groups in terms of race, religion or culture within [nationality] society. For each of the following opinions, could you please tell me whether you tend to agree or tend to disagree:

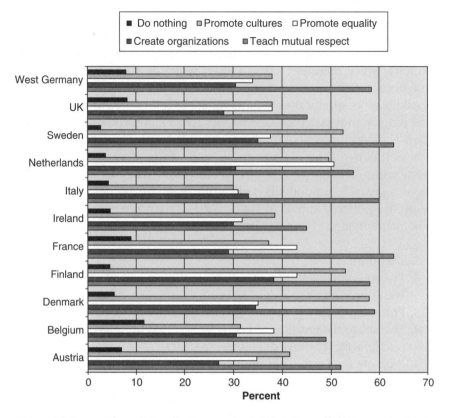

Figure 3.2 Support for policies affecting people of different races, religions, and cultures

Survey question: 'What do you think ought to be done to improve the relationship between people of different races, religions or cultures in [your country]?'

Source: Eurobarometer 53 (2000).

1. In two or three generations' time, people belonging to these minority groups will be like all other members of society.
2. In order to be fully accepted members of [nationality] society, people belonging to these minority groups must give up their own culture.
3. [Country's] diversity in terms of race, religion or culture adds to its strength.
4. It is a good thing for any society to be made up of people from different races, religions or cultures.'

Figure 3.3 shows rather strong support for what might be called 'multi-culturalist attitudes' such as that diversity adds strength to the nation (on

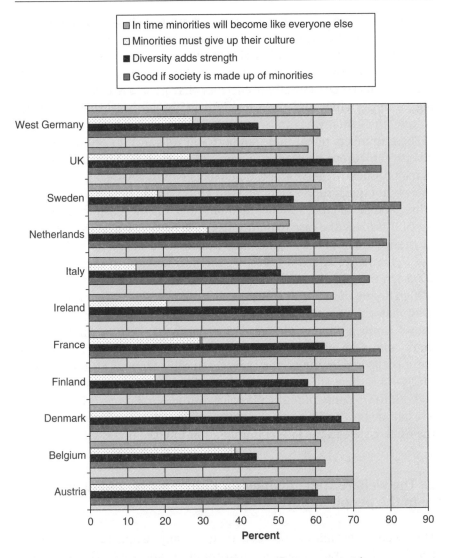

Figure 3.3 Support for diversity and minorities across European countries.
Note: Entries are percentages of those who 'tend to agree' with the respective statement.
Source: Eurobarometer 53 (2000).

average 57 per cent tend to agree with that statement across Europe), that it is good if society is made up of minorities (73 per cent on average), and low percentages of those who believe that in order to be fully accepted members of the dominant society, minorities must give up their culture (around 26 per cent). Respondents also tend to believe that minorities will eventually melt into the larger society. On average, over 63 per cent indicate that in time, members of minority groups will become just 'like other members of society'. This stands in stark contrast to the recent talk about 'parallel societies', 'ethnic enclaves' that are said to develop in many big European cities and the struggle over the term *Leitkultur* (guiding culture) in Germany.

These numbers reveal more support and tolerance for minorities and diversity in Europe than what one may glean from reading the headlines of major American and European newspapers. Still, Figure 3.1 reveals that there is not much support among West European publics for the view that ethnic and racial groups should maintain their distinct customs and traditions. It is likely the case that attitudes have hardened against minorities in the wake of 9/11, the gruesome assassination of Theo van Gogh in the Netherlands, and the terrorist attacks in London in the summer of 2005. On the other hand, to describe multiculturalism policies as meeting a 'high degree of public hostility' as Barry does, seems unwarranted given solid majorities for at least part of such policies. Particularly Figure 3.3 shows a much more widespread prevalence of what might be called 'multiculturalist attitudes' than Barry's comment suggests. These results are especially relevant as they are specifically tapping attitudes about MCPs—and these attitudes are relatively friendly towards MCPs. Having laid out the expanse of multiculturalist attitudes in Europe it is now time to examine how MCPs affect the public's willingness to continue funding the welfare state in the face of immigration-induced diversity.

2. The welfare state, multiculturalism policies, and diversity in the people's court

This section examines whether there is any empirical relationship between MCPs and support for redistribution and trust. The argument is essentially a dynamic one, i.e. it probes whether the support for the welfare state and trust changes over time as a result of the introduction of MCPs. In this chapter every effort is made to capture the dynamic element, although it is not always possible since in some surveys the crucial survey question was posed only once. In such cases, a cross-national design is applied both in aggregate as well as multilevel form.

This contribution concentrates on what Banting and Kymlicka call 'immigrant groups' as opposed to ethno-national groups. For the case of immigrant groups, Banting and Kymlicka (p. 56 above) define multi-culturalism policies as follows: (1) parliamentary affirmation of multicul-turalism; (2) the adoption of multiculturalism in the school curriculum; (3) the inclusion of ethnic representation/sensitivity in the mandate of public media or media licensing; (4) exemptions from dress codes, Sunday closing legislation, etc.; (5) allowing dual citizenship; (6) the funding of ethnic group organizations or activities; (7) the funding of bilingual education or mother-tongue instruction; (8) affirmative action.

The time period for which they examine these policies ranges from '1980 to the late 1990s' and represents the average for this time period. Depending on whether a country adopts most or all of these policies, the country gets either a 'weak', 'modest', or 'strong' rating. The countries with strong multiculturalism policies receive a value of 1, those with modest policies a 0.5, and those with weak policies a 0. Table 3.1 shows these and other relevant data for seventeen industrialized democracies.

Aggregate data analyses

In this subsection, the term 'aggregate' data means individual-level data aggregated to the national level. In terms of attitudes towards redistri-bution, there are few items in the WVS survey that have been asked consistently over time and in enough countries in order to enable fruitful comparison. There is one item, however, that will be used throughout this chapter that aptly captures the essence of the philosophy of the welfare state and that has been asked over time in most countries. The exact wording of the item is as follows: 'Now I'd like you to tell me your views on various issues. How would you place your views on this scale? 1 means you agree completely with the statement on the left, 10 means you agree completely with the statement on the right; and if your views fall somewhere in between, you can choose any number in between. 1: people should take more responsibility to provide for themselves. 10: The government should take more responsibility to ensure that everybody is provided for' (this is variable v127 in WVS 1–3, and e037 in WVS 4). Thus, this variable has a 10-point scale. Entries in Table 3.1 represent the sum of those who have indicated options 6–10 of that variable. The validity of this item derives from the explicit mentioning of who should do the providing ('people' vs. the 'government'). Any misgivings by the public against government-supported MCPs should manifest itself in an increase in support for the 'people' option rather than the 'government' option.

These attitudes should also be affected by the percentage of foreign population in the respective countries.[5] It is intuitive to believe that the higher the percentage of the foreign population the more the effects of MCPs are brought into sharp relief and any 'withdrawal' from public redistribution schemas should be more visible when the percentage of foreigners is higher.

A total of four waves of the WVS have been administered: in 1981, 1990–1, 1995–7, and 1999/2001. Unfortunately, the 'government should provide' question was not asked in 1981 at all. It was asked in the 1990–1 survey and in the 1999/2001 survey while the question was posed in only a few countries in the third wave, i.e. 1995–7. This means that there are basically only two complete time periods in which this question was posed: in 1990/1 and in 1999/2001. This is the reason why the percentage of foreign population was collected for the years of 1988 and 1998. In order to predict attitudes in 1990/1 and 1999/2001, the percentage of foreign population in 1988 and 1998 respectively are used.[6] In order to capture the extent of change of both distributional attitudes as well as percentage of foreign population Table 3.1 also lists the (change) measures for attitudes (measured between the two longest possible time frames in the cases when three observations were given, i.e. 1990 to 1999–2001 as opposed to the cases when data for only two time points were available).

A glance at the per cent change in attitudes (Δ % Att.) in Table 3.1 indicates that, on average, redistributive attitudes have increased by almost 22 per cent between 1990 and 2000. Although there are countries in which support for state-led redistribution has decreased such as in Denmark

[5] The Organization for Economic Cooperation and Development (OECD), on whose database this study relies, defines 'foreign population' as follows: 'The population of foreign nationals may represent second and higher generations as well as first-generations of migrants. The characteristics of the population of foreign nationals depend on a number of factors: the history of migration flows, natural increase in the foreign population and naturalisations. Higher generations of immigrants arise in situations where they retain their foreign citizenship even when native-born. The nature of legislation on citizenship and the incentives foreigners have to naturalise both play a role in determining the extent to which this occurs in practice.' It is important to distinguish between 'foreign population' and 'foreign-born population'. The latter tends to generate higher percentages of the total resident population because it also includes subjects who are foreign born but have attained national citizenship. The OECD defines 'foreign-born population' as follows: 'The foreign-born population can be viewed as representing first-generation migrants, and may consist of both foreign and national citizens' (OECD 2005).

[6] The lead time of two years for the percentage of foreign population is rather arbitrary. How long does it take before a particular percentage of foreign population affects natives' attitudes? This is hard to say. Perhaps one year could have been chosen or even a five-year lead time could have been chosen. Overall however, statistical results would not be drastically affected by different lead times as the percentage of foreign population does not vary dramatically from year to year.

Table 3.1 Public perceptions on 'government should take more responsibility' in 1990, 1995, and 2000

	1990	1995	2000	Δ % Att.	MCP	Foreign population		Δ% FP
						1988	1998	
Australia	n.a.	43.0	43.0	0.0	1.0	22.1	23.2	5.0
Austria	17.8	n.a.	23.1	30.0	0.0	3.9	9.1	33.3
Belgium	35.2	n.a.	39.9	13.0	0.5	8.8	8.7	−1.2
Canada	26.5	n.a.	38.3	44.0	1.0	17.1	17.9	5.0
Denmark	24.0	n.a.	23.5	−2.2	0.0	2.8	4.8	71.0
Finland	24.8	47.2	34.8	40.0	0.0	0.4	1.6	400.0
France	23.7	n.a.	22.6	−5.0	0.0	6.5	5.5	−16.0
Germany	28.3	46.7	37.1	31.0	0.0	7.3	8.9	22.0
Ireland	37.1	n.a.	31.1	−16.0	0.0	1.9	3.0	58.0
Italy	48.5	n.a.	50.3	4.0	0.0	1.1	2.1	91.0
Netherlands	32.5	n.a.	33.7	4.0	0.5	4.1	4.2	2.5
Norway	28.9	50.3	50.4	74.0	0.0	3.2	3.7	16.0
Sweden	14.6	18.9	25.5	75.0	0.5	5.0	5.6	12.0
Switzerland	n.a.	20.8	20.8	0.0	0.0	15.2	19.0	25.0
UK	45.1	n.a.	28.4	−37.0	0.5	3.2	3.8	19.0
USA	17.7	27.5	30.6	74.0	0.5	9.5	10.9	15.0
Average	28.9	36.3	33.3	21.9		7.0	8.25	18.0[a]

[a] This is not the average of the percentage change of each country as the case of Finland, which experienced a 400 per cent increase in foreign population, would dramatically distort that mean. Rather, it is the calculated average increase from 7 per cent to 8.25 per cent foreign population which equals around 18 per cent average increase between 1988 and 1998.

Notes: Entries represent the sum of options 6–10; change in attitudes (Att.); multiculturalism policies MCP (1980 to late 1990s) (0 = weak, 0.5 = modest, 1 = strong); the percentage of foreign population in 1988 and 1998 and its percentage change over the same period.

Sources: Data on attitudes: World Values Survey (1990, 1995–7, 1999–2001). Inglehart et al. (2003); data on multiculturalism policies: Chapter 2, this volume: p. 56; data on foreign population: OECD (1993, 2003).

(−2.2), France (−5), Ireland (−16), and the UK (−37) the overall direction is a positive one. Over the period from 1988 and 1998, on average, the percentage of foreign population has grown by about 18 per cent from 7.0 per cent in 1988 to 8.3 per cent in 1998.

Are these changes in attitudes correlated with the strength of MCPs? Only two countries are indicated to have 'strong' MCPs (Australia and Canada), five countries are indicated to have 'modest' MCPs, and nine are indicated to have 'weak' MCPs. The average per cent change in attitudes for the 'strong' group of MCPs is 22; for the 'modest' group is 40.6; and for the 'weak' group is 20.6. This means that the strongest expansion of support for redistributive policies has occurred in countries with 'modest' MCPs, the next strongest in countries with 'strong' MCPs and the smallest expansion in countries with 'weak' MCPs. These initial descriptive findings are at odds with those who claim that MCPs corrode the welfare state.

Table 3.2 Effects of MCPs and foreign population on redistributive attitudes

	Coefficient	SE	t-test	p-value	
(a) Change model (N = 16): Δ% in Att. is the dependent variable.					
MCPs	3.40	34.90	0.10	0.92	
Δ in foreign population	−0.22	0.44	−0.52	0.61	
Constant	22.50	21.20	1.06	0.31	$R^2 = 0.02$
(b) Cross sectional/time series 'panel' model (N = 32): Δ % in Att. is the dependent variable.					
MCPs	11.50	7.30	1.60	0.12	
% foreign population	−0.18	3.17	−0.45	0.66	
Constant	27.60	3.20	8.70	0.00	$R^2 = 0.03$

Sources: The results are based on data from Table 3.1.

In terms of public opinion, at this stage, there is no systematic negative association between MCPs and redistributive attitudes. If anything, there is a slight positive connection observable.

To analyse this relationship more formally, two methods are applied. First, MCPs are regressed on changes in attitudes (Δ % Att.) as the dependent variable with changes in the percentage of foreign population as an additional predictor. It is possible that societies which experience dramatic increases in foreign population feel especially threatened. If that is the case, according to the critics of MCPs this should undermine the willingness of the public to continue supporting the welfare state.

The second method uses absolute levels of attitudes in 1990 and 2000 as dependent variables and MCPs and absolute levels of foreign population in 1988 and 1998 as independent variables. This doubles the number of observations from 16 to 32 and introduces a short time element in this cross-sectional/time series panel analysis (N = 16, t = 2).[7] The level of foreign population in 1988 is used to explain attitudes in 1990 in country 'A' followed by the same variables but shifted one time frame to 1998 and 2000 respectively in the same country.

Both models in Table 3.2 were estimated using robust regression estimates. This regression technique reduces the impact of outliers and/or leverage points the further away they are from the regression line. Such outlying points can have 'undue' effects on the regression slope, particularly when the number of observations is low as is the case in model *a* with only 16 observations but also in model *b* with 32. Robust regression

---

[7] Here the term 'panel' does not refer to identical individuals who are surveyed over time. Rather, the term panel is used here to examine identical countries over time.

estimates are obtained by using the reweighted least squares method which assigns lower weights to points farther from the regression line. As a result, if there are outlying datapoints, their effect is reduced, thereby increasing the robustness of the findings (Belsley, Kuh, and Welsch 1980). In other words, robust regression estimates ensure that the relationships are not driven either by outliers or points with high leverage on the regression slope.

Neither of the two models in Table 3.2 is statistically significant and their explanatory power is very low. In other words, MCPs do not affect redistributive attitudes either negatively or positively in a significant fashion. These aggregate data analyses do not support the claim that multiculturalism policies adversely affect public support for redistribution even when controlling for the effect of foreign population.

Trusting strangers?

Ever since the publication of Robert D. Putnam's (1993) *Making Democracy Work*, there has been an explosion in studies on 'social capital' and 'trust', its close cousin. The Russell Sage Foundation has sponsored a series of 'trust' books examining both the origins and consequences of trust (Braithwaite and Levi 1998; Cook 2001; Hardin 2002). Why is trust so important? Trust is important because it is impossible to regulate every aspect of human interaction on the basis of legal codes alone. Relationships between people unfold within a framework of social norms of trust and morality. In their absence, as Durkheim so powerfully put it, an 'incoherent chaos' would reign (Durkheim, quoted in Giddens 1971: 69).

When it comes to the provision of public goods trust is crucial because 'contributing' means that at some point one may well be in a situation where the help of the community is needed. One such public good is the welfare state, 'where citizens must trust each other to both take part as contributors and not take advantage as beneficiaries. Trust is aided by identification with fellow citizens. Identification with fellow citizens is easiest in ethnically and culturally homogeneous societies...' (Soroka, Johnston, and Banting 2006: 280). In this account, it is not diversity per se that leads to reduced welfare support, but trust may be reduced as a result of diversity, and this reduced trust may be responsible for lower welfare state support. Thus, 'trust' subtly slips between diversity as cause and welfare state support as an effect. Trust is enhanced when individuals share certain basic tracers such as race, ethnicity, religion, or

Table 3.3 Trust over time 1981–1999/2001

Question: 'Do you think that most people can be trusted or that you can't be too careful?'

	1981	1990/91	1995/97	1999/2001	Δ% Att.
Australia	48.2	n.a.	40.0	40.0	−4.1
Austria	n.a.	31.8	n.a.	33.4	0.8
Belgium	29.2	33.5	n.a.	29.2	0.0
Canada	48.5	53.1	n.a.	38.3	−5.8
Denmark	52.7	57.7	n.a.	66.5	6.9
Finland	57.2	62.7	48.8	57.4	0.0
France	24.8	22.8	n.a.	21.3	−1.8
Germany	32.3	37.8	41.8	37.5	−1.0
Ireland	41.1	47.4	n.a.	36.0	−2.6
Italy	26.8	35.3	n.a.	32.6	2.9
Netherlands	44.8	53.5	n.a.	60.0	7.6
Norway	61.5	65.1	65.3	65.3	1.3
Sweden	56.7	66.1	59.7	66.3	3.2
Switzerland	n.a.	42.6	37.0	37.0	−2.8
UK	43.3	43.7	29.6	29.0	−5.0
USA	40.5	51.1	35.9	36.3	−8.7
Average	43.4	46.9	44.8	42.9	

Note: Entries indicate the percentages of those who say people can be trusted.

Sources: World Values Survey (1990, 1995–7, 1999-2001); Inglehart et al. (2004*a*).

language. Conversely, one might argue that the temptations to cheat and shirk one's duties are enlarged in the provision of public goods when such categorical differences exist.[8] Using the WVS, Table 3.3 shows how trust developed over two decades starting in 1981 to around 2000, very closely matching the time period for which the MCP data have been collected.

A first glance at the averages reveals that trust remains relatively constant over the four time periods. It hovers in the percentage range between the low to middle 40s. Some countries however have seen more dramatic changes over time such as the Netherlands and Denmark, where trust increased on average by around 7 percentage points and the United States where trust dropped on average by almost 9 percentage points.[9] In the

---

[8] Soroka, Johnston, and Banting (forthcoming) understand trust to be a 'state' that is constantly changing depending on the circumstances. As a result trust can be taken as an outcome. This contribution shares this view. However, there are different ways of thinking about trust. Without going into further detail Crepaz (forthcoming) argues that trust can also be thought of as a 'trait', i.e. it is relatively unchanging and enduring and thus can function as a cause for distributional attitudes rather than a consequence.

[9] These averages are averages of change, e.g. four observations across time are available which yields three change measures. They were added up (positive and negative changes) and divided by three yielding a measure of how much change on average has occurred across the four (or three, or two—in which case no average can be calculated) time periods.

Table 3.4 Robust regression estimates of trust (dependent variable) ($N = 32$)

	Coefficient	S.E.	t-test	p-value	
MCPs	11.30	9.70	1.2	0.25	
Foreign population	−0.88	0.55	−1.6	0.12	
Constant	48.30	4.22	11.4	0.00	$R^2 = 0.04$

Source: The results are based on data from Table 3.1.

two countries with the strongest MCPs, Australia and Canada, trust did drop on average by almost 5 points (4.1 for Australia and 5.8 for Canada); the average change in trust was essentially zero in societies with both 'modest' and 'weak' MCPs.

Is that evidence that MCPs undermine trust? To answer this question requires a more systematic analysis of the relationship between trust and MCPs controlling for the percentage of foreign population. Table 3.4 shows the results of a regression analysis with robust regression estimates examining the impact of MCPs on levels of trust controlling for the percentage of foreign population over time. The same time points as in the analysis in Table 3.2 are retained ($N = 16$, $t = 2$) since for the third wave in the WVS (1995–7) there are so many missing data that the number of observations would be unduly restricted.

A cursory look at Table 3.5 indicates again that there is no systematic relationship between MCPs and trust. The relationship is even positive, the opposite of what critics of MCPs would predict, although the relationship is far from being significant. The variable 'foreign population' does indicate the expected sign but is also not significant. Thus, once all observations are taken into account and when the percentage of foreign population is accounted for, there is no systematic evidence indicating that MCPs undermine trust. It is true that if only Australia and Canada are examined, the two countries with the strongest MCPs, trust has declined. However, if they are added to a larger set of modern, post-industrial societies that have engaged in various levels of MCPs, and if the percentage of foreign population is taken into account, there is no systematic negative effect of MCPs on trust observable.

Multilevel analyses

The use of multilevel analysis originated in the field of education. Students of education have long understood that a pupil's performance is not just a matter of their innate capacity and work ethic. Typically, the performance of students, say in the United States is also a matter of, for instance, class size (large or small), the type of school (private or public), the type of county (agricultural or industrial), characteristics of the state (northern or southern), and perhaps even characteristics of the country when compared to other countries. Obviously, such nested data structures do not only occur in the field of education but also in sociology, economics, geography, social psychology, and certainly also in political science.

Similarly, individual attitudes are nested within national contexts and policies. Multilevel analysis is the appropriate methodology for such a question as it allows for the exploration of the effects of state-level differences on individual attitudes. The state-level differences are of course the strength of MCPs, either 'strong', 'modest', or 'weak'. Multilevel modelling can capture these institutional effects, or in the parlance of multilevel modelling, 'level 2' variables, on individual-level attitudes. In order to test the claim that MCPs lead to the erosion of the welfare state, individual attitudes on trust and the redistributive role of the state are used as dependent variables. The multilevel estimation procedures were performed using HLM 6.0 (Hierarchical Linear and Non-linear Modelling) developed by Raudenbush and Bryk (2002).

In Table 3.5 individual responses to the 'trust question' (identical item as used in Table 3.3) are used as the dependent variable at the institutional or structural level (level 2) together with the per cent of foreign population. Additional controls at the individual level are 'life satisfaction', 'interest in politics', self-placement on the political scale, age, education, income, and gender.

Since the dependent variable in this model is dichotomous, a multilevel logit model is the appropriate functional form. The entries in this table show the odds-ratios which are more easily interpretable than the coefficients of a logit analysis. Odds-ratios smaller than one indicate a reduction in probability while odds-ratios larger than one indicate an increase in probability. For instance, the odds-ratio of 1.96 for MCPs means that for a one-unit increase in MCPs (say from 'modest' to 'strong') respondents are 1.96 times more likely to indicate 'trust' as opposed to 'can't be too careful'. The odds-ratio for per cent foreign population of 0.96 on the other hand shows that a one-unit increase in per cent foreign population is associated with a 4 per cent reduction in the probability of people indicating 'trust' over 'can't be too careful'. The odds-ratio for 'female' of 1.06 means that being female increases the chance that respondents choose 'trusting' over 'can't be too careful' by 6 per cent.

Table 3.5 Trust: multilevel logit analysis (HLM)

Question for trust: 'Do you think that most people can be trusted or that you can't be too careful?'

Question for life satisfaction: 'All things considered, how satisfied are you with your life as a whole these days?'

Question for interest in politics: 'How interested would you say you are in politics?'

Question for self-placement on political scale: 'In political matters, people speak of the "left" and the "right". How would you place your views on this scale, generally speaking?'

	Odds-ratios
Structural level (2) variables (N = 15):	
Multicultural policies	1.960**
Per cent foreign population	0.960**
Individual level variables (N = 12,821)	
Life satisfaction	1.130***
Interest in politics	0.860***
Self-placement on political scale	0.930***
Age	1.004**
Education	1.170**
Income	1.180***
Female	1.060***

$* = p < 0.1$, $** = p < 0.05$, $*** = p < 0.01$

Source: Inglehart et al. (2004b).

These are intriguing results! It appears that trust is indeed undermined by the extent of the foreign population. The odds-ratio is significant, indicating that the higher the percentage of population, the lower is trust. Most interestingly, however, is that MCPs counter this trend. Their effect is significantly positive, indicating that those countries with stronger MCPs generate more trust as compared to countries with weaker MCPs. This is inconsistent with the critics of multiculturalism who argue that such policies undermine trust.

Examining further predictors of trust at the individual level highlights other tantalizing results. For example, the more satisfied people are with their life, the older they are, the more educated they are, the higher their income is, and females tend to believe that most people can be trusted, while people less satisfied with their life, younger, less educated and poorer ones, and males, tend to be more distrusting. Interestingly, the less people are interested in politics the less trusting they are, and finally, people who place themselves on the political right are also significantly less trusting than those who place themselves on the political left.

There is an obvious difference between the descriptive results above that showed that in the two countries with the strongest MCPs (Australia

Table 3.6 Support for redistribution: multilevel analysis (HLM)

Structural level (2) variables (N = 15):	
Multiculturalism policies	2.04 (.24)***
Per cent foreign population	−.08 (.017)***
Individual level variables (N = 13,646):	
Satisfaction with life	−.09 (.015)***
Interest in politics	−.008 (.04)
Self-placement on political scale	−.20 (.03)***
Age	−.0086 (.0017)***
Education	−.053 (.021)***
Income	−.25 (.043)***
Female	.19 (.06)***
Proportionate variance explained at level 1	6%
Proportionate variance explained at level 2	36%
Deviance of intercept only model (not shown)	60415.71
Deviance of full model (shown)	59697.68
Deviance reduction: Chi-square	718.03
p-value	.000

Notes: Standard errors in parentheses. * = $p < 0.1$, ** = $p < 0.05$, *** = $p < 0.01$

'People (1) should take more responsibility to provide for themselves' is the dependent variable.

Source: See Table 3.5.

and Canada) trust dropped while in those countries with modest or weak MCPs, trust remained basically unaffected. The difference is explained of course in terms of the methodology applied: in this multilevel analysis, the dependent variable is individual responses to the trust question, controlled for MCPs and per cent foreign population at the national level, while accounting for a whole host of other individual level attributes such as age, gender, education, and income. In other words, once a more systematic look including all countries and controlling for many other potential explanations is applied, the descriptive results no longer appear to be convincing.

Finally, what is the impact of MCPs on people's support for redistribution? As Table 3.2 indicated, there is no evidence of a positive impact of MCPs on attitudes on the welfare state measured at the aggregate level. This final analysis will revisit these results and examine the relationship by using multilevel analysis and controlling for percentage of foreign population at the structural level and a host of additional predictors at the individual level. The item for the dependent variable is the same as the one described in Table 3.1.

Since this dependent variable is measured on a ten-point scale the coefficients in this multilevel analysis can be interpreted just like in an OLS analysis. Another advantage of a continuous dependent variable is that is possible to establish the variance components of the two different levels. In the above model, the proportionate variance explained by level 1 is 6 per cent. In other words, the level 1 predictors explain around 6 per cent of the within-country variance of welfare state support. At level 2, the proportionate variance is 36 per cent. This means that 36 per cent of the true between-country attitude variance in welfare support can be accounted for by MCPs and per cent foreign population. Table 3.5 also reports the 'deviance reduction' measure which is a measure of model fit. Two deviance statistics are presented: the deviance of the baseline model (not shown) which is a simple intercept only model (i.e. with only the country intercepts without any predictors) and the deviance of the full model. The difference in deviance is a Chi-square statistic with associated degrees of freedom. The reduction of 718.03 is significant with a p-value <.000 indicating that this model contributed significantly to the explanation of the variation in support for the welfare state as compared to the simple intercept only model.

Turning to the interpretation of the coefficients, both structural level (level 2) predictors are significant, however in opposite directions. A one-unit increase in MCPs (either from 'weak' to 'modest' or from 'modest' to 'strong' MCPs) tends to increase peoples' support for the welfare state by slightly more than 2 points while a 1 per cent increase in foreign population reduces their support of the welfare state by less than a tenth of a per cent. Both relationships are statistically significant, although the latter, per cent foreign population has a very minor effect on welfare state attitudes. Given these results there is no reason to believe that MCPs undermine support for the welfare state. Clearly, as shown in the negative coefficient of the variable per cent foreign population, immigration driven diversity seems to undercut support for the welfare state, but that tendency is countered by MCPs.

As far as the individual level control variables are concerned, interest in politics does not significantly affect welfare state attitudes. People with higher income, those who are satisfied with their life, who are educated, older, and place themselves on the political right do not believe that the state should ensure that 'everybody is taken care of'. These strata all prefer 'self-help', i.e. that people should take care of themselves. Interestingly only females significantly favour public provision of social benefits. This finding parallels the ones by Svallfors (1997) and Gelissen (2002) who argue that women depend more than men on non-wage income, combined with a gender-specific preference for risk-averse forms of social provision.

Discussion

When Nathan Glazer (1997) claimed that 'We are all multiculturalists now' he was referring to educators in the American academy and not to the public in general. Critics of MCPs have highlighted the 'elitist' character of such policies and observed what they called 'antimajoritarian' biases in the creation of such policies, ultimately endangering, so they argue, the very principle of democracy. It is probably a good thing if politics does not always follow public opinion, but a democracy rests on popular sovereignty and ultimately the 'voice of the people' cannot be denied.

Even so, this chapter shows that claims of elitism notwithstanding, multiculturalist attitudes are resonating with many citizens in modern societies. The teaching of mutual respect, promoting different cultures and equality of people of different cultures, races, and religions is widely supported in modern societies. Similarly, beliefs such as that diversity adds strength and that it is 'good' if society is made up of minorities and that, in time, minorities will blend into the larger society find solid majorities in most modern societies. This is a far cry from claiming that MCPs are policies for elites only. However, it is also true that on average only between a third and perhaps 40 per cent of the publics in modern societies would support immigrants maintaining their distinct customs and traditions, with some notable exceptions such as Switzerland and Italy where there are majorities who feel that way.

In terms of the connection between MCPs and support for the welfare state over time, there is very little indication that such policies undermine the foundation of the redistributive capacity of the state. Redistributive attitudes over time do not show a marked decline as a result of MCPs even when controlling for the percentage of foreign population in aggregate data analysis. Using multilevel analyses and exposing redistributive attitudes to a whole host of potential control variables at the individual level while simultaneously controlling for the size of the foreign population at the second level yields even positive effects of MCPs on redistributive attitudes. These results seem to show that MCPs lower the cultural distance between members of the dominant society and minorities and, as a result, lead to a better understanding between these two groups. MCPs allow access of immigrants into the fold of a liberal society precisely because this society grants cultural autonomy to such groups. It appears that minorities are made a part of the larger society by the state allowing them to be different.

These findings dovetail very closely with the results of the 'trust' model. Critics argue that MCPs undermine trust among natives and without trust public provision of social benefits is not possible. If minorities are perceived to be 'illegitimate receivers of welfare benefits', for example by receiving preference in public housing or free health care, and are perceived as not contributing to the system of welfare, many natives may decide to withdraw from the welfare state by withdrawing support for unions, voting for 'minimal government parties' or even cheating on taxes. Again applying a multilevel model with MCPs and per cent foreign population as predictors at the structural level and a whole host of individual level control variables found a statistically significant *positive* effect of MCPs on trust. In other words, the stronger the MCPs the higher the levels of trust. These findings suggest that MCPs do not threaten the identity of natives and neither do they lead to a fraying of the social fabric that is necessary to support public schemas of redistribution. The widespread notion that MCPs heighten the difference between natives and newcomers and thereby create tensions between the 'in-groups' and 'out-groups' manifesting itself in a decline of interpersonal trust does not appear to be true.

From a policy maker's point of view, MCPs yield more benign interactions between minorities and the dominant members of society. All of this can only bode well for the public support of the welfare state. The biggest enemies of multiculturalism are populist political parties who exploit the uneasiness that particularly less educated and economically more vulnerable people feel as they encounter 'strangers'. Debates on multiculturalism oftentimes lead to emotional flare-ups precisely because the issue is so fundamental to the identity of individuals and nations. Governments, political parties, and civil society must take the concerns of the public seriously, but must resist the temptation to jump on the populist bandwagon for electoral reasons and enforce the public's often misguided opinions about multiculturalism by engaging in fiery populist rhetoric. One of the central findings in this chapter is that more education and higher interest in politics increases trust. More trust implies the capacity to empathize with the life situations of 'others'. Since education is the enemy of ignorance, those with the power to define must inform and educate as they play a central role in the construction of the host society's identity.

Part II

Case studies

4

Multiculturalism and welfare policies in the USA: A state-level comparative analysis

Rodney E. Hero and Robert R. Preuhs

It is widely acknowledged that race has had a strong impact on the development of the welfare state in the USA, with many studies demonstrating strong white resistance to welfare programmes that are seen as primarily, or disproportionately, benefiting racial minorities, particularly African-Americans. Some critics of multiculturalism policies (MCPs) have suggested yet another dimension to the impact of race and ethnicity on welfare policies. The adoption of MCPs may further divide an already fractured polity and erode the coalition that would otherwise support a strong welfare state, resulting in a smaller welfare state as MCPs proliferate. These critics often cite the United States as their main example of the deleterious impacts of MCPs.

In this chapter, we attempt to test this hypothesis by examining the link between MCPs and the welfare state at the state level within the United States. State-level analysis is useful because states vary in their ethno-racial composition, as well as exercising considerable autonomy with regard to both welfare policies and MCPs. This allows us to draw some preliminary conclusions about the impact of MCPs on the welfare state.

In section 1, we review the existing data on the impact of race on the welfare state; in section 2, we identify a range of MCPs that have been adopted at the state level in the USA, as well as what we can call 'anti-MCPs' designed to overturn or pre-empt the possible adoption of MCPs. We then examine the empirical relationships between MCPs and the

121

welfare state, to see whether MCPs impact the welfare state independent of other factors, as critics contend. Our findings suggest that while the impact of MCPs on the welfare state varies from one MCP to another, there is no general tendency for states with stronger MCPs to weaken their welfare policies compared to states with weaker MCPs (or anti-MCP states).

1. Race and the American welfare state

In the American context, the term 'racial minority' most often refers to four distinct groups: (1) African-Americans or Blacks; (2) Hispanics/Latinos; (3) Asians; and (4) Native Americans or (American) Indians. African-Americans (or blacks) are the descendants of forcibly imported slaves. Hispanics or Latinos became an incorporated national minority through territorial 'annexation' (pre-1848 Mexicans; Puerto Ricans before 1898), but currently heavily comprise rapidly growing (legal and illegal or undocumented) immigrant populations. Asians are immigrants from a variety of countries but were also once subject to formal exclusion and subsequently to other types of explicit discrimination. Native Americans are essentially conquered indigenous populations now largely confined to reservations set aside as their land was confiscated for settlement by whites of Western European descent. African-Americans currently comprise about 12 per cent of the US population, Latinos 13 per cent, Asians roughly 4–5 per cent, and Native Americans less than 1 per cent.

Along with differences across groups there is also intra-group heterogeneity. For example, the Latino/Hispanic population encompasses those of Mexican, Puerto Rican, Cuban, and other Latin and South American countries. The Asian category includes those of Chinese, Japanese, Korean, and a number of other Asian countries. Both the Latino and the Asian subgroups have had different historical experiences, different socio-economic circumstances, and vary on other dimensions as well.

American racial politics has been popularly understood and studied by scholars almost entirely through a 'white–black paradigm' because slavery and its legacy have understandably been seen as the defining event in the American racial order. This is true both of research on racial politics in general, and of research on the racial politics of the welfare state in particular. The impact of white resistance to welfare programmes that are perceived as benefiting blacks has been intensively studied, as we describe below. Less research has been conducted in relation to the other racial groups. However, for the substantially large and rapidly growing Hispanic/Latino populations there is some evidence of some similar, if less consistent and weaker, dynamics. Research on Asians is sparser and their impacts on state (and urban) politics are not well understood. This is primarily because Asian groups are still relatively small in number, with large geographic concentrations in only a few states, seemingly less of a threat to white majorities than blacks and Latinos in contemporary American politics, and have assimilated to a greater extent than Latinos where numbers are less concentrated (cf. Huntington 2004).

Despite these important differences within and across these racial minorities, we can identify some general trends that have affected racial politics in the United States. Over the last forty years, racial and ethnic minorities gained political and civil rights at an unprecedented level in US history. Civil and voting rights were guaranteed in the mid-1960s, with increasing enforcement through the 1970s and 1980s. At the same time, MCPs, such as bilingual education, bilingual ballots, and affirmative action, began to be encouraged and were adopted at all levels of government. The adoption of civil and political rights policies also coincided with an expansion of the welfare state in the 1960s and 1970s. In this period, then, there was a tendency for both welfare policies and MCPs to improve.

By contrast, the last two decades have witnessed a retreat from both welfare provision and MCPs. Direct payments to welfare recipients were subject to new restrictions under the 1996 'Welfare Reform' legislation, which created the Temporary Aid to Needy Families (TANF) welfare programme to replace the previous welfare programme, Aid to Families with Dependent Children (AFDC).[1] The last decade was also one of policy changes in many states that clearly undermined MCPs, such as the ending of affirmative action in several states.

This ebb and flow of policies aimed at helping racial and ethnic minorities, or even policies that are *perceived* to disproportionately help these groups, is a consistent facet of American racial politics (Klinkner and

---

[1] Even the names of the two programmes highlight the differences in approach. TANF's emphasis on 'Temporary' is the key issue, with both incentives and maximum enrolment times that are meant to discourage long-term reliance on the welfare state. Furthermore, recipients are no longer dependent children, but needy families.

Smith 1999). This suggests that if a relationship exists between welfare policies and MCPs, a positive relationship may be as plausible as a negative one—i.e. they may stand or fall together. Our empirical analysis in section 2 will attempt to test this hypothesis.

The specific nature of state-level cultural policies in the USA adds an interesting complication to our analysis. As the term is used elsewhere in this volume, 'MCPs' imply policies that provide benefits to individual groups in an attempt to overcome past discrimination, increase the cultural acceptance of the group, and provide basic services that are culturally sensitive. In the USA, however, there have also been a number of policies that are explicitly cultural in nature but which clearly diverge from, indeed, seek to overturn or pre-empt the diversifying goals of MCPs in general. These may be thought of as *anti*-multiculturalism policies'. For instance, consider the widespread adoption in the 1980s and 1990s of Official English policies that formally affirm English as the official language of state government. This is clearly a cultural policy, but one aimed at pre-empting multiculturalism language policies. Some states have also prohibited the use of race and ethnicity in state hiring and higher education admissions, abandoning affirmative action in general. California and Texas are the best-known examples of this anti-multiculturalism policy shift, as both states ended affirmative action in 1996.

The adoption of such pre-emptive and anti-MCPs seems more common in the last ten to fifteen years, making them an important element in the debate regarding the relationship between MCPs and the welfare state. If MCPs act to displace welfare state support, as critics allege, does the removal of or pre-emptive action regarding MCPs allow for renewed expansion of the welfare state? Our analysis will address this important aspect of MCPs as well.

The role of race in the development of the American welfare state

Before examining the impact of MCPs (and anti-MCPs) on the welfare state, it is important to understand the profound impact of race on the development of, and variation in, the welfare state. There are two key sets of empirical findings. First, welfare policies in the American context are historically racialized, which differentiates welfare state development from many European countries. This racialization of welfare politics, in turn, has led to a great deal of variation in welfare policy at the state level, depending on the ethno-racial composition of each state's population. Second, research has consistently demonstrated that racial backlash, or white resentment, is at the core of this variation. We will briefly summarize these two key findings.

A substantial body of scholarship has demonstrated that race fundamentally shaped the structure and macro-evolution of the American welfare state (Lieberman 2003). The urban 'machines' of the early 1900s partly addressed the social policy concerns of the immigrant 'white ethnics', but they did so in non-ideological, pragmatic, largely non-redistributive ways that had the effect of blunting the development of class-based politics and, in contemporary parlance, emphasized 'recognition' over 'redistribution', or treated the latter as a type of the former (Katznelson 1981; Wolfinger 1974; Lineberry and Sharkansky 1978). As a result, welfare policies as such were not developed, much less institutionalized until well into the twentieth century.

America's 'racialized' perspective on welfare policy was, arguably, broadened and became more explicit over time. Until the 1960s, poverty appeared overwhelmingly as a 'white problem' in the American news media. But, as Martin Gilens points out, 'beginning in 1965, the media's portrayal of American poverty shifted dramatically. Although the true racial composition of the American poor remained stable, the face of poverty in the news media became markedly darker between 1965 and 1967' (Gilens 2003: 101). Gilens attributes these changing perceptions to several developments. Massive Black migration from the South to the North, particularly prevalent during the 1940s to 1960s, was an 'initial link in a chain of events that led to the dramatic changes in how Americans thought about poverty'. Between 1940 and 1970 the proportion of Blacks among welfare (AFDC) recipients grew steadily, and 'as the welfare rolls expanded sharply in the 1960s and 1970s, the American public's attention was drawn disproportionately to poor blacks'. With this backdrop, the 'more proximate events' that led to major changes in Americans' views of the poor 'were a shift in the focus within the civil rights movement from the fight for legal equality to the battle for economic equality, and the urban riots that rocked [the USA] during the summers of 1964 through 1968' (Gilens 2003: 101).

It thus appears that the implications of greater Black *participation in* the welfare state, as recipients of welfare policy, and Black demands for greater equality of outcomes, rather than simple equal opportunity, profoundly affected views of AFDC, 'the most conspicuous program to aid the poor'. If the early formulation of the American welfare state substantially excluded or underserved Blacks, the extent of their later formal inclusion into the American welfare state was exaggerated, resulting in distorted perceptions of their presence among welfare recipients (Gilens 2003: 102–4). To an important degree, the welfare state and race became conflated almost to the point that welfare and race, and later race-specific policies, were seen as closely linked.

Race, public attitudes, and welfare policy in the pre- and post-reform periods

A substantial body of scholarly research has demonstrated the direct importance of race for welfare policy in the American states. Several studies have shown that states with larger racial minority groups tend to have less generous welfare states. In one recent study, Johnson (2001) examined a state's average AFDC payment per recipient in 1990 and found that racial diversity in states has a direct influence on those payments, i.e. as racial diversity increased, welfare payments decreased. This study examined welfare policy *before* the 1996 reform, in which TANF replaced AFDC. But Johnson has reaffirmed the basic findings in another study of the *post-reform* period (Johnson 2003), in which racial diversity was shown to have a negative impact. In this instance, the per cent of welfare recipients who are black was shown to be associated with lower average monthly welfare benefits in the post-reform period. Johnson concludes this analysis by saying that 'it appears that policymakers have a different relationship with the racial majority in their states than with the racial minority: They *respond* to whites and *react* to the presence of African Americans' (2003: 161–3, emphasis in original). At the same time, Johnson finds that where racial attitudes are more tolerant and there is a more liberal 'mass ideology' in states, there are higher benefits payments.

Other analyses have further demonstrated the importance of race in the policy formulation and implementation of the post-1996 welfare state. Soss and his colleagues (2001) found that higher percentages of African-Americans on welfare rolls were related to stricter sanctions, stricter time limits, and family caps. In addition, states with higher percentages of Latino populations tended to have stricter time limits and family caps. Both groups tended to negatively affect benefit levels as well. They also found evidence that strict sanction policies were significantly more likely in states with conservative governments, in states with less vigorous political party competition, in states with higher unmarried birth rates, in states that engaged in policy innovation by making earlier requests for AFDC waivers, and states that maintained smaller AFDC caseloads. This latter set of variables, however, did not have much impact on state policy regarding work requirements, time limits, or family caps. In short, race/ethnicity was most consistently associated with the various welfare policies examined, along with spending decisions (Soss et al. 2001: 385–9).

In yet another analysis, Fellowes and Rowe (2004) largely reaffirm 'the strong role of race in TANF politics', which is evident in three dimensions of the policy: a higher percentage of African-American recipients leads to (*a*) stricter rules governing initial eligibility, (*b*) less flexibility in new welfare work requirements, and (*c*) lower cash benefits to welfare recipients. This study also affirms the negative relationship between the percentage of welfare recipients who are Latino and cash benefit levels, suggesting that the racialization of the welfare state is no longer confined strictly to the black–white dichotomy.

Finally, Keiser, Mueser, and Choi's (2004) analysis focuses on the *implementation* dimension of TANF policy through a case study in one state, Missouri. Missouri has an African-American population that is on the whole slightly larger than the national average, and the state's sanction policy is administratively similar to other states in the level of discretion given to bureaucrats responsible for direct implementation. Their analysis of how bureaucrats in Missouri apply sanctions—that is, of the way they reduce case grants to recipients for failing to meet training, work, or other requirements—finds that 'sanction rates increase as the nonwhite [i.e. minority or African-American] population increases' (although that pattern is altered when a threshold is reached where non-whites achieve political power). In short, the profound importance of race has been repeatedly confirmed in both the formulation and implementation of state-level welfare policies.

Race and multiculturalism

A similar story can be told about the role of race in shaping public policy in the area of multiculturalism, although this field has been less researched. As with welfare policies, there is evidence that public attitudes towards MCPs have been affected by racial prejudice, and that this has affected the sustainability of such policies, leading to important variations across the states. Indeed in recent decades, multicultural policy in the USA, and within the states themselves, can be characterized by a retreat from multiculturalism, as much as it is marked by the adoption of MCPs.

One example is the adoption of Official English policies, or English as an official state language, during the 1980s and 1990s. These Official English laws represent a retreat from a stream of federal and state laws, judicial decisions, and administrative regulations that had been largely sympathetic to language rights from the 1960s into the 1970s. The 1967 Bilingual Education Act (BEA) was a pivotal element in this earlier movement towards a more multicultural approach to language, and so it became the 'main catalyst for opposition' for critics of multiculturalism. Symbolically, the BEA's ostensible emphasis on cultural maintenance 'repudiated the "melting pot" as a normative ideal in favour of a "multiculturalism" conception'. To the English-speaking majority in the mass public, bicultural education apparently implied a diminished respect for American culture as a whole (Citrin et al. 1990).

The 1980s and 1990s witnessed widespread adoption of Official English laws in the states. In states with substantial language minority populations, determined resistance by minorities was able to prevent the passage of such laws by state legislatures, despite often widespread public support for such laws in the majority community, but conservative states and states which allowed for mechanisms of direct democracy generally adopted such laws (Preuhs 2005; Tatalovich 1995). In all, twenty-five of the fifty states now have an Official English law. Hawaii, which is not included in that total, recognizes both English and Hawaiian as its official languages.

Like welfare reform, adoption of Official English laws is most closely tied to white resentment of racial/ethnic minority groups. Tatalovich's (1995) qualitative study concludes that while institutional factors in the policy-making process ultimately led to the ability of English-speaking majorities to succeed in pressuring for adoption of these laws, the underlying motive was steeped in racism. Schildkraut (2001) presented statistical confirmation of Tatalovich's conclusion, by demonstrating that higher percentages of foreign-born populations were associated with a greater probability of adoption of English Only laws. However, in a more nuanced study, Preuhs (2005) demonstrates that while the initiative and legislative representation were key elements in adoption, the backlash was not aimed at the foreign-born population broadly conceived. Instead, Latino populations were the specific target of backlash, thus mitigating the importance of Asian immigrants as a source for contemporary racial and ethnic resentment in the American states generally.

The pervasive impact of race and ethnicity on American public policy

As the previous section has demonstrated, the impact of race and ethnic diversity on state politics is widespread, consistent, and, under most

conditions, is reflected in a negative relationship between minority populations and 'liberal' policies. While the focus here is on welfare policies
and multicultural policies, many studies show that racial diversity is a
factor in a wide array of policy outputs and outcomes in the American
states. Hero's (1998) study demonstrates the centrality of racial and ethnic
diversity by showing ties not only to state policy outputs, but also to
outcomes as diverse as minority graduation and infant mortality rates.
Scholars now commonly include indicators of race and ethnic population size or diversity when modelling state policy outputs, outcomes,
and political behaviour—even when race and ethnicity is not a central
question in their study.

In short, what makes the American context relatively distinct from
the European context is the common impact of race on both welfare
policies and MCPs. Race, welfare, and multiculturalism are all intertwined,
particularly at the state level. The question is whether we can find a way to
separate out the influence of these factors, and in particular to determine
whether the presence of MCPs helps or hinders the already difficult task
of sustaining welfare programmes in racially heterogeneous states. That is
the task of section 2.

2. Empirical analysis of MCPs and the welfare state

The central orienting question posed in this study is whether adopting
MCPs undermines welfare policies—that is, whether 'the politics of recognition' displaces or erodes 'the politics of redistribution'. We examine this
question at the state level. Specifically, our empirical analysis examines
the assertion that the adoption of MCPs leads, or allows, states to reduce
the size of their welfare state.

This analysis is complicated by the fact that both federal and state
governments are actively involved in these policy areas. In fact, the federal
government played a lead role in the initial formulation of MCPs. Many
MCPs were adopted on a country-wide basis as the USA shifted towards
increasing the strength of civil rights policies in the 1960s and early 1970s.
During this period, state-level MCPs—such as affirmative action plans,
educating immigrants and their children (often in their own languages),
and providing ballots and voting instructions in different languages—
were often directly required by the federal government or compelled
through fiscal policy strings. Subsequent state action regarding MCPs is
thus often best characterized as a retreat from or pre-emption of MCPs,

as states began to eliminate some elements of policies that were not expressly required by the national government.

In short, while state policies vary in significant ways, many of the key policies often highlighted by studies of MCPs were either adopted broadly or applied through top-down incentives. We attempt to overcome this analytical obstacle by examining a number of policies where state governments have a significant level of policy discretion. The clearest cases concern policies regarding support for immigrants and for minority languages, as well as some aspects of affirmative action. The policies we examine below do not represent a comprehensive index of MCPs, nor do they provide the robust variation that a cross-country comparison allows. They are, however, among the most highly controversial policies that have been the focus of debates over multiculturalism during the last few decades.

Before introducing the analysis and presenting results, we should make a few clarifications and qualifications. First, we are examining the actual policies adopted by state governments, not public perceptions about the existence of such policies. While we have chosen high-profile policies, it is possible that the general public, in some states, has a mistaken or exaggerated view of what MCPs are in fact in place, and that this misperception impacts on welfare policies. A different sort of analysis would be needed to test this hypothesis. Our analysis focuses on the claim that MCPs themselves have a negative impact on welfare policies, which we believe to be at the heart of the critics' complaint.

Second, it is important to note that MCPs differ in their intended target group. For instance, language policies are typically aimed at recent immigrant groups, while affirmative action is aimed at a wider range of disadvantaged racial and ethnic minorities (as well as women), and was initially designed to benefit the historically disadvantaged African-American community. MCPs aimed at different target groups might have differing effects on the welfare state. Some minorities might be seen as more 'deserving' of state support in the form of MCPs, either because they are seen as the victim of historic injustice, or because they are seen as 'hard-working' and 'loyal'. If so, MCPs targeted at such 'deserving' minorities may be less likely to generate the corroding effects claimed by critics.

Ideally, a full analysis of the impact of MCPs on welfare policies would attempt to control for such variations in target group. In our analysis below, we take a step in this direction, by presenting the results for affirmative action and for language/immigrant policy separately. However, in the context of state-level policies, the reality is that most MCPs are aimed primarily at two main target groups—blacks and Latinos. While Asians and American Indians may benefit from language, affirmative action, and immigrant policies, there is ample empirical evidence that contemporary policies are most often construed as benefiting blacks or Latinos at the state level. (Local issues, of course, may vary.)

This is certainly true of the MCPs we analyse. Blacks and Latinos are the primary beneficiaries in the case of affirmative action. Popular accounts and the empirical evidence discussed above strongly suggest that Latinos are the perceived primary beneficiaries of language and immigrant-oriented policies at the state level. These two groups also are the main targets of backlash against MCPs. Thus we are confident that while the populations that MCPs benefit may vary, the majority's reactions to those groups, and related group-based policies, vary little in the American context.

Ultimately, our goal is to provide a reasonable range of tests of the hypothesis that MCPs are negatively related to the size of the welfare state. If this hypothesis is correct, as critics suggest, then we ought to find a general pattern that reflects this relationship across a variety of MCPs, with effects on most or all indicators of the welfare state. Many of the critics of MCPs point directly to policies in particular states that they believe have eroded the politics of redistribution (e.g. Gitlin 1995). We provide a more systematic and rigorous, albeit initial, test of the hypotheses by leveraging the variation across the states.

Our analysis focuses on three MCPs: (*a*) language policies, (*b*) immigrant support policies; and (*c*) affirmative action. We have chosen these because they are among the most visible and contested policy areas in the last few decades, making them the most likely to affect the degree of support for the welfare state. In addition, these policies are characterized by much variation across states. The following sections describe these policies, and test their relationship to welfare policies. We begin with an analysis of immigrant and language MCPs, using a multivariate analysis of welfare spending in all fifty states. We then examine affirmative action, and in particular the states of California and Texas, which abolished affirmative action in higher education.

Immigrant and language policies: Defining the policies

One of the central issues in debates around multiculturalism in the USA (as in other countries) concerns the integration of immigrants, and

131

the extent to which they should be 'recognized' or 'accommodated'. In the American context, an important dimension of this debate concerns language policy. State-level policies regarding language are, therefore, a useful dimension for assessing a commitment to multiculturalism. For our purposes, we can distinguish two different dimensions of language policy: (*a*) the existence of 'Official English' policies; (*b*) the provision of public education in minority languages. We briefly describe each of these policy areas, before testing their impact on the welfare state.

The 1980s and 1990s witnessed growing variation in state language policies, particularly in the use of English in official government practices, correspondence, and documentation. By 2000, twenty-one states had adopted policies that to some extent formally recognized English as the official language of the state. Official English, or English Only laws, generally affirmed the de facto dominant status of the English language in government communication and documentation. We should note that some government communications, such as ballots used during elections, are mandated to be published in multiple languages under certain circumstances by the federal government. Nevertheless, the passage of English Only was highly controversial and, as discussed above, was generally opposed by language minorities in the states. In assessing the relationship between MCPs and the welfare state, Official English policies may be considered as a pre-emptive policy aimed at undermining language MCPs, restricting the possibilities of greater state efforts toward flexible or permissive language policies. If MCPs lead to a reduced welfare state, then anti-MCPs, such as Official English, may be associated with a state's willingness to extend welfare state benefits as an indirect consequence of removing the MCP issue.

The provision of public education in languages other than English is an additional dimension of multiculturalism that we include in our analysis. States vary in the degree to which they provide educational programmes for students who are not native English speakers. More specifically, states differ in whether they do and do not: (1) mandate limited English proficiency (LEP) programmes, (2) fund LEP programmes, (3) certify English as a second language (ESL) instructors, and (4) certify bilingual education instructors. These programmes have been visible and often controversial. LEP programmes reflect a wide array of educational policies aimed at educating students that lack an age-appropriate mastery of the English language. Funding for these programmes is not necessarily guaranteed through state funds, and thus, we treat the programmes themselves and funding as separate MCPs. LEP programmes generally follow two main approaches, which differ in actual implementation. ESL programmes teach students with LEP in English, and certified instructors often do not need to be fluent, or even functional, in the students' native language. For instance, an ESL programme might offer remedial English instruction beyond general courses taught in English, and do so through classes with students from a variety of language backgrounds at the same time (i.e. Laotian- and Spanish-speaking students attend the same ESL classes). Bilingual certification requires that the instructor be competent to teach the subject in both English and an additional language. Courses are taught in the students' native language or their native language as well as English. They generally do not offer more than the two languages, however, and students with the same native languages attend the same courses. Given these differences, we include all four indicators separately in our analysis. If the critics are correct, the presence of these four MCPs should be negatively correlated with welfare spending at the state level.

We should note that these language education programmes are not wholly, and perhaps not at all, comparable to native-tongue instruction outside the United States. Such programmes need to be understood in the context of the historic evolution of education in the USA, especially the role of separate schools. While separate schools for various cultural minorities have been used by other nations to emphasize and celebrate cultural differences, the long history of separate schools in the United States strays far from these noble underpinnings. The states in the south-western portion of the United States employed 'Indian Schools' and 'Mexican Schools' until well into the twentieth century, ostensibly to provide educational opportunities to Native Americans and Mexican-Americans. In the case of the former, Native American students were stripped of their language and cultural history. In the case of the latter, no English instruction was provided, which left students unprepared to communicate in the United States' social, political, and economic realms. De jure and de facto segregation of black and white schoolchildren is the most pronounced case of severe disparities in the provision of educational opportunities. In short, separate schools in the United States were not part of a liberal policy of providing recognition and support to ethno-cultural minorities, but rather operated to severely curtail minority groups' social, economic, and political opportunities, as part of a larger scheme of racial inequality.

Given this history, the struggle for multiculturalism in the USA has not typically been a struggle for separate minority-language schools, but rather for greater respect and accommodation of linguistic minorities within mainstream schools. One important manifestation of this struggle is the LEP programmes, whether under the ESL or bilingual models. These programmes provide additional educational opportunities, albeit in varying degrees of multicultural recognition, that otherwise would not be provided under an assimilationist model (with no provision of additional instruction oriented to those with limited English proficiency). While LEP, ESL, and Bilingual Education programmes in the American context are not necessarily thought of as primarily aimed at cultural recognition, they do support the differential needs of ethno-cultural minorities. Thus, in light of the possible policy alternatives, these programs add a layer of recognition to education policy, even though they also have, to varying degrees, programme elements that are aimed at assimilation.

Our first empirical test, therefore, examines the impact of this set of language-related MCPs—ranging from pre-emptive Official English laws to various minority-language education policies—on welfare spending. The results are described below. However, for the sake of completeness, we have also included one further immigrant-related policy: namely, the provision of food stamps for immigrants. After the passage of the 1996 Welfare Reform Act that replaced AFDC with TANF, states could decide whether they would provide food assistance to documented immigrants by funding food stamps for these potential recipients. In 1999, thirteen states chose to provide food stamps to legal immigrants; and thirty-seven chose not to. We have classified the provision of food stamps to immigrants as an MCP, although we recognize that some people may question this label. It is clearly a pro-minority policy but it may not qualify as an 'MCP' by those who challenge such policies. For these critics, granting food stamps to immigrants can be seen as removing a form of differential treatment, and replacing it with an approach that focuses on economic need, thereby encouraging cross-ethnic coalitions focused on redistribution. It is our view, however, that examining this policy is useful and appropriate, since in public debate and political coalitions it plays a role that is structurally similar to that of other MCPs. To the extent that Americans view or conflate 'immigrants' with *Latino* and/or other minority group immigrants, and, further, to the extent that immigrants are not differentiated in people's minds as legal or 'illegal' (undocumented)—and there is evidence that many Americans do have such perceptions—consideration of this policy is worthwhile.

Language and immigrant policies: testing the impact on welfare

Thus, there is one anti-MCP (Official English) and five MCPs (LEP programs; LEP funding; ELS certification; Bilingual Certification; and immigrant food stamps) with which to evaluate the relationship between MCPs and the welfare state. These are the key variables in our analysis. To provide a fair test of the critics' claims, two sets of analyses are conducted. The first relies on an *index* of MCPs based on these six indicators, which was created as follows. Each state was given one point for each of the five MCPs they had implemented by 1999. A score of −1 was given to states that had adopted an Official English policy by 1999.[2] The index can range from −1 for states with no MCP in place and an English Only policy, to 5 for states with all five MCPs and no Official English policy. The index captures the basic character of the indicators, and is internally consistent. Cronbach's alpha, the inter-item reliability coefficient or average correlation between each item and the index, is a fairly strong 0.66. The fifty states reflect a full range of scores on the index. Three states had scores of −1; three states had scores of 0; six states were scored 1; nine states were scored 2; eleven states scored 3; thirteen states scored 4; and five states were coded with the highest score of 5. Table 4.1 presents the states categorized as 'weak', 'moderate', and 'strong' MCP states, with their actual MCP index score in parentheses. The second analysis treats each MCP and the anti-MCP as discrete policies to uncover any specific effects that might be masked by the aggregate index.

The measures of the welfare state are the rates of change in the proportion of state expenditures dedicated to welfare and education as percentages of gross state product (GSP). Relative change provides a means to control for the confounding factor of preconditions that may have led a state to have a relatively larger welfare state even before the impact of MCPs. We focus on the relative change for two indicators: (1) welfare expenditures as a percentage of gross state product, and (2) education expenditures as a percentage of gross state product. Spending relative to GSP provides an indicator of overall state commitment to welfare and education relative to a state's production capacity, and is roughly equivalent to cross-country indicators standardized by gross domestic product. The time frame in this analysis is from 1984 to 2000, roughly the period

[2] The reference year is chosen primarily due to the lack of data for the specific year each policy was adopted for each state. English Only laws were adopted broadly throughout the 1980s and 1990s, and most states had immigrant and language policies in place sometime before this reference year. We recognize that this forces the analysis to focus on general tendencies, rather than a specific temporal impact of adoption of these policies.

Table 4.1 Multicultural policy scores across the states and change in welfare and education spending

	Weak MCP states (MCP index scores of −1 to 0)	Moderate MCP states (MCP index scores of 1 to 3)		Strong MCP states (MCP index scores of 4 to 5)
	Louisiana (−1)	Alabama (1)	Arizona (3)	California (4)
	Mississippi (−1)	Hawaii (1)	Florida (3)	Colorado (4)
	South Carolina (−1)	Kentucky (1)	Indiana (3)	Connecticut (4)
	South Dakota (0)	Montana (1)	Michigan (3)	Delaware (4)
	Tennessee (0)	Pennsylvania (1)	North Carolina (3)	Iowa (4)
	West Virginia (0)	Wyoming (1)	Nebraska (3)	Illinois (4)
		Alaska (2)	Ohio (3)	Kansas (4)
		Arkansas (2)	Oklahoma (3)	Massachusetts (4)
		Georgia (2)	Oregon (3)	Maryland (4)
		Idaho (2)	Rhode Island (3)	Maine (4)
		Missouri (2)	Utah (3)	New Mexico (4)
		North Dakota (2)		Nevada (4)
		New Hampshire (2)		Wisconsin (4)
		Virginia (2)		Minnesota (5)
		Vermont (2)		New Jersey (5)
				New York (5)
				Texas (5)
				Washington (5)
% change in welfare spending as % of Gross State Product	Mean: 120.91 Standard deviation: 57.86	Mean: 77.08 Standard deviation: 53.18		Mean: 35.44 Standard deviation: 47.39
% change in education spending as % of Gross State Product	Mean: 18.03 Standard deviation: 7.90	Mean: 25.41 Standard deviation: 26.95		Mean: 10.53 Standard deviation: 10.80
N	6	26		18

Note: States are presented by category, alphabetically by score. MCP Index scores are displayed within parentheses.

Source: Compiled by authors. See Data Appendix.

that captures adoption of English Only laws, language education, and immigrant food stamps.[3]

An initial analysis of the patterns between MCP categories and welfare and education expenditures is also presented in Table 4.1. The mean increase in welfare expenditures in weak MCP states is much higher than in strong MCP states, providing what might seem like initial evidence

[3] The baseline year of 1984 provides for a broader set of data on other independent variables included in the model. Removing those variables and replacing the baseline year with 1980 do not change the substantive results of the analysis.

supporting the critics' claims. However, there is wide variation within each group as indicated by the standard deviations, and thus the means are somewhat deceiving. In fact, even the apparently large difference in average relative change in welfare expenditures between the strong and weak MCP states is not statistically significant at conventional levels in a one-tailed t-test. In other words, the differences between means are very likely to be due to chance rather than being systematically related to the degree of MCPs held within each group. Also note that there is no clear pattern between MCPs and change in education expenditures. This initial test does not control for potential important alternative explanations, however, and thus we now turn to a more rigorous test of the critics' claims through a regression analysis.

In addition to the key independent variables discussed above, our multivariate statistical model also takes into account several alternative explanations for changes in the indicators of the welfare state. We include a citizen ideology score, *Ideology*, from Erikson, Wright, and McIver (1993), which accounts for a general ideological disposition toward the welfare state. Higher scores on this scale indicate more liberal states. Southern states have traditionally been reluctant to provide generous welfare benefits, and this dummy variable is added to the model. South is coded 1 for the eleven states of the former Confederacy, and 0 otherwise. We also account for the impact of change in several variables with readily available data to measure temporal change during this time period. Change in these independent variables is measured in the same ways as the dependent variable from 1984 to 2000, with values as a percentage of 1984. We include change indicators for racial and ethnic groups as the percentage of the population in each state that is Latino (Δ *% Latino*) and the percentage of the population that is black (Δ *% Black*) because the discussion above presented a variety of evidence that race and ethnicity affects welfare provision. Finally, we include a bank of social, economic and demographic indicators that are generally associated with state policy (Gray and Hansen 2004). The demographic characteristics include: Δ *Income* in constant dollars; Δ *Unemployment* rate; Δ *Education* which is measured as the per cent of a state's population with at least a highschool degree; and Δ *Population Density*, which is the population per square mile.[4] In addition to the above variables, we also include the average value for the overall period (1984–2000) for each of these variables to control for the

---

[4] These state-level data were provided by the *State Politics and Policy Quarterly* data archive, available at: **www.ku.edu/pri/SPPQ/research.shtml**.

effects of the size and magnitude of the indicators along with that which is attributable to change.

Finally, we include a constant to capture the general national trend in welfare state policy change as well as the level of the dependent variable in 1984 ($t = 0$). The latter captures the tendency of states to follow a process of regressing towards the mean, with negative coefficients indicating that states with higher original welfare levels tended to decrease their welfare provisions at a higher rate than states with lower original levels. Forty-eight states are included in the analysis since ideology scores are not available for Alaska and Hawaii.

Table 4.2 reports the results of some initial models of the baseline control variables for welfare and education spending. The baseline models first include only the change variables (Models 2a and 2c) for welfare and education, respectively. We then add the average levels in Models 2b and 2d. The levels do add some explanatory power, and they will be included in the remaining analyses when we specifically address the impact of MCPs on welfare and education spending.

Table 4.3 presents the results of the OLS regression analysis of the models of the two indicators of the welfare state, with the summary MCP index as the key independent variable. Overall, the models perform reasonably well, explaining a large portion of changes in welfare expenditure indicators and inequality, with less explanatory power for change in education provision. As the focus of the analysis is on the impact of MCPs on the welfare state, this is reasonable. The results suggest that MCPs are *not* a major factor in state changes to welfare policy expenditures. While the coefficient is negative for the model of education spending, it is actually positive for the model of welfare spending. The coefficients are not statistically significant, however, and thus there is no relationship between MCPs and the welfare state evident in these models.

The MCP index, however, may mask the independent effects of each MCP on the welfare indicators examined. This could occur if the components of the index differ greatly in the degree of their effect, or if they operate on different dimensions; either is plausible. Thus, the two models are reanalysed and the MCP index is replaced with each of the MCP indicators and English Only as separate independent variables in a series of models including only one MCP indicator at a time. Each is coded as 1 if the state had the policy in place in 1999, and 0 otherwise. The hypothesis that MCPs erode the welfare state is supported if the indicators for the MCPs are negative in each of the expenditure models. As an anti-MCP, the coefficients for English Only would support the hypothesis if they are

Table 4.2 Baseline models of relative change in welfare and education expenditures

	Δ Welfare as % GSP		Δ Education as % GSP	
	Model 2a	Model 2b	Model 2c	Model 2d
Ideology	−.26	2.41	−.31	.51
	(1.35)	(1.51)	(.62)	(.80)
South	20.35	29.99	5.22	4.11
	(23.56)	(24.82)	(9.68)	(11.98)
Δ % Latino	−.16*	−.11*	−.02	.01
	(.07)	(.06)	(.04)	(.04)
Δ % Black	.19	.24	.12	.13
	(.13)	(.15)	(.13)	(.14)
Δ Income	.28	1.30	−.15	.00
	(.85)	(.98)	(.45)	(.42)
Δ Unemployment	.56	1.60*	−.55	.01
	(.54)	(.82)	(.33)	(.60)
Δ Education	3.33*	−.62	−.04	−.78
	(1.92)	(1.79)	(.89)	(1.53)
Δ Population density	−.11	−.63*	−.11	−.30**
	(.29)	(.28)	(.11)	(.11)
% Latino		−.65		.22
		(1.28)		(.56)
% Black		−1.19		.47
		(1.02)		(.63)
Income		−.01*		−.004*
		(.00)		(.002)
Unemployment		10.74		7.27
		(12.09)		(8.67)
Education		−3.48		1.16
		(2.24)		(1.15)
Population density		−.02		−.01
		(.03)		(.02)
Level of dependent	−56.93***	−71.94***	−8.91	−17.07**
variable at $t = 0$	(15.54)	(12.15)	(5.50)	(6.45)
Constant	132.51	713.51***	25.98	75.64
	(51.12)	(183.81)	(21.38)	(119.60)
N	48	48	48	48
R^2	.52	.77	.19	.36

Note: * $p < .05$, ** $p < .01$ and *** $p < .001$ in a one-tailed test of significance. Robust standard errors in parentheses.

Source: See Table 4.1.

positive. Tables 4.4 and 4.5 consider the effects of individual MCPs on welfare and education expenditures, respectively.

It seems that the index masked only one relationship, that between immigrant food stamps and education expenditures. This relationship is perhaps the least consistent with the critic's claims for two reasons. First, food stamps provision is well removed from education policy as such. Second, immigrant food stamps can be seen as much as a redistributive

Table 4.3 Estimated effects of the MCP index on relative change in welfare and education expenditures

	Δ Welfare as % GSP	Δ Education as % GSP
MCP index	1.37	−1.11
	(5.38)	(4.01)
Ideology	2.44**	.52
	(1.52)	(.80)
South	30.46	3.71
	(25.11)	(12.79)
Δ% Latino	−.12**	.02
	(.06)	(.05)
Δ% Black	.24*	.14
	(.15)	(.14)
Δ Income	1.32*	−.02
	(.99)	(.41)
Δ Unemployment	1.61**	−.00
	(.84)	(.61)
Δ Education	−.51	−.85
	(1.81)	(1.64)
Δ Population density	−.63**	−.30***
	(.28)	(.11)
% Latino	−.79	.33
	(1.42)	(.68)
% Black	−1.20	.48
	(1.05)	(.64)
Income	−.01**	−.004*
	(.00)	(.002)
Unemployment	10.33	7.58
	(12.17)	(8.93)
Education	−3.59*	1.23
	(2.35)	(1.13)
Population density	−.02	−.01
	(.03)	(.02)
Level of dependent variable at $t = 0$	−72.86***	−16.61**
	(12.40)	(6.40)
Constant	727.22***	63.89
	(194.47)	(123.95)
N	48	48
R^2	.77	.37

Note: $^* p < .05$, $^{**} p < .01$ and $^{***} p < .001$ in a one-tailed test of significance. Robust standard errors in parentheses.

Source: See Table 4.1.

policy as a multicultural policy. Furthermore, the remaining MCPs had no effect on a state's relative change in welfare expenditure as a percentage of GSP. Thus, there is scant evidence that MCPs have a direct effect on welfare provisions. If MCPs have the general effect of eroding the welfare state, it is not manifested in these models.

We briefly note the effects of other variables considered in this study. Change in the size of the Latino population is consistent in most of the

Table 4.4 Estimated effects of individual MCPs on relative change in welfare expenditures

	Model 4a	Model 4b	Model 4c	Model 4d	Model 4e	Model 4f
Immigrant food stamps	.04 (15.68)					
LEP programme		−17.29 (34.00)				
LEP funding			20.58 (15.26)			
ESL certification				−3.48 (15.26)		
Bilingual certification					1.79 (12.40)	
English Only law						−1.33 (10.37)
Ideology	2.41 (1.54)	2.30 (1.54)	2.83* (1.42)	2.49* (1.47)	2.45 (1.50)	2.40 (1.55)
South	29.98 (25.28)	26.37 (29.50)	31.48 (23.39)	30.59 (24.70)	30.47 (24.56)	30.43 (24.37)
Δ % Latino	−.11* (.06)	−.09 (.08)	−.15* (.06)	−.11 (.06)	−.11* (.06)	−.11* (.06)
Δ % Black	.24 (.15)	.21 (.17)	.24 (.15)	.23 (.15)	.24 (.15)	.24 (.16)
Δ Income	1.30 (.99)	1.21 (1.01)	1.46 (.94)	1.32 (.98)	1.32 (1.01)	1.30 (1.00)
Δ Unemployment	1.60* (.90)	1.51* (.88)	1.72* (.86)	1.56 (.93)	1.64* (.81)	1.58* (.90)
Δ Education	−.62 (1.81)	−.45 (1.84)	−.05 (1.75)	−.65 (1.83)	−.54 (1.84)	−.59 (1.85)
Δ Population density	−.63* (.30)	−.61* (.29)	−.70** (.27)	−.63* (.29)	−.64* (.29)	−.63* (.29)
% Latino	−.65 (1.34)	−.50 (1.33)	−1.00 (1.24)	−.60 (1.32)	−.70 (1.37)	−.68 (1.27)
% Black	−1.19 (1.03)	−1.37 (.99)	−1.21 (1.02)	−1.20 (1.02)	−1.21 (1.05)	−1.20 (1.03)
Income	−.01* (.00)	−.01* (.00)	−.01* (.00)	−.01* (.00)	−.01* (.00)	−.01* (.00)
Unemployment	10.73 (12.88)	8.16 (14.88)	11.54 (12.20)	10.20 (13.13)	10.76 (12.22)	10.22 (13.55)
Education	−3.48 (2.26)	−3.15 (2.23)	−3.67 (2.24)	−3.44 (2.22)	−3.49 (2.28)	−3.50 (2.29)
Population density	−.02 (.03)	−.02 (.03)	−.02 (.03)	−.02 (.04)	−.02 (.03)	−.02 (.03)
Level of dependent variable at $t = 0$	−71.95*** (12.45)	−69.28*** (13.52)	−76.94*** (11.94)	−72.30*** (12.42)	−72.29*** (12.16)	−72.01*** (12.24)
Constant	713.64*** (186.29)	686.48*** (183.29)	747.26*** (186.90)	712.18*** (184.01)	716.53*** (192.04)	715.77*** (186.70)
N	48	48	48	48	48	48
R^2	.77	.78	.78	.77	.77	.77

Note: $^*p < .05$, $^{**}p < .01$ and $^{***}p < .001$ in a one-tailed test of significance. Robust standard errors in parentheses.

Source: See Table 4.1.

Table 4.5 Estimated effects of individual MCPs on relative change in education expenditures

	Model 5a	Model 5b	Model 5c	Model 5d	Model 5e	Model 5f
Immigrant food stamps	−19.21* (8.10)					
LEP programme		22.36 (18.38)				
LEP funding			20.32 (13.90)			
ESL certification				−8.02 (10.51)		
Bilingual certification					−8.40 (9.91)	
English Only law						−2.97 (7.37)
Ideology	.64 (.77)	.49 (.77)	.70 (.83)	.68 (.86)	.38 (.81)	.50 (.80)
South	10.62 (12.70)	10.61 (14.24)	6.69 (11.81)	5.87 (11.76)	2.25 (12.98)	4.95 (12.16)
Δ% Latino	.02 (.04)	−.02 (.05)	−.03 (.05)	.02 (.04)	.00 (.05)	.01 (.05)
Δ% Black	.16 (.13)	.15 (.13)	.11 (.11)	.11 (.13)	.15 (.14)	.12 (.13)
Δ Income	−.01 (.40)	.11 (.43)	.14 (.43)	.06 (.44)	−.09 (.42)	.01 (.42)
Δ Unemployment	.48 (.62)	.17 (.58)	.16 (.58)	−.07 (.65)	−.17 (.66)	−.03 (.64)
Δ Education	−.64 (1.42)	−.90 (1.46)	−.22 (1.29)	−.83 (1.64)	−1.04 (1.69)	−.75 (1.53)
Δ Population density	−.39** (.13)	−.27* (.12)	−.31* (.13)	−.29* (.12)	−.29** (.11)	−.29** (.11)
% Latino	.57 (.43)	−.04 (.59)	−.14 (.61)	.32 (.64)	.39 (.55)	.16 (.58)
% Black	.43 (.58)	.61 (.65)	.37 (.57)	.43 (.60)	.55 (.67)	.44 (.61)
Income	−.00 (.00)	−.004* (.002)	−.01* (.00)	−.004* (.002)	−.00 (.00)	−.004* (.002)
Unemployment	12.12 (8.78)	10.77 (9.95)	8.25 (8.27)	6.05 (8.42)	7.17 (8.85)	6.09 (9.59)
Education	1.52 (1.12)	.79 (1.10)	1.07 (1.13)	1.26 (1.25)	1.16 (1.18)	1.13 (1.17)
Population density	−.01 (.02)	−.01 (.02)	−.02 (.02)	−.02 (.02)	−.01 (.02)	−.02 (.02)
Level of dependent variable at $t = 0$	−16.31** (5.60)	−16.24** (6.49)	−18.53*** (6.28)	−16.96** (6.60)	−15.30** (6.98)	−17.42 (6.44)
Constant	22.83 (101.18)	87.86 (120.39)	99.33 (118.23)	67.90 (127.58)	53.45 (116.39)	83.01 (120.04)
N	48	48	48	48	48	48
R^2	.44	.40	.43	.38	.38	.37

Note: $*p < .05$, $**p < .01$ and $***p < 001$ in a one-tailed test of significance. Robust standard errors in parentheses.

Source: See Table 4.1.

models of welfare expenditures, but the size of the black population is not. The lack of an effect from black populations does not seem consistent with previous findings. Yet there is very little change in the size of the black population, and policy affected by the size of the black population was established well before the period of our study (Gilens 2003; Lieberman 2003). It is striking that minority population size, albeit the Latino population rather than the black population, continues as a factor in the decline of the welfare state. The most consistent indicator across all of the models is national trends captured by the constant, suggesting that welfare and education expenditures generally increased as states have taken on greater responsibilities after the 1996 welfare reforms. Finally, it seems that states tended to converge on the value of welfare spending, as indicated by the negative and significant coefficients for the level of the dependent variable at the baseline year ($t = 0$). States with higher levels of initial welfare spending reduced their relative expenditures at greater rates than those that had lower levels during the baseline year. These findings imply that changes in the welfare state may be more sensitive to national trends than state-specific trends, and critics' arguments about the effect on liberal coalitions in states underestimate the effects of national trends.

Affirmative action in higher education–California and Texas

Affirmative action programmes based on racial and ethnic backgrounds are the most obvious forms of MCP in the states. An analysis of two high-profile policy changes in the late 1990s, in California and Texas, add an additional test of the MCP question. These two states are important cases, because they are the two most populated states in the United States and they have population sizes that are larger than or comparable to many of the worlds' nation-states. California's gross product would place it fifth in the world if it were a separate country, outpaced by only the rest of the United States, Japan, Germany, and the UK. Also highly important is that California and Texas are among the most racially/ethnically diverse states in the USA.

In 1996, these two states ended major components of their affirmative action programmes. California did so through the passage of a citizen initiative, Proposition 209, which garnered 60 per cent of the statewide vote. Proposition 209 effectively ended affirmative action programmes in state hiring as well as admissions to public universities. The use of affirmative action in higher education admissions in Texas ended after the federal courts ruled the programme unconstitutional in *Hopwood* v. *Texas*. In both cases, the most widely anticipated consequence was in public university admissions. If affirmative action, as an MCP, is said to lead states to reduce support for the welfare state, then in the period following the removal of affirmative action, especially in such a highly visible way as these two states did, increased support for welfare policies might be expected.

In order to test this hypothesis, we examine the degree to which welfare provisions changed in the period following the *Hopwood* decision (in Texas) and the passage of Proposition 209 (in California), relative to other states. Specifically, we compare the change in measures of welfare and education spending as a percentage of GSP between 1996 and 2000 as a percentage of 1996 levels. The 1996 baseline is used since this should be the point where California and Texas are most likely to diverge in their spending as the MCP of affirmative action was abandoned. Given the widely publicized concern regarding higher education in the case of California, and the direct impact of the *Hopwood* case on higher education admissions in Texas, education expenditures provide an indicator of welfare provision that is most likely to be affected by such a change. Public welfare expenditures are included in the analysis to examine the broad impact of this particular policy change on the welfare state more generally.

Again, the key hypothesis tested is whether MCPs and the welfare state are inversely related. In this case, California and Texas should display a greater relative increase (or a smaller relative decrease) in welfare provisions as affirmative action is removed compared to other states. California and Texas diverged from this expectation quite drastically in the direction of their welfare state from 1996 to 2000. Both decreased welfare expenditures as a percentage of GSP. Thus, the major shift that might be anticipated after the removal of a major MCP did not occur. Regarding the narrower question of the impact on education spending, the two states differed in the direction of education expenditure changes during this period, with California increasing their education expenditures as a percentage of GSP, while Texas decreased education expenditures in the four years following the *Hopwood* decision.

These findings, however, should be placed in a broader context to further test the hypothesis, by comparing the rate of change in other states, since general social, economic, and political trends may account for these changes. Perhaps all states were reducing welfare spending in this period, as a percentage of GSP. Thus, the question asked is: did

California and Texas reduce their welfare expenditures at a relatively lower rate than other states during this period? Contrary to the critics' hypothesis, the answer is no. In fact, California's 53.5 per cent decrease in welfare expenditures as a percentage of GSP in this four-year period was the second largest decrease of all fifty states. Texas, with a reduction of 21.4 per cent in welfare as a percentage of GSP, was the tenth largest decrease. Both states' rates of change were well below the mean of relative changes in welfare as a percentage of GSP (−6.7 per cent) for all fifty states.

The results for education expenditures compared to other states are more mixed. Comparatively, California's relative *increase* in education expenditures as a per cent of GSP (20.8 per cent) ranked as the fifteenth largest increase in the fifty states. Texas, however, *decreased* its education expenditures during this period; its 15.3 per cent decrease in education spending as a percentage of GSP places it in the bottom third of the states in relative change from 1996 levels.

Of course, there may be other factors that explain why California and Texas did not reap the predicted increase in welfare expenditures from removing affirmative action. Controlling for all potential variables is difficult, given their unique status as the two states that experienced this policy shift. However, we can gain some further insight by comparing expenditures in these two states with other comparable states that did not abandon their affirmative action programs. In particular, we can compare California and Texas to other states with similarly sized minority populations—in particular, Latino and African-American populations. Blacks and Latinos are the highest-profile targets of affirmative action in California and Texas, and as we have discussed earlier, it is the size of such minorities (and white attitudes towards them) that provide the most likely link between welfare policies and MCP policies. If affirmative action as an MCP erodes support for redistribution, then California and Texas should be doing better on welfare expenditures, post-1996, than other states with comparably sized minority populations.

Table 4.6 presents the ten states with the largest percentage of Latinos, and the ten states with the largest percentage of African-Americans and Latinos combined. The cells provide each state's ranking within the group for each measure of the welfare state, with the highest ranking for the largest relative increases, and the actual percentage change in welfare state indicators in parentheses.

Did relative welfare expenditures in California and Texas increase to a greater extent (or decrease to a lesser extent) than the most comparable states? If so, both states would be expected to consistently rank at or near

Table 4.6 Comparison of California and Texas with other racially and ethnically diverse states

States ranked by Latino population as a % of total population	% population Latino	Rank and (percentage) change in welfare as percentage of GSP	Rank and (percentage) change in education as percentage of GSP
1. New Mexico	37.9	1 (6.2%)	1 (64.9)
2. Texas	**25.5**	**4 (−21.5)**	**7 (−15.3)**
3. California	**20.6**	**10 (−53.5)**	**2 (20.8)**
4. Arizona	14.6	7 (−28.1)	4 (7.0)
5. Colorado	14.0	6 (−25.9)	5 (−3.3)
6. Nevada	13.0	3 (−11.6)	3 (8.8)
7. Florida	13.4	2 (−3.9)	6 (−7.3)
8. New York	12.3	8 (−37.2)	9 (−32.2)
9. New Jersey	10.0	9 (−45.2)	10 (−35.8)
10. Illinois	9.0	5 (−27.4)	8 (−17.2)

States ranked by Latino and Black population as a % of total population	% population Black and Latino	Rank and (percentage) change in welfare as percentage of GSP	Rank and (percentage) change in education as percentage of GSP
1. New Mexico	39.8	4 (6.2)	1 (64.9)
2. Texas	**36.8**	**8 (−21.5)**	**8 (−15.3)**
3. Mississippi	36.5	2 (16.3)	3 (43.5)
4. Louisiana	32.5	7 (−14.0)	4 (22.3)
5. California	**32.2**	**10 (−53.5)**	**5 (20.8)**
6. South Carolina	31.0	3 (6.8)	6 (20.5)
7. Georgia	30.3	6 (−12.3)	7 (7.2)
8. Maryland	28.2	5 (4.6)	9 (−21.2)
9. New York	27.9	9 (−37.2)	10 (−32.2)
10. Alabama	26.8	1 (24.1)	2 (50.0)

Note: States are ranked within each group. Per cent change is the relative per cent change as described in the text.

Source: See Table 4.1.

the top of each group. As rankings in Table 4.6 indicate, this is not the case. While California ranks second in change in education as a percentage of GSP within states with the largest Latino population (Column 4), it also had the greatest *decrease* in welfare expenditures as a percentage of GSP. Texas generally fell at the lower end of the rankings, with the exception of being ranked fourth in welfare expenditure change as a percentage of GSP among the states with the largest Latino populations. In all, even when making comparisons among states with similar minority populations, there is no systematic movement towards increasing welfare provisions when MCPs have been eliminated in these two cases. In many instances, Texas and California were in the bottom half of their peer states on key indicators.

Table 4.7 Summary of the effects of MCPs on the welfare state in the American states

	Does the effect support (Yes) or undermine (No) the argument that MCPs displace the welfare state?	
	Δ Welfare expenditures as a per cent of Gross State Product	Δ Education expenditures as a per cent of Gross State Product
Affirmative action	No	No
MCP index	No	No
Immigrant food stamps	No	No
LEP programme	No	**Yes**
LEP funding	No	No
ESL certification	No	No
Bilingual certification	No	No
English-only laws	No	No

Source: See Table 4.1.

3. Summary and conclusion

Do MCPs undermine support for welfare state policies? Based on the extensive evidence we have marshalled and analysed on the states of the USA, the most straightforward answer to this question is 'no'. Considering states that adopted or had not adopted various MCPs, as well as instances where states had certain MCPs in place but repealed them, there is little or no evidence that in the aggregate the presence of MCPs is related to lower welfare spending or other indicators of state social equality, nor, on the other hand, that the repeal of MCPs leads to an increase in support for welfare. Table 4.7 summarizes the findings; as shown, fifteen of the sixteen findings do *not* support the claim that MCPs are related to lower welfare support and education expenditures within the states.

What challenges might be made to these findings? Some challenges quickly come to mind, though there are surely others. One is that there are other, perhaps 'better' ways to measure important variables. For instance, one might measure policies such as welfare and education spending on a per capita or other basis different from that used here. Perhaps this would lead to different findings; but different indicators may be more or less appropriate depending on the assumptions and specific theory to be examined. Nonetheless, this and other measurement issues should not be dismissed. We have provided an initial analysis, and invite additional research that is both systematic and rigorous to add to, and perhaps challenge, our findings.

While our findings do not support the critics, it is also important to note that our findings provide little support for the opposite hypothesis that MCPs and the welfare state reinforce one another. Instead, it appears that there is simply no systematic linkage between level of MCPs and level of welfare expenditures.

This may seem surprising, given our earlier discussion of the significance of racial/ethnic diversity historically for both welfare and cultural policies. As we saw, similar racial dynamics appear to underpin the adoption and retrenchment of both welfare policies and MCPs. Given this, we might have expected MCPs and welfare expenditures to co-vary—i.e. to rise or fall together. How then is it that race affects welfare policies, and that race *also* affects MCPs, but that MCPs and welfare policies seem unrelated?

The general lack of relationships may be attributable to several factors. It may be that the policies themselves are complex and that those policies cannot be adequately captured by yes/no indicators, such as measures regarding the presence or absence of Official English, bilingual education, and so forth. Another possibility is that a number of institutional factors alone or in combination muffle the relationship between welfare policies and MCPs, although race is relevant to each set of policies. For example, federal programmes both constrain and enable states. Federal policies constrain states by assuring certain levels of uniformity, perhaps moderating a welfare/MCP relationship in the process. On the other hand, federal programmes enable states by providing considerable discretion within policy areas and it may be that is where the impact of race is manifest, but the impacts do not cross over from one set of policies to another (MCPs to welfare policies). Along with federalism, another institutional feature may be important. Recall that in two important instances where MCPs were overturned—namely, affirmative action in Texas and California— this was done outside the traditional venues of political representation and lawmaking. Specifically, the repeal of California's affirmative action programme, as well as its adoption of Official English, occurred through referenda and the initiative process; the state legislature had been protective of more permissive language policies. And the elimination of affirmative action admissions in Texas higher education was achieved by a court decision, *Hopwood*. But note that Texas is a state with a small welfare domain, while California has traditionally had substantially larger welfare provision. Federalism and the separation of powers (at both the state and national levels) may together separate the two types of policies, although the importance of race remains for each domain individually.

Howard (1999) has argued that in assessing the American welfare state, particularly as shaped by federalism, it is not correct to speak of *the* welfare state, but it instead should be viewed as welfare states in the plural. That is, Howard asserts that each type of welfare policy, whether it be Medicaid, TANF/AFDC, or other redistributive policy, and/or particular dimensions of such policies, *has its own politics and political dynamics*. Assuming Howard is correct about welfare policies, perhaps his assertions also extend to MCPs. Not only does each MCP have somewhat different policy goals, aims, and mechanisms, but each MCP also has different consequences for different minority groups and subgroups. Therefore, there is almost certainly not one, but numerous, MCP regimes. The analysis above indicates a central trait those MCPs may share is that none seems to significantly affect the welfare states.

Critics of multiculturalism have advanced a 'master narrative' about the trade-off between recognition and redistribution in the United States. According to this narrative, the tendency of the progressive wing of the Democratic Party to indulge in 'identity politics' (including support for MCPs) has made it more difficult to build or sustain a pan-racial coalition in favour of redistribution (e.g. Gitlin 1995; Barry 2001). On this view, there are many working-class Americans—particularly white members of the working class—who would support a stronger redistributive welfare state, but who are neglected or turned off by the Democrats' embracing of cultural rights and multiculturalism. The evidence in this chapter casts doubt on this narrative, but does not yet explain why it is wrong. Further research is needed to explore why the various mechanisms posited by the critics—such as the crowding out, corroding, and misdiagnosis effects of MCPs—have not manifested themselves. However, one possible explanation why there does not appear to be a trade-off between MCPs and welfare policies—at least at the state level—is that the voters who are likely to be antagonized by MCPs have *already* left the Democratic Party. The critics seem to be assuming that there is a large pool of voters who would support colour-blind redistribution (even if it disproportionately benefits Blacks and Hispanics), as well as supporting strong anti-discrimination for racial minorities, but who are put off by MCPs. This may actually be a small pool, or at least a smaller pool than assumed. It may be that the voters who reject MCPs are also opposed to welfare policies that disproportionately benefit minorities. And these voters have already left the Democratic Party, such that the only way to recruit these voters would be to abandon not only support for MCPs but also support for strong anti-discrimination and welfare policies. It is important to remember, in this respect, that the 'white flight' from the Democratic Party began, in at least some parts of the country, in the 1960s when the Democrats embraced basic civil and political rights for Blacks.

To summarize, previous research indicates that race has a profound influence on the size and the nature of welfare policies in the USA. Prior research also suggests that race affects whether or not MCPs will be adopted and extended, or repealed. But the findings of the present chapter suggest that MCPs appear unrelated to the general level of welfare expenditures. The analysis here also suggests that to reverse or abolish MCPs would not necessarily mean that welfare expenditures would increase. Our study is simply a first step in investigating these links, and its limitations will undoubtedly become clear as further research examines these issues. For the time being, however, the evidence presented here indicates that the pursuit of recognition through MCPs has not eroded the politics of redistribution in US state politics.

Appendix 4.1. Data Sources

Table A 4.1 Description, summary statistics, and sources for data used in the analyses

Variable	Description and summary statistics	Sources
LEP programmes	1 if state has policy, 0 otherwise. 43 States (84%) coded 1.	National Clearinghouse for Bilingual Education (1999).
LEP funding	1 if state has policy, 0 otherwise. 37 states (74%) coded 1.	National Clearinghouse for Bilingual Education (1999).
ESL certification	1 if state has policy, 0 otherwise. 36 states (72%) coded 1.	National Clearinghouse for Bilingual Education (1999).
Bilingual education certification	1 if state has policy, 0 otherwise. 27 states (54%) coded 1.	National Clearinghouse for Bilingual Education (1999).
English-only laws	1 if state has policy or ever had policy, 0 otherwise. 25 states (50%) coded as 1.	Preuhs (2005).
Immigrants eligible for state-funded food stamps.	1 if state has policy, 0 otherwise. 17 states (34%) coded as 1.	Tumlin, Zimmerman, and Ost (1999).

(Continued on next page)

Table A 4.1 Continued

Variable	Description and summary statistics	Sources
Δ Welfare expenditures as a percentage of GSP	Per cent change from the baseline year in total state expenditures on welfare policy areas as a percentage of Gross State Product (GSP). Measured as: $100*[($Welfare as % GSP_t – Welfare as % GSP_{t0})/ Welfare as % GSP_{t0}], where t is the end year and $t0$ is the baseline year. Mean: 67.35 SD: 57.79 Range: −33.97 to 210.4	For GSP: US Department of Commerce; Bureau of Economic Analysis. For Welfare Expenditures: US Census Bureau; Census of Governments.
Δ Education expenditures as percentage of GSP	Per cent change from the baseline year in total state expenditures on education as a percentage of Gross State Product (GSP). Measured as: $100*[($Education expenditures as % GSP_t – Education expenditures as % GSP_{t0})/ Education expenditures as % GSP_{t0}], where t is the end year and $t0$ is the baseline year. Mean: 19.17 SD: 21.58 Range: −9.65 to 92.71	US Census Bureau; Census of Governments (various years). For GSP: US Department of Commerce; Bureau of Economic Analysis. For Education Expenditures: US Census Bureau; Census of Governments.

5

Is multiculturalism eroding support for welfare provision? The British case

Geoffrey Evans

Introduction

This chapter examines the argument that there is a 'trade-off between the extension of multiculturalist policies and public commitment to a universalistic welfare state' (Banting and Kymlicka, introduction to this volume). According to some authors the increasing enactment of multicultural policies has supposedly contributed to an increase in tensions between majority and minority groups, a decline in levels of social trust, and the undermining of support for universalistic welfare provision. These changes in public opinion thus provide a mechanism that links the adoption of multiculturalist policies to a decline in the institutions of the welfare state. Our primary focus is on these aspects of public opinion, particularly those concerning attitudes towards minority rights on the one hand and welfare provision on the other, and how they have changed in recent decades in the British social context. As we shall see, in the British case, at least, there is so far little or no empirical support for predictions derived from the trade-off argument, though future developments consistent with these claims cannot be ruled out.

A case study of Britain can of course provide only the slimmest of grounds for preferring one account over another in such a general debate. It is also an area that is characterized by conceptual proliferation, with the arguments advanced by advocates of the idea that multiculturalist policies undermine welfare states (e.g. Gitlin 1995; Barry 2001; Goodhart 2004) weaving together features of current politics and policy with a range of putative mechanisms that have not yet been empirically evaluated.

Examination of the role of public attitudes in accounting for any relationship between multiculturalist policies and a supposed decline of the welfare state is also made difficult by a lack of clarity regarding the precise attitudes that it might be useful to examine: exactly which sorts of issues (immigration; multiculturalist policies; integration versus the preservation of cultural differences)—and for which minorities? Similarly, it is not clear exactly which aspects of the welfare state—unemployment benefit; social security; wealth redistribution; levels of social spending; public health care; education; public sector employment; taxation? Then there is the even more tortuous task of disentangling the plausible factors which might impact on those attitudes: the precise point at which multiculturalist policies supposedly have become salient (not necessarily when they were enacted) in the public consciousness; the size and behaviour of the minorities themselves; the presence of increasing numbers of asylum seekers; pronounced variations in economic performance; a dramatic change in political ascendancy of the main parties; global terrorism and geopolitical conflicts; and doubtless others.

Despite these complexities we can engage directly with one influential account, that of David Goodhart (2004), which analyses public resentment about welfare provision for immigrants in Britain and from this derives more general inferences concerning the dangers that diversity might bring for the welfare state. His interpretation is based primarily on evidence taken from a single British survey conducted in late 2003 by Mori (see Duffy 2004*a*), which therefore has considerable limitations as a basis of inference in that it cannot tell us if these issues have become more important over time. After all, people have always had categories of the 'undeserving' for whom welfare payouts are not seen as just— single teenage mothers, 'the workshy', the 'rough rather than respectable' working class, 'sturdy beggars' have all featured in one way or other through time as objects of resentment with respect to state handouts (as Duffy 2004*a* illustrates). That some should feel like that about immigrants is probably not a new attitude, nor is it specific to immigrants. Goodhart's paper also focuses on diversity, rather than multiculturalist policies themselves, and gives considerable attention to attitudes towards immigration and asylum, issues that have been increasing in significance in line with rising immigration and increases in the number of asylum seekers but which are not necessarily linked to multiculturalism as a political programme. And while the rise of Islamic militancy since the turn of the millennium has probably made people more aware of cultural differences than might otherwise have been the case, their primary reaction is more likely to be a justifiable fear of possible terrorist attacks than a concern over the workings of multiculturalist policies.

The main weakness of Goodhart's evidence regarding the corrosive effects of diversity on support for welfare is that it has little over-time basis on which to make comparisons. In contrast, our empirical terrain is Britain during the last 20–30 years, our tool of investigation is the most extensive set of high-quality social surveys conducted over this period—the British Social Attitudes (BSA) series and the British Election Studies (BES) series from 1974 to 1997, with supplements from selected Mori polls. The welfare state will be narrowed down to issues concerning unemployment benefits, spending on poverty, redistribution, and the NHS, but will not attempt to cover the full range of welfare state issues. The classic definition of a multiculturalist policy has not been much examined in social surveys, so though we will examine one question asked at two points in time on that issue, this will be supplemented by examining the attitudes of the majority to minorities and immigrants more generally.

1. The predictions

According to Banting and Kymlicka (Chapter 1, this volume), critics of multiculturalism polices postulate three main mechanisms to account for how multiculturalism might undermine the welfare state, which they label the 'crowding-out', 'misdiagnosis', and 'corroding' effects. The first two predict that multiculturalism has a negative impact on the *political salience* of redistribution; the third predicts that multiculturalism has a negative impact on *public support* for redistribution. Is there a way to test these hypotheses using public opinion data?

The 'crowding-out' hypothesis appears to focus on activists, who shift from the politics of redistribution to the politics of recognition, but it also has implications for mass opinion to the degree that such opinion is influenced by the issues activists choose to promote to general salience.[1] One consequence is a possible decline in the political significance of traditional left-right issues concerned with the 'slice of the cake', and an increase in the political prominence of social and cultural issues. In

---

[1] 'Misdiagnosis' cannot easily be examined using this sort of data, though as with crowding out it might also carry with it the implication that cultural themes replace economic ones as the movers of the popular vote, and thus impact on the policies emphasized by parties competing for that vote.

its most extreme form this could be associated with a decline in the emphasis given to redistribution when making political choices by the traditional left-wing support base in the working classes, for whom an emphasis on the rights of minorities would appear to be particularly unappealing (see for example, Sniderman et al. 2001; Lipset 1981; Evans 2000). One prediction, then, is that the rise of multiculturalism has led to the increased salience of cultural issues over redistributive issues in determining popular support for different political parties, with negative consequences for left-wing parties.

The 'corrosion' thesis appears to relate to Miller's (1995) argument that diversity produces a decline in trust—echoed in the Goodhart paper cited above and in Putnam's well-known US evidence that diversity is associated with lower social capital. In this context, the adoption of multiculturalism policies is said to reinforce and exacerbate this negative impact of diversity on trust and solidarity, by further emphasizing our differences rather than our commonalities. A second prediction then is that the rise of multiculturalism has contributed to a decline in social trust and a decline in support for universalistic provision via collective contribution.

In summary, the implications of the various strands of the anti-multiculturalist thesis are that, *ceteris paribus*, we would expect attitudes towards welfare to become more negative over time as multiculturalism becomes an increasing reality. Levels of trust should be in decline. There should be evidence of increasing resentment at multiculturalist policies and the minorities who benefit from them. These minority rights issues should over time form a stronger component of models of voting at the expense of redistributive, welfare-related issues, thus providing a basis for anti-welfare electoral success.

We attempt to test these hypotheses below. We also note an alternative view that is sceptical of the plausibility of the mechanisms that link premises to conclusions in these theories. It would instead link attitudes to welfare to the perceived level of provision in place given the demands upon it: welfare provision is valued more when it is needed. Thus support for social security and unemployment benefits is likely to be higher when unemployment is a serious threat to many among the public, but recede when the economy is booming. Similarly, if spending on welfare is perceived to be high, then further spending will be seen as less important than if spending has been retrenched. We would thus expect attitudes to track typical indicators of economic performance, unemployment, and welfare spending. From this perspective, to pursue explanations of variations in public support based in the subtleties of the multiculturalist critics would seem unproductive. Let us examine some evidence.

2. The evidence

We pursue this set of questions in two different ways. In the next section, we examine what has happened to British attitudes towards ethnic rights, multicultural policies, and immigrants over the twenty-year period covered by the British Social Attitudes surveys. The following section then moves on to focus in more detail on the possible political impact of these attitudes towards minorities with respect to support for welfare policies and the parties who advocate them. In effect, we start with the independent variables in these assertions: public attitudes towards minorities and multiculturalist policies. We then move on to the dependent variables: public support for the welfare state, and the voters' choices.

We are aware, of course, that a possible criticism of our emphasis on survey evidence of this sort is that respondents may simply be unwilling to demonstrate 'politically incorrect' views to an interviewer even if they hold them. But this argument does not stand up to close examination. In the first case, many questions examined on these topics are in the self-completion part of the British Social Attitudes questionnaire which is usually only filled in after the interviewer has left—these views do not need to be expressed face-to-face and thus do not involve potential embarrassment or awkwardness in the interviewer–respondent encounter. Secondly, a tendency not to express negative views towards minorities because of an awareness of and compliance with what is seen to be politically correct can be taken as an indicator of what people consider legitimate to express in social encounters. It is therefore a measure of a changing social climate with respect to racial tolerance and is likely to be 'real in its consequences', both in terms of everyday interaction and because response to public opinion polls informs policy makers and the strategists of parties competing for political office.

3. Public attitudes about multicultural diversity

Has there been increased resentment and hostility towards ethnic minorities and multiculturalism policies, reduced feelings of social trust, and a backlash against immigration, which critics fear weaken support for redistribution? This section examines each of these dimensions of contemporary multicultural experience.

Attitudes towards multiculturalism and ethnic minority rights

Although there has been concern about the presence of ingrained, supposedly 'institutional', racism, especially since the murder of Stephen Lawrence and the subsequent Macpherson Report concerning its investigation (Macpherson 1999) and, particularly since 11 September 2001, evidence of intolerant acts towards groups such as Muslims, immigrants, and asylum seekers, there are at least some grounds for believing that tolerance of minority rights is likely to have increased in recent years. First, it is generally argued that tolerance of minorities is linked to higher levels of education (Hyman and Wright 1979; Bobo and Licari 1989; Nie, Junn, and Stehlik-Barry 1996), and the last twenty or so years have seen a great leap in the proportion of young people going on to higher education. Secondly, there has been pressure from above, in the form of the Commission for Racial Equality, Parliament, and many other institutions in society which seek to protect and extend the rights of minorities. In consequence, although there are still debates on these matters, empirical studies of expressed prejudice seem to indicate that it has indeed been on the decline (Evans 2002a; Heath and Rothon 2003). Whether this might also translate into public endorsement of specifically multicultural policies is less clear—as Banting and Kymlicka note, one can have multiculturalist policies without multiculturalist rhetoric, and to some degree this has been the case in Britain, where in 2004 the then Home Secretary David Blunkett explicitly expressed his dislike for the term 'multiculturalism', but where there has been increasing attention to such policies by the government.

Let us first examine some evidence of attitudes towards minorities and their rights. The most extensive time-series question providing evidence on tolerance of racial minorities in Britain asks respondents: 'How would you describe yourself... as very prejudiced against people of other races, a little prejudiced, or, not prejudiced at all?' Although we have provided evidence of the validity of these responses, and used them to demonstrate a decline in prejudice in Britain over twenty years from the early 1980s (Evans 2002a), we will restrict the evidence presented here to responses to questions that do *not* use self-definition. There are a range of such questions that have been asked at various points in the history of the BSA,

157

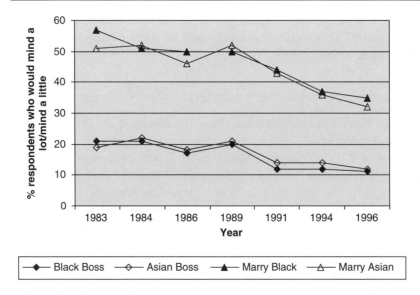

Figure 5.1 Acceptance of minorities
Question: 'Would you mind or not mind if a suitably qualified person of Black or West Indian (Asian) origin were appointed as your boss?'
Question: 'Would you mind or not mind if one of your close relatives were to marry a person of black or West Indian (Asian) origin?'

though they have been discontinued in recent years. Responses to these questions confirm an increasing and majority tendency to acceptance of racial minorities (which might be part of the reason why they were discontinued). As Figure 5.1 indicates, the proportion of respondents who would mind if a suitably qualified black/Asian were appointed as their boss had disappeared into insignificance by the 1990s. Levels of disapproval at interracial marriage by a close relative were higher but still evaporating by the time these series were dropped from the BSA in 1996.

These figures point to greater acceptance. A series on immigration from the same era suggests that increasing acceptance doesn't mean mass endorsement of further immigration, a point to which we return below. However, it is important to note here that there has been a marked closing of the gap between attitudes towards Asian and Australian/European immigrants during the period as opposition to further Indian and Pakistani settlement declined (see Figure 5.2).

But what of minority rights? Equality of opportunity has been the main interest of British researchers over the years and both the BES and BSA have relevant questions (see Table 5.1). The BSA trends on this show

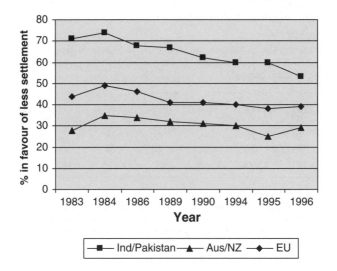

Figure 5.2 Immigration
Question: 'Please say, for each of the groups below, whether you think Britain should allow more settlement, less settlement, or about the same as now: Indians and Pakistani; Australians and New Zealanders; Common Market/European Community/European Union countries'.

majority acceptance of equality of opportunity for people of different races, opposition to this having fallen to around 20 per cent by the 1990s. A differently worded question asked in 2001 found only 3 per cent who thought race discrimination was 'usually or always right'. We can also see that in the 1990s, and increasingly during the latter part of the decade, our respondents perceived substantial legal discrimination against minorities, which was presumably seen as unjust.

A longer though sparser time series in the BES asks a different question—whether 'attempts to give equal opportunities to *black people and Asians* in Britain have gone much too far/gone a little far/about right/not quite far enough/not gone nearly far enough'. As Table 5.2 reports, distributions of responses to this question remain effectively constant through time—despite the very clear changes that took place over the period in question. In other words, at no point is there evidence of an increase in the proportion of people who thought things had 'gone too far', which indicates that there was no reaction against the improvements in equal opportunities attained over the period.

Equal treatment is accepted, but multiculturalist policies are about rather more than being treated equally. Table 5.3 shows responses to two questions that address multiculturalism more precisely. These have only

159

Table 5.1 Equal treatment for minorities

Support for equality

Question: 'There is a law in Britain against racial discrimination, that is against giving unfair preference to a particular race in housing, jobs and so on. Do YOU generally support or oppose the idea of a law for this purpose?'

	1983	1984	1986	1989	1990	1991	1994	1996
Support	69	70	65	68	68	76	73	75
Oppose	28	26	32	28	29	21	22	21
Base	1,761	1,675	1,548	1,461	1,397	1,473	2,302	2,399

Perceived racial discrimination

Question: 'Suppose two people—one white, one black—each appear in court, charged with a crime they did not commit. What do you think their chances are of being found guilty ... the white person is more likely to be found guilty, they have the same chance, or, the black person is more likely to be found guilty?'

	1990	1994	1998
White person more likely	3	4	3
Same chance	49	49	41
Black person more likely	42	44	51
Don't know	6	4	5
Base	1,397	1,137	2,071

been asked in 1995 and 2003, but they give us a further eight years to assess change following on from those covered in the previous table. The first of these questions asks for a basic integrationist vs. multiculturalist preference from respondents.[2] In both years most people opt for the integrationist answer. However, between 1995 and 2003 the gap between integration and multiculturalism dropped by a substantial 15 per cent. The second question raises the role of government assistance in furthering the multiculturalist agenda. In both years most people disagree with this

---

[2] This question has been criticized as offering a false choice (see, for example, Miller's chapter in this volume). Most defenders of multicultural policies argue that when public institutions accommodate a minority's customs and traditions, this actually makes it easier for immigrants to participate in those institutions, and thereby assists their integration. Moreover, even the most enthusiastic defender of multiculturalism does not suppose that immigrants should be able to maintain all of their customs and traditions, regardless of their content or conformity with human rights standards. So they tend to frame the issue as not one of 'maintaining customs' versus 'integration', but rather as one concerning what kinds of accommodations are compatible with what kinds of integration. It is unlikely however that these nuances are perceived and shared by the general public, nor is there evidence that they feature strongly in public disputes between advocates of pro- and anti-multiculturalist policies. Regardless of political theorists' concerns, in the real of world of political competition the choice between integration vs. multiculturalism is usually how the debate is framed.

Table 5.2 Attitudes regarding equal opportunities for blacks and Asians in Britain

	1974	1979	1983	1987	1992	1997
Attempts have gone...						
Much too far	11	11		7	5	5
Too far	15	17	19	21	18	20
About right	42	39	49	40	38	42
Not far enough	21	20	27	24	29	25
Not nearly far enough	6	7		4	4	3
Base	2,305	1,871	3,955	3,826	3,534	3,615

Note: The question had only three response categories in 1983.

proposition—but again, the 58 per cent registering disagreement in 1995 drops to 51 per cent in 2003. Despite the majority disapproval, these shifts in a pro-multiculturalist direction provide, at very least, no evidence of increasing resentment at such policies.

So, we find no support for a 'backlash' against minorities or their rights whether with respect to equal treatment or maintaining cultural distinctiveness. Equal treatment is clearly far more widely endorsed than

Table 5.3 Attitudes towards multiculturalism

Question: 'How much do you agree or disagree with the following statement? Ethnic minorities should be given government assistance to preserve their customs and traditions'

	1995	2003
Strongly agree	2	2
Agree	13	15
Neither agree/disagree	23	27
Disagree	39	38
Strongly disagree	18	13
Base	1,058	873

Question: 'Some people say that it is better for a country if different racial and ethnic groups maintain their distinct customs and traditions. Others say that it is better if those groups adapt and blend Into the larger society. Which of these views come closer to your own?'

	1995	2003
Maintain customs	16	20
Adapt and blend into society	65	54
Can't choose	18	24
Base	1,058	873

multiculturalism, but both have demonstrated positive changes over the years.

Declining social trust?

A different element of the critique of the effects of multiculturalism on welfare focuses on declining trust as a result of increasing diversity. Levels of trust are almost impossible to calculate with confidence—trust in whom, when, for what? But there are rough indicators. Trust is not measured over any period of time in the BSA series unfortunately, but there is a useful time series conducted by Mori that indicates some aspects of such orientations over an extensive period.

In these data, trust is measured as believing in what people say, which is a rather limited operationalization of the notion of trust but the only one for which we have a lengthy time series (see Figure 5.3). The most relevant item is that concerning 'the ordinary man and woman in the street'—which clearly shows no evidence of decline through time—but information on trust in the representatives of institutions makes interesting reading and useful comparators. Civil servants, doctors, teachers, scientists, and especially trade unionists became more trusted over this

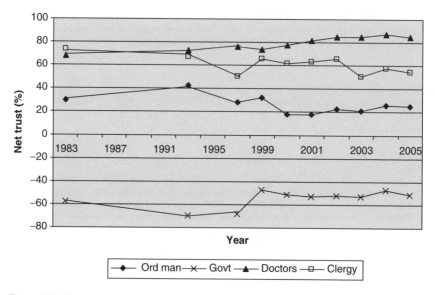

Figure 5.3 Trust

Net trust in different groups of people—illustrative examples (% respondents who trust group to tell truth − % respondents who do not trust group to tell truth)

period. Clergymean, arguably, were less trusted—presumably as fewer and fewer people participated in institutionalized religion, though this relies heavily on the very restricted measurement points in the early years of the series—and other groups including the government and politicians, and 'the ordinary man and woman in the street' fluctuated trendlessly. Figure 5.3 illustrates some of these (others are available on request).

So not only is there no sign of a decline in trust in other citizens in general, but the agents of the welfare state have in several cases gained in credibility among the general public. Clearly, as noted above, ideas about social trust probably require greater examination over time than these data supply, but without the availability of such evidence we must conclude the case for decline is unproven.

Immigration and diversity

Levels of trust do not appear to be in decline, and we have already seen that attitudes to minority rights and multiculturalism have if anything become more positive. However, there is evidence that asylum and immigration are issues that the public has become more concerned about. Mori polls show how immigration has become rated as the most important issue facing Britain in recent years by an increasing (though erratically so) proportion of the population, but it is still only a very small proportion (Duffy 2004a). Our own BSA data also show some evidence of an increase in concern between 1995 and 2003, though this is not dramatic in its extent, with the most noticeable change being a ten-point increase in those who want to see immigration reduced by 'a lot' (Table 5.4).

To explain even this change requires little imagination and no need for recourse for arguments about reactions to multicultural policies. Figure 5.4 shows the recent trends in immigration and in asylum seekers— both have been on a marked upward sweep until very recently (the number of asylum seekers declined precipitously in 2003/4). Given these increases and the media attention they have inevitably garnered, it would be surprising if at least some of the population hadn't become more concerned.

In summary, then, it is difficult to depict British public attitudes as moving consistently in the directions anticipated by critics of multiculturalism. There is no evidence of a backlash against minorities or minority rights, or of a decline in general levels of trust in other citizens. There was some increase in opposition to immigration between the mid-1990s and 2003. However, increased opposition to immigration is not the same

Table 5.4 Immigration

Question: 'Do you think the number of immigrants to Britain nowadays should be...'

	1995	2003
Increased a lot	1	2
Increased a little	3	4
Remain the same as it is	27	16
Reduced a little	24	23
Reduced a lot	39	49
Can't choose	6	6
Base	1,058	873

Question: 'There are different opinions about immigrants from other countries living In Britain. (By "immigrants" we mean people who come to live in Britain.) How much do you agree or disagree with each of the following statements?'

	1995	2003
Immigrants increase crime rates		
Strongly agree	7	13
Agree	17	25
Neither agree/disagree	34	31
Disagree	31	24
Strongly disagree	7	3
Immigrants are generally good for Britain's economy		
Strongly agree	1	1
Agree	15	20
Neither agree/disagree	42	35
Disagree	31	31
Strongly disagree	5	8
Base	1,058	873

as opposition to multiculturalist policies for minorities already settled in Britain. While such policies cannot be described as popular, public attitudes about them softened in the same period. Nor as we shall see, can increased opposition to immigration easily be interpreted as translating into opposition to welfare policies.

4. Multiculturalism and the welfare state

In this section, we turn to the bottom line: support for the welfare state. Has public support for redistribution weakened in Britain? If support has declined, is it reasonable to blame immigration and multiculturalist policies, or are alternative explanations more convincing? And

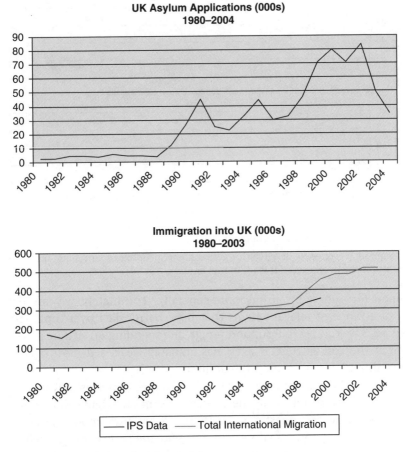

Figure 5.4 Immigration and asylum trends

Note: The Office of National Statistics changed how it measured immigration in the 1990s and so figures for total immigration (including asylum seekers) are only available from 1992 onwards. Earlier data are from the International Passenger Survey (IPS).

is there evidence that attitudes towards immigration and multiculturalism have had an impact on voter choices between different political parties?

Declining public support for universalistic provision?

Attitudes towards the welfare state are multifaceted. Immigration is a growing issue, and there is some recent evidence of disapproval of immigrants getting full welfare rights (Duffy 2004a). But does this impact on

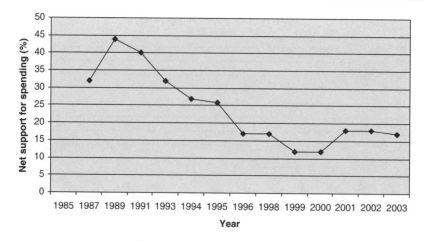

Figure 5.5 Attitude towards spending on welfare

Net Support (% agree–% disagree) for government spending more money on welfare benefits for the poor, even if it leads to higher taxes

support for welfare provision more generally? Fortunately, we can make use of a range of relevant items that have been asked over time. From Figure 5.5 we can see that support for 'greater spending on welfare benefits even at the cost of higher taxes' has arguably weakened most over the years, though it has apparently stabilized recently.

Similarly, there is some evidence that the public is increasingly sceptical about whether people truly need welfare support. Figure 5.6 presents responses to several questions about this. Scepticism about the deservingness of people on social security has remained constant, though disagreement with the statement has dropped a little since the late 1990s. Disagreement with the idea that the welfare state encourages people to stop helping each other also weakened in the mid-1990s, and more people likewise thought that if welfare weren't so generous more people would learn to stand on their own two feet.

In short, since the mid-1990s, public support for increased welfare spending has declined and attitudes towards welfare recipients have hardened. These trends do lend some credence to the concern that the 'politics of redistribution' has weakened.

But should we attribute these patterns to multiculturalist policies, or even immigration? It hardly seems justified—at all time points there is a slight positive correlation between being pro spending/redistribution and believing minority rights haven't gone far enough/support for multiculturalism. However, the relationship is weak and it does not increase over

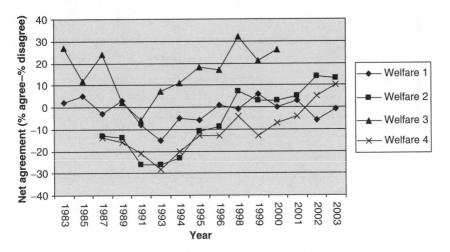

Figure 5.6 Attitudes towards welfare provision
Net agreement (% agree–% disagree) with the following statements:
1. The welfare state encourages people to stop helping each other
2. If welfare benefits weren't so generous, people would learn to stand on their own two feet
3. The welfare state makes people nowadays less willing to look after themselves
4. Many people who get social security don't really deserve any help

time, which is what would be expected if a reaction against ethnic rights had, as a result of the implementation of multicultural policies, become linked with opposition to the welfare state. Thus, for example, support for redistribution and a belief that more should be done for minorities are correlated 0.11 in 1974 and 0.06 in 1997. Similarly, support for increased welfare spending and support for multiculturalism are correlated 0.12 in 1995 and 0.09 in 2003. This is clear evidence that the linkage between welfare and multiculturalism has not increased and has not become more politically relevant in recent years.

More importantly, there are alternative ways of explaining these patterns, which require little in the way of interpretative creativity or explanatory contrivance. One hint about this alternative explanation is the timing of the decline in public support for welfare, which occurred mainly in the mid-1990s, when unemployment was dropping and Britain was moving into the period of growth and affluence it has been in since that time. This explanation for these slight shifts in attitudes can be discerned from an item asking about perceptions of job opportunities (Figure 5.7). After 1996 there was a step change in the proportion of respondents who thought 'people could find a job if they really wanted

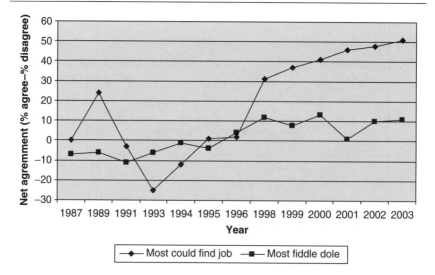

Figure 5.7 Perceptions of job opportunities and unemployment
Net agreement (% agree–% disagree) with the following statements:
1. Around here, most unemployed people could find a job if they really wanted one
2. Most people on the dole are fiddling in one way or another

one'. And this was accompanied by a switch round in the belief that 'people on the dole are fiddling'.

Figure 5.8 provides more general support for the proposition that declining support for welfare was related to economic factors, not cultural ones. The figure shows the trend in support for welfare and the trend in affluence (as measured by GDP per person) and unemployment figures. The fit is quite close. Views on the importance of welfare spending and the need for such provision change roughly in line with the improving economic situation of the 1990s and new Labour arrived with a package of policies that included greater expenditure on reducing poverty, thus weakening the need to spend yet more on a diminishing problem. As unemployment declined so did support for more spending on welfare.

If an area of public policy stops being as much of a problem, the public are sensible enough to change their view of the priority it should be given and also to infer that the extent of genuine hardship is lessened. This can hardly be seen as evidence of a decline in support for the welfare state.

Moreover, this evidence on the reduced relevance of welfare provision under conditions of affluence and low unemployment shouldn't blind us to the continuing and extremely positive view of the welfare state

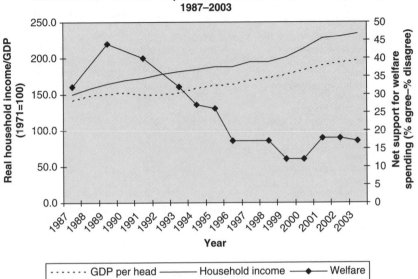

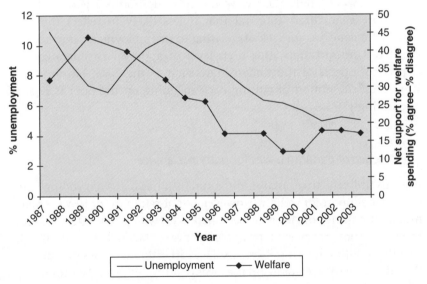

Figure 5.8 Support for welfare by trends in affluence/unemployment over time
Sources: Office of National Statistics 2004a and 2004b.

Table 5.5 Attitudes to the welfare state

	00	01	02	03
The creation of the welfare state is one of Britain's proudest achievements				
Strongly agree	18	19	16	17
Agree	39	38	37	41
Neither agree/disagree	30	30	31	29
Disagree	10	10	11	8
Strongly disagree	2	2	2	3
Cutting welfare benefits would damage too many people's lives				
Strongly agree	10	11	9	9
Agree	49	47	44	46
Neither agree/disagree	24	25	27	27
Disagree	14	13	16	16
Strongly disagree	2	2	2	1
Base	2,980	2,795	2,900	873

held by the British public. A recent, short time series asks for respondents' reactions to the claim that 'the creation of the welfare state is one of Britain's proudest achievements'. As can be seen in Table 5.5, this is overwhelmingly their view and this question is a good indicator of a more generalized approval that is less likely to reflect the more immediate concerns (or lack of) relating to unemployment, poverty, and the like. Unsurprisingly, this high level of approval is reiterated with respect to aspects of the welfare state such as the NHS, but as can be seen, even the notion of cutting back spending on the poor is rejected resoundingly.

The salience of minority issues for party preference

It seems unlikely, then, that multiculturalism has had a 'corroding' effect on public support for welfare. However, it is also important to ask whether multiculturalism policies may have had a 'crowding-out' effect on redistributive issues. As noted at the outset, critics of such policies have worried that the 'politics of recognition' displaces attention to issues of redistribution, dividing the electorate on the basis of attitudes toward cultural issues rather than economic and welfare issues. Although multiculturalism does not seem to have weakened public support for welfare, it is possible that contemporary events such as immigration and terrorism have raised issues of multiculturalism onto the political agenda—especially as the traditional right–left ideological conflict has declined in intensity with Labour's successful occupation of the middle ground since the mid-1990s.

Is there evidence of such a 'crowding-out' effect? As ever, we can only examine this in a relatively schematic manner. The tables below present models of party support conditioned by attitudes on key areas of dispute in contemporary politics. These models are logistic regressions, which estimate the effects of a set of independent variables—attitudes towards multicultural and other issues—on the likelihood (or 'odds') of choosing one political party or another. The models focus on the primary axis of British electoral competition—the Labour Party vs. the Conservative Party. As is common practice, the effects of the independent variables are represented as 'log-odds', with a positive coefficient indicating an increased likelihood of voting for the Labour Party, and a negative coefficient indicating an increased likelihood of voting for the Conservatives. However, our primary interest is in the statistical significance of the coefficients for attitudes towards minority rights and multiculturalism. Following convention, we use the 5 per cent level of significance to indicate an effect that is probably not simply a chance occurrence.

One set of models (presented in Table 5.6) covers the 1974–97 period using the BES surveys, which include a question about whether minority rights have 'gone too far'. This also employs a set of regularly repeated questions measuring attitudes on key political issues that can be taken to indicate respondents' positions on left–right and liberal–authoritarian issues, which are the core dimensions of political division values underlying political disputes in Britain over this period (e.g. Heath et al. 1990). The second set of models (Table 5.7) are estimated for 1995 and 2003 and contain the most direct measure of support for multicultural policies available over time in the BSA as well as a measure of attitudes towards immigration and multi-item scales measuring left–right and liberal–authoritarian values (see Evans, Heath, and Lalljee 1996).

Have minority rights become more important relative to other concerns over the years when deciding which of the two main UK parties to support? The longer-term data suggest that there was no change between 1974 and 1997. The general pattern is for issues concerning economic inequality to predict in a relatively consistent and trendless form, with little effect from the liberal–authoritarian issues. A similar weak and inconsistent pattern is observed for ethnic minority rights. Attitudes towards the EU are unusual, in that their relationship with party support reverses

171

Table 5.6 The effect of attitudes towards minorities on Labour–Conservative voting 1974–1997 (multivariate analysis with standard errors in parentheses)

	1974	1987	1997
Ethnic minorities	**0.08**^{ns}	**0.25**	**0.13**^{ns}
	(0.07)	(0.06)	(0.07)
Poverty	0.09^{ns}	0.48	0.40
	(0.07)	(0.08)	(0.07)
Workers	0.32	0.15	0.17
	(0.06)	(0.06)	(0.05)
NHS	0.20	0.90	0.59
	(0.07)	(0.09)	(0.09)
Wealth	0.79	0.83	0.76
	(0.06)	(0.06)	(0.06)
Women	−0.08^{ns}	0.04^{ns}	0.16^{ns}
	(0.07)	(0.08)	(0.08)
Abortion	0.14	−0.12^{ns}	0.04^{ns}
	(0.06)	(0.07)	(0.07)
Stiffer sentences	−0.01^{ns}	0.22	0.04^{ns}
	(0.04)	(0.05)	(0.07)
Withdraw from EU	1.29	0.58	−0.67
	(0.14)	(0.12)	(0.12)
Model chi^2	577.0	884.8	658.4
N	1483	2140	2102

Notes: Coefficients give log odds of having Labour vs. Conservative party identification. All coefficients significant at $p < 0.05$ unless indicated

Questions on Left–Right attitudes: 'Should the government spend more money to get rid of *poverty*? Should the government put more money into the *National Health Service*? Should the government give *workers* more say in running the places where they work? The government should redistribute income and *wealth* towards ordinary people. Responses on a five-point scale: very important/fairly important/doesn't matter/fairly important not done/very important not done (response codes for wealth in 1987, 1997 are strongly agree/disagree)'.

Questions on Liberal–Authoritarian attitudes: 'How do you feel about attempts to give equal opportunities to *women* in Britain? How do you feel about the availability of *abortion* on the NHS? How do you feel about *stiffer sentences* for people who break the law? How do you feel about attempts to give equal opportunities to *black people and Asians* in Britain? Responses on a five-point scale: gone much too far/gone a little far/about right/not quite far enough/not gone nearly far enough (response codes for sentencing in 1987, 1997 are strongly agree/disagree)'.
Variables coded so that higher values indicate left wing/liberal attitudes.

Questions on EU: 'Should Britain stay in the EEC on present terms/stay but try to change/change or leave/get out? (1974) Do you think Britain should continue to be a member of the European Community/Union or should it withdraw? (1987, 1997)'.

substantially over the period as the parties themselves swap positions on the question of closer EU integration (Evans 1999; Evans and Butt 2005). There is nothing here to suggest a growing political salience for ethnic rights.

However, if we examine the relation between party support and attitudes towards left–right and liberal–authoritarian dimensions of political values, the EU, and multiculturalism at the two recent time points for which we have comparable measures, 1995 and 2003, we do find

Table 5.7 The effects of attitudes towards multiculturalism and other issues on Labour–Conservative Party identification 1995/2003 (multivariate analysis with standard errors in parentheses)

	1995		2003	
	Model 1	Model 2	Model 1	Model 2
Multiculturalism	**0.09**^{ns}	**0.10**^{ns}	**0.28**	**0.20**^{ns}
	(0.10)	(0.12)	(0.11)	(0.11)
Immigration attitudes	—	**−0.04**	—	**0.41**
		(0.17)		(0.16)
Left–Right attitudes	1.65	1.65	1.08	1.11
	(0.15)	(0.15)	(0.15)	(0.16)
Lib–Auth attitudes	1.29	1.30	0.61	0.44
	(0.18)	(0.20)	(0.19)	(0.20)
Attitudes towards EU	0.22	0.23	0.55	0.53
	(0.09)	(0.09)	(0.11)	(0.11)
Model chi^2	254.8	254.8	111.9	118.6
N	689	689	505	505

Notes: Coefficients give log odds of having Labour vs. Conservative party identification. All coefficients significant at $p < 0.05$ unless indicated.

Left–Right attitude scale comprised of 5 agree/disagree items (see below for details). Scale ranges from 1 to 5 with high scores indicating 'left-wing' position.

Liberal–Authoritarian attitude scale comprised of 6 agree/disagree items (see below for details). Scale ranges from 1 to 5 with high scores indicating 'libertarian' position.

Questions on EU attitudes: 'Do you think Britain's long term policy should be to: Leave EU/stay in and reduce powers/leave things as are/stay and increase powers/work for formation of single European Union?'

Questions on attitudes to multiculturalism: 'Ethnic minorities should be given government assistance to preserve their customs and traditions. Responses coded on a five point scale—strongly agree/agree/neither/disagree/strongly disagree—where higher values indicate agreement with statement.'

Questions on immigration attitudes scale comprised of items shown in Table 5.4. Scale ranges from 1 to 5 where higher values represent pro-immigration stance (alpha = 0.70)

Left–Right scale items

- The government should redistribute income from better-off to those who are less well off
- Big business benefits owners at expense of workers
- Ordinary people do not get their fair share of nation's wealth
- There is one law for the rich and one for the poor
- Management will always try to get the better of employees if it gets the chance

Liberal–Authoritarian items

- Young people today don't have enough respect for traditional British values
- People who break the law should be given stiffer sentences
- For some crimes the death penalty is the most appropriate sentence
- The law should always be obeyed even if a particular law is wrong
- Censorship of films and magazines is necessary to uphold moral standards
- Schools should teach children to obey authority

evidence of change. Model 1 in Table 5.7 shows that as might be expected from other analyses, the left–right and libertarian–authoritarian divisions between Labour and Conservative are less predictive in 2003 after six years of 'Blairism' than in 1995, when the Conservatives were still in power. In contrast, the EU has increased its predictive power—again as would be expected given what we know of political developments over this period (Evans 1999, 2002b)—but so, intriguingly, has multiculturalism, which had no significant net effect in 1995, but was clearly significant and at over twice the magnitude in 2003: in 2003 voters who had negative attitudes towards multiculturalism were more likely to choose the Conservatives than Labour.

This is a potentially very interesting change in the political character of multiculturalism. However, it is possible that rising concern over immigration, as well as global Islamic terrorism and the war in Iraq account for this increased salience rather than any heightened concern over multiculturalist policies. Evidence for this hypothesis is provided by including immigration attitudes in the models and seeing how they affect attitudes towards multiculturalist policies. Model 2 includes a scale of attitudes towards immigration which is constructed by adding together responses to the questions shown in Table 5.4. It can be seen that in 1995 attitudes towards immigration had no significant effect on the likelihood of voting Labour vs. Conservative. However, in 2003 they had strong and highly significant effects. Even more interestingly, the inclusion of attitudes towards immigration reduces the coefficient for attitudes towards multiculturalism so that it is no longer quite significant at $p = 0.05$. This suggests, then, that a substantial component of the effect of attitudes towards multiculturalism is derived from concerns about immigration rather than with multiculturalist policies themselves.

In short, we see little evidence of 'crowding out', at least at the level of electoral choices of the public. Supporters of redistribution continue to attach great significance to that issue when deciding which party to support. There is evidence that some pro-redistribution voters would consider switching parties if they felt that Labour was unable or unwilling to control immigration levels. This fact has not been lost on Labour Party strategists, who have responded by asserting their commitment to cracking down on illegal immigration and controlling the borders. But while immigration control may sometimes crowd out redistribution in determining people's voting behaviour, there is scant evidence that multiculturalism policies for already settled minorities are having this effect.

Conclusions

During a period where multiculturalist policies have been implemented, immigration has increased, and where asylum and immigration have produced a negative popular reaction, we have seen both a reduction in expressed prejudice towards ethnic minorities and a small upward shift in support for multiculturalism. At the same time, attitudes towards welfare appear to map more closely onto fluctuations in economic performance, such as unemployment levels, and more than likely, Labour incumbency, in rational self-interested ways. Temporally, there is no connection between declining support for welfare and increasing resentment of minorities or multiculturalist policies. There is no evidence that negative attitudes towards minority rights provision have become more closely linked to a rejection of welfare. Finally, when modelled in a multivariate analysis of vote choice/party preference, there is only slim evidence that attitudes towards multiculturalism have become more important in recent years. And this increase appears to relate more to concerns about increasing immigration than multiculturalist policies themselves. On the basis of this evidence we must cast doubt on the prognosis of a trade-off between multiculturalist policies and commitment to the welfare state, at least to the degree that the mechanism which accounts for any such link involves the processes of transformation in public opinion specified in such theses.

We can infer therefore that the possible tensions identified in Evans's (2000) analysis of the gap that has arisen between the Labour Party and its traditional working-class base as the party has adopted more 'progressive' policies on social and minority issues have not so far been costly for the party and its programmatic aspirations. Clearly some sections of the working class are unreceptive to pro-minority positions, but these issues are not usually decisive for their choice of party. The very limited success of the British National Party even among marginalized groups testifies to this. Moreover, the manual working class is less than half the size it was only forty years ago and is simply far less significant as the basis of Labour's electoral success than it used to be—a lack of significance accentuated by the party's successful courting of middle and intermediate class voters in the last decade.

Perhaps we should not be surprised at these, on the whole, null findings. Over time, evidence suggests that the population in general is getting more tolerant and looks likely to continue to do so. The reasons for this cannot easily be pinned down, but generational replacement, and increased access to higher education (Hyman and Wright 1979; Bobo and Licari 1989; Evans 2002*a*; Heath and Rothon 2003) would appear to provide part of the explanation, via the entry of new cohorts of tolerant people into adulthood, the growth of more highly educated groups as a proportion of the population, and the general tendency for the more highly educated to be on the progressive edge of attitudinal change, with new ideas becoming accepted more gradually by people with lower levels of education. Other research has provided substantial evidence that among the main factors linked to tolerance (or intolerance) of minorities are religiosity, and social class (e.g. Sniderman, Brody, and Tetlock 1991; Sullivan and Transue 1999). The pronounced decline in levels of religiosity and in the size of the working class over the second half of the twentieth century are thus likely to have contributed to this increased tolerance.

All of these factors can help to explain why the British are more tolerant of racial minorities than they were twenty years ago and why opposition towards multiculturalist policies have softened in recent years. Nevertheless, despite these trends, there is still evidence that increasing immigration has been linked to its perception as a problem by some people, and recent comparative research suggests that the reasons for this are likely to relate to concerns about the erosion of cultural traditions and linguistic unity (Ivarsflaten 2005). However, there is nothing to indicate that this concern translates into a rejection of universalistic welfare provision, nor even of the rights of already present ethnic minorities.

These conclusions must, of course, be treated as provisional, not only because of the data limitations and the interpretative uncertainties indicated in the introduction, but because of the as yet unknown implications of any changes in the relationship between minorities and the majority. Thus according to the 2001 Census Britain has only around 8 per cent of racial minorities—though this figure is typically considerably overestimated by the general public. Should that figure increase substantially the conclusions here might well need to be revised. But given current rates of immigration and taking into account the recent dramatic fall in asylum applications, this seems at very most a temporally remote possibility. Also, of course, the impact of recent Islamic terrorist acts on attitudes towards multiculturalism remains to be seen. But again, given that it is generally acknowledged that such acts are undertaken by very few individuals and do not in any way represent the views of Britain's Muslim minorities, it is not clear how the negative responses that they might have incurred would translate into a rejection of the widely supported institution of universal welfare provision.

6

The parallel decline of multiculturalism and the welfare state in the Netherlands

Han Entzinger

Introduction

A study on the relationship between policies of multiculturalism and the welfare state would be incomplete without a chapter on the Netherlands. For many years this country had a reputation not only as a shining example of a respectful and successful institutionalization of cultural difference stemming from immigration, but also as a strong welfare state. At first glance, therefore, the Netherlands seems to contradict this book's point of departure, which is that multiculturalist policies and the welfare state may be incompatible. In recent years, however, some rather dramatic shifts have occurred in this country. Two politically inspired murders of well-known critics of multiculturalism—Pim Fortuyn in 2002 and Theo van Gogh in 2004—have encouraged a reappraisal of Dutch public policy towards immigrants, both by the government and by the general public. Meanwhile, assimilation has become the watchword. The Dutch welfare state has also undergone significant trimmings, albeit over a somewhat longer period. In 1980, Dutch public social expenditures as a percentage of GDP were higher than in any other of the seventeen countries in Europe and North America that are mentioned in the table in Appendix 2.3 to Chapter 2 of this book, with the exception of Sweden and Denmark. That same table shows that between 1980 and 2000 the Netherlands dropped from third place to the middle of the pack, ranking alongside a traditional neoliberal state, the United Kingdom. Since 1998 the level of welfare provisions has decreased even further.

In this chapter I will try to assess whether there is a causal relationship between the recent changes in Dutch multiculturalist policies and the decline of the Dutch welfare state. If this is the case, which has provoked which? First I will describe and analyse Dutch policies for immigrant minorities and apply the eight criteria to them that the editors of this volume have developed in Chapter 2. I will then continue with a description of the way in which immigrants have been qualifying for welfare state provisions and have made use of these. Does the Dutch experience indicate that multiculturalist policies indeed erode the welfare state, as some observers cited in Chapter 1 of this volume seem to believe? In the Netherlands we have witnessed multiculturalism and welfare state provisions decline more or less simultaneously. Does this mean that in the Dutch case the 'recognition or redistribution' dilemma has been solved by abandoning both of these as political objectives? Or is this sheer coincidence, and must we conclude that recognition and redistribution are less directly linked to one another than some observers suggest (e.g. Bommes 1999; Brochmann and Hammar 1999)? I will try to shed further light on these questions on the basis of the three lines of argument that Keith Banting and Will Kymlicka have developed in Chapter 1.

The recent history of immigration to the Netherlands and the immigrant presence in the country are not drastically different from those in neighbouring West European countries. Currently, more than 11 per cent of the Dutch population of 16.4 million people are foreign born and for that reason can be qualified as immigrants. If one includes the second generation the percentage goes up to 20. This means that one in five persons living in the Netherlands is either an immigrant or a child of an immigrant. These figures include people with a background in other EU countries, in Western countries outside the EU, as well as in pre-independent Indonesia. The number of residents with 'non-Western origins', as official Dutch statistics call them, stands at close to 1.7 million, one-tenth of the population. Among these 'visible minorities'—to use a Canadian term—three communities stand out in size: Turks, Surinamese, and Moroccans each number between 300,000 and 350,000. The Turkish and the Moroccan communities are legacies of the 'guest worker' policies in the late 1960s and early 1970s, which were followed by a rather generous programme of settlement and family reunion. Meanwhile, many people of Turkish or Moroccan origin have taken up Dutch citizenship. Most migrants from Suriname arrived in the 1970s, when this former

Dutch colony acquired political independence. Their Dutch passports enabled them to do so without much difficulty.

In the 1990s immigration to the Netherlands went up and its origins became much more diverse. The end of the Cold War led to a significant growth of East European migrants as well as of asylum seekers, some of whom later acquired refugee status. Besides, growing numbers of Dutch and foreign residents find their spouses in other countries. More recently, immigration of highly skilled 'knowledge workers' has gone up, but most of these do not stay on. Meanwhile, immigration among the three largest communities, the Turks, the Surinamese, and the Moroccans, continued as well, albeit at a slower pace than before. In the past few years, immigration to the Netherlands has declined significantly. This is believed to be the combined outcome of a stagnant economy and stricter immigration laws and policies. Since 2003 the migration balance has been negative, a phenomenon unknown since the early 1960s (except in 1967).

1. *Pillarization* and social policy as guiding principles

The beginning of large-scale immigration to the Netherlands and the emergence of the welfare state coincided more or less in time.[1] No wonder that, back in the 1950s, it was mainly through a number of well-chosen social policy measures that large numbers of so-called 'repatriates' from Indonesia were encouraged to assimilate to Dutch society, with which they already had a certain familiarity. Later, in the 1960s and 1970s, social policy again played a crucial role in the reception and guidance of newly arriving immigrants, guest workers from the Mediterranean as well as people from Suriname. A major difference, however, was that these migrants' residence was seen as temporary, both by the authorities and by most migrants themselves. As a consequence, no efforts were made this time to promote their integration. On the contrary, the migrants were encouraged to retain their own cultural identity. The official justification for this was that this would help them reintegrate upon their return to their countries of origin. One of the clearest expressions of this approach was the introduction of mother-tongue teaching for migrant children in Dutch primary schools as early as 1974. The authorities also facilitated migrants in setting up their own associations and consultative bodies.

---

[1] I have analysed the development of Dutch policies for immigrants, particularly during the last few years, in more detail in Entzinger (forthcoming).

To the Dutch this approach of creating separate facilities based on community identities was nothing new. Under the well-known system of 'pillarization' (*verzuiling*) various religious and ideological communities in the Netherlands had long had their own institutional arrangements, such as schools, hospitals, social support agencies, newspapers, trade unions, political parties, and even broadcasting agencies for radio and television. Each community or 'pillar' (e.g. Catholics, Protestants, Jews, but also socialists, liberals, humanists) may set up its own institutions, largely paid for by the state. The state itself can then remain neutral, since it is obliged to treat all communities in exactly the same way. Within its own institutions each community is reasonably free to make its own arrangements. This enables them to preserve their specific identity and to 'emancipate' their own members. This approach is based on the subsidiarity principle, or—to use a classical Dutch Protestant term—on 'sovereignty in one's own circle', which in a more contemporary variant would be 'living apart together'. The unifying element in this institutionalized diversity is to be found at the top: the elites of all pillars meet regularly to discuss issues of common concern and to build coalitions that are needed for majority decision making. Hence the metaphor of pillarization: the elites constitute the common roof that the pillars support (Lijphart 1975).

Since the late 1960s pillarization has been losing ground in the Netherlands, partly as a result of secularization and partly because of the rising level of schooling of the population as a whole. Unconditional obedience to paternalistic leaders, a prerequisite for a proper functioning of the system, could no longer be enforced. Yet, it was generally believed that what did not work any more for the population as a whole might be good for the migrants who, after all, were perceived as fundamentally different from the Dutch and as people in need of emancipation. Until about 1980 the promotion of institutional separateness could be justified easily with an appeal on the migrants' presumed temporary residence. However, this institutional separateness persisted even after the Dutch government acknowledged in that year that, contrary to earlier beliefs, most migrants would stay in the Netherlands and that their integration should therefore be encouraged.

The path that was envisaged for integration was remarkably similar to the one that had worked in the past for the religious and ideological 'pillars'. It was a combination of combating social deprivation through selected support measures provided by the generous welfare state, promoting equal treatment, and encouraging 'emancipation', while aiming at the preservation of the communities' cultural identity. To this purpose the migrants were labelled *ethnic minorities*, and the policy on their behalf became known as the Minorities' Policy. It was interesting to observe how a country which until then had been remarkably homogeneous from an ethnic perspective now introduced the notion of ethnicity as a basis for differential policy making.[2] The authorities and a vast majority of the population were convinced that this was the best way to work on the migrants' 'emancipation'. However, there were also critics who claimed that stressing ethnic differences would risk perpetuating these and therefore become an obstacle to the migrants' fuller social participation, a phenomenon known as *ethnicization* or *minorization* (Rath 1991).

In the 1980s the term multiculturalism was still not very common in the Netherlands. The Dutch government never really used it. In hindsight, however, the Dutch Minorities' Policy of the 1980s can certainly be labelled as multiculturalist. In a number of spheres it provided institutional arrangements that operated parallel to existing mainstream arrangements. Some of these will be discussed in more detail later in this chapter. The parallel institutions were generously supported with public funds. The Minorities' Policy, therefore, can be seen simultaneously as the hallmark of pillarization and of the welfare state. It was this approach that drew worldwide attention from protagonists of multiculturalist policies. However, in the Netherlands itself doubts began to rise about its effectiveness.

2. From multiculturalism to integration

The restructuring of Dutch industry in the early 1980s had left large numbers of low-skilled workers without a job and many of them were of immigrant origin. By the end of the decade more than one-third of all Turks and Moroccans in the Netherlands were unemployed. In contrast to policies pursued by other European countries, such as Germany and Switzerland, most of the Dutch considered it inappropriate to encourage the return of these people, to whom the Dutch economy owed so much.

---

[2] Of course, regional differences exist and persist between different parts of the Netherlands in spite of the country's relatively small size. Most Roman Catholics, for example, live in the south-eastern half of the country, while the north-west is predominantly protestant. The only community that could be qualified as a regional minority are the half a million Frisians in the northern province of Friesland/Fryslân. Most of them speak not only Dutch, but also Frisian. This language can be used in contacts with public authorities in the province and teaching in Frisian primary schools is partly in Frisian. However, it would be an exaggeration to say that there is a strong movement for a further recognition of Frisian distinctness in the province.

As a consequence, immigration became a growing burden for welfare and social policy regimes, but making mention of this in public was widely considered to be politically incorrect, if not racist.

Under the surface, however, dissatisfaction grew. In 1991 the then parliamentary leader of the opposition Liberal Party (VVD), Frits Bolkestein, triggered a first public debate on immigration. The debate did not focus on welfare arrangements, but rather on the presumed incompatibility of Islam and 'western values' (Bolkestein 1991). It was influenced by the Rushdie affair in Britain and the conflict over wearing headscarves in state schools in France. The debate calmed down after a while, but some uneasiness with the strong cultural relativism that lay at the basis of the Minorities' Policy remained. Didn't this approach promote the ethnic minorities' isolation from mainstream society rather than their integration into it? Wasn't it, therefore, responsible for the minorities' continuing, possibly even growing reliance on welfare state provisions?

After the 1994 parliamentary elections the Christian Democrats (CDA) remained outside the government for the first time in almost a century. Traditionally, they had been the champions of pillarization. This explains why the incoming 'purple' coalition of the three major non-religious parties, headed by Labour Party leader Wim Kok, was able to shift the focus of its policies from respecting cultural diversity to promoting the immigrants' social and economic participation.[3] Quite significantly, the Minorities' Policy was rebaptized Integration Policy. From that moment on culture was largely seen as a private affair; providing jobs to immigrants had become the main objective. Mother tongue teaching was removed from the core curriculum and later disappeared altogether from the schools. Besides, it was recognized that the migrants' lack of integration was also due to their insufficient familiarity with the Dutch language and society. A programme of mandatory Dutch language and *inburgering* ('civic integration') courses was launched which every newly arriving migrant from outside the European Union would be obliged to attend.

The ambition to improve the migrants' position in employment, education, housing, and a few other significant spheres of society proved to be quite successful. In the second half of the 1990s registered unemployment among people of immigrant origin dropped dramatically, though

---

[3] This government was actually a coalition of the main liberal parties (in a philosophical sense). In the Netherlands it is commonly referred to as the 'purple' coalition, since purple is the colour that results from the blending of the colours of the three constituent parties: red (Labour), blue (Liberals), and green (Democrats).

it still remained substantially above the national average. It is generally assumed, however, that it has been the prospering economy rather than targeted government policies that have led to this improvement. Also in education the position of immigrants, particularly the second generation, improved significantly during the later 1990s. They are still over-represented in lower forms of secondary education, but their participation in higher education is rising and school dropouts among immigrants have become less frequent. The housing situation of immigrants no longer differs significantly from that of the native population of similar income levels (Dagevos, Gijsberts, and van Praag 2003).

However, certain problems related to immigration turned out to be more persistent. Rising expectations about the migrants' Dutch language proficiencies could not be met by the still rather amateurish integration courses. Even more worrying were the high delinquency rates among certain immigrant communities (Junger-Tas 2002). These were generally seen as a sign of the weakness of integration, but also the weakness of opportunities. Equally worrying, but perhaps less noticed, was the finding that interethnic contacts at a personal level had decreased rather than increased during the 1990s (Dagevos, Gijsberts, and van Praag 2003: 334–9). To a large extent this may have been an effect of a growing segregation in cities, where immigrants continue to take the places of native Dutch who have moved to the outskirts (Uitermark and Duyvendak 2004). School segregation has become an even more serious problem than segregation in housing. In certain neighbourhoods only few native Dutch children are left anyway and the pillarized school system allows publicly funded confessional schools to refuse children of a denomination that is not their own. As a consequence, many schools have become even more segregated than the neighbourhoods in which they are located. In addition to this, concerns were also growing, though seldom expressed, over the relatively strong reliance on various social policy provisions among ethnic minorities. Later in this chapter we will see to what extent such concerns were justified.

3. The changeover to assimilation

At the start of the new millennium two contradictory narratives competed in the Dutch public debate on integration. One was the 'official' one of a considerable progress that had been achieved on all major indicators, such as participation in the labour market, in education, housing etc. In the years 1990 to 2000, for example, registered unemployment among people of Turkish and Moroccan descent went down from around 40 to 12 per cent. Overall, the second generation was doing considerably better than their parents, particularly among the Surinamese (Veenman 2002, Dagevos, Gijsberts, and van Praag 2003). The continuing identification among Turks and Moroccans with their countries of origin and also with Islam was taken as a sign of a successful multiculturalism: institutional integration could indeed go hand in hand with a preservation of the original cultural identity. The sharp rise in naturalizations during the 1990s was yet another sign that growing numbers of immigrants saw a future for themselves in the Netherlands.

The competing view was much less optimistic. Paul Scheffer, a publicist and a prominent member of the Labour Party, was among the first to voice this view, thus risking the wrath of the established order. In a much-debated article called 'The Multicultural Tragedy' published in January 2000 in the leading newspaper NRC Handelsblad he stated that Dutch multiculturalism had failed (Scheffer 2000, 2003). Instead, a new ethnic underclass was emerging of people who did not feel attached to Dutch culture and society, and who were unwilling and unable to integrate. Scheffer voiced the concern that many Dutch people felt, but did not express about continuing immigration, stagnant integration, increased segregation, high dependency on welfare provisions, and a rapidly growing Muslim population. Eventually, in Scheffer's view, this would undermine social cohesion and the functioning of the liberal-democratic state, particularly because of the supposedly illiberal ideas of the Muslims among the immigrants. Scheffer accused the Dutch elite of having remained largely indifferent to these developments. Their cosmopolitanism and their cultural relativism had allegedly prevented them from demanding that the newcomers adapt. Respect for cultural difference had prevailed over defending the principles of liberal democracy.

Scheffer's outcry initially met with a lot of opposition, but five years later it is widely seen as the beginning of a dramatic turnaround in the Dutch public debate and in policy making regarding immigration and integration. In this climate of increased sensitivity regarding immigration in general and Islam in particular, the events of 11 September 2001 clearly had a catalysing effect. Around that same time Pim Fortuyn's star began to rise in the Netherlands. Until then he had been a relatively marginal academic, known for his powerful anti-immigrant and anti-Muslim columns in a right-wing weekly (Pels 2003). In the post-'9/11' climate his radical views and his charisma quickly made him into a media star. He decided to participate in the May 2002 parliamentary elections with his own party, List Pim Fortuyn (LPF).

Fortuyn's programme was quite radical and not very coherent in many places, but he appealed to feelings of dissatisfaction present among the electorate after eight years of 'left–right' coalition, that was seen as having swept all controversies under the carpet (Fortuyn 2002). Large segments of the electorate had become weary of public authorities and dissatisfied with their policy making and with the provision of public services. This proved to be a good breeding ground for populism. Fortuyn's views about immigration became a central element in his programme, but not the only one. Unlike politicians such as Le Pen in France, Haider in Austria, or De Winter in Flanders Fortuyn was not really against immigrants as such. His primary concern was the assault on democratic liberties that might result from the presence of so many people unfamiliar with Western values, particularly Muslims (Wansink 2004). In fact, with almost one million the Netherlands has the second highest per capita share of people of Muslim origin in Europe, after France (Phalet and ter Wal 2004). Fortuyn also took a rather strong position against the generosity of the welfare state, but he did not explicitly link this to immigration and certainly not to multiculturalism. Instead, his main argument was that the welfare state had become too bureaucratic and therefore too costly. In his view people, including those of immigrant background, should be encouraged to assume more responsibilities for their own lives—the classical neoliberal argument.

The sudden rise of Pim Fortuyn ended even more abruptly when an animal rights activist assassinated him on 6 May 2002. In the parliamentary elections, nine days later, his party list LPF obtained 26 out of 150 seats in parliament, thus becoming at once the second largest party after the Christian Democrats. They took the lead in a new right-wing government, headed by Jan Peter Balkenende, along with the Fortuynists and the Liberals. Curtailing immigration and promoting a more coercive integration policy were high on the new government's agenda. The predominant view was that primarily the immigrants themselves were to blame for their lingering integration. However, the new government was very unstable and it fell within three months.

In the new elections, in January 2003, the Fortuynists fell back to only eight seats and a new coalition was formed, once more headed by Balkenende, who swapped the Fortuynists for the Democrats as a junior partner. Like its predecessor, this government also opted for a rather populist agenda regarding immigration and integration (De Heer 2004). In immigration policy the combat against illegal immigration was reinforced and family migration from outside the European Union was severely curtailed. Asylum policies became much stricter and procedures for obtaining residence permits were made more cumbersome and much costlier. In integration policy a new approach has been developed as well. The overall idea is that migrants are to blame for their slow integration, while efforts to step up the process must come from their side. Acquiring Dutch citizenship, for example, has been made much more difficult and costly, which has provoked a dramatic plunge in naturalizations.

A significant change in the mandatory integration courses has also been announced. These courses will no longer be offered free of charge by the local government. In line with free market ideologies it will be the newcomer's own responsibility to find a course, to register and pay for it, and, eventually, to pass a mandatory language-and-culture test that has to be taken within three and a half years after the initial settlement in the Netherlands. Immigrants who fail that test will be fined and will be disqualified from permanent settlement (Entzinger 2004). In many other fields of government policy similarly compulsory measures have been taken or announced that aim at stepping up the migrants' integration. Most of these leave little or no room for a public recognition of the migrants' cultural identity. The Christian Democrats in particular, traditionally champions of pillarization and therefore of multiculturalism, emerged from their eight years in opposition as fervent nationalists and as proponents of immigrant assimilation. This led to the paradox that migrants who initially had been encouraged to preserve their own identity were now blamed for insufficiently identifying with Dutch culture. Today, acknowledging religious and ethnic diversity is no longer considered a public responsibility, let alone facilitating its institutionalization.

Regular surveys by the Social and Cultural Planning Office of the Netherlands indicate a decline in acceptance of multiculturalism among the Dutch population (Dagevos, Gijsberts, and van Praag 2003). More than before, immigrant integration appears to be defined in terms of their loyalty to and identification with 'Dutch values and norms', rather than in terms of their social and institutional participation. Several observers have noticed a decrease in mutual understanding and acceptance between the native Dutch and the immigrant communities. The killing on 2 November 2004 in Amsterdam of film-maker Theo van Gogh, reputed for his powerful anti-Muslim statements, by a Muslim fundamentalist born and raised in the Netherlands led to a public outcry comparable to that after the Fortuyn assassination. It set in motion a countrywide series of assaults against mosques and Muslim schools, thus adding to the pre-existing social and political instability in a society apparently in search of a new identity.

4. The rise and fall of multiculturalist policies

In Chapter 1 of this volume Banting and Kymlicka notice a general trend in most immigration countries, particularly in Europe, that goes from assimilation to a gradual introduction of more multiculturalist elements in their policies. It shall be clear from the preceding paragraphs that this is not the situation in the Netherlands. On the contrary, this country started off on a strongly multiculturalist agenda. In the last few years it seems to have turned into one of the most assimilative countries of Europe, a trend that it shares above all with Denmark. Yet, it remains to be seen to what extent this development is reflected by concrete policy measures. In Chapter 2 of this volume Banting and Kymlicka list eight policy fields as potentially the most common or emblematic forms of multiculturalism for immigrants. Even though their selection has a Canadian flavour, it is still worthwhile to see how these eight have been faring in the Netherlands.

1. *Constitutional, legislative or parliamentary affirmation of multiculturalism, at the central and/or regional and municipal levels.* During the 1970s and 1980s multiculturalist policies for immigrants were supported by almost the entire political spectrum in the Netherlands. This can be explained primarily in the light of the Dutch history of pillarization. Without much reflection the pillarization model was applied to the new immigrant ethnic minorities. Pre-existing constitutional and other legislative arrangements in a number of areas enabled the creation of separate facilities for these minorities and accounted for their funding, particularly in education and in public broadcasting. In the 1990s multiculturalism gradually lost some of its shine, and in the new millennium it almost completely disappeared from the Dutch political agenda. Nevertheless, and in spite of the current rhetoric, the practice of Dutch integration policy still bears significant aspects of multiculturalism, particularly at the municipal level. Local authorities often find it difficult to involve immigrants in policy making without acknowledging their specific ethnic background as a relevant factor. Consultative bodies for immigrants have continued to exist nationally and sometimes also locally, but they have lost much of their influence.

2. *The adoption of multiculturalism in the school curriculum.* Under the pillarized system Dutch schools are free to decide their own curriculum; only the final exams are centralized. However, from the very onset the public authorities have encouraged schools to accommodate ethnic diversity as a fact of society in their teaching. On the whole this has been more successful in ethnically mixed areas, where it is impossible to close one's eyes to the dramatic social and cultural changes. Besides, Dutch law guarantees equal treatment of all religious communities wishing to establish a school, provided, of course, that certain requirements have been fulfilled. As a consequence of this law some fifty Muslim primary schools and two Muslim secondary schools have been founded in the past twenty years, as well as several Hindu schools. All are fully subsidized by the state. Many Muslim schools are looked upon with growing suspicion, but closing them would require a constitutional change that will also affect Protestant, Catholic, and other forms of non-public education.

3. *The inclusion of ethnic representation/sensitivity in the mandate of public media.* Here too, the Dutch tradition of pillarization has made it easy to accommodate pluriformity that stems from immigration. Most public broadcasting at a national level is in the hands of associations or agencies that are founded on commonly shared religious or ideological beliefs. Meanwhile, two Muslim, a Hindu, and a Buddhist agency have been added to the pre-existing patchwork, each with a few hours of radio and television time per month. Additional legal provisions have been made to ensure that a certain percentage of public broadcasting time is dedicated to issues of multiculturalism. However, the government recently announced that it would discontinue this arrangement, yet another sign of a growing scepticism about multiculturalism.

4. *Exemptions from dresscodes, Sunday-closing legislation, etc.* This issue at times gives rise to heated disputes, particularly on headscarves. The general rule here is that private institutions, including schools, are free to decide for themselves about dress codes. In a vast majority of cases the wearing of headscarves is allowed and unproblematic. There have been a few interesting cases before the Commission for Equal Treatment, which has ruled a ban on wearing headscarves as part of a uniform—e.g. in court, or by the police—to be discriminatory. However, the Commission only has a consultative status and the public authorities have refused to follow that ruling. Occasionally a row arises when local authorities forbid their desk clerks to wear headscarves. In late 2005 the Dutch Parliament

adopted a motion forbidding women to wear a burqa in public places. After this had occurred some MPs realized that they had never really seen this happen: a clear illustration of the current anti-Muslim climate in the Netherlands. Sunday-closing laws do not seem to be an issue in the Netherlands, probably because these have been relaxed anyway. An issue that does lead to strong disputes regularly is the construction of mosques. How 'exotic' are they allowed to look and how much noise may they spread? The very strict rules for physical planning, construction, and the environment in the Netherlands, combined with opposition from the neighbours, often make mosque building a very tedious process. In recent years, the changing mood in the country has not made this easier.

5. *Allowing dual citizenship.* During the heydays of the Minorities' Policy, in the 1980s, migrants were not encouraged to acquire Dutch citizenship. The leading principle was that foreign residents should be treated like citizens in as many areas as possible. This explains, for example, the introduction of local voting rights for foreigners in 1985. The idea that encouraging migrants to acquire a Dutch passport might enhance their loyalty to Dutch society was alien to the strong cultural relativism that prevailed in those days. In 1992 this approach was replaced by one that allowed dual citizenship for anyone who opted for a Dutch passport. This led to an enormous increase in naturalizations. Many new citizens did not object to becoming a citizen of the Netherlands, but they also wished to preserve ties with their country of origin, for emotional or for pragmatic reasons. In 1997 dual citizenship policies were dropped again, since a majority in the Senate felt that one could only be loyal to one country at the time (De Hart 2004). However, many exceptions to this rule continued to exist and obtaining a Dutch passport still remained rather easy. This changed once more in 2003, when the current government introduced a very strict—and rather costly—naturalization exam in which language proficiency and knowledge of Dutch society were tested. Since then the annual number of naturalizations has plummeted to a quarter of what it used to be.

6. *The funding of ethnic group organizations to support cultural activities.* In the 1970s and 1980s this was one of the most outspoken elements of Dutch policy for ethnic minorities. Since then it has become increasingly disputed and funding has almost stopped, particularly at the national level. Funding of *inter*cultural activities that aim at promoting a better understanding between communities has remained slightly more gener-ous. At times, interesting dilemmas may arise, for example when sports

clubs with an almost exclusively single-ethnicity membership ask for public support.

7. *The funding of bilingual instruction or mother-tongue teaching.* Both forms of instruction were introduced in the 1970s when the idea prevailed that migrants would return home. After this idea was dropped, mother-tongue teaching in particular continued to exist as an expression of recognition. It even became one of the hallmarks of the Minorities' Policy (Lucassen and Köbben 1992). At primary school level all major migrant communities were entitled to five hours of mother-tongue teaching per week, fully funded from public sources. To this end hundreds of teachers were recruited, particularly from Turkey and Morocco. In the early 1990s, however, doubts began to rise about its effectiveness. Mother-tongue teaching did not seem to enhance school achievement and it was seen as detrimental to the children's acculturation. The number of hours was gradually reduced and mother-tongue teaching was removed from the core curriculum, until the present government discontinued its funding altogether.

8. *Affirmative action for disadvantaged minority groups.* Affirmative action in the Netherlands has been focused largely on the labour market, not on education, as in countries with a more selective educational system. Throughout the 1980s a large number of targeted employment projects on behalf of the most disadvantaged communities were launched as part of the Minorities' Policy. These efforts became more systematized in 1993 with the introduction of a law copied from the Employment Equity Act in Canada. This law obliged employers to report regularly on the breakdown of their staff by ethnic origin as well as on their efforts to increase the number of employees with a minority background. Quotas were not set; mandatory reporting was thought to encourage employers sufficiently. The law was not a great success, largely because many employers refused to send in their annual reports. It was withdrawn in 2004. Nevertheless, during the years that the law was in force minorities' labour force participation rose dramatically. This, however, is widely seen as an effect of the booming economy, rather than of any of the targeted measures.

In conclusion, this overview of what Banting and Kymlicka see as the most emblematic forms of multicultural policies for immigrants confirms what we have seen in the earlier sections of this chapter. When first faced with large-scale immigration, the Netherlands set out on a truly multiculturalist course. Gradually, however, multiculturalism has lost some of its appeal, but in a number of fields it certainly has not disappeared altogether. Today's assimilative rhetoric, particularly at the national level, disguises the perpetuation of certain multicultural practices. Many of these find their roots in pillarization, others in a pragmatism which is based on the view that ethnic diversity has become a characteristic of Dutch society that cannot be ruled out altogether, even if one might wish to do so. The authors of Chapter 2 of this volume quite rightly qualify the Netherlands as modestly multiculturalist.

5. Minorities and the welfare state

We will now focus more sharply than so far on the welfare state, the second main element of the central hypothesis of this volume. As indicated before, the relative decline in public social expenditures has been larger in the Netherlands than in any other major Western country, especially during the 1990s. This was partly an effect of the above-average growth of the Dutch economy, particularly during the second half of that decade. The GDP went up faster than in most other European countries and unemployment, which was in double digits during much of the 1980s and still hovered around 8 per cent in 1995, dwindled to less than 4 per cent in 2000. However, this does not fully explain the decline in social spending which has occurred in the Netherlands since 1983. That year was an all-time high with 19.9 per cent of GDP being spent on social security provisions. Twenty years later, in 2003, this percentage had gone down to a mere 12.3 (Bos 2006: 32). Table 6.1 shows the share of each programme in total social security spending for the two years considered, 1983 and 2003, as well as the absolute and relative decline in these during the two decades that separate those years.

It must be noted that in most cases the decline in social security is due to a drop in the number of persons entitled, rather than to a lower level of the provisions. In the Netherlands most social security benefits are linked by law to the statutory minimum wage. Although the minimum wage has been increasing less rapidly than the average wage level, this alone cannot explain why the share of social security spending in the Dutch GDP went down by almost two-fifths in twenty years' time. Since the late 1980s consecutive governments have pursued very active policies to encourage people on social security to return to the labour market. This explains much of the dramatic drop in persons entitled to unemployment benefits and to public assistance ('welfare'). The substantial drop in family allowances is largely due to demographic effects and to the introduction

Table 6.1 Social security spending in the Netherlands as a percentage of Gross Domestic Product, 1983–2003

	1983	2003	1984–2003	
			Change in % of GDP	1983 = 100
All social security spending	19.9	12.3	−7.6	62
Public old age pensions	6.1	5.3	−0.8	87
Family allowance	1.8	0.7	−1.1	39
Sickness allowance	1.4	0ᵃ	−1.4	—
Disability allowance	3.7	2.5	−1.2	68
Unemployment benefits	2.9	1.2	−1.7	41
Public assistance	2.6	1.6	−0.9	62
Individual rent subsidies	0.4	0.4	−0.1	—
Other	1.0	1.3	0.3	130

[a] The sickness allowance scheme has been privatized.

Source: Bos (2006: 32).

of a new grant scheme for students. The access to disability schemes has also been made more difficult. In the 1980s these schemes were often used as unemployment schemes 'with a golden rim'.

In the period 1983–2003 total public spending on distributive policies went down from 36.3 to 27.3 per cent of the GDP, i.e. by nine percentage points (Bos 2006: 14). This means that distributive policies other than direct income transfers (i.e. social security) have almost kept pace with the growth of the economy. Such policies include education and health care, but also 'workfare' and other programmes aiming at redirecting the unemployed to the labour market as well as mandatory language classes and 'integration courses' for new arrivals. The decrease in social security spending has not led to more poverty, but rather to higher labour force participation rates. The provisions of the welfare state have not really been reduced, but access to them has been made much more difficult than before and many of the beneficiaries have been successfully redirected to employment.

Our interest here lies primarily in the relationship between changes in the welfare state and the decline of multiculturalism. The underlying idea is that the welfare state requires a redistribution of scarce resources, which can be achieved more easily in a society that is culturally homogeneous. Such a society is assumed to generate stronger feelings of mutual solidarity than one in which multiculturalism is publicly recognized or even institutionalized, as in the Netherlands. Of course, this argument is only valid if the use of welfare provisions is unevenly spread over the different communities, since this generates intercommunity income transfers. To what extent is this the case in the Netherlands?

The answer to this seemingly simple question very much depends on the programme considered as well as on the period studied. Besides, there are also significant differences between the different communities. Initially, large-scale immigration of low-skilled workers from Turkey and Morocco was extremely beneficial to the welfare state. In the 1960s and 1970s these hard-working people contributed to it, but they seldom used any of its benefits. This changed drastically when many of them lost their jobs in the 1980s and became entitled to unemployment or disability allowances, and later also to public assistance. Some observers have argued that the generosity of these allowances kept many former 'guest workers' trapped in the Netherlands and made them decide to let their families join them (Entzinger and van der Meer 2004: 115). Going back would have meant losing one's only source of income, but staying on without any prospects prevented them from integrating. There can be little doubt that this has also had a negative impact on the opportunities for many of the 'guest workers'' children.[4]

The absolute number of people with an immigrant background has gone up substantially during the past decades, particularly of people with a non-Western background. In 1980 about 0.5 million people in the Netherlands had a non-Western background, while this number had risen to 1.7 million in 2005. It is not surprising, therefore, that their share in social policy benefits has also gone up. But are they also over-represented among the beneficiaries? A study carried out in 2003 by the Netherlands Bureau for Economic Policy Analysis (CPB) revealed that the relative claim on disability allowances among migrants of non-Western origin was 24 per cent higher than among the Dutch (Roodenburg, Euwals, and Ter Reele 2003: 66). The corresponding figure for unemployment benefits was 57 per cent, for rent subsidies 184 per cent, and for public assistance 337 per cent. At present almost 40 per cent of those who are entitled to public assistance ('welfare') are of non-Western origin, while this category constitutes only 10 per cent of the population of the Netherlands (de Beer 2004). Contrary to common belief, large segments of the second generation are doing much better than their parents. In 2001, 7 per cent of all second generation immigrants of non-western origin between 15 and 35 years of age were living on social security, as against 5 per cent for the non-immigrant Dutch and 17 per cent for first-generation immigrants of that same age group (CBS 2003: 109).

---

[4] For other migrant communities, particularly those with post-colonial origins, the situation is less dramatic. On average, they are better educated and, as a consequence, they have had more opportunities and encountered less discrimination.

The over-representation of minorities is not confined to the social security system, but can also be found among those who benefit from other social policy instruments. Given their relatively high levels of unemployment, it is not surprising that people of migrant background were heavily represented in the 'workfare' programmes that were introduced by the 'purple' coalition government (1994–2002), but that have been discontinued since then. Special teaching facilities make expenses on primary education 48 per cent higher for a pupil of non-western origin than for a Dutch pupil. However, this over-representation does not hold for all public services. The CPB study mentioned earlier found no differences in expenditure on health care, while the per capita costs of higher education for ethnic minorities were actually lower than for the Dutch, an effect of their under-representation in this form of schooling. The same applies to the most costly of all social security provisions, the public old age pension scheme. Relatively few minority members are 65 or older, so overall minority entitlements under the scheme are well below those for the population as a whole. Besides, many immigrants who are over 65 have not contributed to the system long enough to draw the full benefits from it.

Notwithstanding these nuances, the overall picture is that the minority share in social security and in other social policy instruments is well above the national average. Has this precipitated the introduction of cuts and stricter policies in the past twenty years? This question is very hard to answer. Total public spending on schemes with relatively high minority participation (unemployment, public assistance) has indeed been reduced by a larger percentage than spending on other schemes. However, this is the outcome not of a dramatic reduction in the level of benefits, but rather of successful reintegration policies into the labour market. It is interesting to note that some of the most authoritative analyses of trends in social security hardly point at the immigrant factor in their explanation of the changes in the Dutch social security system of the past decades. A much stronger emphasis is put on many other good reasons why the welfare state needed to be reformed, such as individualization, increased flexibility in labour relations, rising levels of education, rising levels of expectations, and the need to counter a natural tendency for expansion (Beltzer and Biezeveld 2004; Arts, Entzinger, and Muffels 2004). Immigration may only be one of many factors. However, the relative success of the reform of the Dutch welfare state has produced a situation where only those who really are at a great distance from the labour market can make use of social benefits, particularly public assistance and disability benefits. These are precisely the two schemes that include comparatively many people of immigrant origin with low skills, insufficient linguistic competencies and social abilities, or with war traumas, as in the case of refugees. So we find ourselves in the paradoxical situation that the immigrant share in some of the most prominent parts of the social security system has increased as a result of the successful reform of that system.

This paradox is likely to become even more outspoken in the coming years, since an increase of the immigrant population of non-Western background is to be expected as a result of continuing immigration, relatively high birth rates, and the high incidence of single-parent families among many of these communities. This prospect serves as a justification for the present government in curtailing family migration and fighting illegal immigration. In 2004 the Social and Cultural Planning Bureau conducted a survey in which the Dutch were asked about their views on the future of social security. Seventy-four per cent of the respondents thought that social security would go down even further during the next fifteen years. Asked about the major reasons for this, 37 per cent referred to the need for general cuts in the public budget, 25 per cent to the ageing of the population, and only 12 per cent to immigration. All other answers (e.g. a further EU expansion, large-scale unemployment, or a decrease in solidarity among the population) scored less than 5 per cent (SCP 2004: 331). This finding contrasts strikingly with the answers to another question in the same survey, in which 74 per cent of the population acknowledged that 'the social security system will have become unaffordable in 2020 because of continuing immigration' (SCP 2004: 168). In an attempt to explain this discrepancy the Planning Bureau hypothesizes that 'continuing immigration may be seen by many as one of the factors putting strains on social security, but not necessarily as the major factor' (SCP 2004: 355).

6. Recognition vs. redistribution: The Dutch case analysed

Can we conclude, therefore, that the case of the Netherlands illustrates that multiculturalism and the welfare state are indeed incompatible, and that the Dutch way of resolving this tension has been to set limits to both? For a more precise answer to this question let us review the three lines of argument that Banting and Kymlicka present in Chapter 1 of this book. The first argument, the *crowding-out effect*, is certainly the most political of the arguments they discuss. It assumes that the energy that advocates of multiculturalism spend on this issue diverts attention from enhancing economic redistribution. In other words, while the political left tries to achieve its multiculturalist agenda, the political right is dismantling the welfare state. In the Netherlands, like anywhere else, the strongest advocates of the welfare state certainly are on the political left, but their multicultural efforts were not at the expense of their redistribution objectives. On the contrary, the idea of 'equity'—each ethnic community should have its proportional share in the distribution of scarce resources—was crucial to them. The main issue of the Minorities' Policy was how to reconcile striving for diversity with striving for equality. In addition, multiculturalism was also endorsed quite strongly by the Christian Democrats, who had always been in the political centre. As convinced communitarians they are the traditional vanguards of pillarization. When, in 2002, they returned to government after an unprecedented interruption of eight years, they had moved somewhat to the right and their views had changed from multiculturalist to nationalist. There is very little evidence, however, that the minorities' apparent over-representation in the use of social benefits played an immediate role in this change of political priorities.

Rather, it was the view that multiculturalism perpetuates the migrants' social and economic marginality that had generally been gaining momentum. The Minorities' Policy, however good its intentions for recognition may have been, confirmed the newcomers in their being different and therefore tended to exclude them from mainstream Dutch society, instead of including them. The pillarization model that had worked so well in the past for emancipating indigenous religious and ideological minorities did not at all have the same effect for the immigrant ethnic minorities. Their numbers were too small. It was impossible to create sufficient institutional arrangements for each community and the ethnic minorities were never needed for coalition building. Above all, however, classical pillarization only worked because the pillars, in spite of an absence of contacts at the grass roots level, shared enough commonalties. For most immigrant minorities this was not the case: many did not speak Dutch and they were not encouraged to do so until the mid-1990s. An active citizenship policy was also lacking until then. When it turned out that the strong emphasis on multiculturalism might have prolonged the migrants' minority status, publicly sponsored institutional separatism was gradually abandoned and replaced by an integration policy that tried to play down the culture card. From the early 1990s onwards culture was declared a private affair, the concept of ethnic minority became less prominent, and improving the immigrants' labour force participation, their linguistic abilities, and their level of education became central policy objectives. The idea was that a fuller social and economic participation of migrants would foster their integration and also decrease their dependence on social policies. Actually, this shift can be interpreted with what Banting and Kymlicka label as the *misdiagnosis effect*: the focus on cultural difference displaced the attention to class.[5] One could say that the delicate balance between diversity and equality, characteristic for Dutch policy making in the 1980s, gradually shifted towards promoting more equality, even if this was at the expense of diversity.

Meanwhile, however, some dramatic changes took place in Dutch society, which at first remained largely unnoticed by most observers. While politicians of the 'purple' coalition in the 1990s prided themselves for having facilitated a much better integration of immigrants into the major institutions of Dutch society, such as the labour market and the school system, the definition of what integration actually meant appeared to change. This change can probably be understood best with another line of argument suggested by Banting and Kymlicka, *the corroding effect*. In this line of argument, stressing differences between communities would erode solidarity, lead to interethnic tensions, and hence undermine public support for redistribution.

The answer that the present government has formulated to this challenge is to stress the need for assimilation to mainstream culture and to require the migrants to identify more strongly with the Netherlands. This, indeed, has long been overlooked as a relevant issue. Perhaps this is one of the biggest differences between classical immigration countries such as Canada, the United States, and Australia on the one hand and countries that have been confronted with immigration more or less against their will, as in most European states. Indeed, only few immigrants identify more strongly with the Netherlands than with their country of origin, particularly among the Muslim communities. In a survey among Rotterdam youngsters of Turkish and Moroccan origin—first and second generation—we found that more than three-quarters of them claimed that they felt Turkish or Moroccan, rather than Dutch (Phalet, van Lotringen, and Entzinger 2000). To many observers this came as a surprise; others saw

[5] Banting and Kymlicka also mention *race* as a possible alternative to culture in diagnosing the true reasons for the problems minorities face. All examples they mention refer to the African-Americans in the United States, and indeed, race, though not totally absent from the public discourse in the Netherlands, does not have the same relevance in public policy making as it does in the USA.

it as a logical consequence of decades of cultural recognition and social marginalization. In any case, the idea that Dutch multiculturalism has failed has become broadly accepted in the past five years. It has become manifest that successful multicultural policies presuppose a sufficient degree of loyalty to the nation-state where the migrants actually live. This is in line with what Castles and Miller have observed for a number of immigration countries (Castles and Miller 2003: 44). In the Dutch case, however, that aspect had been systematically overlooked. More recently, therefore, efforts have been stepped up to make migrants identify more strongly with the Netherlands, for example by intensifying their integration courses and by discontinuing much of what had remained of multiculturalist policies.

Yet, one may wonder how far a government in a liberal democracy can reach out in imposing a new national identity upon immigrants. Exerting too much force in this direction can easily become counter-productive and it may widen rather than narrow the divide. This is what many believe to be happening right now. So, while in the past the debate was largely on the tension between diversity and equality, it now seems to have shifted to the tension between diversity and unity. Unity, then, is interpreted by the current political majority in terms of national solidarity, which is also seen as a prerequisite for a perpetuation of the welfare state, albeit in a trimmed-down form.

Conclusion

Recognizing and facilitating multiculturalism was a major characteristic of Dutch policy making for immigrants from the beginning of large-scale immigration until about ten years ago. Since then it has quickly lost its momentum, particularly in the past three or four years. The Dutch welfare state has equally undergone substantial trimmings. Income redistribution was at its peak in 1983. Since then the income gap between the wealthiest and the poorest segments of the population has grown, though differences are still smaller than in most other European countries. The emphasis in distributive policies has shifted quite successfully from providing social security to developing social policy instruments meant to encourage labour participation. Overall public social expenditure as a percentage of GDP has gone down by one-quarter in the last twenty years, almost exclusively because of a decrease in the number of social security beneficiaries. Was this change in the welfare state precipitated by its earlier persistence on multiculturalism? This is the major question the editors of this book are asking.

The relatively high reliance on social policy instruments among immigrants, as well as growing feelings of dissatisfaction about this among the native-born population of the Netherlands, make one tempted to answer the leading question in the affirmative. Yet, I do think that in the Dutch case the relationship between multiculturalism and the welfare state is more complex. Institutionalized multiculturalism was long seen as the best possible form of recognizing the consequences of immigration; this was the case virtually throughout the political spectrum. In reality, however, it also provoked forms of social, economic, and cultural exclusion. Initially, this unintended effect was not recognized: the welfare state served as a safety net for those who were excluded. It was seen as politically highly incorrect to criticize the immigrants' over-representation in this safety net. The standard response to such criticism was that the country owed so much to the immigrants' hard work in the past—in the case of former 'guest workers'—and that the 'burden of colonialism' had to be carried—in the case of post-colonial migrants. However, as welfare provisions gradually became less generous and as the migrants' expectations rose, the safety net no longer worked adequately.

As a reaction to this, policy efforts to promote immigrant participation in the country's major institutional areas, such as employment, schooling, and housing were stepped up. These efforts have been relatively successful, even though this success was largely facilitated by very favourable economic conditions, especially in the 1990s. The immigrants' growing numbers and their claims for a fuller participation demanded from the original population a degree of acceptance that until then had not been necessary. It also required from the migrants a stronger orientation towards Dutch society and the understanding that their future would lie in the Netherlands rather than in their country of origin or in that of their parents. Both sides found it hard to come to terms with the new situation. Against this backdrop perpetuating multiculturalism as a major element of public policy would have been counter-productive. The emphasis in policy making shifted from recognition of cultural difference to redistribution of economic opportunities.

The reaction to this came sooner than expected. The definition of integration as the general public expected it to happen shifted from promoting institutional participation to acculturation, in many cases even to assimilation. Dropping multiculturalism was interpreted as 'becoming like us'. However, cultural differences did not disappear as quickly as

199

many in the dominant population had expected and it remains to be seen how far this really is a requirement for the proper functioning of a liberal-democratic society. In recent years, the worldwide climate of polarization, in which fears of terrorism and of Islam play a dominant role, have activated latent interethnic tensions, and made the government opt for a more assimilationist course, which can easily become counter-productive. At the same time, however, some major conditions that are known to foster immigrant assimilation are not fulfilled. The hurdles towards Dutch citizenship have been made much higher, newcomers will soon have to pay for their own integration courses, and permanent residence will only be granted after a successful language-and-culture test. Fines for not complying with these rules will be hefty. On the whole, the anti-immigrant rhetoric of the present government, particularly when addressed at Muslims, is not likely to produce the desired effects, unless its hidden ambition would be to keep migrants in the margins of society.

Looking back on the past decades the link between recognition and redistribution only seems to be an indirect one in the Dutch case. Indeed, multiculturalism was dropped at a time when welfare claims among immigrant communities were high and when some major cuts in social policy were carried through. This empirical link, however, does not nec-essarily imply a causal relationship. Multiculturalism seemed to foster the migrants' dependency on welfare arrangements, but this was not a signif-icant reason for the reforms in redistributive policies. The analysis in this chapter shows that those who advocated a break with multiculturalism used the welfare state argument only sparsely. Much more significant were the wish to prevent a further marginalization of immigrants and the desire to stress unity rather than difference as a binding element in society. However, unity fosters solidarity, and solidarity also lies at the basis of the welfare state. Thus, in an indirect manner the Dutch case still seems to confirm the central hypothesis of this book.

Still, as an afterthought to this conclusion on the Netherlands, it remains interesting to observe that, in comparative terms, a rather strong empirical relationship exists between multiculturalist policies and the welfare state, while logically the two cannot be reconciled so easily. The intervening variable here seems to be the state. Multiculturalism and redistributive social policies both require a strong state. This explains why in Europe we find (or found?) the most outspoken examples of both in the Nordic countries and in the Netherlands, and much less so in the southern countries. Canada also has a lot more of both than the United States does. However, the Dutch example shows that the combination of the two can only survive if some additional conditions are fulfilled. A basic requirement is that the migrants identify sufficiently with their new country. Another requirement is a sufficient degree of solidarity between the communities that together build society. Both were neglected for too long in the Netherlands. Paradoxically, the drastic break with multiculturalism and the recent emphasis on assimilation are not very likely either to help achieve this objective.

7

Multiculturalism in Germany: Rhetoric, scattered experiments, and future chances

Peter A. Kraus and Karen Schönwälder

In the German public debate, multiculturalism has fallen out of favour. But at the same time, the concept—or rather the spectre—of multiculturalism is more present than ever before. While few people nowadays commit themselves to an explicitly multicultural agenda, conservatives and the far right hardly miss a chance to confirm their determination to stand in the way of Germany's allegedly threatening transformation to a multicultural society.

In fact, multiculturalism in Germany has so far mainly existed at the level of discourse and not as a consistent political programme. No present or past federal or regional government has subscribed to an explicitly multicultural agenda. And yet, elements of multiculturalism policies do exist. This chapter will discuss how this is possible, and why it is at the same time unlikely that multiculturalism policies will in the near future be extended. It will further offer a discussion of how this may be related to the structure and development of the welfare state. Currently, developments seem to be determined by the new emphasis on the social and cultural integration of immigrants which, in Germany as in other European countries, reflects a growing concern with the overall integration of an increasingly heterogeneous society. While there are competing conceptions of integration, at least one line of argument claims that cultural diversity and social integration are incompatible and that, in

Thanks to Thomas Faist, Will Kymlicka, Keith Banting, and the participants of a Kingston workshop for many helpful comments and suggestions.

order to defend the German social model, it is necessary to counter trends towards more ethnic diversity.

1. Emergence and meaning of 'multiculturalism'

Multiculturalism emerged late in West German debates, and it was and remains mostly a slogan rather than a precise policy. Although some contemporaries already in the early 1970s realized that immigration would result in a more plural society, an active promotion of cultural pluralism and minority rights within Germany was not an issue. Within the Social Democratic and Liberal coalition governments of the period from 1969 to 1982 only some outsiders were willing to openly accept that immigration was about to transform German society (see Schönwälder 2001). When the Social Democrats reluctantly began to move towards an acceptance of given realities, they soon lost the opportunity to shape government policy. The programme of the Conservative-led Kohl government, which took over in autumn 1982, emphasized nation and national identity, and this ruled out explicit multiculturalism policies.

Nevertheless, in the 1980s and early 1990s the 'multicultural society' became an influential idea in intellectual and, to some extent, political discourses. The first to pick up the term were social workers and pedagogues who responded to international debates. From the late 1970s, academics and teachers discussed concepts of 'intercultural education' (Schulte 1990; Nitzschke 1982). A breakthrough came around 1980 when 'multiculturalism' became a symbolic rallying point for many left-wing or liberal-minded West Germans who wanted to resist a shift of public opinion against immigration (see Schönwälder 1991) as well as oppose a conservative policy turn towards national identity and a new line of argument in the public debate according to which Germans and some immigrant groups could never coexist harmoniously (Fijalkowski 1991: 245; Schönwälder 1996b: 166–9). 'In the Federal Republic, we live in a multicultural society,' exclaimed a programmatic document for the 1980 'Tag des ausländischen Mitbürgers' (Day of the Foreign Co-citizen) (Ökumenischer Vorbereitungsausschuss 1980).[1] Germans were called upon to accept the undeniable fact of immigration and to embrace the new cultural plurality. As the declaration suggested, it was time to replace

---

[1] The paper stated: 'Wir leben in der Bundesrepublik in einer multikulturellen Gesellschaft.' The Day of the Foreign Co-Citizens was introduced in 1970 by a Committee of the two major Churches.

the notion that West Germany was part of a German community of fate, bound together by language, culture, history, and ethnic descent, with a new self-perception based on pride in the liberal and democratic constitution.

About ten years later, the slogan of a multicultural German society reached the peak of its influence. Around 1990, many left-wing and liberal Germans felt a need to counter a potential resurgence of nationalism accompanying national unification. By emphasizing that Germany was a multicultural country, they wanted to express that the times of national homogeneity were over (if they had ever existed), that immigration and ethnic plurality within German society were unchangeable facts, and that this ethnic plurality was a positive element Germans should embrace and shape—rather than continuing to deny the fact of immigration. Throughout, rather than a precise political concept, multiculturalism signified a general attitude, a commitment to tolerance and anti-racism.

Support for multicultural ideas and concepts came from the Green Party,[2] from within the Churches, welfare organizations concerned with counselling services for foreigners, parts of the trade unions, and from individual Social Democrats as well as Christian Democrats (Cohn-Bendit and Schmid 1992; Frank 1995; Geißler 1990). Some scholars assume that the concept of the multicultural society originated in the framework of the Lutheran Church's academies (Fijalkowski 1991: 244), and it certainly found major supporters among Christians who emphasized the need for mutual acceptance of and interchange between cultures and religions.[3] Even the Christian Democratic Union, on the initiative of their general secretary Heiner Geißler, in 1982 organized a Conference at which the question whether Germany was 'on its way to a multicultural society' played a prominent part (Geißler 1983). While Geißler invested considerable energy in propagating the idea of multiculturalism, his party, from 1982 the leader of a new government coalition under Chancellor Helmut Kohl, overall remained hostile to such an approach. Until 1998, there was no real chance that wide-ranging and explicit multiculturalism policies would be implemented on the federal level. Apart from the composition

[2] In 1990 they explained that multiculturalism referred to a conception of society that involved the reshaping of all spheres of life. It did not mean the mere coexistence of cultures but intercultural involvement with each other (Die Grünen 1990: 19).

[3] See e.g. the conference publication edited by Jürgen Micksch (1983), a leading spokesperson of the Lutheran Church (EKD) on the issue. It is however a misconception that the debate originated in the conservative Christian Democratic Party and that Heiner Geißler introduced the term 'multicultural society' to West German debates.

of the governing majority, other developments contributed to conditions unfavourable for MCPs: the breakdown of the wall had renationalized the terms of political debate in an enlarged Federal Republic. In the critical period of autumn 1989, East German protest movements had rediscovered not only democracy but also the German nation and switched from the slogan 'We are *the* people' to 'We are *one* people'. Huge financial transfers from West to East have, since 1990, been justified by continuous appeals to national solidarity among Germans. Not before 1998, when the Social Democrats and Green Party were elected into power, were conditions created which enabled the transformation of the previously exclusive citizenship regime (in 1999) and the passing of a law acknowledging past and future immigration (in 2004)—but even then multiculturalism did not become official policy (see e.g. Kruse, Orren, and Angenendt 2003; Schönwälder 2004).

2. Traces of multiculturalism policies

Given this background, it is hardly astonishing that there is very little in Germany that deserves to be described as multiculturalism policies (MCPs) as defined by Banting and Kymlicka, i.e. policies that 'go beyond the protection of the basic civil and political rights guaranteed to all individuals in a liberal-democratic state, to also extend some level of public recognition and support for ethno-cultural minorities to maintain and express their distinct identities and practices' (this volume). At least this is true if we refer to policies linked to an explicit programme of recognizing and promoting ethnic plurality. However, if we consider the eight policies Banting and Kymlicka list as the most common forms of immigrant MCPs, we find that some of these policies do in fact exist in Germany.

First, there is a strong relation between multiculturalism policies and traditional minority rights. The Federal Republic has, on the international stage, in the past decades been a supporter of collective rights for established national minorities. Already in the interwar years, Weimar Germany had pressed for such rights in order to strengthen the position of ethnic German groups in Central and East European countries (Schönwälder 1996a). To some extent, this tradition forms a basis for an acceptance of the legitimate claims of ethnic or linguistic minorities to public recognition and support for the preservation of their cultural identities. Considerable efforts were made to distinguish between established and immigrant minorities and to deny the latter minority rights. And yet, elements of a minority rights approach were, in the 1950s and 1960s, applied to the so-called *Heimatlose Ausländer*[4] and to foreign refugees. Specific attention was paid to helping them practise and retain their culture, educational system, and 'their ethnicity' (*Volkstum schlechthin*). Integration (*Eingliederung*) was the proclaimed aim, which was set against assimilation (*Einschmelzung*). In 1968, for example, federal and regional states made about 3.9 million marks available for this purpose (Bundesregierung 1969: 468–9). Soon after, this policy promoting the ethnicity of refugees and former Displaced Persons was discontinued. It had originally been motivated by the assumption that some groups would return to their homelands as well as by organicist conceptions of the *Volk* which linked the integrity of the individual to his or her *Volkstum*. Additionally, some small national or linguistic minorities, such as the Danes and the Sorbs, were granted explicit minority rights, and such rights are enshrined in the constitutions of a number of regional states (for more details see Hahn 1993). Foreign policy considerations were a major motivating factor.

Up to the 1980s, the idea had never come up that minority rights might be applied to the new immigrant groups. Given that they were not officially recognized as permanent residents, this is not astonishing. However, in the early 1990s calls were put forward to the effect that the protection of minority rights should be extended to all ethnic groups, and only last-minute interventions prevented the introduction in the German constitution of a general article on the protection of minorities (in 1994).[5] Its supporters had argued that a constitutional commitment to tolerance and the preservation of cultural and linguistic diversity would be a powerful symbolic act and an appropriate response to the racist violence of the early 1990s (see Guggenberger, Preuß, and Ullmann 1991: 128, 44; *Bericht der Gemeinsamen Verfassungskommission* 1993: 72). Explicitly, individual rights were regarded as insufficient. In the end, conservative opposition

---

[4] Literally 'homeless foreigners', the official term adopted in West German law for the Displaced Persons, i.e. mostly former forced labourers and Concentration Camp inmates.

[5] 'The state respects the identity of the ethnic, cultural and linguistic minorities' was the wording of a proposed article supported by a two-thirds majority in the Joint Committee on the Constitution (a parliamentary committee of Bundestag and Bundesrat) and a majority of the regional states (*Länder*). The intended article represented a much watered-down version and fell short of an effective minorities policy: a symbolic declaration of respect would not have given the minorities a right to funds for cultural activities or political representation. Still, it would have represented a strong symbolic form of recognition.

against any step towards pluralistic integration of immigrant minorities was crucial (see Schönwälder 1995; 1997: 203–12).[6] But in spite of its eventual failure, this example shows that, within German politics, there is considerable support for the right of national or ethnic groups to a preservation of their cultural identities.[7]

Dual citizenship is officially still unwanted, and the current citizenship law includes strict measures against its expansion. Nevertheless, as exceptions were granted, for example, to ethnic Germans who were allowed to retain their Polish citizenship, to Iranians who were not released from their former citizenship, as well as, for a time, a significant number of Turks, estimates put the number of Germans also holding another citizenship at several hundred thousand.[8]

Multiculturalism—or rather intercultural education—is an element of several school curricula. In 1996, the Kultusministerkonferenz (the body of the regional ministers for culture and education) passed recommendations on intercultural education in German schools. As Krüger-Potratz (2004) argues, ministers responded to internationalization, European integration, as well as an increasing cultural plurality within Germany. Aims include the promotion of tolerance and humanitarian principles, knowledge about and respect for other cultures, and the ability to deal peacefully with potential conflicts arising from the encounter of different ethnic, religious, and cultural groups. The regional authorities are encouraged to make sure that in school education no society or culture is marginalized or denigrated and that non-German students are offered opportunities for positive identification.

Mother-tongue education does exist—although there is considerable regional variation and it is not necessarily an element of multiculturalism policies.[9] Mother-tongue education is sometimes part of public education, but in some states organized by the sending states' consulates.[10] It is usually not integrated with regular education and attendance is voluntary

---

[6] Interior Minister Kanther insisted that he would not accept a policy leading to 'group egoism and separatism' (see Bundestag 1994: 20978).

[7] We do not, however, agree with the position that the German authorities, by organizing counselling services according to religion and nationality, deliberately encouraged ethnic group formation (Ireland 2004).

[8] After the introduction of the new citizenship law in 2000, conditions have in some respects become more restrictive. Those who, without the consent of the German authorities, retain or regain their previous citizenship after naturalization in Germany automatically lose their German citizenship.

[9] In the 1960s and 1970s mother-tongue education was part of a policy which envisaged the return of the migrant children to the countries of origin. Since the early 1980s, this objective is no longer pursued (see Reich 2000: 114).

[10] Due to Germany's federal structure, the situation varies in the different *Länder*.

(see Gogolin, Neumann, and Reuter 2001). Altogether the languages of the immigrant minorities play, at best, a marginal role in state education. The German educational system has responded only in a very piecemeal way to the challenges of heterogenization and its linguistic dimensions. No major structural reforms were introduced, teachers are not systematically prepared for teaching in ethnically plural classes, and adequate programmes for the education of non-native speakers have not been implemented.

Several cities with a high percentage of foreigners among their inhabitants, such as Essen (11.4 per cent in 2001), Cologne (18.8 per cent), Stuttgart (24.4 per cent), and Frankfurt on Main (22.5 per cent), have committed themselves to multicultural or intercultural policies. Detailed research on local policies is scarce. It seems there is often no clear agenda or policy statement, and the content and purpose of such policies remain vague. Typically, policies include measures intended to support the process of language acquisition and to improve the educational performance of children with an immigration background, the introduction of intercultural elements in school curricula, the development of community-based institutions and projects devoted to promoting contacts and exchange between native Germans and immigrants. More recently, attempts to adapt the structure of the local administration to a changed socio-cultural environment ('intercultural opening of institutions') have been at the centre of local policies (Filsinger 2002: 16–19; see also Ireland 2004: 60–115).

At the level of institution building, the most prominent example of local multicultural policies in Germany is the Office for Multicultural Affairs (OMCA, or, in German, Amt für Multikulturelle Angelegenheiten, AMKA), established in Frankfurt in 1989. The OMCA was created with the deliberate aim of coordinating the work of all administrative bodies in relation to issues of cultural pluralism. At the same time, through the composition of its staff, it was meant to act as a body that would give immigrants a voice within the local administration. It was considered an innovative institutional response to the city's pronounced multicultural profile. One of OMCA's main tasks has been to convince local government bodies of an agenda of anti-discrimination. Its approach, which depends entirely on persuasion, involves mediation, conflict resolution, counselling services, campaigns for tolerance, support for migrant organizations, the promotion of cultural activities, and measures to increase labour market participation of immigrants (see Amt für Multikulturelle Angelegenheiten 1990; Leggewie 1993: 46–60; Radtke 2003: 63–6).

There are bodies to consult with ethnic communities—or rather foreign citizens in Germany.[11] In the regional state of Northrhine Westphalia currently (autumn 2004) 97 such local bodies exist, elected by, on average, 13 per cent of the eligible electorate and organized in an umbrella organization now called Landesarbeitsgemeinschaft der kommunalen Migrantenvertretungen Nordrhein-Westfalen (LAGA NRW) (see www.laga-nrw.de). In Berlin a new body consisting of representatives of immigrant communities was formed in 2003, but it is too early to assess its impact. To some extent, the new bodies express the search for alternatives to the older Foreigners' Advisory Councils (*Ausländerbeiräte*). Assessments of the basis and role of these councils are more or less devastating—due to a set of different factors including their limited popularity with foreign citizens and their extremely limited rights (Hoffmann 2002).

Ethnic group organizations or activities are funded by the federal and the regional states as well as some local authorities. Thus the government of the regional state of Nordrhein-Westfalen regards the 'strengthening of the foreigners' ability to represent themselves' as an issue of great importance. It provides funding for a regional umbrella organization of the local representative bodies of migrants (*Migrantenvertretungen*) as well as for several projects (about 20) of ethnic group organizations (NRW 2000: 29, 32; Rütten 1998: 26–7). The new Conservative-led regional government promises extended support for the 'promotion of the cultural practices of immigrants'. A new *Aktionsplan Integration* states that the regional government pursues a policy that aims at 'achieving social, economic and legal equality accompanied by respect for cultural and religious differences'. Exactly the same phrase was used by the previous government led by the Social Democrats (NRW 2004, 2006). Other states and some local authorities also provide funding for such initiatives, but an overview for Germany and evaluations of the effects of such support on ethnic group organization or consciousness do not exist.

Bodies controlling the public broadcasting stations may include representatives of the foreign population—as in the case of the Rundfunkrat of the Westdeutscher Rundfunk.

There is no affirmative action in Germany. Following European Union legislation, an antidiscrimination law was finally passed in 2006, but it does not include elements of 'positive discrimination'.

---

[11] In some regional states, naturalized German citizens remain eligible to vote and to be elected.

There are no relevant exemptions from dress codes, other than those based on individual rights (like the right, on certain conditions, to wear a headscarf as a sales assistant).

All in all, at least some policies considered typical of the multiculturalism approach exist outside an explicit MCP framework.[12] Joppke and Morawska (2003) have described similar observations as '*de facto* multiculturalism', a phenomenon they distinguish from 'official multiculturalism policies'. They explain the coexistence of both—as is now common—with reference to a 'logic of liberal states'. Surely the norms any liberal democracy subscribes to, in particular respect for individual rights, religious freedom, and the freedom to practise one's own language and culture, are an important basis for the development of a plural society. Tolerance of other cultures and peaceful coexistence are nowadays common ideals in education, and not necessarily linked to policies aiming to actively promote the confidence and public recognition of minorities. But in order to explain the coexistence of integrative and exclusionary mechanisms and the sometimes seemingly contradictory processes at work, we need more complex and more country-specific explanations. They will have to take the interests and influence of different societal actors into account—who for instance in particular cities and regions have pushed for representation of immigrants and measures against discrimination. Additionally, further research is needed to determine what difference explicit and comprehensive multicultural programmes made—in comparison with the partial and muted implementation of partly similar measures in the absence of an explicit multicultural programme, as described here for Germany. In the recently revived debate about migrant integration explanatory frameworks relying on assumed 'models' of integration or exclusion have been found wanting and hopefully more complex explanations for differences and common features will be developed. For the time being, the authors of this chapter will continue to assume that policies aiming, on the one hand, at assimilation, i.e. the disappearance of group differences, and, on the other, at pluralism, i.e. a continued relevance and recognition of ethnic diversity, have contributed to the development of different frameworks for the incorporation of immigrants into host societies.[13]

[12] A somewhat parallel observation has recently been made by scholars of integration policies who noted that, in spite of rather different concepts of membership, European states pursued fairly similar policies in order to further the social integration of immigrants.

[13] Joppke and Morawska take the legitimate criticism of the concept of national models of immigrant incorporation too far when they state that differences between liberal states are largely to be located on the level of 'political surface rhetoric' (2003: 7).

Consequently the question remains relevant what barriers may, in West Germany, have stood in the way of an adoption of explicit and more fully developed multiculturalism policies. Of a number of factors, some are linked to welfare state issues.

3. Multiculturalism, MCPs, and the welfare state

Obviously, explicit and comprehensive MCPs were unlikely to be introduced as long as it was officially assumed that no long-term immigration had occurred. However, the official insistence on Germany not being a country of immigration was always part of a contradictory approach. As early as the 1960s, discussions had begun about the consequences of the permanent immigration of at least some of the guest workers. In the early 1970s, it was a widespread consensus in the newspapers that the government's declared policy of integration could hardly mean anything but the eventual naturalization of the long-term immigrants. Hardly anyone, however, envisaged an ethnically plural German society. Rather than recognition of minority identities, social integration was seen as the key challenge (see Schönwälder 2001: 505–15, 616–17 with detailed references).

Among other factors, this focus on social integration rather than—as, for instance in Britain—on discrimination and rights was a reflection of traditions favouring a paternalistic attitude to the migrants and of the corporatism typical for the West German state at the time (Streeck 1997; Katzenstein 1987). From the 1950s, labour migrants were granted fairly wide-ranging social rights and more or less equal access to the work-related social insurance system. West Germany thus demonstrated that labour recruitment now was a different thing than forced labour under the Nazi regime. The German government additionally responded to demands of the sending states. But it was also relevant that West German corporatism was based on consensus building, and the consent of the trade unions to foreign recruitment depended on arrangements which ensured that foreign migrants would not be cheaper workers and endanger 'German' jobs. Social inclusion developed its own dynamic. As for instance Bade and Bommes (2000: 166, 172) have argued, a pragmatic policy of integration within welfare state structures contributed to a fairly advanced process of integration.

Arguably, the weight of corporatist structures in the German welfare state reduced the chance that the impact of immigration on social policy would become a controversial issue. In corporatist welfare regimes, social rights are, to a large extent, insurance based (Esping-Andersen 1990). Entitlements to welfare provisions are closely linked to participation in the labour market and the continuous payment of the required contributions to the unemployment, health, and pension insurances. Thus it was more difficult to accuse the guest workers of exploiting the German welfare system.

Furthermore, due to its plural structure and the large number of organizations involved, the German welfare system could be assumed to be more open to minority organizations. On the other hand, however, the established actors in such a corporatist welfare system are likely to defend their stakes against newcomers. Organizations linked to the social democratic movement and the churches still play an important role in the implementation of social integration policies targeting immigrants.

Even among those advocating migrants' rights, social inclusion was usually regarded as more important than cultural issues or civil rights.[14] While for instance in the United Kingdom the debate about immigrant and minority rights was strongly influenced by the Civil Rights struggles in the USA (and this encouraged the adoption of anti-discrimination measures and multicultural programmes), in Germany a similar parallel between American and European developments was not drawn. Rather, Germans felt reminded of their own experience with Polish migration and minority conflicts. At least for several post-war decades it was widely if falsely believed that minority conflicts had caused the First World War and in the long run Germany's decline towards Nazism and territorial dismemberment. When around 1980, Social Democratic Chancellor Helmut Schmidt publicly emphasized that West Germany would not, as a consequence of guest-worker immigration, follow the Yugoslav path towards a *Vielvölkerstaat* (a multinational state), he surely evoked associations of the Balkans as the site of nationality conflicts and the region where the First World War originated.

In the labour movement, the need for unity was one of the major lessons of the experience of Nazism. Any trend towards separation, like migrants' lists in elections for factory representatives, was eyed with great suspicion. To the present day, there is significant resistance within Social Democracy and the trade unions to policies promoting ethnic plurality. This partly has its roots in nationalism, but is also related to the great importance placed on unity as the basis of strength and welfare rights.

---

[14] See e.g. the position of the social democratic Arbeiterwohlfahrt (1973).

Historical experiences also to some extent explain why there is strong opposition against plural concepts within the German left and among liberal-minded people. Group rights and the promotion of a multicultural society are sometimes seen as expressions of nationalistic, biological, or at least culturalist conceptions of ethnic or national communities, conceptions which are seen as conflicting with the principles of a liberal society (see e.g. Oberndörfer 1994). Given the German past of extreme nationalism and Nazism, a particular sensitivity exists among anti-nationalists as regards a possible revival of *völkisch* perspectives. In intellectual debates a line of argument is influential which claims that multiculturalism policies might lead to even stricter separations within society and that individuals are in danger of being allocated a group identity which limits their freedom of choice. Like in the North American debate, the point is made that a focus on culture distracts from the more fundamental questions of social rights (e.g. Radtke 1991*a*).

In view of Germany's historical experiences, the refusal of left-wing analysts to make any concessions to a *völkisch* type of discourse is perfectly understandable. In some cases, however, this attitude seems to involve a strong antipathy against all kinds of political claims based on cultural identities (Radtke 1991*b*; Kaschuba 1995). Ultimately, the insistence on the priority of the social and the rejection of cultural explanations of inequality and injustice make it very difficult to develop an approach to diversity that acknowledges the independent weight cultural factors can have in the structuring of social and political relations in modern societies.

More recently, in 2004 and 2005, arguments against policies promoting group identities have assumed a new urgency. One key term in this debate is *Parallelgesellschaft* (parallel society)—a term summarizing fears of self-secluding ethnic communities, islands of non-Western values, social exclusion, and urban conflicts. The debate is related to worries about the overall integration of the increasingly heterogeneous Western societies—given various developments that threaten social cohesion and the welfare state ideal of equal opportunities and limited inequality. The fear exists that ethnic communities are contributing to disintegration by withdrawing into secluded communities or 'parallel societies'. There are obvious parallels between debates in different European countries and among European social democrats. The German debate is to date not as heated and the attack on multiculturalism not quite as urgent as in the Netherlands or in the UK, where of course multiculturalism has had more impact on policy. But there is a trend towards a closer

213

interconnection of debates in different European countries, and clearly developments mainly in the Netherlands do influence developments in Germany.[15]

As in the Netherlands and in the United Kingdom, intellectuals have played a part in stimulating the re-evaluation of multiculturalism. Parts of the left-liberal spectrum in Germany seem to have shifted from a multiculturalist discourse towards a growing emphasis on social integration, which is frequently related to cultural adaptation—or even assimilation. The German debate about segregation and 'parallel societies' can be traced back to a study directed by social scientist Wilhelm Heitmeyer (Heitmeyer, Müller, and Schröder 1997).[16] Published in 1997, the study drew attention to perceived dangerous developments on the edges of the majority society and to ethnic concentrations which—in this view— provided fertile ground for Islamic fundamentalism and an acceptance of violence among young Muslims. Although the study met with a lot of criticism, the concept of a 'parallel society' kept reappearing in discourses on immigration and integration policies. The Social Democratic Party, for instance, in its 'Government Programme, 2002 to 2006', declared that it was opposed to any consolidation of cultural parallel societies—thus alleging that such societies do exist in Germany (SPD 2002: 137).

The term 'parallel society' is not always used as a clearly defined concept which could be tested empirically. One, almost the only, systematic definition was offered by Thomas Meyer, an influential Social Democratic intellectual (2002).[17] In his view, the term 'parallel society' refers to social collectivities with a high degree of ethno-cultural homogeneity. Their situation vis-à-vis the majority society is characterized by spatial segregation and the development of a separate infrastructure close to institutional completeness. As Meyer (2002: 210–21) argues, there is a real danger that such structures may evolve in particular areas of Cologne, Hamburg, and Berlin. From his perspective, developments in the Netherlands, where, to some extent, the cultural 'pillarization' of immigrant groups received the support of political institutions, should be a warning for Germany. Like several academics today, he believes that the maintenance of cultural differences is one reason for the unsatisfactory social, economic, and

---

[15] In particular after the murder of Dutch film-maker van Gogh, references to developments in the Netherlands have become common in the German public debate. Even before, influential interventions, such as articles by Dutch author Paul Scheffer, used to be published in German newspapers.

[16] Heitmeyer is an influential voice in the social democratic debate in Germany.

[17] He is a member of the SPD Grundwertekommission, a committee concerned with defining and interpreting the 'basic values' in the party's political programme.

political integration, as the thus consolidated 'parallel societies' block the creation of interlocking opportunity structures conducive to the formation of social capital and trust.

Typically, Meyer's, like Heitmeyer's, concern is with social integration. Given the range of pressures exerted on the welfare state and the European social model, ethnic differences are seen as a further, potentially dangerous source of disintegration.

Furthermore—and this is the second strand from which current debates originate—ethnic differences are increasingly seen as one major cause of continuing social disadvantages on the part of children and young people with a migration background. As is argued, institutionalized ethnicity may provide alternatives to the cultural and social assimilation necessary for equal life chances (e.g. Heitmeyer 1998). Public debates about such social and educational disadvantages were revived by the publication of the results of the PISA 2000 study on student achievements in selected subjects (see Baumert and Schümer 2001). Compared to children in many other OECD countries, the results of those educated in the German system were disappointing. One recurrent motive in the public discourse following the 'PISA shock' has been the possible connection between the unsatisfactory performance of German schools and the number of children with a migration background and a non-German mother tongue. Indeed, in some parts of German towns and major cities, the share of children from immigrant communities already exceeds 25 per cent. In Frankfurt on Main, for instance, more than one-third of students in schools hold a foreign citizenship (35 per cent in 1998, see Straßburger 2001: 74). Their command of the German language, when entering school education, is often limited,[18] and the German education system fails to compensate quickly and adequately for such deficits.

Public discussions about the consequences of multilingualism for urban schooling frequently display a tendency to blame the victims. Thus an alleged unwillingness of some immigrant groups, the Turks in particular, to learn German, combined with ethnic concentrations enabling a withdrawal into secluded Turkish communities, are frequently held responsible for the problems occurring in school. The immigrants' allegedly insufficient cultural and social assimilation is seen as the root cause of their failure to achieve equal chances in the employment system. Even

---

[18] In Berlin, for instance, a recent assessment of the language competencies of all children about to enter school found that about one-quarter were in need of special support. A previous test had found that among children from families with a non-German language background about 80 per cent had only a limited knowledge of German.

worse, the presence of a large group of immigrant children is regarded as one cause for overall deficits of education affecting all children.

While obviously a certain extent of scapegoating and general anti-immigrant attitudes are involved, the German-language proficiency of immigrant children and possible connections between academic achievements, residential segregation, and ethnic community ties are serious problems which anyone interested in equal life chances should address. To date, knowledge about these connections is not very far advanced. It is, however, safe to assume that residential segregation occurs to a lesser extent in Germany than in some other countries (such as the USA, the UK and the Netherlands) (Häussermann and Siebel 2001) and that links between dense ethnic community ties and low academic achievement have not been established. When a recent study for the Bertelsmann foundation (Hörmel and Scherr 2004) claims that, in Germany, multicultural education contributed to a consolidation of group differences it is reiterating common objections against MCPs but surely not presenting an empirically based finding. After all, multicultural education hardly existed. Nevertheless, current trends point to a clear emphasis on the teaching of the German language. Under the pressures of a politically unfavourable climate as well as budgetary restrictions, mother-tongue education may be reduced even further.

To be sure, attitudes to integration and the resulting policy approaches are not uniform. Even within the government of Social Democrats and Green Party (1998–2005) different approaches coexisted. Thus Otto Schily, the Social Democratic Minister for the Interior, has in the past rejected any public support for the maintenance of Germany's new minorities. As he thinks, it would be wrong to promote the establishment of 'new homogeneous minorities' which he seems to identify with parallel societies, tensions, and conflicts ('Es ware verfehlt, wenn wir die Entstehung neuer geschlossener Minderheiten fördern würden.'). Instead, in his view 'The aim of integration is incorporation in the German cultural space. We cannot promote all kinds of other languages on top of that. This would lead to total chaos.' And, even more harshly: 'I tell you quite frankly: The best form of integration is assimilation' (2002a).[19] For Schily, linguistic integration is the key to social integration; the Turks' mother tongue should in future be German.

---

[19] Surprisingly, the interview cannot be found in the long selection of interviews with Otto Schily offered on the Minister's homepage (www.otto-schily.de). Schily has given other speeches in which he presented a more tolerant and plural idea of integration (see e.g. Schily 2002b).

The previous Federal Government's Commissioner for Migration and Integration, however, supported a more pluralistic conception,[20] and the Social Democratic Party has also on several occasions confirmed its commitment to a policy which emphasizes equal access to educational and other opportunities and refrains from any assimilatory pressures.[21] This programmatic platform leaves space for regional organizations to develop a more assimilationist policy or one that includes at least multicultural elements.

Overall, the leading principle of official government policy is nowadays expressed in the slogan of *Fördern und Fordern* ('promote and challenge' or: provide support and demand individual efforts)—a typical New Labour phrase. It legitimizes a focus on the individual who is offered some help but is also required to prove his or her willingness to cooperate and, for example, attend language classes. On a new government website, 'integration' is explained by emphasizing that individuals who desire to stay permanently in Germany have to fulfil certain requirements, first of all to learn German. German society, on the other hand, should grant permanent immigrants a wide-ranging participation in its societal, political and economic life, 'if possible' on an equal footing.[22] Group rights and legitimate claims to recognition do not really feature in this concept, rather the claim that no society can tolerate 'an internal separatism which is based on cultural divisions' may be read as a rejection of multiculturalism.[23] For the previous Interior Minister himself, the existence of ethnic communities and infrastructures is incompatible with integration and would lead to major divisions in German society (Schily 2002*a*).

It is not easy to identify the factors influencing Social Democratic and trade-union thinking on multiculturalism as frequently positions remain

[20] The (now renamed) Federal Government's Commissioner for Foreigners Affairs defined integration as a 'permanent process of consensus-building about the common fundaments and rules of co-existence in a community', a process that involves society as a whole. Equal chances and participation as well as the absence of discrimination are strongly emphasized (*Bericht der Beauftragten der Bundesregierung* 2000: 202, 205–6); see a similar conception in *Integrationspolitisches Memorandum der Bundesarbeitsgemeinschaft Freier Wohlfahrtspflege* (*c*.2001).

[21] See, for instance, a position paper of the parliamentary faction which emphasizes that ethnic minorities should be able to find themselves and their cultures represented in German social life. Cultural integration should involve a greater emphasis on the plurality of cultures and on cultural identities (SPD-Bundestagsfraktion 2001).

[22] See the new government website www.zuwanderung.de (accessed 10 Mar. 2005) which explains 'Zuwanderern soll eine umfassende, möglichst gleichberechtigte Teilhabe in allen gesellschaftlichen Bereichen ermöglicht werden. Zuwanderer haben die Pflicht, die deutsche Sprache zu erlernen sowie die Verfassung und die Gesetze zu kennen, zu respektieren und zu befolgen.'

[23] 'Einen inneren Separatismus, der auf kulturellen Trennungen beruht, hält eine Gesellschaft nicht aus.' www.zuwanderung.de (10 Mar. 2005).

clouded in vague declarations. To a considerable extent Social Democratic migration and integration policy is always determined by considerations as to xenophobic and racist attitudes among their supporters.[24] SPD politicians have been aware of the political developments in neighbouring countries such as Denmark, the Netherlands, and Austria, where populist and xenophobic right-wing groups were successful in attracting important portions of both the lower- and the middle-class vote, including segments traditionally supporting the socialists. The case of Austria was followed with particular concern by German social democrats, not only for reasons of cultural proximity, but also because the SPÖ had been substantially weakened in the course of the ascension of Haider's FPÖ in the 1990s (see Pelinka and Rosenberger 2003). Any measures of support for immigrant groups might be regarded as preferential treatment of newcomers and as competing with more legitimate claims of the German working class. Multiculturalism policies might endanger the political basis of Social Democracy and thus, in a way, also the basis for welfare state policies. Are such fears justified?

Implications of immigration for the welfare state have, for about thirty years, been a major issue in the (West) German political debate. In the early 1970s, the allegedly limited absorptive capacities of West German society provided one major justification for the stop to foreign labour recruitment. Later on, the accusation that immigrants and asylum seekers, in particular, make illegitimate claims on welfare state provisions became an established feature of the public discourse. However, links between multiculturalism, or more specifically, multiculturalism policies, and support for the welfare state are more difficult to establish. Empirically founded knowledge about the social acceptance of specific welfare state arrangements is altogether rather limited (Ullrich 2000a: 22). We do however know that the welfare state in general enjoys an extremely widespread acceptance among the populations of all Western industrialized societies, and that its acceptance is even higher in Europe than in the United States. Worries regarding a threatening welfare state backlash have altogether turned out to be unjustified (Ullrich 2000b: 132–4). We know less about what specific qualities of a welfare state system are likely to increase or to reduce its acceptance among the population. As it seems, social benefits targeted at only some groups of the population tend to be

---

[24] We are, however, not aware of a recent explicit debate on the potential electoral consequences of multiculturalism policies. It is more common for politicians to refer in a more general way to the voters' demand for strict immigration controls and effective integration policies.

less popular. But this is not true for all targeted programmes—student grants and housing benefits enjoy more support than unemployment benefits. It thus seems plausible that acceptance also depends on views of those benefiting from the programmes and of their needs and that, consequently, views of the ethnic minorities and of the legitimacy of their claims would be crucial.

Again, hard empirical evidence is scarce and we only have some hints: in a survey conducted by Munich's city authorities people were asked about issues the city should spend more or less money on. A surprisingly large share of almost 50 per cent of respondents thought that more money should be spent on the 'integration of foreign co-citizens', and only about 10 per cent wanted to see expenditure reduced (the rest thought it should stay the same) (Landeshauptstadt München 2002: 102). Surely 'integration' is not identical with multiculturalism policies, but at least these figures indicate that there may be considerable support for some measures immigrants would benefit from. At the same time, however, demands for a better adjustment of the foreigners' lifestyles to the German have, since the 1980s, consistently enjoyed majority support (*Datenreport* 2004: 585–6)—an observation that indicates resistance to ethnic pluralism. Asked whether they supported equal rights for selected immigrant groups, between 11 (for asylum seekers) and 44 per cent (for ethnic Germans from Eastern Europe) of respondents said that they should in all spheres have the same rights as Germans (figures were 23 per cent for Turks and 40 per cent for Italians). A large proportion were indifferent, but a maximum of 53 per cent opposed the granting of equal rights for asylum seekers (*Datenreport* 1997: 461).[25]

Generally, of welfare state aims, 'equality' enjoys less support than 'security' (Ullrich 2000*b*: 133). Andreß, Heien, and Hofäcker (2001: 108–9) further found that of measures aiming to ensure equality of men and women those intending a general improvement of employment opportunities enjoy considerable support; when asked specifically about preferential treatment of female applicants for jobs, only a minority (26 per cent in 1990) agree. The same may occur if people were asked about affirmative action in favour of members of ethnic minorities. But there is no evidence on whether such measures, if implemented against majority opinion, would lead to reduced support for the welfare state in

[25] Note that the question suggested the fairly radical option of equal rights in all respects irrespective of citizenship ('Die in Deutschland lebenden Italiener/Türken/Asylbewerber/Deutschstämmigen Aussiedler aus Osteuropa sollten in allen Bereichen die gleichen Rechte haben wie die Deutschen').

general. Given the stability and complex basis of support for the welfare state, this seems unlikely—and excessive fears of a backlash against possible (moderate) multiculturalism policies not justified.

Concluding remarks

Multiculturalism emerged late in German debates, and it may turn out to be short-lived. Quite possibly multiculturalism will be abandoned without ever having attained great strength as an operational political programme. Presently, as shown above, elements of multiculturalism policies do exist in Germany—albeit not within a concept characterized by a commitment to minority rights and public support for the maintenance and expression of distinct identities. Objections to more fully developed multiculturalism policies arise mainly from three sources. First of all such policies usually require an acceptance of the minority groups as longer-term parts of a given society. Second, the retention of national or ethnic group solidarities is often seen as backward-looking and anti-modern, as unnecessary for the realization of individual rights, and occasionally even as hindering individual development. Thirdly, stronger, more visible, and vocal ethnic communities are seen as a danger to the overall cohesion of modern societies and as parallel societies. Finally, recent transformations of the German welfare state might encourage a shift towards a more assimilationist orientation. The new welfare discourse emphasizes the priority an activating state must assign to the formation of human capital. Education is meant to help increase the employment opportunities of individuals belonging to social strata who, at present, are heavily dependent on welfare benefits, as is the case with important numbers of second and third generation immigrants. The view is gaining ground that, in order to avoid a proliferation of social problems and a further overload of welfare state structures, exclusion and growing social conflicts, German society has to ensure that ethnic communities do not consolidate and that members of Germany's immigrant minorities acquire the German language (and assimilate culturally).[26]

[26] In the context of the debate about a reform of the welfare state, questions of integration policy have attained a much greater saliency than before. Links between multiculturalism and social policy may be addressed more explicitly in the ongoing political debate, as welfare state structures continue to be under pressure. On the other hand, however, in view of the institutional properties of German federalism it seems unlikely that a uniform national policy will emerge.

Currently, the tide seems to be going against any further development of multiculturalism policies. However, as a consequence of internationally stronger calls for extended human rights, the demands of more vocal immigrant minorities, whose members increasingly hold German citizenship and are thus voters whose concerns will be taken into account, and other not yet visible factors, the balance of an overall non-uniform constellation could well turn in a different direction. In the long run, capturing the immigrant vote could turn out to be the more beneficial strategy for the left than making concessions to more traditional segments of the working class.

8

Do campaigns for historical redress erode the Canadian welfare state?

Matt James

In their recent work, Keith Banting and his co-authors have shown that countries with comparatively robust multiculturalism policies have not experienced overall levels of welfare state erosion greater than those seen in their more evidently difference-blind counterparts (Banting and Kymlicka 2004*a*; Chapter 2 in this volume). This is a telling response to an argument that left-wing critics of multiculturalism often make in impressionistic or abstract ways. Captured famously in Nancy Fraser's imagery of 'recognition-versus-redistribution', the charge is that a novel focus on 'cultural or symbolic... injustice... rooted in social patterns of representation, interpretation, and communication' is impeding our capacity to redress 'socioeconomic injustice... rooted in the political-economic structure of society' (1997: 14, 13).

Yet critics are unlikely soon to retract the charge, and perhaps for good reason. While keenly interested in the impact of particular multiculturalism policies on the welfare state, they also have a more diffuse concern. Critics worry about the long-run impact of a vast ensemble of discourses and practices, comprising what we can call 'social-movement multiculturalism', on the civic visions and coalitions that appear necessary to sustain redistribution.[1] Yet it is not immediately clear how one can test

For helpful comments on earlier drafts of this chapter, I would like to thank Keith Banting, the other participants in the 'Multiculturalism and the Welfare State' workshop at Queen's University, and Melissa Williams. Special thanks to Will Kymlicka for helpful comments and encouragement. For great research assistance, thanks to Paul Dyck, Shauna McRanor, and Diane Vermilyea. Thanks also to the Social Sciences and Humanities Research Council of Canada for financial support (grant no. 410-2004-0301).

[1] In addition to Fraser (1997), see Barry (2001), Gitlin (1995), and Rorty (2000).

the proposition that 'social-movement multiculturalism' is eroding redistribution. This chapter proceeds on the assumption that a useful first step is to scrutinize the discourses and practices of particular multiculturalist campaigns for their interplay with political-economy concerns (cf. Carroll and Ratner 2001). To this end, it focuses on one important expression of social-movement multiculturalism in one national context: the politics of historical redress in contemporary Canada.

Often cited as instances of an 'identitarian version of multiculturalism' likely to impair civic solidarity and social cohesion (Torpey, forthcoming; also see Lu 2005; Maier 1993; Nielsen 2001), redress movements provide a useful opportunity for probing claims made by the critics. Indeed, both John Torpey and Charles Maier worry specifically that the emphasis on group victimhood and historic grievance in what I (James 1999) have called 'redress politics' constitutes a threat to the welfare state. Fearing that a 'surfeit of memory' may 'divert from other agendas', Maier states the case this way: 'Every group claims its share of public honor and public funds by pressing disabilities and injustices. . . . I would rather that our society . . . use civic action to meet urgent public needs and diminish the gross inequalities that characterize our life, so that we are all less preoccupied with our memory' (1993: 145, 147, 150).

To explore these concerns, this chapter studies movements that have sought, and in most cases continue to seek, reparations for the following injustices: Canada's past policy of forcing Aboriginal children to attend residential schools; the wartime internment's of Ukrainian and Japanese Canadians; the 'head tax' formerly imposed on Chinese migrants to Canada; and the physical destruction of Halifax's Africville community. In the course of treating the latter case, I also discuss a broader social-movement focus on the historical oppression of Canada's African diaspora, with which it has important thematic continuities and network links. While redress politics and 'multiculturalism' are logically distinct and can be critiqued and defended independently, there appear to be solid grounds—particularly in the Canadian case—for interpreting redress politics as a broadly multiculturalist arena of political discourse and practice. Accordingly, the chapter begins by introducing redress politics as a species of multiculturalism. After summarizing the relevant injustices and using Fraser's (1997) recognition–redistribution distinction to characterize the cases, the chapter then turns to the main task at hand: evaluating the redress campaigns as potential instances of what Banting and Kymlicka identify in this volume as the most plausible means by which multiculturalism might be said to erode the welfare state. These are the misdiagnosis effect (which displaces attention from maldistribution by failing to address its real causes), the crowding-out effect (which saps time and energy that might otherwise be devoted to redistribution), and the corroding effect (which undermines the solidarity that redistribution appears to require). The chapter concludes that redress politics constitutes a species of social-movement multiculturalism whose dynamics are far more complex—and perhaps even more promising—than the misdiagnosis, crowding-out, and corroding charges allow.

1. Characterizing redress politics in Canada

Redress politics as a species of multiculturalism

Although Banting et al. (Chapter 2, this volume) do not themselves include apologies and redress agreements in their list of 'MCPs', I argue that they qualify as a form of social-movement multiculturalism. Redress politics is characterized by a difference-conscious focus on group disadvantage, group restitution, and group responsibilities (Barkan 2000: xx, 161, 308, 319; Cunningham 1999: 290; Torpey 2003: 11–15). Activists seek apologies in the name of ethnic communities or indigenous nations, identify ethno-cultural organizations as anticipated recipients of material gestures of restitution or repair, and speak of the duties that perpetrator or beneficiary groups owe to victim communities. For these reasons, actual redress settlements are likely to include multiculturalist policies as these are defined in Chapter 1 of this volume.

The 1988 Japanese Canadian Redress Agreement (see Miki and Kobayashi 1991), the landmark achievement to which many Canadian campaigns have aspired (James 1999: 259–60), is a case in point. First, Prime Minister Brian Mulroney directed his government's official apology for the racist Second World War Two internment 'to the Japanese Canadian community'.[2] Although the Agreement paid individual compensation to roughly 18,000 internment survivors, this 'many-to-many' apology (Tavuchis 1991: 99–117) conveyed the group recognition characteristic of official multiculturalist affirmations (immigrant MCP #1 in this volume).[3] Second, by establishing the Canadian Race Relations

[2] Mulroney's speech is reprinted in Miki and Kobayashi (1991: 138–9). For an account of the Agreement, see Kobayashi (1992).

[3] If the recipient group is a national minority and the apology acknowledges that status, then the corresponding example would be a parliamentary affirmation of 'multinationalism' (example #5 from that list). Similarly, an apology for injustices of colonialism that

Foundation with a $24 million endowment, the Agreement has helped to promote both multiculturalism in school curricula and ethnic sensitivity in the media (immigrant MCPs #2 and #3 respectively).[4]

A third multiculturalist feature of the Agreement is the $12 million community-development fund elicited by the National Japanese Canadian Citizens' Association (NAJC).[5] The NAJC has used these monies to support cultural activities and group-specific social services (immigrant MCP #6), including a Japanese-Canadian museum, nursing homes, memorial centres, community centres, and commemorative gardens. The NAJC has also drawn on the fund to provide Japanese heritage-language instruction (immigrant MCP #7). As the literary critic and redress activist Roy Miki explains more generally, the community-development fund has been instrumental in strengthening Japanese-Canadian identity, not least by providing 'new social and community spaces... [for] those whose subjectivities had been contained and suppressed' (2004: 62).

Therefore, redress politics would appear to involve advocacy in support of multiculturalist policies oriented towards affirming and nourishing group difference (cf. Barkan 2000: 24, 317). At the same time, and moving beyond the realm of formal policy, redress campaigns also afford a closer look at social-movement multiculturalism's perhaps most controversial feature; its combative approach to dominant majorities. Casting the target nation as the morally compromised beneficiary of racist acts whose echoes continue to structure public life and private power, redress seekers employ an 'adversarial, accusatory history' (Cairns 1995: 24). This approach exemplifies the stance of minoritarian grievance that critics often blame for corroding the solidarity on which welfare states rest (e.g. Gitlin 1995: 229–31). In short, redress politics in Canada have involved both the affirmative state policies that defenders of multiculturalism cite, as well as the potentially antagonistic discourses and attitudes that some critics fear. It therefore provides a good test case for examining claims about the impact of multiculturalism on redistribution.

---

acknowledges a distinct status relationship would correspond to example #7 (affirmation of distinct indigenous status) of the indigenous MCP list.

[4] The Canadian Race Relations Foundation provides multiculturalist resources for educators, such as a quiz testing 'knowledge of racism in Canadian history'. It also promotes Black History Month, Asian Heritage Month, and National Aboriginal Day. See Canadian Race Relations Foundation (2004).

[5] On the NAJC activities enumerated in this paragraph, see Miki (2003: chs. 3 and 4).

The injustices

Let us now consider some of the injustices that have prompted redress politics to appear in the Canadian context.

- Roughly 5,000 Ukrainian Canadians were interned during the First World War, on the dubious ground that their status as former subjects of the Austro-Hungarian empire made them national-security threats (Luciuk 1988). The camps were punitive, inmates were exploited as unpaid labour, and in many cases cash and valuables were seized that were never returned. Ukrainian Canadians were also disenfranchised in the wartime election campaign of 1917.

- From 1942 to 1949, the entire ethnic Japanese population of coastal British Columbia, numbering approximately 24,000 persons, was subjected to a range of racist policies, including internment in the province's interior, forcible 'dispersal' to other areas of Canada, unfree labour, the deportation to Japan of persons who were in many cases Canadian citizens, and the largely uncompensated seizure of homes, property, and businesses (Miki 2004).

- Implemented at the rate of $50 in 1885, the 'Chinese head tax' was raised to $100 in 1900, and then to $500 in 1903 (Bolaria and Li 1988: 107–16). In 1923 it was replaced by a virtual ban on Chinese immigration to Canada, known informally as the 'Chinese Exclusion Act', which, along with a policy of Asian-Canadian disenfranchisement, remained in place until 1947. The prohibitive cost of the tax fostered an informal system of indentured servitude, with labour contractors paying the price of admission in order to acquire indebted and therefore exploitable 'clients'. Because only male workers were typically able to pay the entry tax, and were not generally allowed to bring over other family members once settled, it also ensured that there would be virtually no second Chinese-Canadian generation until the late 1970s.

- Established in the early nineteenth century, the Halifax neighbourhood of Africville quickly became a site for the city's hazardous industries and toxic waste (Africville Genealogy Society 1992). It was also denied such basic services as policing, water, and sewerage. After white Haligonians began to express embarrassment about these conditions, provincial and municipal authorities responded in the late 1960s by razing Africville and dispersing its residents to other parts of the city. This action was taken despite strong protest from what had become a proudly self-sufficient community. Activists cite the Africville experience as a microcosmic example of the mixture of oppression and indifference that African people have endured on Canadian soil (e.g. Saney 2002).

• Canada's century-long residential-schools policy took more than 100,000 Native children from their families and placed them in grossly authoritarian settings (Miller 1996). In addition to suffering family separation and forced culture and language loss, over 12,000 survivors allege in the *Baxter* class-action suit that they were physically or sexually abused by the church personnel whom Ottawa entrusted with running the schools (Canada 2003). The Canadian federal government apologized for the physical and sexual abuse in 1998 (Canada 2004*a*). Indigenous peoples have of course suffered myriad other injustices in Canada, including the imposition of a foreign system of government and pervasive land theft, but because activists usually seek to address these injustices by pursuing self-determination rather than by demanding reparations, I do not directly discuss them here.

Recognition and redistribution in redress campaigns

While all of these campaigns can usefully be seen as examples of social movement multiculturalism, and hence as forms of 'the politics of recognition', there is one crucial difference amongst them. Two of the groups—namely, African Canadians and Indigenous peoples—continue to suffer from serious economic disadvantage, which they trace back at least in part to the acts of historic injustice committed against them. As a result, their redress campaigns exhibit what Fraser calls a 'bivalent' concern to redress injustices of both misrecognition and maldistribution (1997: 19). By contrast, the other groups seeking redress—the Chinese-, Japanese-, and Ukrainian-Canadians—are not on the whole economically disadvantaged when compared to the larger Canadian population.

This distinction is important for my analysis of the cases. In particular, the concern about 'misdiagnosis' only seems to be relevant in the Aboriginal and African-Canadian cases. After all, the charge of misdiagnosis maintains that multiculturalism leads the *victims* of economic injustice to seek wrong-headed 'culturalist' solutions to their economic disadvantage. I will begin my analysis, therefore, by considering whether the preoccupation with seeking redress for historic injustice amongst

Aboriginal and African Canadians has led to a misdiagnosis of their economic condition.

I then turn to consider the possibility of 'crowding-out' and 'corroding' effects, while expanding the scope of the analysis to include the Ukrainian-, Japanese-, and Chinese-Canadian campaigns. While all of the movements that I address have struggled with questions of identity and difference, the latter three are distinguished by a particularly keen focus on cultural recognition. Perhaps most notably, they have fought against group stigma; an unjust and at times disabling inheritance, which episodes such as internment for alleged disloyalty (Japanese and Ukrainian Canadians) or special restriction as 'undesirable' immigrants (Chinese Canadians) may leave in their wake. Campaigns of this sort appear to place particular value on redress settlements as 'symbolic capital' (Bourdieu 1986). Concerned to elicit official recognition that the group's past treatment was wrongful and undeserved, they strive to show authoritatively that their new-found political clout has forced the state to redress the wrong, leaving a precedent-setting contribution towards a more just collective future (James 1999). Accordingly, I will examine whether this preoccupation with recognition and redress has crowded out a broader focus on welfare state concerns. I will also ask whether it appears to have corroded feelings of solidarity across ethnic lines.

To use Fraser's terminology, therefore, this chapter focuses on two distinct types of redress politics: (*a*) the 'bivalent' Aboriginal and African-Canadian campaigns, which struggle against both cultural misrecognition and economic disadvantage; and (*b*) the Japanese-, Chinese-, and Ukrainian-Canadian cases, which are closer to pure instances of recognition politics (cf. Torpey 2001: 335–8).[6] Since issues of cultural recognition arise in all of these cases, concerns about the crowding-out and corroding effects apply across the board. Regarding the Aboriginal and African-Canadian campaigns, we can also ask whether the centrality of cultural concerns has led to a misdiagnosis of the economic injustices facing the group.

---

[6] While it is true that even the Japanese-, Ukrainian-, and Chinese-Canadian movements have sought economic as well as symbolic capital, this alone is not sufficient to claim them for the politics of redistribution. As Anne Phillips points out, if the mere presence of a call on public resources is the criterion then virtually all politics would merit that label (2003: 269).

2. Assessing the impact of redress politics on the welfare state

The misdiagnosis effect

Do the two 'bivalent' cases offer evidence of the misdiagnosis effect? The Aboriginal and African-Canadian campaigns certainly articulate their distributive goals in a 'culturalist' framework that stresses the impact of racist disrespect and colonial assault. For example, a Law Commission of Canada report characterized the concerns of residential-schools survivors with the following summary observation: 'The consequences of residential schools are noted as high rates of alcoholism, suicide, and sexual abuse, the loss of language and culture, low self-esteem and pride, the breakdown of families, the loss of parenting skills, dependency on others, and loss of initiative' (Claes and Clifton 1998: 45). For their part, Africville campaigners argue strongly for the economic importance of community and culture. Noting that the destruction of an established context of group and family support forced many relocatees to turn to welfare for survival, activists see their story as 'a symbol of why black organization and solidarity are necessary' (Clairmont 1992: 74).[7]

For some critics, these arguments and claims may seem to exemplify the naive belief that valorizing disrespected cultures will somehow undo profound socio-economic harm. As Kwame Anthony Appiah famously put it in his critique of multiculturalist responses to the plight of African-Americans, 'Culture is not the problem, and it is not the solution' (see the discussion in Banting and Kymlicka, this volume). However, the expectations that the Aboriginal and African-Canadian campaigns attach to culture are not so self-evidently naive. The campaigns appear to value cultural affirmation not as a solution in its own right, but rather as a means of increasing the group's capacity to vindicate its socio-economic needs—needs that the dominant society has a record of ignoring, to say the least. Activists expect their efforts to contribute to this goal in two major ways; internally, by strengthening the group's solidarity and mobilization capabilities, and externally, by increasing its political influence on the wider society.

The Assembly of First Nations (1994) report, *Breaking the Silence: An Interpretive Study of Residential School Impact and Healing*, emphasizes the internal dimension of group affirmation. A key premiss behind its idea

---

[7] Clairmont (1992: 72), finds that only 10 per cent of Africville residents were on social assistance at the time of the relocation, with over 50 per cent in receipt of benefits shortly afterwards.

of 'breaking the silence' is that grappling with past trauma through enterprises of community healing will promote self-esteem and group solidarity, encouraging participants 'to lead healthy, prosperous lives' and contribute 'to the well-being of their families and communities' (141, 137). A similar focus on rebuilding community as a step towards tackling unemployment and poverty informs the Africville campaign (e.g. Cox 2001; *Shunpiking* 2002).

Externally, the residential-schools and Africville redress campaigns focus on persuading the dominant society to respond more energetically and appropriately to their respective communities' social-welfare needs. For example, activists stress the contemporary economic impact of Africville's destruction and of the dispossession and discrimination visited on the African diaspora more generally. They do so in the hope that teaching other Canadians about the ongoing effects of historical racism might create the political basis for a 'Marshall-plan' response to African-Canadian underemployment and poverty (African-Canadian Legal Clinic 2004; Barnes 2004; *Shunpiking* 2002).

Many Native advocates are similarly concerned to educate the dominant society about the continued impact of the residential schools. Indeed, researchers Rhonda Claes and Deborah Clifton have found that the reparative priority most commonly cited by survivors is for greater 'public recognition and awareness' of the effects of the schools, to be promoted 'in the form of an inquiry' (1998: 61). Often speaking in redistributive terms, advocates hope that such a process might lead Canadians and the federal government to embrace their duty to help repair the devastation that they have caused. For example, the Assembly of First Nations (1990) demands that Ottawa provide a 'full range of [health and counselling] services to victims... their families and communities', and that it strive more vigorously to redress a key legacy of the schools: 'inadequate education reflected in high unemployment rates.'

Africville and residential-schools campaigners also insist that Canadian welfare planners committed severe injustices in pursuit of what unblushing authorities and activists alike once called civic integration. For instance, they remind us that Canada's Aboriginal education policy was little more than an instrument of attempted cultural genocide (Claes and Clifton 1998: 31–39), and that 'integration' and 'urban renewal' in Halifax meant destroying a Black community (Clairmont 1992). The point is not to deny any distinction between the contemporary importance of the residential-schools legacy in Aboriginal arguments for self-determination, as against the more obviously integrative concerns of many African-Canadians. It is that their common focus on criticizing the Marshallian welfare state, particularly its more aggressive attempts 'to integrate people into a common national culture' (Kymlicka 2002: 328), does not imply a rejection of distributive politics. Rather, it constitutes an attempt to promote a more effective and culturally sensitive redistributive agenda.

In summary, Aboriginal and African-Canadian participants view redress campaigns as internal opportunities for rebuilding and mobilizing fractured communities. This work is often seen as a contributing step towards autonomous processes of community economic development. Externally, activists hope that their campaigns will teach historical lessons which foster a climate of moral urgency and forge a more sensitive appreciation of community economic problems and needs. Amply aware that progress on these fronts will require what Phillips (2003) calls 'political voice', the residential-schools and Africville redress campaigns seek to vindicate their communities' historically neglected and improperly addressed distributive needs. This may not be the approach that multiculturalism's left-wing critics prefer. But it is a far cry from ignoring economic injustice altogether or believing naively that cultural respect on its own will solve it.

Before treating the questions of crowding out and corrosion, I want to consider what Banting and Kymlicka call the 'Machiavellian version' of the misdiagnosis argument. Of course it seems unlikely that members of a historically oppressed group would go to the trouble of launching a redress movement in a devious attempt to distract attention from maldistribution. However, there is evidence that neoliberal and traditional right-wing political parties promote a narrow 'heritage' approach to redress as a substitute for more ambitious remedies for injustice.

As Yasmeen Abu-Laban and Christina Gabriel have shown, during the mid-1990s the governing federal Liberals instituted steep budget cuts to multiculturalism programmes and downgraded the former ministry into a toothless and administratively sidelined division of the new Department of Canadian Heritage (2002: ch. 4). These measures served neoliberal goals by helping to weaken, both financially and in terms of political influence and access, a variety of progressive advocacy groups. This 'heritage' approach to marginalizing social-movement multiculturalism also encompasses redress. Since 1994, when Secretary of State for Multiculturalism Sheila Finestone declared that her department would not pay reparations or apologize for historical injustices (Canada 1994), the federal Liberal government steadfastly resisted activist calls for apologies, 'Marshall-plan' responses to group disadvantage, and community anti-racism projects.[8] Instead, it has established commemorative markers at Ukrainian-Canadian internment sites, designated Africville as a site of 'national historic significance', and marked 28 July as 'A Day of Commemoration' of the Acadian deportation (see James, forthcoming).

The phrase 'heritage redress' itself comes from the 2004 election platform of Canada's opposition Conservatives (see Ukrainian Canadian Civil Liberties Association 2004). Although party leader Stephen Harper has not elaborated on its meaning, Conservative MP Inky Mark's private member's bill, the Chinese Canadian Recognition and Restitution Act, provides some indication (Canada 2004b). Mark's proposed Act rejects two of the main reparative goals pursued by the Chinese Canadian National Council since 1985: federally funded community anti-racism projects and financial compensation for former head-tax payers and their families. Instead, the Act speaks of 'restitution', which, on its rather narrow reading of that term, means funding 'educational materials on Chinese Canadian history and on the promotion of racial harmony'. The Act stipulates further that these materials be developed and delivered by the National Congress of Chinese Canadians; a low-profile organization which supports Mark's bill but appears to have little serious history of advocacy on head-tax redress.[9]

For the Conservatives, a party often portrayed as hostile to the welfare state and insensitive to diversity, championing heritage redress may be a way of attempting to appear more centrist and compassionate.[10] The Conservative stand certainly won praise from the Ukrainian Canadian Civil Liberties Commission, whose research director, Lubomyr Luciuk, paid tribute in the following terms: 'This is a remarkable development, confirming as it does that this is a new party with a commitment to social

---

[8] The only exception is the 1998 Statement of Reconciliation and 'healing fund' for residential-schools survivors. However, this response is best interpreted as an attempt on the part of the federal government to avoid responding to the unwelcomely demanding 1996 report of the Royal Commission on Aboriginal Peoples. On this point, see James (forthcoming).

[9] For example, a Google search (23 October 2004) for 'National Congress of Chinese Canadians' + 'head tax' garners 28 hits, while 'Chinese Canadian National Council' + 'head tax' yields 216. Furthermore, virtually all mentions of the former group come after the initial introduction of Inky Mark's private member's bill in 2002.

[10] Following the completion of this paper, the Conservative Party emerged from the 2006 federal election with a parliamentary minority. Interestingly, one of its first actions in the area of domestic policy was to adopt a redress agreement for the Chinese Canadian head tax. Although it follows the main lines of the 'heritage redress' model, the agreement also contains a significant formal apology and includes rather than sidelines the activist Chinese Canadian National Council. These latter developments suggest that social-movement multiculturalism maintains a limited but still important capacity to modify officialdom's preferred 'heritage' approach.

justice' (Ukrainian Canadian Civil Liberties Association 2004).[11] Given Ottawa's own attack on multiculturalism programmes, to say nothing of the sweeping mid-1990s cuts that brought federal social spending to levels not seen since the 1950s (Johnson 1997), Luciuk's response may also suggest the potential attraction of heritage redress for the governing Liberals.

Therefore, heritage redress appears to be an instance of multiculturalism in the service of neoliberalism. But what makes it useful in this role is precisely its capacity to undermine social-movement multiculturalism. Heritage redress aims to marginalize activist priorities by replacing serious negotiations over the dominant society's contemporary reparative responsibilities with scattered depoliticized acts of national 'commemoration' instead. This Machiavellian tactic exemplifies the neoliberal drive to depose social-movement organizations from their former status as accepted state interlocutors (Jenson and Phillips 2001; Smith 2005). Far from being complicit, most Canadian redress movements strongly resist it.[12]

Nevertheless, redress campaigns may still contribute to what I (James 2004) call the reshaping of the moral contours of contemporary citizenship. The reshaping appears to be double-sided. On the one hand, as poverty becomes all but proscribed as a focus of government concern it seems to resume some of its Victorian social meaning as a straightforwardly stigmatic emblem of personal failure. This development can be grasped in terms of Ulrich Beck's stress on 'moral individualization' in late modernity (1992: ch. 3) and Janine Brodie's notion of the 'demise of the social' (2002). On the other hand, recent scholarship suggests that reconfigured discourses of civic compassion are emerging (Brodie 2003). As Xiaobei Chen (2003) argues, for instance, we appear to be witnessing a heightened sensitivity to the plight of suitably 'innocent' victims.

The African-Canadian and residential-schools campaigns are particularly important to consider in the light of these developments. Their emphasis on group-specific anti-poverty measures as reparations for particular acts of colonialism and racism may constitute a problematic adaptation to a political climate hostile to social-democratic appeals and obsessed with innocent desert. After all, even right-wing 'libertarians' can

---

[11] The present-day Conservatives were created by a 2003 merger between the former Progressive Conservative and Canadian Alliance parties.

[12] In addition to the aforementioned National Congress of Chinese Canadians, the other apparent exceptions are the Ukrainian Canadian Civil Liberties Association and Ukrainian Canadian Congress. The apparent openness of the latter two organizations to heritage redress may reflect the facts that there are very few survivors of the First World War internment and that Ukrainian Canadians do not generally suffer systemic or patterned disadvantage.

accept a limited notion of redistribution in the form of incident-specific responses to unjust past transfers (see Valls 1999). Thus, social-movement framings that portray poverty as a result of the prior victimization of particular groups of innocents, and which articulate solutions in the businesslike language of rectifying illegitimate transfers, may offer unwitting assistance to some of the broader ideological currents eroding welfare states.[13]

Yet it would be self-serving for a privileged white author to suggest that Aboriginal and African-Canadian poverty and underemployment can be meaningfully discussed without addressing histories of racism and colonialism. It would also be wrong-headed to say that actually existing welfare states have ever posed a remotely adequate solution to the problem. Analysts and activists are certainly well advised to track the ways in which discourses of reparation may be complicit in the neoliberal reshaping of contemporary citizenship. But rejecting redress politics simply for harbouring this potential would seem reminiscent of a one-sided economism amply guilty of its own misdiagnoses (cf. Banting and Kymlicka, this volume).

The crowding-out effect

The crowding-out argument should not be pushed too far: it seems unlikely that a sudden end to multiculturalism would send teams of newly enlightened activists scurrying off to defend the welfare state. But could social-movement multiculturalism, and in this case, Canadian redress movements, somehow be sapping time and energy that might otherwise be devoted to redistribution?

In an ongoing series of open-ended, non-attributable interview conversations, I have been asking high-level redress-movement participants how they view the relationship between their campaigns and the welfare state. These encounters have focused on two broad issues: how redress activism might be shaping the political behaviour of group members on welfare-state issues, and how it may be influencing the societal values and coalitions that undergird the welfare state. Animating this approach is a desire to attenuate the often false objectivity of scholarly distance (cf. Bourdieu and Wacquant 1992) by hearing activists convey their own sense of the character and impact of their endeavours. Of course, the responses are in one sense predictable: redress campaigners would be

---

[13] For a philosophical critique of the notion of 'restitution', see Vernon (2003).

highly unlikely to endorse the argument that multiculturalism erodes the welfare state. But the responses also bring us into closer contact with some of the more elusively diffuse mechanisms and valences that concern the critics.

As one might expect, activists strongly supported Banting and Kymlicka's point that political mobilization is not a zero-sum affair. Recall that Banting and Kymlicka (this volume) suggest that the real task may be to get people engaged 'on any issue worth fighting about. Once they are involved, and have [a] sense of political efficacy, they are likely to support other progressive issues as well'. Participants illuminated this point in a variety of ways. One long-time Chinese-Canadian advocate pointed out that most activists he knows are highly involved politically and often work on several social-justice campaigns at once (Chung 2004). A younger Chinese-Canadian leader told me that learning about the head tax and its impact was what motivated her to join the Chinese Canadian National Council in the first place (Kang 2004). She has since become a Council executive member, and now participates in Toronto-area campaigns and coalitions around issues of immigration and refugee policy.

The Chinese-Canadian leaders told of several individuals spurred on by the redress campaign to other political involvement. For instance, a York University student came to their organization for help researching an essay about the head tax, and then wound up joining and getting involved in refugee advocacy (Chung 2004). Several young head-tax campaigners have recently become active in the peace movement (Chung 2004). In addition, some participants have protested to Public Security Minister Anne McLellan about the post-11 September treatment of Arab and Muslim Canadians (Kang 2004), while others have helped to organize a National Forum on Race and Homophobia (Chinese Canadian National Council 2004a). The common theme in these accounts is that learning in an activist context about the origins and impact of the head tax has encouraged Chinese Canadians to act on other social-justice concerns as well.

The nascent struggles around African-Canadian redress exhibit a slightly different dynamic. As a founding member of the African-Canadian Coalition Against Racism explained, initiating discussions around reparations for Canadian Blacks has meant gathering activists from diverse communities, already working in their own separate organizations on their own specific concerns, and trying to focus them on how to 'more effectively mobilize, strategize and work together'. She argued that this attempt is 'important because ... the diverse composition of African Canadian communities... [is] at times... used to divide the communities' (Barnes 2004).

The Africville campaign illustrates this desired trajectory from local activism to a more expansive focus on African-Canadians as members of a common diaspora. The movement emerged in the early 1980s when former residents reacted to their sense of lost community and endangered identity by forming the Africville Genealogy Society and initiating a tradition of annual picnics (Kimber 1992: 80). Soon, members began lobbying the Nova Scotia and Halifax governments to help them 'return to Africville and re-establish [the] community' (Kimber 1992: 82). But this focus changed. After several high-profile episodes of anti-Black racism in Nova Scotia, Africville Genealogy Society members and other Halifax-area activists began forging links with Toronto-based African-Canadian groups (Kimber 1992: 84). Since then, Africville campaigners have made presentations on reparations to the 2001 United Nations World Conference Against Racism in Durban, South Africa (e.g. Allen 2001) and have collaborated with other African Canadians on the 2001 'Racism and the Black World Response Symposium' in Halifax (see *Shunpiking* 2002).

According to these illustrations and examples, redress-campaign involvement spurs rather than dampens participant activism on other issues. But this effect does not seem to extend to defend-the-welfare-state campaigns. For instance, the mobilization boost that Black redress advocates hope to achieve is oriented primarily towards promoting African-Canadian unity, and perhaps broader disaporic unity as well. Other movements may be similar. For example, although he noted that awareness of the First World War internment makes Ukrainian Canadians particularly strong supporters of anti-discrimination and civil liberties, the Winnipeg-based member of the Ukrainian Canadian Congress whom I interviewed did not provide any evidence of campaign participants moving on to activist involvement beyond the ethnic Ukrainian context (Milavsky 2004).

Activists also replied disapprovingly when I asked whether their group-specific advocacy might crowd out potential action on social-democratic concerns. For instance, my interlocutor from the African-Canadian Coalition Against Racism responded in the following terms:

until we get to a place where... we can say that we fairly understand and appreciate every group's situation... and we can all, reasonably, and in the same way articulate those experiences, and fight for them in the same way... you will always need groups... fighting on particular issues that are specific to their communities and their realities—because nobody can really articulate your issue as you can.

Citing the case of African-Canadian redress as an example, she argued that this sort of sympathetic understanding remains particularly elusive for Canadian Blacks. In her words: the 'resentment, opposition and, you know, the kind of adversarial responses one gets... are not only tied to a general disagreement with reparations... but... also to who is asking for reparations' (Barnes 2004).

The senior Chinese-Canadian leader was similarly unmoved by the crowding-out reproach. He suggested that those who condemn multi-culturalism for sapping social-democratic energies are the ones guilty of unhelpful parochialism: 'I just totally disagree with... the premise of that argument. It's almost a very selfish question because you know... it's sort of like... "I'm not from your group and that's why... I have this problem with [your] campaign." It's almost a very self-centered criticism.' Turning to the specific case of Chinese-Canadian redress, he urged critics to consider the following riposte: 'maybe you have a blind spot for racial issues.... [M]aybe you think this kind of oppression [i.e. the head tax] is acceptable, right?' (Chung 2004).

In short, redress activists were not enthusiastic about being asked to consider the potential impact of their campaigns on the Canadian welfare state. They argued instead that their group-specific focus on community building and self-advocacy is a necessary response to the tendency of non-racialized groups to ignore their views and needs.

The corroding effect

Because white privilege often paints minority protest as a threat to civic harmony, concerns about the corroding effect should be raised carefully. Nevertheless, I will ask: do Canadian redress movements furnish concrete examples of how multiculturalism corrodes the solidarity on which wel-fare states are said to rest?

The previous section noted the dismay and mistrust that redress cam-paigners conveyed when asked about the crowding-out hypothesis. This reaction is significant, because it suggests that aggressive defences of 'com-mon good social democracy' against 'go-it-alone multiculturalism' may be counter-productive, helping to push activists away from engagement with pro-welfare state coalitions. In turn, considering this problem in light of the corrosion hypothesis brings up the question of what might encourage this sort of broader civic engagement among historically marginalized groups. The case of the Japanese Canadian Redress Agreement seems instructive in this respect.

The Agreement has been crucial in helping to reverse the legacy of disengaged mistrust left by the Second World War internment (Omatsu 1992: 67–9). Consider the following list of activities. Since the 1988 settlement, the National Association of Japanese Canadians (NAJC) has intervened in Canadian constitutional debates to support Aboriginal self-government; advised the British Columbia Union of Indian Chiefs and Chinese Canadian National Council on their respective redress campaigns; aided overseas groups suing the Japanese government for its wartime atrocities; held workshops on women's oppression and homophobia; assisted the Ontario Stoney Point band seeking land stolen during the Second World War; supported the Lubicon of Alberta in their boycott of the Daishowa Paper Company; and helped Aboriginal veterans in pursuit of their wrongly denied Armed Forces benefits.[14] The NAJC's post-redress mission statement articulates this new-found sense of engaged civic concern: 'The NAJC has the obligation to speak out and lend support when justice is denied to other individuals and groups' (Miki 2003: 14).

But what about the external impact of redress movements: how might they affect the broader public and the coalitions that support the welfare state? Opinion surveys conducted during the Japanese-Canadian campaign showed results ranging from 42 per cent to 63 per cent in favour of compensating former internees (Miki 2004: 293; Omatsu 1992: 158). The Japanese-Canadian Redress Agreement itself garnered 53 per cent approval shortly after its passage (Omatsu 1992: 158). More recently, an on-line reader 'poll' conducted by the *Globe and Mail* (2003a) yielded 60 per cent support for the principle of apologizing for historical wrongs.[15]

There is certainly ample evidence indicating that redress movements are received favourably by pro-welfare state forces. The left-wing New Democratic Party (NDP), the major national trade unions, and Canadian labour's national umbrella organization, the Canadian Labour Congress, all strongly endorsed the Japanese-Canadian campaign (Canadian Labour Congress 1984: 9; Miki 2004: 286). Labour leaders also played prominent roles in the National Coalition for Japanese Canadian Redress, which

[14] On these activities, see National Association of Japanese Canadians (1991); Miki (1996); Letts (2002); *Globe and Mail* (2003b); and Miki (2003: 115, 172, and 173).

[15] Out of a total 14,283 responses, 7,313 (51 per cent) said that a 'modern apology for a historical wrong' is a 'worthwhile gesture' and a further 2,018 (14 per cent) chose the option, a 'salve for historical wounds'; 3,678 (26 per cent) called apologies 'nothing but lip service', while 1,274 (9 per cent) said they were 'not enough without compensation'.

rallied public backing for internment reparations (Goerzen 2004; Miki 2004: 319). Indeed, Maryka Omatsu's insider's account suggests that the NDP's assistance, particularly in light of the original stance against internment taken by the NDP's predecessor party, the Cooperative Commonwealth Federation, evoked a 'feeling of obligation [and] loyalty' among activists (1992: 139).

In more recent years, left-wing organizations and actors have continued to be a reliable source of redress support. NDP federal and provincial representatives are the only politicians to have spoken out for meaningful Africville redress (e.g. MacDonald 2004; McDonough 2004). The Chinese Canadian National Council's list of 'Canadians for Redress' (2005) includes the antiglobalization Council of Canadians, the British Columbia Federation of Labour, federal NDP leader Jack Layton, Ontario NDP leader Howard Hampton, NDP MP Libby Davies, former NDP MPs Svend Robinson and Margaret Mitchell, and prominent left-wing activists Judy Rebick, Stephen Lewis, Michelle Landsberg, Shirley Douglas, and Naomi Klein—but only one political figure from beyond the ranks of the organized left, Liberal Senator Mac Harb. Even former International Woodworkers of America president Jack Munro, whom many 'new' social movement activists blame for the collapse of the Operation Solidarity coalition against right-wing policies in British Columbia (Carroll and Ratner 1995: 199), has worked for head-tax redress (Chinese Canadian National Council 2004*b*).

In short, it appears that there is a strongly symbiotic relationship between social-movement multiculturalism and traditional-left organizations, at least at the elite level. However, it is less clear whether this dynamic holds true for mass publics. Perhaps the tendency of left-wing organizations to support multiculturalist goals has diminished the enthusiasm of their traditional blue-collar constituency. After all, the New Democratic Party, despite its strong organizational ties to unionized labour, does not in fact receive the majority of votes of union members (cf. Archer 1985).

But suggesting that multiculturalist positions are a significant reason why left-wing parties fail to enjoy strong working-class support would involve attributing a natural disposition among workers towards socialism or social democracy, which those multiculturalist positions are then seen somehow to disrupt. It is perhaps more plausible to expect that workers susceptible to leftist appeals will also be favourably disposed to multiculturalism, while the more economically conservative and politically quiescent among their number—Disraeli's 'angels in marble'—will be likelier to oppose it. A recurrent distinction in labour-movement studies suggests as much. What Kim Moody calls 'business unionism', which 'sees members primarily as consumers and limits itself to negotiating the price of labour', has a history of nativism and indifference towards marginalized people (Moody 1988: xiv, ch. 1). Its 'social' or 'egalitarian' counterpart formations, by contrast, have often been 'champions of the rights of minorities and the rightless of all kinds' (Hobsbawm 1984: 314).[16]

A similar distinction structures many Canadian public interventions on redress. This conclusion comes from a content analysis of forty-one letters on reparations to Canadian newspapers, whose purpose was to probe the kinds of responses that redress campaigns evoke.[17] Obviously, letters to the editor cannot be said to indicate the views of Canadians generally. However, such letters do reflect the views of a politically motivated segment of the population, and may often express the sorts of feelings that might be expected to arise were tensions between redress and solidarity to surface. The most striking finding to emerge from the analysis of these letters was a contrast between redress opponents who expressed a strict ethic of self-regarding individualism and supporters who invoked themes of social responsibility and connection.

Although a slim majority of letter-writers (24/41) was in some sense critical of reparations, 11 of these 24 authors simply commented on the merits of one or another claim and left no indication of their broader views. Among favourable respondents, 12 of 17 exhibited a similarly restricted focus. Two negative letters were judged sufficiently unreasonable as to be unworthy of serious consideration.[18] Thus, 25 of 41 letters were deemed inconclusive. A further group of seven authors argued that redress movements exert a corroding effect. Although they provided no evidence, these writers feared that movements seeking redress for past wrongs are preventing Canadians from 'cooperat[ing] socially and economically' (Bazylevich 2002), thus jeopardizing 'a future of true equality' (Kirby 1987).

---

[16] On the two alternative traditions in the Canadian context, see Carroll and Ratner (1995) and Palmer (1983).

[17] The search procedure (performed between the months of October and December, 2004) involved scanning the ProQuest Canadian Newsstand database for archived letters to the editor containing any of the words 'apology', 'compensation', 'historical injustice', 'reparations', 'redress', 'historical wrongs', 'past wrongs', 'historical grievances', or 'restitution'.

[18] O'Beirne (1997) argued against compensating Japanese-Canadian internees (most of whom were citizens) on the ground that Japan helped to 'start a world war', while Dickey (2001) flatly asserted that 'whiners' should '[g]et real . . . or get out.'

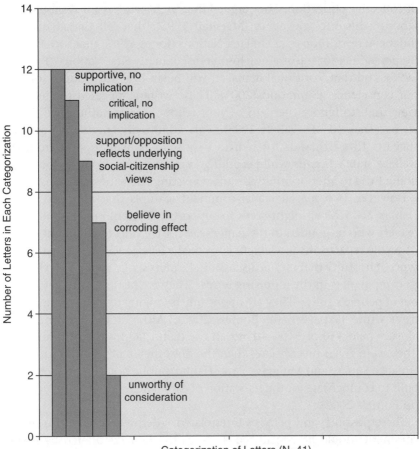

Figure 8.1 Implications of letters to newspapers for social citizenship

Finally, a group of nine letters indicated the tendency of reparations movements to attract responses that reflect pre-existing dispositions towards social citizenship. Among this latter group, four opponents of redress appealed to unqualified notions of individual responsibility. They expressed impatience with people 'wailing for payments from the public purse' (Christie 2001), frustration at 'being continually condemned for the misfortune of others' (MacDonald 2000), and anger towards those who 'harass the government' for funds (Fentie 1995). Their collective message was 'I am not guilty for that which I was not responsible for' (Cyllorn 2000). Conversely, five writers supported redress by appealing to notions of collective obligation. They argued that 'right-wing zealots' should stop ignoring historic grievances (Marshall 1995); that 'all Canadians' owe 'financial restitutions' (*sic*) to First Nations (Jones 1999); that society bears 'responsibility for the ongoing [problems] of many First Nations' (Fournier 1995); and that 'continual denial ... will never heal our wounds [or] free our conscience' (Simmonds 2001). These writers appeared to share the view that 'to ignore the pain of your fellow ... is something we should all be ashamed of' (Pallett 1998). This admittedly speculative account suggests that demands for redress may tend to win support from the welfare state's friends while sparking condemnation from its foes, thus doing little to alter or otherwise affect existing left-wing coalitions.

However, two special reader-comment features that appeared in the Halifax *Daily News* might seem to support a different conclusion. Many readers who responded to the paper's successive calls to comment on the Africville reparations movement conveyed a level, and indeed a particular type, of hostility that merits discussion. Readers spoke about Africville and its campaigners in the following terms: 'They are just trying to get money out of people's guilt'; 'They are opportunists looking to bleed more money from white taxpayers' (in Bornais 2002); 'Most of the residents were already paid $50 or $100—that's all the damn land was worth anyway'; 'they were given nicer homes than the ones they had'; 'I always thought Uniacke Square and Mulgrave Park [Halifax public housing projects] were built to compensate for the relocation of Africville residents. Am I wrong?' (in Bornais 2004).

Three possible, and perhaps interrelated, interpretations of this line of comment should be considered. First, as the remarks offered by Barnes (2004) in her interview on African-Canadian reparations would suggest, the hostile reaction may reflect a racist opposition 'based purely on the fact that Blacks are seeking reparations'. Second, the Africville campaign's focus on the responsibility and guilt of one particular city—a relative rarity in the world of redress politics—may be having a uniquely explosive local effect. Third, and most relevant to the corrosion hypothesis, the responses may reflect the heightened sensitivity of financial reparation in Atlantic Canada; the country's most economically deprived region. This latter interpretation might explain the note of jealousy in many of the remarks. For example, one respondent quite unreasonably inflated the significance of the token payments made at the time of the relocation, while two others portrayed public housing as a form of reward.[19]

---

[19] On the original payments, see Clairmont and Magill (1999: 188–90).

Jealous reactions from people whose own deprivation makes them resent 'special' treatment for others would certainly seem to indicate evidence of a corroding effect. However, the problem goes well beyond the realm of multiculturalism: reactions of this sort are associated with liberal welfare state policies themselves (Esping-Andersen 1990). As Fraser suggests: 'Affirmative [i.e. selective or means-tested] redistributive remedies for class injustices... shift attention from the class division between workers and capitalists to the division between employed and nonemployed fractions of the working class. Public assistance programs "target" the poor, not only for aid but for hostility' (1997: 25). Thus, the potential of targeted solutions to spark or inflame intra-class divisions certainly merits exploration in the context of redress politics. But it is less credibly raised as a plea to defend an existing liberal welfare state against the alleged divisiveness of multiculturalism.

It would be more reasonable to say that a liberal welfare state already straining under its own limitations and contradictions is unlikely to move forward while suffering the additional jealousies and conflicts that redress politics may bring in its wake (cf. Fraser 1997: 28). However, this perspective highlights the importance of a key contribution that the genre's often combative rhetoric may otherwise obscure. In the Canadian context, for example, redress campaigns are promoting precisely what severely fractured societies lack; common civic discussion around contentious aspects of a shared problematic history.

Scholars have criticized past attempts of the Canadian federal government to ground national unity on a 'myopic... ideology of shared values' (Norman 1995: 137). Lamenting what they see as often patronizing incantations to rally around a collective vision of the good, they argue that the country would be better off pursuing a more modest willingness to forge a common stock of historical narratives 'within which we debate our differing values and priorities' (Kymlicka 1998: 174). Canadian redress campaigns make an important contribution to this latter project. Pioneers in what Barkan calls a 'new form of political negotiation that enables the rewriting of memory and historical identity' (2000: xvii), they help to build a common discursive context in which the beneficiaries and victims of historic injustice can better pursue the business of political togetherness.

Redress campaigners make the first move: they initiate the challenge that tries to engage the reconciliatory energies of the dominant society. The move is risky, because the dominant society may fail respectfully to respond, exposing group members to the hurt and even humiliation that can constitute the rebuffed challenger's fate (cf. Bourdieu 1977: 10–12). It is therefore significant that Canadian redress movements are beginning to persuade dominant groups to abandon some of their more grossly self-serving misinterpretations of the country's past. The Japanese Canadian Redress Agreement formally acknowledges that 'the Government of Canada wrongfully incarcerated, seized the property, and disenfranchised thousands of citizens of Japanese ancestry' (in Miki and Kobayashi 1991: 138–9). Although the federal government's limited apology for the sexual and physical abuse suffered by Indigenous peoples in the residential schools is woefully inadequate, at least the doubtful quotation marks once used by newspaper headline-writers, as in, ' "Atrocities" Alleged in Mission Schools' (Aubry 1994), have now given way to a frank admission: 'Residential Schools: A Sad History of Abuse' (*Vancouver Sun* 1998). In a more limited but still significant vein, the Ontario Court of Appeal has described the head tax as 'racist and discriminatory', urging the federal government to make reparation (*Shack Jang Mack*, et al. 2002).

Even without settlements, redress movements are making it untenable for dominant groups to continue to profess ignorance or offer convenient rationalizations for past wrongs. Whereas even twenty years ago many of the more shameful episodes of Canadian history were seldom taught or discussed (Strong-Boag 1994), today a Google search of Canadian web pages yields the following results: 'residential schools', 25,000 hits; Ukrainian + internment, 1,610 hits; Japanese + internment, 6,370 hits; Chinese + 'head tax', 1,950 hits; Africville, 1,910 hits; 'African-Canadian' + slavery, 697 hits.[20] Thus, it appears that redress movements are transforming Canadian memory and historical identity in ways that help to promote a more accurate and inclusive public discourse—an absolutely vital basis for building solidarity and cohesion. If Canada's welfare state depends on solidarity and cohesion, and we wish to reject conformity and quiescence as legitimate routes to achieving it, then redress movements are in this respect contributing to its defence.

Conclusion

Do redress campaigns help erode the Canadian welfare state? This chapter has treated the question by considering the misdiagnosis, crowding-out, and corrosion effects in turn. It has spent considerable time on the

---

[20] Search performed 22 Oct. 2004.

misdiagnosis effect because the perhaps most distinctive political contributions that social movements make are the novel understandings and modes of redressing injustice that they foster. Focusing on the cases of First Nations and African-Canadians, I have noted the tendency of redress campaigns to diagnose socio-economic needs through a cultural lens. Although this approach to injustice is often ridiculed, these campaigns do not pursue cultural affirmation as a stand-alone solution to economic injustice, but rather as a means of solving problems of political voice. The residential-schools, Africville, and broader African-Canadian redress movements all see processes of cultural and group affirmation as ways of building strength and improving the group's capacity to elicit a respectful hearing from the dominant society. With this approach, they aim to pursue more effectively their distinctive and traditionally ignored distributive needs.

Considering the Machiavellian version of the misdiagnosis argument yielded more worrisome results. Although most redress movements resist the attempt to place heritage redress in the service of neoliberal goals, a further problem remains. This problem is that an emphasis on repairing victims of extraordinary episodes of official discrimination may help neoliberal moves to redefine social citizenship as a matter of helping the certifiably 'innocent'. It is important to keep this problem in view without reverting to a one-sided economism that effaces problems of racism and colonialism.

I then asked about the crowding-out effect: whether Canadian redress movements sap time and energy that might otherwise be devoted to redistribution. Evidence gathered from interviews with leading movement participants suggests that the zero-sum view of activism in crude versions of the crowding-out hypothesis is mistaken. Yet redress campaigns do not appear to motivate participant action in the cause of welfare state defence. Indeed, activists seemed quite sceptical about the quintessential save-the-welfare state appeal, which enjoins people to act in solidarity with others to defend cherished components of a common citizenship. This response suggests that the mood of go-it-alone defiance that exponents of the corroding hypothesis worry about is real. It may even lend some limited credence to the concern that a fissiparous social-movement multiculturalism may sometimes undermine the citizen solidarity on which redistribution appears to depend.

So why be sanguine about the impact of redress politics on the Canadian welfare state? The more optimistic picture is initially difficult to perceive. Activists are suspicious of appeals to worry about the broader citizenship or political community. For their part, people who dislike being confronted with problems of social injustice and collective obligation make their own contribution to the picture of a fragmented polity sundered by multiculturalist excess. But more important developments may be taking place. The case of the Japanese Canadian Redress Agreement demonstrates how a polity can earn back some of the civic energy and openness that welfare-state defence requires. Some redress campaigners have found success in reaching out to traditional-left allies. Finally, and of perhaps greatest significance, redress politics appears to be forging a new discursive context in which the beneficiaries and the victims of historical injustice can begin meaningfully to discuss their joint histories and future.

9

Does the recognition of national minorities undermine the welfare state?

Nicola McEwen

1. Introduction

Many established welfare states are also multinational states which encompass one or more national minorities within their territorial boundaries. The multinational character of such states need not be politically significant, and for much of the inter-war and early post-war period, national minorities often seemed content to live within the established institutional structures of the state. This contentment dissipated in the last forty years, with national minorities across many advanced capitalist societies demanding greater recognition of their national status, and articulating their distinctiveness in demands for self-government. States have often responded to such pressures by granting a degree of political autonomy to national minorities, often leading to the establishment or strengthening of substate political institutions (Keating 2001; Guibernau 1999).

Inasmuch as it recognizes and perhaps accentuates their distinctive identities, the granting of limited self-government to national minorities by established national states may be considered an aspect of multicultural policy. However, the territorial nature of national minority demands sets this group apart from the other groups discussed in this book. Unlike groups making non-territorial demands for identity recognition,

I am very grateful to the editors and to Wilfried Swenden for helpful comments on an earlier draft. I am also grateful to André Lecours and Daniel Béland for a preview of their as yet unpublished manuscript.

a national minority has an opt-out solution—ultimately secession from the state—should the existing state fail to recognize its identity and sense of distinctiveness. Granting limited self-government has been an effective tool by which states can manage and appease the demands of national minorities without unduly threatening the territorial integrity of the existing state. However, the establishment or strengthening of substate institutions has usually involved the decentralization of key elements of the welfare state. According to the critics, the welfare state has been weakened as a consequence.

Granting limited self-government is not the only way in which national minorities may be recognized by the state. As Banting and Kymlicka outline in Chapter 2, multiculturalism policies designed to recognize and accommodate national minorities may also include: recognition and support for minority languages; constitutional recognition of the multinational character of the state; enhanced representation for national minorities in central governmental and parliamentary institutions; and permitting the national minority to have a presence in the international arena. Some of these may be considered to have an eroding effect on the welfare state, particularly among those who consider the politics of recognition to 'crowd out' debates over wealth redistribution (Gitlin 1995) or to overlook the 'real' socio-economic problems which are deemed to underlie recognition claims (Barry 2001; see Chapter 1 for a discussion of these debates). However, the demand for self-government has been a consistent feature in the rise of minority nationalism in recent years, and the political autonomy which has often been conceded in an effort to appease such demands arguably poses the greatest challenge to the integrity and scope of the welfare state.

This chapter considers whether recognizing national minorities by permitting a degree of self-government undermines the welfare state. The first section of this chapter sets out the key arguments which suggest that such recognition weakens the welfare state. It then offers counterclaims, or rival hypotheses, which posit that strengthening substate political autonomy need not negatively affect the welfare state, and indeed may even strengthen it. These rival hypotheses are subsequently examined in a comparative analysis of Canada, Belgium, and the United Kingdom, which have granted varying degrees of political autonomy to their respective national minorities by strengthening existing substate institutions or establishing new ones. While each state can lay claim to more than one national minority, it is the effects of policies to accommodate the demands of Quebec, Flanders, and Scotland that are considered here.

2. Minority recognition and the challenge to the welfare state

National minorities have long displayed a dual sense of national identity, feeling a sense of belonging to the minority nation alongside an identification with and attachment to the national state. There is nothing inherently incompatible about such dual national identities. Citizens may feel simultaneously Québécois and Canadian, Flemish and Belgian, or Scottish and British, without any sense of contradiction. However, recent years have seen a weakening in the sense of statewide national identity and a strengthening of substate national identity, which has found expression in demands for greater self-government. States have responded to such demands by extending political autonomy to national minorities, giving substantive recognition to their distinctiveness as nations within the state.

Some observers have suggested that enhancing political autonomy can have a corroding effect on the welfare state. Two distinctive effects can be identified here. Recognition of national minorities—with or without substate government—reinforces their sense of difference from their co-citizens, and may inhibit interregional solidarity, trust, and identity, and undermine popular support for redistribution from richer to poorer regions (Wolfe and Klausen 1997; Miller 1995). A similar criticism has been levelled at all forms of ethno-cultural recognition (see Chapter 1), but the institutional recognition of national minorities poses a particular, additional challenge. Enhanced substate autonomy has often been accompanied by the decentralization of the welfare state, giving considerable responsibility for social policy to substate governments. This may foster intergovernmental competition between regions, which depresses welfare expenditures, and generate institutional barriers to further statewide welfare development (Huber, Ragin, and Stephens 1993; Peterson 1995; Swank 2002). Other critics have argued that a focus upon the recognition of national minorities 'crowds out' more pressing policy issues and fails to address the real socio-economic grievances which are often at the root of demands for self-government (Gitlin 1995; Barry 2001). These concerns will be explored more fully below, before presenting alternative hypotheses on the relationship between minority self-government and the welfare state.

Exploring the negative effects on the welfare state of national minority self-government

The recognition of national minorities by granting enhanced substate autonomy may have two distinctive corroding effects on the maintenance and development of the welfare state: the first is institutional, while the second concerns the shared identity that underpins welfare redistribution.

In the first instance, granting a degree of social policy autonomy to substate governments is considered to have a corroding effect on the welfare state by slowing the pace of welfare development. A substantial literature has presented strong evidence to suggest that the pace of welfare expansion was slower in highly decentralized and federal states than in unitary states. The blame for this retarded development is attributed to the structures of federal states and the competitive environment these structures generate between the constituent units (Huber, Ragin, and Stephens 1993; Swank 2002; Obinger, Leibfried, and Castles 2005). Sharing policy responsibilities between different levels of government multiplies the number of institutional 'veto points', making it more difficult to achieve interregional and intergovernmental consensus in favour of welfare expansion. However, although decentralized state structures may impede welfare expansion, they also appear to slow the pace of welfare retrenchment. Obinger, Leibfried, and Castles's recent study identified a 'ratchet effect' which impedes retrenchment, with the same institutional veto points making it more difficult to generate the consensus required to diminish the scope of the welfare state (Obinger, Leibfried, and Castles 2005).

Political decentralization introduced within established welfare democracies may also shape welfare development and depress welfare expenditures. Indeed, because substate communities are often more vulnerable to the threat of capital flight—'when even a single corporate relocation can devastate an entire community' (Piven 1995: 114)—they may be more reluctant to pursue generous welfare policies that involve raising taxes or impinging on the freedom and flexibility of the market (Pierson 2001). A similar 'exit option' is available to upper income groups on whom the additional tax burden may disproportionately fall. Such a flight of capital and of high-earning, higher-taxed groups may exacerbate the welfare needs of the population while diminishing the resources available to the state to address these needs. To avoid such a scenario, substate governments may be more inclined to limit welfare expenditures in order to maintain a competitive edge vis-à-vis other competitor regions, provoking an interregional 'race to the bottom' in welfare provision (Huber, Ragin, and Stephens 1993; Peterson 1995; Swank 2002).

These criticisms are not confined to decentralization in multinational states. The 'race to the bottom' hypothesis has primarily emerged from empirical studies of federalism in the United States, which is not designed to grant self-government to (territorial) national minorities. Moreover, beyond the United States case, there is little consistent empirical evidence to support it as a general hypothesis on the depressing effects of political decentralization on welfare development (Schram and Soss 1998). Some findings suggest that the effect of decentralization depends upon the divisions of responsibility for revenue raising and spending between the levels of government. Where responsibility for spending is decentralized but responsibility for revenue raising is centralized, other things being equal, social expenditure tends to be higher. By contrast, in countries where both revenue raising and welfare spending are decentralized, expenditure levels tend to be lower (Rodden 2003; Obinger, Leibfried, and Castles 2005).

A second set of criticisms is levelled at the particular impact of identity recognition. The substantive recognition of substate national identities reinforces the sense of difference shared by national minorities, and undermines their sense of identification with their fellow citizens. This may, in turn, have a corroding effect on the welfare state by weakening support for welfare redistribution. According to Wolfe and Klausen, the recent emergence of identity politics, including territorial politics, has contributed to undermining the welfare state by compromising the common culture and sense of national citizenship which makes welfare states possible (Wolfe and Klausen 1997). This view is also aired by liberal scholars of nationalism, who fear that the erosion of statewide national identities weakens support for the welfare state. Miller argued that a shared national identity, because it embodies feelings of solidarity and mutual obligation among members of a national community, represents an essential prerequisite to the functioning of redistributive welfare systems. Without the shared obligations implied by a common collective identity, membership of a political community would be based upon rational self-interest and a relationship of strict reciprocity. Under such circumstances, citizens would expect to receive benefits in proportion to the contributions they make, thus precluding a redistribution of resources on the basis of need (Miller 1995: 71–3; Miller 2000: 105–6). Similarly, Canovan argued that the sense of communal solidarity inherent in national identity explains why goods and possessions should be

251

regarded as shared and defines the boundaries within which they should be redistributed (Canovan 1996: 27–35).

These concerns point to the importance of the welfare state in reflecting, and arguably reinforcing, shared identity and group solidarity. As Keating observed, the relationship between territorial identities and the welfare state cuts both ways: 'Not only does a sense of common identity help sustain the values of mutual help, but the welfare state itself helps foster national identity and unity' (Keating 2001: 40). Public policy designed to recognize the rights and status granted by virtue of one's membership of a national community may in turn reinforce the national identity and sense of national solidarity upon which they are founded. This affects not only feelings of solidarity between class groups, but also feelings of solidarity between regions within the state. As such, the welfare state and the recognition of social rights it entailed may have contributed to strengthening the extent to which national minorities could feel a sense of belonging to the nation-state as well as to their own distinctive nation (McEwen 2006). The decentralization of the welfare state weakens the extent to which it can contribute to strengthening interregional solidarity in this way. This problem may be especially acute where the minority nation is wealthier than other parts of the state. National minorities who no longer feel a strong sense of dual national identity may feel little obligation towards citizens living in other poorer regions of the state, and may resent carrying an additional expenditure burden to meet their greater social and economic needs. A weakened sense of identity and solidarity between regions may thus undermine the capacity of the welfare state to support interregional transfers from richer to poorer regions. Without such transfers, it would be difficult to ensure that citizens throughout the state could gain access to a similar standard of social programmes, or share common social citizenship rights.

Recognition of national minorities, where it takes the form of stronger political autonomy and control over social policy, thus poses a challenge to the principle of social citizenship underlying the welfare state. In T. H. Marshall's analysis, the welfare state marked the evolution of citizenship from the civil and political sphere to the social sphere, ensuring an equalization of status among members of the political community and the provision of uniform social rights (Marshall and Bottomore 1992). The principle of social citizenship underpinning the post-war welfare state was intended to ensure equitable access to health care, education, social security and other public services to all citizens, regardless of their place in society or their place of residence. It is such equitable access that permitted social rights to be a basis of fraternity among the citizens of a state. However, substate autonomy over welfare legislation opens up the opportunity for policy divergence between governments within and across the state, and may lead to the development of distinctive and diverse welfare regimes within the boundaries of a single state. As such, citizens in one part of the country may be entitled to particular social services that are denied to their co-citizens in other regions. The degree to which the state provides for the social and economic security of its citizens—the degree to which it recognizes and guarantees their social rights—may thus be dependent upon where in the state citizens live. Such differing entitlements and rights within the same state may generate a sense of injustice that further erodes interregional solidarity ties (Jeffery 2005).

The focus of this chapter is on the potential corroding effects that the recognition of national minorities by granting limited self-government may have on the maintenance of redistributive welfare states. In addition to these corroding effects, critics have suggested that such recognition claims also produce 'crowding-out' and 'misdiagnosis' effects which undermine welfare systems (Gitlin 1995; Barry 2001). In the first case, demands for identity recognition may consume the energy and time of activists on the liberal-left who might otherwise have campaigned for redistributive welfare. Diverting attention away from redistribution to recognition risks pushing socio-economic issues to the margins of political and legislative debate, and allowing class inequality to prevail. Canadian politics, for example, has long been dominated by the need to balance linguistic and regional interests, and more recently, to accommodate Quebec within the federation without alienating Canadians in the rest of the country, with class-based politics pushed to the sidelines (Banting 2005a). Secondly, it has sometimes been argued that claims for identity recognition misdiagnose the real problem. Here, the root problem underlying the grievances of national minorities or other minority groups is considered to be their relative class or socio-economic status, which cannot be addressed by identity recognition alone. This has been an important historical concern of the British labour movement. Although Scotland and Wales represented the party's heartland for much of the twentieth century, the Labour Party argued that the problems facing the UK's national minorities could only be addressed by commanding control of the levers of central government. When the Labour Party officially abandoned its policy commitment to Scottish self-government (the policy had been abandoned in spirit many years earlier), it justified its position by arguing that 'Scotland's problems can best be solved by social-ist planning on a United Kingdom scale' (Labour Party [Scottish Council] 1958: 1).[1] From this perspective, addressing demands for recognition or special treatment was really a manifestation of deeper socio-economic inequalities which could only be addressed by managing the national economy and employing the tools of central government to support redistributive welfare throughout the country.

In sum, the recognition of national minorities, especially when accom-panied by decentralized political institutions, may have a negative effect on the welfare state in a number of ways. We may identify distinctive corroding effects, whereby political decentralization produces more 'veto points' to inhibit statewide welfare expansion and generates competition between regions which may diminish welfare expenditures, while identity recognition undermines the shared identity and interregional solidarity upon which redistributive welfare systems depend. Devoting attention to demands for recognition may also 'crowd out', or marginalize, debates over redistribution. This is doubly problematic for those who consider that recognition claims 'misdiagnose' the real problem, which can only be addressed by redistributive policies at the centre.

All of these claims can be contested, and we may identify a number of counter-claims and alternative hypotheses to suggest that granting self-government to national minorities need not have a negative impact on the welfare state. Indeed, under certain scenarios, the decentralization of the welfare state which often accompanies regional self-government may even boost welfare expansion.

Can self-government for national minorities strengthen the welfare state?

The recognition of national minorities by strengthening their politi-cal autonomy need not undermine the welfare state. Indeed, we may plausibly present a counter-claim to suggest that granting limited self-government to national minorities may revitalize and strengthen state welfare. Three alternative hypotheses may be identified: (i) national minorities who share a strong sense of solidarity may be better placed to support the development of generous welfare regimes at the substate level; (ii) decentralization may provide an opportunity for policy exper-imentation and innovation at the substate level which can lead to pro-gressive welfare policies throughout the state; and (iii) in multinational

---

[1] The Labour Party renewed its commitment to limited self-government for Scotland and Wales in the 1970s, in response to electoral pressure from the Scottish National Party and Plaid Cymru.

states, the welfare state may represent a tool in the competing nation-building projects of state and substate governments, augmenting rather than diminishing the state welfare.

First, concerns that the decentralization of the welfare state weakens social citizenship and has a corroding effect on the welfare state assume that the state is the relevant policy community for social solidarity, and that the state alone has the capacity for maintaining redistributive welfare systems. However, support for generous and redistributive welfare systems may be more easily maintained at the substate level. National minorities already share a strong sense of identity and belonging together. The governments that represent them may be better equipped than are central governments within multinational states to draw upon feelings of commonality and shared identity to maintain and expand the welfare system. Such societies also tend to benefit from an 'institutional thickness' between government, business, and labour that may nurture mutual trust and facilitate cooperation and compromise between the social partners (Rhodes 1996: 169).

Moreover, advocates of greater self-government for national minorities have often presented themselves as defenders of welfare rights and promoters of the solidarity of the communities they represent (Moreno 2003). Far from being a distraction from 'real' socio-economic problems, or crowding-out issues of social welfare, national minority demands for self-government have often been tied to social and economic objectives, with self-government presented as a means by which the social and economic needs of these nations can best be addressed (McEwen 2006). Thus, the decentralization of the welfare state need not represent a brake on social policy development, but may redefine the boundaries of the welfare community, creating new spaces in which social citizenship may prosper.

Second, political decentralization need not generate interregional competition or produce a 'race to the bottom' in welfare expenditures. Rather, decentralization may stimulate social policy innovation, with substate governments acting as a locus of policy experimentation and a vehicle for change at the national level. For example, several social programmes underpinning the post-war Canadian welfare state were pioneered in the province of Saskatchewan (Banting 2005a; Béland and Lecours 2005a). The extension of political decentralization within established welfare democracies may also stimulate policy innovation. Where substate governments have autonomy over aspects of the welfare state, some degree of social policy divergence may be inevitable, implying a variation in the social rights and social services available to citizens in different parts of the state. However, the effects of social policy divergence may be offset by a 'demonstration effect' that minimizes the detrimental consequences for interregional solidarity (Moreno and McEwen 2005). For example, when the Basque government launched a minimum income programme (Plan de Lucha contra la Pobreza), it sparked the other Spanish *communidades autónomas* into establishing similar programmes, in a form of 'competitive state-building' (Arriba and Moreno 2004).

Third, in multinational states which have multi-level government, social policy may serve as a tool in the competing nation-building projects of state and substate governments. Nation building is not only evident in the period of nation and state formation. Rather, nation building is a continuous process, a form of politics designed to maintain a sense of identity and belonging to the national community, and strengthen the legitimacy of the political community. It is especially significant in multinational states, when a state's claim to represent a nation or people is challenged by the presence and voice of a national minority. The nation-building role of welfare may be identified in three ways (McEwen 2006). Welfare state institutions can serve a symbolic function, representing a common heritage, a symbol of shared risks and mutual commitment, and a common project for the future. This may be particularly effective in supporting statewide national identities in multinational states, allowing such identities to develop alongside substate cultural or historic national identities. In addition, welfare service provision entails recognition of the social rights of citizenship, and may reinforce the ties that bind the citizens to the institutional level which guarantees these rights. The provision of social services enhances the ability of governments to appeal directly to their citizens and to nurture loyalty on the basis that they represent the source and guarantor of their social well-being. The development of the welfare state also enhanced the relevance of the institutions of the state in the everyday lives of its citizens. Welfare development led by the centre may heighten the importance of statewide 'national' political parties and leaders operating within statewide 'national' institutional frameworks, shifting the focus away from substate political institutions and marginalizing the territorial dimension of political debate.

The nation-building function of the welfare state may be evident at the level of the state as well as the substate level, depending upon the locus of social policy control (Banting 1995: 270–1). Where power rests with central government, social policy can be utilized to mediate regional conflicts and reinforce national integration, strengthening the authority and legitimacy of the state in the face of challenges from territorial minorities. Conversely, where social programmes are developed and managed at the substate level, they may strengthen regional cultures and enhance the significance of regional governments in the everyday lives of their citizens. In the context of multilevel government, responsibility for policy development is often shared between state and substate governments, with a degree of interdependence between the different governmental levels. Control over social policy development has emerged as an area of tension in intergovernmental relations, especially as nationalist-leaning governments at the substate level seek to extend their policy jurisdiction while central governments seek to preserve their scope for intervention in the social policy sphere. Of course, social policy is not the only area of policy to be the subject of such disputes, but its role in the politics of nation building may make it particularly significant. Rather than crowd out issues of social welfare, such intergovernmental competitiveness may push them to the top of the political agenda. And, instead of corroding the welfare state, competitive nation building between state and substate governments may generate increased social welfare provision.

Thus, granting self-government to national minorities may have positive consequences for the welfare state, enhancing the scope of substate welfare regimes and promoting policy innovation and experimentation which, when successful, may be extended throughout the state. The welfare state may also serve as a tool in the competing nation building projects of state and substate governments, promoting welfare expansion as both levels of government compete for the loyalty and attachment of the citizens. These claims and counter-claims can now be tested empirically in our three case studies.

3. The welfare state and the politics of self-government in Canada, Belgium, and the United Kingdom

Canada, Belgium, and the United Kingdom are multinational states and advanced welfare states which have had to respond to demands for recognition and autonomy from nations within their boundaries. In particular, nationalist movements in Quebec, Flanders, and Scotland have emerged to demand greater self-government, and ultimately to challenge the territorial integrity of their respective states. As such, they offer useful case studies in which we can examine whether granting autonomy to national minorities erodes or enhances the welfare state.

There are a number of dissimilarities between the cases which should be borne in mind. Canada is a historic federation in which Quebec and the other nine provinces have enjoyed a long period of self-government. Although in theory a symmetric system, in practice federalism is asymmetric, with Quebec exercising more policy and fiscal autonomy than the other provinces. A formerly unitary state, Belgium adopted a federal constitution in 1993 and while the three regions and communities enjoy similar status and powers, the fusion of the Flemish region and community introduced asymmetry into the system. The United Kingdom is not a federal system and the devolution initiated in 1999 is highly asymmetric. Whereas Scotland, Wales, Northern Ireland, and Greater London have been granted varying degrees of autonomy, there is no institution to represent the rest of England separate from the UK parliament and government.

There are important differences, too, in the relative strength of the nations within these states. Within Canada, Quebec's status as a distinctive nation has been disputed, but its geographic centrality, size, and its position as the home of the majority of Canada's francophone population has made it difficult for Canadian governments to ignore Quebec's self-government demands. Flanders arguably has even greater significance to the future of Belgium. Strictly speaking, categorizing Flanders as a national minority is inaccurate, given that it is the largest and wealthiest region of Belgium, and home to the Dutch-speaking majority. Scotland's status as a nation within the UK has never been seriously questioned, but its peripheral location and relatively small proportion of the UK population has at times facilitated the marginalization of Scottish issues in UK political debate. Still, no state welcomes challenges to its territorial integrity, and the growth of the Scottish self-government movement prompted the state to respond with proposals to devolve power over domestic affairs.

These contrasts between the cases influence the extent to which, and the manner in which, the recognition of their national identity in the establishment or strengthening of autonomous political institutions shapes the politics and development of the welfare state.

Canada and Quebec

Canada is a long-established federation in which powers and responsibilities are constitutionally divided between the federal government and the provinces. Control over social welfare provision falls largely within provincial jurisdiction, but the fiscal strength of the federal government has enabled it to devise a role for itself in developing a pan-Canadian welfare state (Guest 1997).

As a historic federation, Canada offers an important insight into the effects of political decentralization on welfare development. The development of the Canadian welfare state has been shaped by the federal division of powers, sometimes prompting innovation and welfare development, while at other times representing a block to expansion. For example, innovative policy experiments in the province of Saskatchewan in the 1940s arguably served as a catalyst for federal government proposals to establish a comprehensive pan-Canadian welfare state (Banting 1987; 2005a). However, the institutional veto points inherent in the federal system saw the federal government's post-war package of welfare proposals (the Green Book proposals) blocked by opposition from the provincial governments of Ontario and Quebec. This delayed rather than prevented post-war welfare expansion, although Quebec lagged behind the rest of Canada in this regard (Vaillancourt 1988: 116–17). As a result of the intransigence of the Union Nationale government, Québécois were denied access to many federal social welfare initiatives implemented in the 1940s and 1950s. These programmes were rejected in the name of provincial autonomy, but the Quebec government's opposition also reflected the regime's fiscal conservatism. The slow pace of welfare development in Quebec is thus best explained by ideological rather than institutional factors.

When federal governments have been able to bypass provincial opposition or secure provincial consent, they have been able to develop policies that generate comparable levels of social provision across the state. A federal Equalization Program was introduced in 1957 to provide payments to poorer provinces to enhance their capacity to meet social need, while a system of conditional transfer payments supports the development of equivalent programmes in health care, post-secondary education, and social assistance. Although delivered at the provincial level, shared-cost programmes permit the federal government to impose national standards as a condition of its fiscal transfers. The 1984 Canada Health Act, for example, reinforced national standards in health care, underlining that the federal government's financial support was conditional upon provincial programmes meeting five principles: universality, portability, comprehensiveness, accessibility, and public administration. Most controversially, the federal government has used its spending power to bypass provinces altogether by providing direct benefits to individual Canadians as a right of citizenship (Banting 1998: 41–7; Guest 1997: 207–12; Vaillancourt and Rault 2003). Some observers have noted a trend in recent years of an increased reliance on the federal spending power to achieve social policy goals, reflected in initiatives such as the Canada Child Tax Benefit and the Millennium Scholarships Fund (Noël 1999).

Canada also offers insight into the effects of territorial identity politics on welfare development. A territorially based nationalism has been evident in Quebec since the early 1960s, yet there is little evidence to suggest that the assertion and recognition of Quebec's distinctive identity has had a corroding effect on the welfare state. Indeed, the immediate impact within Quebec was to strengthen welfare provision. During Quebec's Quiet Revolution, the Quebec Liberal government of the day sought greater control of Quebec's economy and society and demanded increased autonomy over social and fiscal policies in order to allow the Quebec 'state' to act as an instrument for improving the status and living standards of francophone Québécois (McRoberts 1993; Coleman 1984: 157–70). Responding to these demands, the federal government permitted the government of Quebec to opt out of a broad range of shared-cost and conditional programmes in health, education, and welfare, receiving fiscal compensation and enhanced revenue-raising capacity to initiate its own (similar) programmes. The Quebec government also negotiated an agreement to introduce its own Quebec Pension Plan, albeit closely tied to the plan offered to Canadians outside Quebec (Simeon 1972: 58–9). Such opting-out of shared-cost social programmes enhanced Quebec's political autonomy and represented a de facto recognition of Quebec's status as a national minority.[2] The provincial government used its autonomy to ensure that Québécois gained access to similar social programmes already available to other Canadians, and in some cases, social welfare provision in Quebec superseded provision in other provinces. Among other developments, the Quebec government standardized and expanded health-care provision, extended compulsory schooling and post-secondary education, and increased income security provision. State intervention was embraced as the means by which Quebec could not only survive but flourish as a distinctive nation (Laurin-Frenette 1978: 126–38; McRoberts 1993: 128–41). Thus, the enhanced autonomy granted to Quebec in the 1960s arguably expanded rather than diminished welfare provision within Quebec.

---

[2] Opting out was offered to all provinces but accepted only by Quebec. It thus represents an informal special status within the context of a formal equality of the provinces.

The politics of territorial identity may also have had positive effects for the welfare state in the rest of Canada. Although institutional veto points have sometimes blocked federal initiatives that require provincial consent, the nation-building or 'statecraft' potential of pan-Canadian welfare has been recognized and exploited by federal governments, especially when responding to nationalism in Quebec. For example, Pierre Trudeau's tenure as Liberal Prime Minister was dominated by a drive to foster the idea of Canada as one national community, and strengthening the federal government's role in welfare provision was a key aspect of this project. A series of federal proposals in the late 1960s sought to enhance the federal government's social policy role, with one working paper arguing that a sense of Canadian solidarity justified an enhanced federal role in income distribution which, in turn, would give 'additional meaning in the minds of those who receive the payments to the concept of a Canadian community' (Canada 1969: 68). McRoberts suggested that these ill-fated proposals (the proposals fell with the 1971 Victoria Charter) were bound up with Trudeau's hostility to Quebec nationalism and his efforts to strengthen Québécois' attachment to the federal state—a strategy which 'made it important for them to receive direct services and benefits from the federal government' (McRoberts 1997: 144).

Successive federal governments, particularly under the Liberal Party, have similarly sought to defend and expand the federal government's presence in the social policy arena. One study accused successive federal governments of attempting to purchase national unity through continual increases in social programme spending, a practice which was perhaps only temporarily interrupted in the 1990s by the need to rein in the deficit (James and Lustzig 2002). Indeed, the Liberal government was re-elected in 2004 with a commitment to renewed state intervention in the social policy arena, especially in health care. This included pledges to introduce universal shared-cost programmes in pharmacare and child care, extending to the rest of Canada programmes which are already operating in Quebec. As well as providing evidence of a 'demonstration effect', these initiatives may also reflect the use of social policy in Canadian nation building. Quebec will secure an opt-out to continue to run its own programmes, but the fiscal compensation provided by the federal government will ensure that Quebec's programmes remain broadly in line with those extended to the rest of Canada.

Notwithstanding ongoing debates regarding a vertical fiscal imbalance in the Canadian federation with respect to the revenue-raising capacity and spending obligations of the federal and provincial governments

(Boadway 2004; Lazar, St-Hilaire, and Tremblay 2004), Quebec remains a recipient of substantial equalization payments, representing implicit transfers from richer to poorer provinces.[3] If Quebec's territorial demands and claims for recognition had corroded interregional solidarity, we might expect that support for these payments would be undermined. Yet, although the operation of the programme is not without criticism (Finance Ministers 2003), support for the principle of equalization remains strong across provincial governments and within the wider population. In a joint statement issued in 2003, provincial and territorial Finance Ministers reiterated their support for the maintenance and strengthening of the Equalization Program, and stressed that 'the ability to obtain relatively comparable public services, regardless of province of residence, is a value Canadians cherish' (ibid. 14). Indeed, survey evidence suggests strong support across all provinces for the federal Equalization Program, with support ranging from 78 per cent (Alberta) to over 90 per cent (Nova Scotia and British Columbia) (CRIC 2004).

Quebec's demands for recognition and autonomy have dominated Canadian politics in the last forty years. Critics may wish to suggest that this provides evidence of a 'crowding-out' effect, with the dominance of constitutional issues pushing social and economic issues off the political agenda. Indeed, the constitutional upheaval of the 1980s[4] coincided with a period of welfare retrenchment, which saw the federal Conservative government reduce social expenditure, especially in fiscal transfers to the provinces (Rice and Prince 1993: 391–6). In its early years, the succeeding Liberal government continued the trend towards the retrenchment of state welfare programmes, overhauling (and effectively cutting back) fiscal transfer payments. Some observers expressed concern that a diminished federal role in social welfare weakened Canadian nationhood and solidarity (Banting 1995: 287–90; Rice and Prince 1993: 399). Welfare retrenchment, however, was provoked by ideological pressures and a desire to

---

[3] In fact, equalization is a vertical programme and is entirely funded by the federal government from consolidated federal revenues. Three provinces (Alberta, British Columbia, and Ontario) are identified as 'have' provinces and do not receive any payments, while the others are identified as 'have not' provinces and receive varying entitlements based upon standard calculation. There are no direct transfers from 'have' provinces to 'have not' provinces (Hobson 2002: 4; Vaillancourt and Rault 2003: 135–6).

[4] In 1982, in the face of the unanimous opposition of the Quebec National Assembly, the Trudeau government repatriated the Canadian Constitution and introduced a Charter of Rights and Freedoms. The subsequent decade was dominated by ill-fated attempts to give constitutional recognition to Quebec as a distinct society and to facilitate its reintegration into the constitution, first with the intergovernmental Meech Lake Accord and later in the defeated referendum on the Charlottetown Accord (Gagnon 1993; McRoberts 1993: 190–221; Boismenu 1993).

reduce the deficit, not by Quebec's demands for recognition. Indeed, notwithstanding the degree to which ideologically motivated retrenchment pressures had also been evident within Quebec, federal cuts to social programmes and fiscal transfers shaped the discourse of those arguing for self-government in the 1995 referendum on Quebec sovereignty, in which the pro-sovereignty camp was defeated by less than 1 per cent of the vote. The perceived threat to social programmes from the federal government's neoliberal restructuring permitted sovereigntists to argue that the social and economic security of Québécois would be threatened in the event of a NO vote. Sovereignty, then, was presented as a *projet de société*, and a means of protecting and delivering social welfare for Québécois (Gagnon and Lachapelle 1996; Venne 1996; McEwen 2006).

Thus, there is little evidence to suggest that the politics of territorial identity in Quebec has had a corroding effect on the welfare state. The decentralized nature of Canadian welfare has sometimes presented institutional barriers impeding welfare development, while at other times presenting opportunities for policy innovation and policy transfer. The assertion of Quebec's distinctiveness and claims for recognition, meanwhile, does not appear to have eroded the sense of shared solidarity upholding interregional transfers. More evident is the manner in which social welfare has been drawn into the competing nation-building projects of Quebec and Canadian governments. Both levels of government have been keen to defend their control over social policy development and to present themselves as the defender of the social rights of their citizens. The effects have often been to augment rather than diminish welfare provision.

Belgium and Flanders

Belgium was founded and developed as a unitary state until a multi-stage devolution process, beginning in 1970, gave way to a formal federal structure in 1993. Its complex federal structure is composed of two overlapping types of constituent unit: three territorially defined regions (Flanders, Wallonia, and Brussels-Capital region) and three linguistic communities (the Dutch-speaking, French-speaking, and German-speaking communities). At the same time, Belgian federalism is also bipolar, structured around the two main linguistic communities, and asymmetric, most notably in the fusion of the institutions of the Flemish Region and Community, a process not replicated in the rest of the country (Swenden 2002). Although the Belgian federal system is highly decentralized, the key pillars of the post-war welfare state remain primarily the responsibility of the federal level. Indeed, in Belgian political debate, the term 'social security' has historically been used in preference to the term 'welfare state'. The pillars of Belgium's welfare system were founded upon four social insurance schemes: family allowances, unemployment insurance, health insurance, and old age insurance. Federalism has not fundamentally altered this system, as the federal level retains control over social insurance and the bulk of social spending. The communities have competence over 'personal matters', including education, social assistance, health services, family policy, and old age policy, but often within strict parameters set by the federal state. The regions have control over aspects of employment policy, but employment-related social insurance and labour law remain within the jurisdiction of the federal government (de Cock 2002; Dandoy and Baudewyns 2005).

The rise of Flemish nationalism and the polarization of the French-speaking and Dutch-speaking linguistic communities has been the driving force in the federalization process. The Flemish nationalist movement first emerged as a reaction against the cultural and political dominance of the francophone elite, and was strongly associated with demands for linguistic and cultural equality. Granting a degree of self-government to the constituent units was a concession which it was hoped would appease Flemish demands while maintaining the integrity of the state. The continued centralization of the Belgian welfare system has constrained the degree to which identity recognition has produced a corroding effect on the welfare state. However, demands for self-government have remained, and in recent years have centred on calls for a regionalization of social security, particularly in the areas of health care and child allowances.

Two key factors account for the emergence of demands for greater autonomy over social security. First, the process of federalization was accompanied by a disintegration of the party system along linguistic lines, creating a dynamic whereby Flemish-based parties seek to outbid each other in the defence and promotion of Flemish interests. The fragmentation of Volksunie, a nationalist party on the left, into groups which formed alliances with the other main parties, coupled with the need to respond to the rise of Vlaams Blok, a nationalist party on the far right, ensures that a nationalist dimension permeates the political spectrum in Flanders (Béland and Lecours 2005b). Secondly, in the latter half of the twentieth century, Flanders moved from being the poorest to the wealthiest region in Belgium, altering the direction of interregional transfers. Whereas Flanders was once a net recipient of fiscal transfers, a series of studies in the 1980s and 1990s found that Flanders had become a net contributor of transfers to Wallonia and Brussels-Capital region (Caruso et al. 2002; Cattoir and Docquier 1999). These are implicit interregional transfers. The Belgian social security system operates on the basis of solidarity between persons, with contributions based upon employment status and earnings, but a regional dimension emerges when one region consistently has higher income and employment levels than the others. Walloons benefit disproportionately in unemployment allowances, family allowances, health-care allowances, invalidity allowances, and pensions, with Flanders only receiving a net contribution in transfers for early retirement pensions (Cattoir and Docquier 1999: 250–1; Dandoy and Baudewyns 2005).

For francophone political elites resistant to demands for a regionalization of social security, the flow of fiscal resources to Wallonia and Brussels is justified by relatively greater need, and reflects the principle of solidarity underpinning the Belgian welfare system. Such a system is justified in a national community by the feelings of identity and mutual responsibility one feels for her fellow citizens. For political elites in Flanders, however, interregional differences in social spending also reflect distinctive cultural behaviour patterns. A nationalist discourse, often combined with a neoliberal discourse, has depicted Walloons as having a culture of dependence on the state, with habitual tendencies to overuse (and misuse) social services and social security benefits (Béland and Lecours 2005b: 272–5). More moderate Flemish politicians agree that cultural preferences play a part, especially in health care, citing a greater tendency for francophones to seek specialist services, and a greater propensity of francophone medics to engage in expensive medical practices (de Cock 2002: 61–3). Autonomy over health insurance and child allowances has also been sought as the logical next step in the process of federalization, which would bring coherence to the policy spheres under the jurisdiction of the regions and communities, as well as facilitate policy development in accordance with distinctive regional preferences. These different regional perspectives on the issue of social security regionalization may also reflect distinctive conceptions regarding the boundaries of the nation and the relevant community of social citizenship. Whereas for francophone political elites in Wallonia and Brussels, federal control over social security is an important basis of the solidarity of the Belgian nation and part of the cement holding this otherwise highly decentralized state together, the primary national and citizenship community of most Flemish political elites is Flanders, not Belgium (Poirier and Vansteenkiste 2000).

Inasmuch as the granting of limited self-government through federalization may have accentuated Flemish regional identity and institutional distinctiveness, it may lend support to the hypothesis that the politics of recognition can have a corroding effect on the welfare state by weakening the solidarity underpinning the welfare state, at least with respect to solidarity between regions if not necessarily between persons. It is impossible to say whether welfare expenditures would diminish were the demands for a regionalization of social security to be granted; all we can conclude is that, on the basis of current revenues and expenditures, Flanders would have more fiscal resources at its disposal and Wallonia would have fewer. The recent Flemish initiative of an insurance scheme covering long-term elderly care, and the Walloon push to have such a scheme adopted at the federal level to prevent an imbalance in the Belgian social security system (Béland and Lecours, forthcoming), suggests at least the prospect for autonomy to give rise to competitive nation building and demonstration effects in the development of social policy.

There are, however, a number of barriers blocking any such moves towards the regionalization of social security. The consociational nature of the Belgian political system, as well as the fragmentation of the party system, is such that governments are made up of coalitions between matching Flemish and Francophone parties, and legislative progress can only be secured with the consent of ministers representing the two main linguistic communities (Swenden 2002). Francophone parties concerned for the consequences for social and national solidarity thus represent an important institutional veto preventing the regionalization of social security. In addition, it is important to underline that these demands are primarily voiced at the elite level. According to the 2003 election study, although support for social security regionalization was greater among Flemish than Walloon respondents, at 41 per cent and 27 per cent respectively, the majority of Flemish respondents were either opposed to such a reform (34 per cent) or had no position either way (25 per cent) (Dandoy and Baudewyns 2005). Political elites, however, have an important role in shaping public opinion and these ongoing debates may yet influence perceptions of social and national solidarity across Belgium's linguistic divide.

The United Kingdom and Scotland

Until 1999, the United Kingdom was a politically unitary state, with power centred in Westminster and Whitehall. The UK was also a 'union state' (Rokkan and Urwin 1982), as it afforded some recognition of distinctive nations within its boundaries. Recognition of Scotland's status as a national minority could be seen in enhanced representation in the House of Commons, the preservation of distinctive public and civil society institutions, and the development of a distinctive system of public administration centred around the Scottish Office, a territorial department of the UK state. Although it has been argued that administrative autonomy permitted the welfare state to assume a distinctive form in Scotland (Paterson 1994), the absence of an autonomous substate government ensured that post-war welfare expansion could develop without the need to overcome institutional veto points or secure intergovernmental consensus (McEwen 2002). Nor did the presence and recognition of national minorities have any discernible corroding effect on welfare development. For much of the twentieth century, Scots demonstrated a dual sense of national identity, feeling Scottish and British at the same time. Indeed, the development of the post-war welfare state may have reinforced British identity in Scotland, by establishing a set of recognizably British institutions, elevating the importance and relevance of the state for political parties and the public, and providing a level of welfare provision that offered a new reason for Scots to feel a sense of belonging and attachment to the United Kingdom state (Bennie, Brand, and Mitchell 1997: 5–6; McEwen 2002).

The issue of self-government in Scotland has periodically arisen since the Treaty of Union united Scotland and England in 1707, but it has been particularly salient since the late 1960s, amid British economic and political decline, the failure of regional policy, the discovery of North Sea oil, and (following the election of the Thatcher government) the retrenchment of the welfare state. This latter association may lead one to suggest that the politicization of Scottish national identity may have had a corroding effect on the British welfare state, yet the heightened demands for Scottish autonomy in the 1980s and 1990s were much more a consequence than a cause of welfare retrenchment. In Scotland, opposition to Thatcherism was associated with expressions of Scottish distinctiveness and a demand for self-government. The politics of territorial identity did not 'crowd out' issues of welfare; rather, the two were powerfully combined in a demand for Scottish self-government. A Scottish Parliament thus came to be regarded and promoted, not just as a vehicle for the expression of Scottish national identity, but as a prerequisite for better public services and progressive social and economic change (McEwen 2002; Mitchell and Bennie 1996).

The establishment of the Scottish Parliament in 1999 altered the structure of the UK state, involving the decentralization of substantial areas of the welfare system. The Scottish Parliament has policy responsibility for health, education, and personal social services, although the UK Parliament retains control over social security, taxation, and finance. The Scottish Executive's fiscal resources are transferred *en bloc* from the UK Treasury but, unusually for a multilevel state, there are few conditions attached to the transfer, nor is there any framework legislation to constrain the Executive's policy development. This opens up the opportunity for policy divergence between the state and substate level, and a variation in the social rights of citizenship across the state.

Although policy divergence has been constrained by the shared values and agendas of Labour-led governments at each level, some divergence has emerged. There are two main forms of policy divergence. In the first instance, the Scottish Executive has initiated distinctive policies, most notable in the abolition of up-front tuition fees for university students and the adoption of a universal programme of free personal care for the elderly (Keating et al. 2004; Woods 2002). In the second instance, policy has diverged when the Scottish Executive has chosen not to replicate policies pioneered by the UK government, such as foundation hospitals or 'top-up' tuition fees for higher education. Although the Labour Party is in government at each level, it faces distinctive ideological, institutional, and popular pressures. In Scotland, Labour's coalition partners, the Liberal Democrats, the main opposition party (the nationalist Scottish National Party), much of civil society, and the public remain broadly committed to a universal, social democratic welfare state. At the UK level, the Blair government, whose main opposition is the Conservative Party, has embraced a market- and consumerist-driven notion of public sector delivery.

There is little evidence, then, to suggest that Scottish self-government has had a corroding effect on the welfare state. Indeed, the universal dimension in social programmes has become stronger in Scotland. This has been facilitated by substantial increases to the Scottish block grant generated by the Blair government's spending priorities in health and education, areas devolved to the Scottish Parliament.[5] However, policy divergence implies different rights of access to social services, depending

[5] Changes to the Scottish block grant are determined by a population-based formula, the Barnett formula, which sees Scotland get an equivalent share of additional spending (or facing an equivalent share of expenditure cuts) allocated to equivalent UK departments. Additional spending in health and education therefore automatically produce 'Barnett consequentials', bringing a proportionate increase in the Scottish budget.

on where in the UK one lives, and this may challenge social citizenship and interregional solidarity. According to Keating, the British welfare state was founded on a solidarity principle that holds that broadly equivalent services be available, as a right of citizenship, to all citizens according to their needs. This may limit the extent to which the system could cope with diverse social citizenship rights, generating pressure for policy convergence and the maintenance of common standards in service provision (Keating 2002: 11–12). In addition, although the fiscal strength of Scotland vis-à-vis the rest of the UK is hotly contested, Scotland is a net beneficiary of identifiable public expenditure. Extensive variation in the social rights and services available to British citizens in different parts of the UK may in time erode the sense of solidarity that, to some extent, underpins these fiscal transfers. However, some divergence in welfare provision has always been tolerated within the British welfare state (Paterson 1994; Wincott 2005). Devolution may have accentuated these differences and led to a growing divergence in social citizenship rights north and south of the border, but there is little evidence to suggest that has generated concern among the wider population (McEwen 2006).

The integrity and scope of the British welfare state is also supported by political leaders in Scotland and the UK. With Labour in power at each level, there is no environment of competitive nation building. The territorial objectives of the Scottish Executive and the UK government are the same. In political discourse, the Scottish Executive emphasizes its partnership with the UK government and shares many of its social policy goals. Leading Labour figures at both governmental levels emphasize the 'community of shared values' that continues to bind Scotland and England together (Brown 1999; Blair 2003). The welfare state features prominently in this discourse, elevating the National Health Service, pensions, and social security to symbols that reflect the solidarity of the British people. For example, the UK Chancellor, Gordon Brown, himself a Scottish Labour MP, insisted in a speech that 'Today, when people talk of the National Health Service, whether in Scotland, Wales or England people think of the British National Health Service: here national is unquestionably British . . . And its most powerful driving force is that every citizen of Britain has an equal right to treatment regardless of wealth, position or race, and indeed, can secure treatment in any part of Britain' (Brown 1999: 11). This discourse has been substantiated by substantial investment in public services since 1999. In addition, under the devolution settlement, the UK government retains control over social security and most revenue raising. The continued intervention of the UK government (notably, the Treasury) in developing redistributive social services, such as the Child Tax Credit and the Family Income Tax Credit, direct to individual citizens and families throughout the UK, permits the maintenance of a pan-UK dimension to the welfare state.

Conclusion

The particular institutional, territorial, and political configuration in each of the multinational states examined here has shaped welfare development and debates over the future of the welfare state in different ways. There is little evidence, however, to suggest that either the demand for self-government voiced by national minorities, or the recognition of their territorial distinctiveness in new or strengthened autonomous institutions, has had a corroding effect on the welfare state. Indeed, in some cases, we can plausibly argue that the need to accommodate and appease national minorities has supported welfare expansion, with the welfare state used as a tool of territorial integration.

Returning to our initial hypotheses, there is little evidence of a 'race to the bottom' in any of the cases examined, although there is some evidence to suggest that decentralization has generated institutional veto points affecting welfare development, especially in federal states. This was especially apparent in the early years of Canadian post-war expansion, although the development of pan-Canadian social programmes continues to require intergovernmental negotiation and compromise. In Belgium, by contrast, the institutional veto points work to preserve the integrity of the Belgian welfare state, with francophone parties in the federal government acting as a barrier against Flemish demands for the social security regionalization.

Similarly, there is little evidence from our case studies to suggest that the recognition of national minorities has eroded social citizenship and social solidarity. In Scotland and Quebec, social policy decentralization has to some extent redrawn the boundaries of the social citizenship community, offering governments an opportunity to draw upon a stronger sense of social solidarity and mutual belonging to support welfare expenditure.

Redefining the relevant community for social citizenship, however, may pose challenges for solidarity between regions, especially where the self-governing region is wealthier than the others. Although the extent to which Scotland and Quebec benefit financially from the distribution of resources from their respective states is fiercely debated, it is reasonable to conclude that, at least in terms of identifiable public expenditure, both are net recipients. Flanders, by contrast, is a net contributor, and fears that the regionalization of social security would diminish interregional solidarity are particularly prevalent among political elites in Wallonia and Brussels. Social security is also seen as one of the last institutional ties binding Belgium together, lending support to the view that the welfare state can play a role in the politics of national unity. There is little evidence of competitive nation building in social policy (or in any other policy area) between the Scottish Executive and the UK government; the party leading both governments wants to make devolution work towards strengthening the UK state. Competitive nation building, however, has been much in evidence in Canada–Quebec relations, with social policy used as a means by which governments at each level might strengthen their institutional legitimacy and maintain the consent of their citizens. The competitive nature of such efforts may have neutralized its effects on the politics of national unity, but it may have contributed to sustaining, and at times expanding, the welfare state at the federal and provincial level.

10

Multiculturalism versus neoliberalism in Latin America

Donna Lee Van Cott

Apart from the industrialized Western countries and the post-Communist countries of Europe, Latin America is perhaps the region where multi-cultural policies (MCPs) have been most widely adopted in the last two decades. As in the first two regions, there has been a great deal of public and scholarly debate concerning the appropriateness of these policies and the connection between movements in favour of multiculturalism and movements favouring economic redistribution. Is there evidence that the politics of MCPs crowds out a discussion of redistributive justice or divides groups that might otherwise coalesce in coalitions supporting greater eco-nomic equality? Is there evidence that indigenous peoples misdiagnose their problems, pursuing cultural recognition when their problems are really rooted in economic exploitation? On the contrary: multiculturalist movements have articulated a new discourse that links ethnic and eco-nomic claims and, in so doing, have revitalized low-income/leftist reform coalitions.

In Latin America MCPs focus almost exclusively on the situation of indigenous peoples, the descendants of the peoples who populated the western hemisphere prior to the arrival of Europeans.[1] During the 1980s

The author wishes to thank Keith Banting, Will Kymlicka, Shannan Mattiace, David Miller, and John Myles for their helpful comments on a previous draft, and Tony Pereira and Kurt Weyland for assistance locating measures of structural reform.

[1] Indigenous peoples constitute approximately 8–10 per cent of the population of Latin America, or approximately 40 million people. The proportional size of the indigenous pop-ulation ranges from almost none in Uruguay and most Caribbean islands, to one-quarter or one-third of the population in Ecuador and Peru, and a majority in Bolivia and Guatemala (Sieder 2002: 1).

and 1990s indigenous peoples movements became increasingly important collective actors in many Latin American countries. By the 1990s they had consolidated national organizations. Their maturity as political actors coincided with the decline of unions and leftist political parties, leaving indigenous movements in some nations the most cohesive actor on the left, with the most coherently articulated alternative to a neoliberal model that had caused widespread suffering. Indigenous peoples traditionally have organized as both an oppressed ethnic group and an exploited economic class and have not limited their political activism to the promotion of MCPs. In the 1990s class issues often supplanted cultural claims as the structural reforms that swept the region—the weakening of protections for workers, the loss of subsidies for agriculture, the promotion of agribusiness at the expense of small farming, the privatization of water rights—hit indigenous peoples particularly hard. What is new is the increasing weight of indigenous peoples' organizations within anti-neoliberal coalitions and the fact that their claims are now made within an institutional framework that is increasingly sensitive to cultural difference.

Virtually all Latin American countries with indigenous populations recognize some constitutional rights for indigenous peoples. Twelve recognize a distinct status for indigenous peoples and most recognize some type of collective land rights and the right to exercise customary law. Twelve countries—including all of the larger countries with the exception of Chile—have ratified International Labour Organization Convention 169 on the rights of indigenous and tribal peoples (see Table 10.1). The only other ethnic group that receives constitutional attention is Afro-Latin Americans, the descendants of African slaves.[2] Constitutional attention to Afro-Latin American rights often mimics that provided for indigenous peoples. Therefore, I focus primarily on MCPs with respect to indigenous peoples.

Like Banting and Kymlicka, I develop a taxonomy of MCPs affecting indigenous peoples, using similar criteria and classifying Latin American countries' support of such policies as 'strong', 'modest', or 'weak'. Since all of these reforms are relatively recent (the earliest occurred

---

[2] There are approximately 120 million Afro-Latin Americans, or approximately 30 per cent of the population of Latin America. Blacks range from a majority of the population in most Caribbean islands to a significant portion of the populations of Brazil, Colombia, Guyana, Suriname, and Venezuela (Inter-American Dialogue 2002). Latin American countries recognizing African-American rights include Colombia, since the 1991 constitutional reform (Arocha 1992; Asher 1998; Van Cott 2000); Ecuador, since the 1998 constitutional reform (Van Cott 2002); and Brazil, since the adoption of affirmative action policies in 2001 (Htun 2004).

Table 10.1 Multicultural policies for indigenous peoples in Latin America

Country	Date of Constitution/ recognition	Collective land rights	Self-govern. rights	Cultural rights	Customary law	Rep. in central govt	Affirmation of distinct status	Ratified ILO 169	Affirm. action	Total number
Argentina	1994	Y	N	Y	Y	N	Y	2000	N	5
Belize	1981	N	N	N	N	N	N	N	N	0
Bolivia	1995	Y	Y, L	Y	Y	N	Y	1991	N	5.5
Brazil	1988	Y	N	Y	Y	N	Y	2002	Y	6
Chile	1993 by statute	Y	N	N	Y, L	N	N	N	N	1
Colombia	1991	Y	Y	Y	Y	Y	Y	1991	Y	8
Costa Rica	Laws passed in 1977/93/99	Y	N	Y	N	N	N	1993	N	3
Ecuador	1998	Y	Y	Y	Y	Y	Y	1998	N	7
El Salvador	1983/91–2	Y	N	N	N	N	N	N	N	1
Guatemala	1986	Y	N	Y	Y	N	Y	1996	N	5
Guyana	1980/96	Y	N	N	N	N	N	N	N	1
Honduras	1982	Y	N	Y	Y	N	N	1995	N	4
Mexico	1917/92/2001	Y	Y	Y	Y	N	Y	1990	N	6
Nicaragua	1987/95	Y	Y	Y	Y	N	Y	N	N	5
Panama	1972/83/93–4	Y	Y	Y	Y	Y	Y	N	N	6
Paraguay	1992	Y	Y	Y	Y	N	Y	1993	N	6
Peru	1993/2003–4	Y, weakened in 1993	Y	Y	Y	N	N	1994	N	5
Suriname	1987	N	N	N	N	N	N	N	N	0
Venezuela	1999	Y	Y	Y	Y	Y	Y	2002	N	7

Source: Author's compilation from constitutions.

"L" means adopted in a limited manner

in 1991), and they occurred after economic crisis in the 1980s led to sharply curtailed welfare spending, it is difficult to discern an impact with respect to the economic and social indicators studied by Banting and Kymlicka. Moreover, reasons for changes in these measures since 1980 are largely attributable to factors other than the institution of MCPs. Finally, the welfare state in most Latin American countries historically has been exceedingly weak or non-existent. Thus, it makes little sense to perform the same correlation between MCPs and the indicators of welfare state erosion used by Banting and Kymlicka. The more relevant comparison is between the codification of MCPs and the enactment of neoliberal structural reforms. In Latin America these reforms were instituted in the 1980s and 1990s at the behest of multilateral institutions, to whom most Latin American countries owed enormous debts.

I argue that the relationship between multiculturalism, neoliberalism, and the ability to make redistributive reforms in Latin America is derived in part from the relative strength and cohesion of three key collective actors: neoliberal elites, the electoral left, and indigenous peoples' social movements. I argue that the relative strength of these actors has changed over the last fifteen years, with interesting implications for states' ability to adopt, implement, and maintain neoliberal structural reform programmes. I first discuss the nature of and forces giving rise to MCPs and neoliberal reforms in Latin America. I then examine the relationship between coalitions in favour of and opposing both sets of policy changes and assess the implications of these relationships for policy outcomes.

1. Multicultural policies in Latin America

Banting and Kymlicka identify nine policies emblematic of Western democracies' new approach to recognizing indigenous peoples' rights. Two of these policies do not travel well to Latin America. First, treaties between indigenous peoples and European powers, or the independent states that succeeded them in the nineteenth century, were less common in Latin America than in North America. Constitutional recognition replaced treaties after independence as the primary source of indigenous corporate rights (Clavero n.d.: 2). Indigenous communities today press mainly for recognition of collective land titles secured during the colonial period, but this component of MCPs is already encompassed under the

275

category of collective land rights. Second, there are few 'affirmative action' policies targeted toward any population in Latin America.[3] Therefore, Table 10.1 refers mainly to the other seven policies. Cultural rights usually denotes rights to bilingual education and/or to official recognition of indigenous languages.

Based on the information presented in Table 10.1, Latin American countries are ranked as follows with respect to the adoption of MCPs:

STRONG: Colombia, Ecuador, Panama, Venezuela
MODEST: Argentina, Bolivia, Brazil, Costa Rica, Guatemala, Honduras, Mexico, Nicaragua, Paraguay, Peru
WEAK: Belize, Chile, El Salvador, Guyana, Suriname

Those countries classified as 'strong' recognize at least six of the nine MCPs for indigenous peoples. All countries in this group recognize some form of meaningful autonomy for indigenous peoples—that is, control over a territorial space and public resources and the power to make and enforce norms—as well as the right to hold land collectively, the right to exercise customary law, and some type of educational or language rights.[4] Although Brazil and Paraguay also recognize six MCPs, in these countries the extent of recognition, particularly with respect to land rights and self-government, is considerably weaker than in the other countries. In Brazil, affirmative action rights instituted in 2001 accrued to blacks rather than to Indians. Thus, although Banting and Kymlicka weight all of their nine policies equally, I give relatively more weight to the creation of meaningful autonomy regimes that confer jurisdictional powers and economic resources. All countries that ratified ILO Convention 169 recognize the right of indigenous peoples to hold land collectively, govern themselves, exercise customary law, and to receive some type of language recognition and an appropriate educational policy. The 'strong' set of cases affirmed these rights in their constitutions or ordinary legislation as well. 'Weak' countries recognized no or only one type of MCP. The 'modest' countries fall between these two extremes. Various scholars and agencies have ranked Latin American and Caribbean countries with respect to MCPs, producing different results. Table 10.2 presents two such rankings. Given

[3] Brazil recently embraced such policies for its significant Afro-Brazilian population, and Colombia has some programmes in the area of higher education for indigenous peoples and blacks (Htun 2004).

[4] Guatemala might have joined this category if not for the failure of voters to approve a 1999 referendum on constitutional reform that included a broad set of indigenous rights based on one of the peace treaties that ended the long-running civil war.

Table 10.2 Alternative rankings of Latin American countries with respect to constitutional rights for indigenous peoples

Barié ranking		Inter-American Development Bank ranking	
Country	Score	Country	Score
Ecuador	21	Ecuador	45
Colombia	20	Mexico	33
Venezuela	18	Colombia	32
Paraguay	18	Venezuela	30
Peru	14	Nicaragua	27
Mexico	14	Bolivia	17
Argentina	14	Brazil	17
Brazil	13	Peru	13
Guatemala	11	Paraguay	12
Bolivia	11	Panama	12
Panama	10	Guatemala	12
Nicaragua	10	Argentina	7
Honduras	5	Guyana	4
Guyana	5	Honduras	4
El Salvador	4	Costa Rica	3
Costa Rica	3	El Salvador	2
Suriname	0	Suriname	1
Chile	0	Belize	1
Belize	0	Chile	0

Sources: Barié ranking from Barié (2003: 560). Inter-American Development Bank ranking from **www.iadb.org**, as cited in Barié (2003: 560).

the variation in ordinal placement, all rankings should be considered rough estimates rather than definitive measures.

Whereas in the advanced industrialized countries MCPs are for the most part implemented once adopted, in Latin America the weakness of judicial institutions, and the fragmentation and intentional obstruction of legislatures charged with writing implementing legislation for multi-cultural constitutional reforms, means that in some cases these policies only exist on paper. The policies that are least likely to be implemented faithfully are indigenous self-government and collective land rights. Not only do powerful political and economic forces restrict the exercise of indigenous collective land rights, in Latin America subsoil rights belong to the state. Thus, while honouring collective land rights, states are able to gain access to minerals, petroleum, and other valuable resources. Self-government rights often are restricted to levels of government where resources and powers are reduced or overridden by competing powers

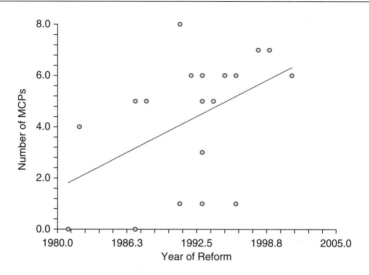

Figure 10.1 Adoption of MCPs during the 1990s.

of non-indigenous governments.[5] Thus, the rankings above are based mainly on the *codification* of constitutional rights that in some cases have yet to be implemented. For example, in Ecuador new, autonomous electoral districts for indigenous peoples and Afro-Ecuadorians have yet to be established, partly due to the lack of consensus within the indigenous movement on the particulars. Venezuelan Indians have yet to realize the implications of their constitutional right to form Indigenous Municipalities. Nevertheless, the comprehensive nature of the Ecuadorian and Venezuelan constitutional indigenous rights regimes, and the extent of rights implemented thus far, clearly places these two countries above the 'modest' group.

As Figure 10.1 illustrates, the tendency to recognize indigenous rights in Latin American constitutions increased during the 1990s, demonstrating a pronounced policy diffusion effect. The small sample size makes linear regression a blunt tool for analysis, but the bivariate statistical relationship between the year that MCPs were adopted and the number of reforms adopted is statistically significant.[6] In addition to this longitudinal trend, we can detect an inverse relationship between the size of the indigenous population and the political and economic impact of the MCPs adopted. Countries with relatively small indigenous populations

[5] For more information on multicultural constitutions in Latin America, see Assies, van der Haar, and Hoekema (2001), Clavero (2000), and Sieder (2002).

[6] At the 0.05 level, with an R-squared of 0.22.

adopted the most extensive regimes of multicultural policies (Colombia, Venezuela, Panama), while countries with relatively large indigenous populations (Bolivia, Guatemala, Mexico, Peru) adopted more restrictive regimes. Ecuador—a country with both a large indigenous population and a strong regime of MCPs—is an outlier, probably due to the greater effectiveness during the constitutional reform of its indigenous movement, the only one that boasted a strong electoral vehicle and an effective and hegemonic national indigenous organization during this crucial period of MCP adoption.

This inverse relationship is to be expected because the implications of shifting economic and political power to a minority group increase as that group grows larger. This is particularly the case with groups whose central claims have to do with territory and autonomy. Latin American indigenous people typically claim territory far in excess of their proportion of the population. For example, Colombian Indians constitute less than 3 per cent of the population but their autonomous reserves cover one-quarter of the national territory. Similarly, providing a few reserved seats for Indians in a large national assembly will not generate a radical shift in the balance of power or the allocation of government resources, whereas providing equitable reserved seats to Bolivia's 65 per cent indigenous population would turn relations of power upside down. Although Banting and Kymlicka found a positive relationship between indigenous population size and the number of MCPs, the variation in size of the indigenous populations included in their sample was not great, and all are relatively small.

2. Neoliberalism in Latin America

Since the 1970s, most Latin American countries have enacted a series of neoliberal economic reforms intended to restart growth after decades of inefficient inward-oriented, state-centred development policy. In most cases multilateral banks and lender-country governments imposed structural adjustment programmes as a condition for access to capital after Latin American countries began in 1982 to be unable to make scheduled payments on foreign debt. Reallocating government expenditures toward debt payments required the dismantlement of fragile social safety nets. In Latin America, these typically consisted of pension and health-care programmes, which comprised between two-thirds and 100 per cent of social welfare spending. In addition, government subsidies or price controls with respect to food, energy, and transportation constituted an important part of government social assistance. Pensions and health care typically have been associated with formal employment, with different classes of benefits accruing to different labour categories (public/private) and sectors of the workforce, resulting in significant inequalities and gaps in coverage. Whereas employment-based welfare programmes can be effective in industrialized countries, Latin American economies' industrialized labour forces range from 25 to 35 per cent, far below the European average, leaving the majority of the population uncovered (Huber 1996: 158; Huber and Stephens 2000). This is a particularly regressive option for Latin America, where a large portion of the population is unemployed or working in the informal sector and, thus, cannot benefit from employment-derived social benefits, and where there are large rural populations receiving no benefits whatsoever (Huber 1996: 142).

Most of these social-welfare programmes were developed in the context of Latin America's import substituting industrialization (ISI) economic model, which enabled well-organized, urban, middle-class groups to demand social insurance schemes specifically targeted to them. Protected markets enabled employers to pass the costs on to consumers (Huber 1996: 144). These programmes were largely dismantled after the collapse of the ISI model in the early 1980s because they were no longer economically sustainable. Structural adjustment policies that decimated organized labour and public sector employment reduced the amount of contributions, while inflation and falling real wages reduced the value of what contributions could be made. Governments could not take over private pension schemes, given the severe debt crisis and fiscal crisis experienced by virtually all countries in the region, as well as mandates from international financial institutions to reduce and privatize such programmes and to cut subsidies and remove price controls (Huber 1996: 144–5; Huber and Stephens 2000).

The Southern Cone countries[7] were first to initiate structural reform in the 1970s. This spread to the rest of the region after 1985, following the initial shock of the debt crisis, and accelerated in the 1990s (Morley, Machado, and Pettinato 1999: 5, 14). Structural reforms included tax reform to raise government revenues and remove distortions in the market, liberalization of trade restrictions, privatization of inefficient

---

[7] That is, the countries in the southernmost part of South America: Argentina, Brazil, Chile, and Uruguay. The index of structural reform cited below is a combined score aggregating separate indexes of 'trade reform, domestic and international financial liberalization, tax reform, and privatization' (Morley, Machado, and Pettinato 1999: 10).

Table 10.3 Relative intensity of structural and MCP reforms

Intensity of MCPs	Intensity of structural reforms		
	Strong	Moderate	Weak
Strong			Colombia, Ecuador, Venezuela
Moderate	Argentina, Costa Rica, Peru	Bolivia, Brazil, Guatemala, Mexico, Paraguay	Honduras
Weak	Chile, El Salvador		

state-owned businesses, regulatory reforms of the financial sector, and reductions in spending on education, health care, and poverty alleviation (Cornelius 2003: 199). Table 10.3 presents a correlation of my ranking of the intensity of MCPs with Morley, Machado, and Pettinato's (1999) ranking of the intensity of structural reforms, for those countries appearing in both rankings. No countries making a strong effort at neoliberal economic reform in the 1980s and 1990s also enacted a strong set of MCPs, and no countries making a weak structural reform effort also enacted weak multicultural policies. The three countries that Paunovic identifies as having the strongest record of macroeconomic stabilization and most intense structural reforms—Argentina, Chile, and Peru—have relatively weak MCPs, while the two countries that he identifies as being the greatest laggards in the region—Ecuador and Venezuela—have the most ample and deep set of MCPs (Paunovic 2000: 34). Thus, there seems to be an inverse relationship between the strength of multicultural and structural reforms.

Latin American economies for the most part did not respond as expected to the change in economic model. The loss of investment capital, climatic disasters, and a steep decline in the terms of trade for exports exacerbated economic stagnation or caused contraction, leading to economic growth rates significantly lower in the 1980s and 1990s than in the three previous decades (Cornelius 2003: 201). Higher interest rates on existing foreign debt led in the 1990s to extremely high debt burdens, which have yet to subside. For example, Argentina and Brazil in 2002 had public debt burdens equal to 55 per cent of GDP (Cornelius 2003: 219). Although most Latin American countries increased exports as a percentage of GDP between 1980 and 2000 (on average, from 12.4 per cent to 17.3 per cent) this has not been sufficient to offset the cost of adjustment. As a result, public spending on education, health care, and subsidies for the most disadvantaged and vulnerable groups was slashed in the 1980s and early 1990s as governments bowed to pressure from international lenders (Huber 1996: 162). Thus, most Latin American states entered the era of multicultural constitutionalism after the introduction of structural reforms and with little welfare state to speak of. The timing of the adoption of MCPs—mainly after 1994—actually coincides with an increase in welfare-state spending in response to sharp increases in poverty and inequality throughout the region—on average from 10.4 per cent to 13.1 per cent of GDP, although this is only slightly above the amount of social expenditure in 1980 (Hershberg 2003: 22; Huber and Solt 2004: 161).

3. The debate about neoliberalism and multiculturalism

What is the relationship between these two important trends: the tendency of Latin American states to codify constitutional rights for indigenous peoples and to undertake neoliberal reforms? Both outcomes are responses to crises in the prevailing political and economic models. The degree of elite convergence on the need for structural reform is partly determined by the intensity of fiscal crises and hyperinflation in the pre-reform period (Paunovic 2000: 20–1), just as the tendency to adopt far-reaching rights for disadvantaged groups and to create mechanisms to promote democratic participation is partly determined by the intensity of the democratic legitimacy crisis faced by political elites prior to major constitutional reforms (Van Cott 2000). In countries undergoing a serious economic crisis prior to constitutional reform, neoliberal elites were relatively stronger and more cohesive than anti-neoliberal and pro-indigenous coalitions. The correlation between hyperinflation and the strength of neoliberal elites during constitutional reforms that considered indigenous rights is particularly interesting. Of the four countries with quadruple-digit inflation, none enacted 'strong' MCPs. Conversely, the three countries with the strongest recognition of indigenous rights (Colombia, Ecuador, Venezuela) experienced only moderate, two-digit inflation in the pre-reform period.[8] Thus, intense

[8] Inflation rates are as follows: Argentina (1,383 per cent), Bolivia (2,199 per cent), Brazil (1,332 per cent), Peru (2,465 per cent), Colombia (28 per cent), Ecuador (60 per cent), and Venezuela (36 per cent). Data from Paunovic (2000: 21).

economic crisis may strengthen neoliberal elites, making it more difficult for indigenous peoples to secure ample multicultural regimes, whereas relatively low levels of economic crisis give more leverage to anti-structural reform coalitions and lower the barriers to securing indigenous rights.

The relationship between the adoption of MCPs and the defence of redistributive economic policies against the juggernaut of neoliberalism is different in Latin America compared to the other regions studied in this volume owing to the larger size of the population that would benefit from both types of policy. Whereas indigenous peoples are a minuscule minority in most advanced, industrialized countries, in Latin America there are two countries where indigenous populations constitute a majority (Bolivia, Guatemala), and at least three where the population ranges between 10 and 40 per cent of the total (Mexico, Ecuador, Peru). Moreover, in Latin America, in a context of high and increasing inequality in the 1990s, on average half of the population lives in poverty—50.7 per cent according to a 2000 Inter-American Development Bank report; slightly less according to 2002 ECLAC data.[9] Poverty tends to be even higher in countries with larger indigenous populations (Székely et al. 2000: table 1; see also Walton 2004).[10] Thus, rather than the diamond-shaped distribution we see in industrialized countries, in which a large middle class must be convinced to transfer income to small, impoverished, minority groups, in Latin America we find a pyramid. The majority of Latin Americans would benefit greatly from redistributive policies and the ethnic minority in question, indigenous peoples, shares class interests with the non-indigenous poor. Thus, there are more possibilities for cross-ethnic, intra-class coalition building in Latin America.[11] As Huber and Solt argue,

A coalition of the poor and the working-class, . . . accounts for 60–70 percent of the population in Latin American countries. Basic health care, nutrition, education, and a minimum income in case of illness or old age, targeted toward this population, with entitlement based on citizenship and financed out of general tax revenue, would be an effective and politically sustainable approach [to poverty reduction]. (Huber and Solt 2004: 161)

---

[9] Huber and Solt, citing 2002 ECLAC data, reports that 'poverty fell from 48.3 per cent of the population in 1990 to 43.8 per cent in 1999' (2004: 152).

[10] Bolivia 1996 (65.1); Ecuador 1995 (57.0); Mexico 1996 (58.8); Peru 1997 (43.3). No data was listed for Guatemala, among the poorest and most indigenous countries in the hemisphere (Székely *et al.* 2000).

[11] I thank David Miller for pointing this out.

Some anthropologists working with indigenous movements view the relationship between MCPs and economic policies differently. They argue that political elites endorse a minimal set of multicultural rights in order to deflect demands for more radical challenges to neoliberalism and that indigenous movements that 'settle for' multicultural constitutional regimes risk sacrificing progress on the more important goal of blocking or overturning the neoliberal economic model and, thus, altering fundamental relations of power (see e.g. Gustafson 2002; Hale 2002; and Postero 2003). This argument is essentially the Machiavellian version of the crowding-out argument exposed by Banting and Kymlicka in the introduction to this volume.

Based on his observations of the Nicaraguan and Guatemalan cases, Charles Hale (2002) argues that neoliberals recognize a limited set of cultural rights as part of a strategy for moderating cultural demands and defusing anti-neoliberal protests. Recognizing a more modest set of cultural rights delegitimizes more 'radical' demands. Co-opting moderate indigenous leaders by giving them space within formal politics delegitimizes leaders who refuse to assimilate into the formal political system and to accept the prevailing market-based economic model. This strategy enables neoliberals to divide cultural movements into 'acceptable', 'moderate' indigenous subjects, and 'threatening', 'dangerous', 'radical' indigenous subjects. Radical indigenous subjects are those calling for a complete restructuring of political and economic relations, including the prioritization of communal, traditional, and non-market economic decision-making processes, the protection of collective property rights, and a greater emphasis on redistribution relative to economic growth. Hale argues that the danger of accepting a limited set of multicultural rights is that the larger agenda will be unattainable.

Bret Gustafson (2002) makes a more nuanced argument. Based on his study of Bolivia, Gustafson argues that 'multicultural neoliberalism', or 'neoliberal interculturalism' fails to transform unequal political and economic relations. However, when indigenous movements participate in the creation of these reforms, unexpected and often empowering processes are unleashed that elites are unable to control. For Gustafson, 'neoliberal interculturalism'

is not a uniform process of 'inclusion' of previously excluded Indians, but rather a set of uneven, contradictory shifts of political languages and institutions that seek to reorder and legitimate changing expressions of social difference, citizen identity, and hierarchical forms of participation. These new tactics of governments represent a transformative renewal of discourses and institutions through which elites seek to insulate centralized power (spatially, conceptually, and institutionally) from various forms of 'indigenous' and other 'popular' forms of political engagement. Certainly laudable for a reformist sensibility, interculturalist reforms do not, however, pursue robust versions of indigenous rights or overhaul structures of economic inequality. Nonetheless, new forms of social mobilization and paradoxes of the reforms themselves suggest that, as in the past, governmental projects are hardly guaranteed to obtain that which they seek and may in fact produce new and unexpected outcomes. (Gustafson 2002: 269–70)

Although it is easy to read what Hale calls a 'wider calculated logic' into elites' intentions, Gustafson shows how this is belied by the fragmented and contradictory nature of the reforms, their 'implementation, meanings and effects' (Gustafson 2002: 277).

Hale, Gustafson, and Postero present a distorted view of the relationship between MCPs and neoliberal elites because their case selection—chiefly Guatemala and Bolivia—is biased toward the 'modest' end of the MCP continuum, and because their analysis stops before Bolivian Indians had had an opportunity to fully take advantage of the Sánchez de Lozada-era reforms (1993–7). An analysis of multicultural policy reforms in South America, where they are more widespread and indigenous peoples are relatively more powerful vis-à-vis neoliberal elites and the state than in Central America or Bolivia in the 1990s, does not support the view that MCPs have deflected demands for more radical challenges to fundamental power relations. Indigenous leaders in South America interviewed between 1993 and 2002 argued that the recognition of the limited set of rights achieved, and the access to formal politics that these have facilitated, will make possible the eventual acceptance of more 'radical' forms of autonomy and self-government. As Andolina puts it in his study of Ecuadorian multicultural reforms, newly won multicultural rights are viewed as '"tools in the struggle" and new sites of negotiation and contention' (2003: 749). Thus, rather than foreclosing more radical proposals, the limited set of MCPs realized provides a foothold in the formal political system for the articulation of more radical, transformative alternatives.

In his contribution to this volume, Matt James reports a similar finding with respect to redress movements in Canada. Such movements increase group solidarity, strengthen collective identity, enhance the ability of the group to mobilize politically and, when successful, create a positive image of the group in the wider society. Thus, movements for cultural rights enhance the ability of disadvantaged cultural minorities to successfully advance redistributive claims. Even if the MCPs go unimplemented, their successful codification has positive political effects. The leaders of historically disadvantaged groups

view redress campaigns as internal opportunities for rebuilding and mobilizing fractured communities. This work is often seen as a contributing step towards autonomous processes of community economic development. Externally, activists hope that their campaigns will teach historical lessons that foster a climate of moral urgency and forge a more sensitive appreciation of community economic problems and needs. (James, this volume.)

These observations apply equally well to indigenous campaigns for constitutional rights in Latin America.

Hale's analysis oversimplifies the complexity and variation within coalitions supporting the original adoption of MCPs and the contested nature of multiculturalism within states. It also elides the intense opposition to these policies expressed by state actors and other elites during constitutional reform processes. Indigenous peoples and their allies bargained, engaged in civil disobedience, employed brinkmanship, and manipulated the media and international supporters in order to achieve even modest recognition of indigenous rights. They linked their demands to important elite goals, such as extending the reach of public law, establishing a regime of internationally approved human rights, and recuperating the legitimacy of exclusionary democratic regimes. Once rights were codified in constitutions, indigenous peoples had to battle again to secure implementing legislation, much of which remains unwritten. Within the neoliberal governments and political parties that ultimately endorsed MCPs, fierce debates raged over the scope and details of the reforms, debates *among* diverse political elites, not just between neoliberals and indigenous actors. Hale's assertion that neoliberals have a coherent 'project...to harness and redirect the abundant political energy of cultural rights activism' (2002: 498) gives too much credit to neoliberals, who are internally divided over the issue of cultural rights and tend to respond reactively and opportunistically to such demands as political conjunctures unfold.

As Matt James (this volume) observes with respect to redress movements in Canada, conservative elites in Latin America promote restrictive 'cultural heritage' rights agendas as a substitute for more radical transformation. They champion more moderate indigenous organizations, whose leaders are easier to co-opt, in an effort to weaken more radical actors.

And in countries where conservatives are united and their opponents are weak they often succeed. Nevertheless, indigenous peoples themselves do not 'misdiagnosis' the basis of their exploitation. Rather, they frame the discourse on social justice in new ways. Although most indigenous organizations denounce neoliberalism and globalization, their economic claims can be satisfied within the context of a generous capitalist welfare state. They seek greater political and administrative autonomy within their own territories, combined with a significant increase in economic redistribution toward the impoverished and state programmes that would enable them to compete within the prevailing model (e.g. access to credit, market assistance, and agricultural subsidies like those available to farmers in the West).

In fact, neoliberalism and globalization have not brought only harm to indigenous peoples. The policy reform that facilitated the Bolivian and Colombian multicultural constitutional reforms was decentralization, a key component of contemporary neoliberal economic and state reforms. Decentralization shifts authority and resources to municipalities and regions where resources can be used more transparently and efficiently and authority can be exercised with greater accountability and responsiveness to public needs. It was the mechanism that provided the structural basis for fulfilling indigenous peoples' most important demand: self-government. The establishment of local and, in Colombia, regional direct elections enabled indigenous peoples in both countries to dominate municipal governments in areas where they are concentrated and, in Colombia, to use the flexibility provided by multicultural reforms to employ culturally appropriate governance norms. In addition to a tendency toward decentralization, the global diffusion of policy norms from the advanced industrialized countries brought with it international norms of cultural recognition and human rights upon which indigenous movements have based their rights claims.

If political elites approved MCPs with the expectation that they would forestall direct confrontation of the state and the economic model, they have been bitterly disappointed. Indigenous social movements in South America continue to engage in the full range of protest activities, undeterred by the limited nature of the MCPs thus far achieved. They lead and participate in numerous demonstrations that challenge relations of power and economic distribution. Ecuadorian and Bolivian indigenous organizations, for example, have toppled neoliberal presidents and blocked neoliberal policies while demanding the creation of a 'multinational state'.[12] Events in the last decade actually support the converse of Hale's argument. State recognition of a modest set of cultural demands encourages more radical demands. In the 1990s, rather than 'crowding out' leftist movements and class-based claims, or 'corroding' the solidarity that redistributive coalitions require, Latin American indigenous movements revitalized the left and became integral parts of coalitions opposed to structural adjustment and trade liberalization. From the indigenous perspective, neoliberal reforms and trade liberalization are modern forms of imperialism having historical continuity with foreigners' colonization of the Americas and their extraction of its vast mineral wealth: a 'second colonization' (Houghton 2004: 12; see also Postero 2003). Today, new Conquistadors—multinational corporations, US embassies, and IMF officials—impose policies on Latin American governments that further the economic dependence and impoverishment of indigenous peoples while distorting the traditional economic and social structures on which indigenous cultures depend for their autonomous development. Indigenous organizations in Mexico, Ecuador, and Chile have been particularly vocal in their opposition to free-trade agreements.[13]

Throughout the Americas indigenous peoples are fighting back. In Bolivia indigenous organizations participated in a 2000 mobilization that prevented the privatization of water in Cochabamba by a foreign company (Bechtel), and led a movement in 2003 to prevent the sale of natural gas to foreign corporations (Assies 2004; *Economist* 2004). In Ecuador, indigenous organizations led a broad-based national mobilization in

[12] On these movements in Bolivia, see Assies (2004) and Gustafson (2002). On Ecuadorian indigenous protests, see *Boletín ICCI* (2002: 2); Collins (2000); Dávalos (2003); León (2001); Lucero (2001).

[13] For example, in September 2003, representatives of indigenous organizations throughout the world met in Cancún, Mexico, during the Fifth Ministerial Conference of the World Trade Organization in order to protest the negative impact of the WTO on their communities. In a Declaration issued on 12 September, the indigenous organizations made the following statement: 'With the creation of the World Trade Organization and with the continued imposition of structural adjustment policies by the World Bank and International Monetary Fund, our situation, as indigenous peoples, has gone from bad to worse. The corporations receive more rights and privileges at the expense of our rights. Our right to self-determination, which consists of determining freely our political status and seeking our own economic, social and cultural development, and the exercise of our rights over our territories and resources, over our indigenous knowledge, culture and identities, are flagrantly violated.' (Declaración Internacional Cancún de los Pueblos Indígenas 2003, author's translation.) Among the damages identified are: the loss of livelihood for Mexico's indigenous corn producers, attributable to the dumping of subsidized corn from the United States, and the contamination of traditional strains of corn due to genetic modification; increasing conflicts between mining, gas, and petroleum companies and indigenous peoples in Ecuador, Guyana, Colombia, and Venezuela; militarization and environmental devastation in indigenous communities caused by extractive industries; and infrastructural projects that destroyed sacred and ceremonial places in Guatemala and Mexico.

February 2004 opposing the proposed Free Trade Area of the Americas, continued payment of the foreign debt, privatization of the petroleum, telecommunications, electricity, social security, health, and education sectors, and the weakening of public sector labour rights (Agencia de Noticias Plurinacional del Ecuador 2004). Indigenous-movement-based political parties, like Bolivia's Political Instrument for the Sovereignty of the Peoples,[14] Ecuador's United Plurinational Pachakutik Movement, and Colombia's Indigenous Social Alliance, emphasize class as well as ethnic issues and identities. Rather than 'crowding out' or eroding support for economic and social welfare issues, indigenous movements revived these issues and helped to form more robust coalitions for economic and social justice in the context of declining electoral strength and dynamism on the left. As Banting and Kymlicka observe with regard to the advanced industrialized countries, the emergence of multicultural issues and policies 'provided a context for the left to get involved in politics again, by providing an issue on which progressives felt it was possible to make a difference. Getting involved in making a difference helped revive confidence in the possibility of challenging economic inequalities' (Chapter 1, p. 16 above).

Indigenous peoples' organizations have a long history of relations with leftist parties and unions. Prior to the 1990s, such relations generally were tense, with indigenous leaders complaining that parties and unions failed to address their issues, excluded indigenous people from leadership roles, and expressed racist attitudes. Nevertheless, as Mexican indigenous rights activists Margarito Ruiz Hernández and Araceli Burguete Cal y Mayor argue, relationships with leftist parties and movements had a profound ideological and organizational influence on contemporary indigenous movements. The experience

was fundamental in fuelling a broad segment of the contemporary *indianista/autonomista* movement. The political biographies of a significant number of *indianista/autonomista* indigenous leaders over the age of 40 today highlight the roots of their training in the worker/peasant movements and/or in the communist or socialist parties—or even the guerrilla movements, in Guatemala, Nicaragua and Chile—of their respective countries. (2001: 25)

---

[14] Coca growers and other indigenous leaders formed the Assembly for the Sovereignty of the Peoples in 1995 to compete in municipal elections. Unable to successfully register due to difficult barriers, the ASP borrowed the legal registration of the United Left. Prior to the 2002 national elections the party split. The larger faction, the Political Instrument for the Sovereignty of the Peoples, headed by coca growers' leader Evo Morales, borrowed the legal registration of the Movement toward Socialism. See Van Cott (2005).

After 1989, the global decline of socialism made it difficult for Latin American leftist parties to put forward socialist platforms as a viable alternative (Alcántara Sáez and Freidenberg 2001; Roberts 1998: 20–2). At the same time, the neoliberal reforms of the 1980s and the massive public sector job losses they engendered reduced the size of the organized working classes and debilitated the union and peasant organizations that had previously served as a base of support and as key organizational mechanisms for leftist parties. These parties saw their vote share reduced dramatically in most countries as socialism experienced a dramatic fall in public support after the fall of the Berlin Wall (Levitsky and Cameron 2001: 26). The decline of traditional leftist actors gave relatively more leverage to indigenous organizations within anti-neoliberal coalitions.

4. Four cases

These arguments about the complex and changing relationships among indigenous peoples' movements, neoliberal elites, and the left can be illustrated by comparing four key cases: Colombia, Bolivia, Ecuador, and Venezuela.

In Colombia, three indigenous delegates participated in the 1990–1 National Constituent Assembly: two were elected, while a third was appointed to represent the demobilized Quintín Lame guerrillas. An unusually large number of Assembly delegates—nearly a third—represented the left and centre-left. However, the cohesion and numerical dominance of neoliberal elites convinced leaders of the leftist bloc not to challenge the prevailing neoliberal economic model in exchange for support for its programme to open up the closed two-party system and to promote political and administrative decentralization. Indigenous peoples in that assembly allied most often with the centre-left bloc and with Liberal Party neoliberals seeking to promote decentralization and to strengthen the rule of law. Thus, because the consensus between the two major parties on neoliberalism seemed unshakeable, leftist and indigenous delegates chose to focus on more achievable goals. The result was a set of indigenous peoples' rights that was unprecedented in its boldness and scope. Afro-Colombians gained lesser rights, primarily having to do with collective land rights in a limited region of the Pacific Coast, where the ancestors of slaves have developed distinct rural cultures. Since Afro-Colombians had no representative in the Assembly, indigenous representatives advocated their rights. These largely mimic in weaker form rights granted to indigenous communities (Van Cott 2000: 67–98).

As in Colombia, indigenous organizations in Bolivia in 1994–6 faced a strong neoliberal coalition headed by a popular president. President Gonzalo Sánchez de Lozada had come to office in an unprecedented coalition with a small indigenous party, the Tupaj Katari Revolutionary Movement of Liberation. Explicit recognition of the importance of indigenous issues gained Sánchez de Lozada the largest victory margin for a presidential candidate in a decade. However, as Xavier Albó observes, this 'surprising and bold alliance' of neoliberals and multiculturalists was awkward at best (Albó 1994), and it did not outlast the president's four-year term. Indigenous representatives did not have the opportunity to participate as equals in a constituent assembly; instead, the Bolivian Constitution was reformed behind closed doors and passed by a Congress that the president's party dominated (Van Cott 2000). Thus, not only did Indians receive a much weaker set of rights, particularly with respect to self-government and political representation, neoliberal reforms proceeded that eroded the flimsy social safety net. As Gustafson (2002) observes, instead of economic benefits, neoliberals offered Bolivia's impoverished indigenous majority less costly multicultural reforms. The inadequacy of Bolivia's multicultural model was made apparent in the years that followed, as indigenous organizations successfully led massive mobilizations in favour of a constituent assembly to secure the expansion of their self-government rights, as well as changes to the economic model (*Economist* 2004: 33; Gustafson 2002: 283–91; Schultz 2003: 8–10).[15]

Constitutional reform processes and their results in Ecuador and Venezuela were different. In Ecuador, the Confederation of Indigenous Nationalities of Ecuador (CONAIE) led the popular demand for a National Constituent Assembly. CONAIE's political power was surging following the successful creation in 1996 of an indigenous-movement-based political party (Pachakutik), the spectacular ouster of President Abdala Bucaram, and a series of effective mobilizations with respect to a wide range of policy issues.[16] By 1996 CONAIE had established

[15] Indigenous peoples protested in favour of a constituent assembly with prominent indigenous participation in the summer of 2002, and during often violent demonstrations that toppled President Gonzalo Sanchez de Lozada in October 2003. On 20 February 2004, President Carlos Mesa promulgated a reform of the Bolivian Constitution that will allow the convocation of a constituent assembly in 2006 (ALAI 2004).

[16] For example, in 1994 CONAIE defeated the government's proposed agrarian reform policy, and in 1995 was a key partner in a movement to change electoral laws through a nationwide referendum.

itself as the core of a revitalized left, which worked together more-or-less coherently during the Assembly that began in December 1997. CONAIE's platform included a set of ethnic rights more expansive than the Colombian regime, as well as the destruction of the neoliberal economic model. Although outnumbered at the beginning of the Assembly, CONAIE's indigenous-rights platform prevailed after the largest conservative party (the Social Conservative Party) walked out following disputes over social security reform and the extension of the Constituent Assembly beyond its 30 April 1998 mandate. As in Colombia, indigenous representatives in the Assembly and their leftist allies achieved recognition of a weaker set of cultural and self-government rights for Afro-Ecuadorians (Andolina 1999, 2003; Van Cott 2002). The Ecuadorian constitutional reform differs from the Bolivian and Colombian experiences in that the indigenous party Pachakutik was the third largest force in the Constituent Assembly and the centre of the opposition bloc. As a result, indigenous themes had relatively more support than in Bolivia or Colombia. In addition, Ecuadorian elites were weaker and more divided by region and political party. Although elite congressional representatives attempted to manipulate or pre-empt the reform process, social movements and influential opinion makers, who perceived the Assembly as the legitimate expression of Ecuadorian society, outmanoeuvred them.

Similarly, in Venezuela in 1999 indigenous peoples took advantage of the collapse of the traditional elite parties and the president's affection for the history and culture of indigenous peoples. Buoyed by a resounding electoral victory that granted him a mandate for sweeping constitutional reform, President Hugo Chávez decreed electoral rules that favoured his own left-leaning movement—62.5 per cent of the vote in Constituent Assembly elections was converted into 121 of 128 seats, while the two neoliberal parties that had dominated politics in Venezuela for the previous half-century earned only one seat between them. This resulted in an Assembly overwhelmingly dominated by the president and his allies from the military, the left, and the human rights movement. Three indigenous representatives participated through reserved seats for indigenous peoples and two more gained election to the Assembly on their own. Despite the relative weakness of Venezuela's indigenous movement, the five indigenous delegates successfully demanded the region's most progressive regime of indigenous constitutional rights (Van Cott 2003a). During the 1999 Assembly, the president's coalition took on the neoliberal model and dismantled the privileges of the business elite. Thus, indigenous peoples did not have to waste energy fighting neoliberal elites, who were too weak to challenge their multicultural demands. Instead, their stiffest opposition came from Chávez's military allies, who expressed the fears of their counterparts in other Latin American countries, i.e. that granting rights to indigenous peoples would threaten the country's territorial integrity. The issue of indigenous rights provoked a four-day confrontation between conservative ex-officers and the Commission on Indigenous Rights. After language was inserted explicitly denying the possibility of territorial dismemberment, the indigenous rights platform passed with 128 votes in favour and 3 abstentions (Van Cott 2003*a*: 61–2).

In sum, indigenous peoples gained multicultural rights in Bolivia and Colombia by allying with a centre-left that did not challenge the neoliberal economic model but successfully pressured for decentralization and the opening of the democratic regime. In Ecuador and Venezuela elites resisted the imposition of neoliberal reforms for years in the hope that future oil revenues would make them unnecessary. Indigenous peoples achieved an ample regime of indigenous rights by allying with the anti-neoliberal left: in Ecuador as the core of the centre-left bloc; in Venezuela, as a privileged friend of the leader of the left. In every case, although some elites supported the multicultural rights codified, indigenous peoples had to fight hard against strong opposition and indigenous rights were among the most controversial rights ultimately recognized.

Whereas constitutional reform occurred in South America during periods of intense political crisis regarding the legitimacy of the democratic regime, in Guatemala, Nicaragua, Panama, and Mexico indigenous constitutional rights were recognized as a direct result of successful military pressure from indigenous (and non-indigenous) combatants. In the meso-American cases, neoliberal elites remained relatively strong and unified during the period when indigenous peoples movements were best able to press their multicultural claims. In all four cases the left was too weak to serve as an effective ally in the struggle against neoliberalism. Indigenous peoples only secured a strong set of multicultural constitutional rights where they successfully exerted military pressure and had the backing of the United States (Panama, Nicaragua) (Van Cott 2001). Nicaragua is an exceptional case that proves the rule: the Atlantic Coast Autonomous Regions were established in 1987 under Marxist Sandinista rule. Neoliberals that took control of the government shortly thereafter have impeded their full implementation.

5. Conclusion

Latin America in the 1990s witnessed two major trends: (1) the adoption of neoliberal economic restructuring, which exposed millions of people to hardship and weakened the modest and uneven social security systems that had developed in some countries in earlier years; and (2) indigenous movements' successful campaign for cultural rights, resulting in the widespread codification of multicultural policies. Critics have argued, along the lines of the critics of MCPs in developed countries, that neoliberal elites conceded modest MCPs in order to forestall radical challenges to their economic model.

In fact, the relationship among neoliberalism, indigenous political mobilization, and the adoption of MCPs is more complex.[17] Since the adoption of MCPs followed the original neoliberal momentum, there is little evidence that MCPs crowd out redistribution. Rather, the causal chain runs in the other direction: the politics of economic crisis and neoliberalism tended to open political space for indigenous mobilization and the adoption of MCPs. Indigenous movements gained strength in the context of economic hardship. They revived leftist-popular coalitions that opposed structural adjustment and trade liberalization. Thus, the pursuit of MCPs did not divide social justice coalitions; rather, it helped to build them. Indigenous movements have been more successful in obtaining MCPs than in forestalling neoliberal agendas. In part, this reflects the fact that indigenous groups and their priorities became stronger within leftist coalitions as economic crisis weakened unions and socialist parties. In some cases indigenous movements and their allies recognized that they were too weak to reverse neoliberalism but were strong enough to win some MCPs. Moreover, some indigenous demands—particularly for self-government—were compatible with the neoliberal emphasis on decentralization and state restructuring. Indigenous movements did not misdiagnose their problems; rather, they captured gains that were attainable in particular political contexts.

---

[17] Attempts to correlate MCPs with either the human development index or measures of economic competitiveness are inconclusive due to limitations of the data and the small sample size. There is a weak statistical correlation between the measure of macroeconomic competitiveness in 2002 and the number of multicultural policies adopted, at the 0.06 level, with an R-squared of 0.22. With respect to the impact of MCPs on the welfare state, the results are even weaker. All countries in our sample improved their level of human development during the 1990s, according to the Human Development Index prepared by the United Nations Development Programme. There is no statistical relationship between change in HDI between 1990 and 2001 and the number of MCPs adopted. There is also no correlation between the HDI in 2001 and the number of MCPs adopted.

Whether indigenous movements and the MCPs they have attained will strengthen or weaken future campaigns for economic redistribution will depend upon the relative strength of indigenous peoples' organizations, neoliberal elites, and the left in each country. The severe hardships that neoliberal reforms have caused have cost neoliberal elites and the political parties that represent them support. Meanwhile the left has recuperated some of its electoral strength; for example, leftist presidents recently were elected in Brazil, Ecuador, Uruguay, Venezuela, Bolivia, and Chile. Indigenous movements are also gaining force, particularly in countries where they have joined forces with popular movements to create new electoral vehicles.

Given the recent inception of both MCPs and structural reforms in Latin America, the future offers a range of possibilities. Latin American states that instituted both sets of reforms fall between two modal types. On one end of the spectrum are states like Chile, Argentina, Peru, and Guatemala, in which neoliberal reforms were undertaken vigorously and now coexist with a modest set of MCPs, the latter limited primarily to language, education, and limited collective land rights. We can call this 'neoliberal multiculturalism', borrowing from Hale and Gustafson. On the other end of the spectrum are countries like Ecuador and Venezuela with more expansive sets of multicultural policies that include considerable political representation and autonomy rights. In these countries popular, as well as elite, resistance has delayed the imposition of neoliberal reforms and has been accompanied by political and economic instability, party system fragmentation and decomposition, and widespread social protest. We can call this 'populist multiculturalism' to convey the political context in which multicultural reforms were adopted in those countries.

The political and economic equilibria described by the 'neoliberal' and 'populist' types is by no means stable, given the changing relations among the three key collective actors and the dissatisfaction with the status quo that all three express. Three further outcomes are, thus, foreseeable. The first is the resurgence of the economic and political elite, who lead a backlash against and rollback of MCPs. I call this option 'neoliberal reaction'. In fact, this occurred during the Banzer-Quiroga administration in Bolivia (1997–2002). The second outcome entails a radical ethno-nationalist development of MCPs with considerably more self-government powers for ethnically defined subnational governments and some scheme of national-level ethnic power sharing. This could result in the ethnic utopia that many indigenous organizations envision, in which all ethnic groups have voice and representation through mechanisms compatible with their culture and redistributive measures provide basic social welfare for all: the 'multinational democratic state'. In the alternative, given the existing extreme inequalities in Latin American societies, and the divergent interests of light-skinned elites and the dark-skinned majority, it could lead to a constant state of social upheaval, economic stagnation, and legislative and executive gridlock, an outcome we can call 'protracted ethnic conflict'. Should an indigenous majority emerge from this battle and seize executive power, it is likely that neoliberalism will be significantly curtailed. It is too soon to tell whether this is occurring in Bolivia, where indigenous leader Evo Morales was elected president in December 2005 with an unprecedented absolute majority of 54 per cent of the vote.

The direction that each country takes ultimately will depend upon the relative strength of neoliberals, the left, and indigenous peoples' movements, on the capacity of fragile political party systems to aggregate and channel coherent policy alternatives, and on economic conditions—domestic and international—which largely determine the resources with which Latin American states can address multicultural and welfare demands.

11

Neoliberalism and the re-emergence of ethnopolitics in Bolivia

Willem Assies

Bolivia, although a much poorer country than most of those studied in this book, was not a stranger to welfare policies. During the middle decades of the twentieth century, it had taken steps towards the development of programmes dedicated to economic and social security. Although the system was limited in many ways, it did provide elements of protection to at least some parts of the population. In the 1980s and 1990s, however, two major trends transformed the Bolivian political landscape. One was neoliberalism, which exposed the population to significant economic hardship and reduced the limited social programmes that had been inherited from the past; the second was the political mobilization of indigenous people and the adoption of multiculturalism policies. Given the debates addressed in this book, the key issue is the relation between multiculturalism and neoliberalism. Did multiculturalism in Bolivia contribute to the advance of the neoliberal agenda or not?

To address this issue, in the first place we have to distinguish clearly between identity politics 'from below' and recognition policies 'from above' or, to put it crudely, between 'demand' and 'supply'. What are indigenous movements demanding and what is a neoliberal state willing to concede? Framing the question this way also leads us to explore the relationship between policies of recognition and redistributive policies.

This chapter is based on research carried out in the framework of the project 'Indigenous Peoples and State Reform', funded by the Consejo Nacional de Ciencia y Tecnología (CONA-CyT), Mexico (Project No. 45173). I would like to thank the editors and the participants in the workshop at Queen's University, Kingston, for their helpful comments on an earlier draft of this chapter.

In his article on what he calls 'neoliberal multiculturalism' Hale (2002) has argued that neoliberal states may be willing to proactively recognize a minimal package of cultural rights, while equally vigorously rejecting the rest of indigenous demands. He proposes that the acceptance of certain cultural demands may lure indigenous movements into a limited form of identity politics that forsakes redistributive issues and thus in the end contributes to neoliberal governmentality. He furthermore suggests that the relationship between 'cultural' and 'redistributive' issues may be more complex than an either-or question. The emergence of identity politics poses the challenge of rethinking the relation between redistribution and recognition as two, not mutually exclusive, forms of achieving social justice (Fraser 2003) and, in the case at hand, invites an exploration of the complex relations between ethnicity and class (status and class) in a post-colonial society.

This chapter argues that Bolivia provides no significant evidence of a 'crowding-out' effect in the sense that culturalist demands took precedence over a more general redistributive agenda. Neoliberalism was well established before the effective mobilization of indigenous peoples and the strength of the neoliberal position was not significantly enhanced by the emergence of indigenous movements and parties involved in identity politics. Instead, the dominant pattern seems to be that: (*a*) neoliberalism was generated by other forces such as the multilateral agencies, but that (*b*) neoliberal restructuring in turn helped trigger indigenous mobilization and ethnically charged politics. If neoliberal politicians came to adopt multiculturalism policies, this was basically what Van Cott (this volume) calls a reactive and opportunistic response.

The question of the 'corroding' effect is difficult to answer for the Bolivian case if it is framed in terms of indigenous mobilization weakening relations with other groups that would otherwise have coalesced to resist neoliberalism and support wider popular coalitions. In fact, it was neoliberal restructuring that obliterated the existing trade union structures and ethnically charged politics blossomed in the vacuum thus created. A major characteristic of contemporary popular protest in Bolivia is that it is highly fragmented. Typically, protest peaks, or what Bolivians call 'social convulsions', emerge out of a temporary fusion of dispersed mobilizations that coalesce around some issue that emerges as overarching and representative of neoliberal economic policies and the system of governance that allows such policies to be implemented. This, however, at best gives rise to tactical alliances among more or less 'radical' groups or leaders, be they indigenous or not.

Do indigenous peoples in Bolivia 'misdiagnose' their situation and do they pursue cultural policies that cannot really solve their deep-seated socio-economic problems? It is difficult to speak of misdiagnosis in this sense in the Bolivian case because there are no indigenous movements that are limited to 'cultural' issues. If Bolivia can be characterized as a post-colonial society, is it a case of misdiagnosis if indigenous peoples consider themselves as both culturally oppressed and economically exploited and dispossessed of the resources for cultural and economic reproduction?

To develop the argument, the chapter traces the historical development of these issues through several critical cycles. After a brief introduction to the history of Bolivia, the first major section examines the National Revolutionary Cycle which began in 1952 and established certain welfare policies. The second section examines the development of neoliberal policies and the political constellation that allowed this development. It then traces the emergence of ethnically charged opposition to these policies and the adoption of multiculturalism as an aspect of a second generation of neoliberal reforms in the mid-1990s. It finally shows how these multiculturalism policies failed to enhance support for the neoliberal project as became increasingly clear by the end of the 1990s when indigenous peoples came to play an important role in the resistance against neoliberalism, leading to the Bolivian crisis of 2003. Indigenous movements often played a key role in the opposition to neoliberalism. The final section briefly sums up the argument and considers possible future scenarios.

1. A post-colonial society with an indigenous majority

Although data on numbers of indigenous people are notoriously controversial and difficult to interpret (Gonzalez 1994) it is commonly assumed that indigenous people constitute the majority of the Bolivian population. According to Bolivia's 2001 census, the country counted nearly 8.3 million inhabitants of which 62 per cent[1] declared themselves to belong to some indigenous people, principally the Quechuas (31 per cent) and the Aymaras (25 per cent) of the Andean highlands and the colonization areas in the eastern lowlands, while the remaining 6 per cent accounts for some thirty different indigenous peoples in the eastern Amazonian

---

[1] Of those over fifteen years.

lowlands (Bolivia 2003). According to estimates up to 45 per cent of the indigenous population lives in urban areas. Thus, while equating the indigenous population with the rural population—about 38 per cent of the total population—is erroneous, it is commonly agreed that 90 per cent of the rural population is indigenous (Calla Ortega 2003a: 198; MACPIO 2001). While about 54 per cent of the urban population is poor and 26 per cent extremely poor, in the rural areas 81 per cent is poor and 55 per cent extremely poor (UDAPE 2003: 51). Being indigenous and being poor are clearly correlated (PNUD 2004: 108).

Bolivia is a post-colonial society that still has to come to terms with its colonial legacy. It is beyond the scope of this article to thoroughly discuss Bolivian history, but it should be pointed out that after the arrival of the Spaniards a highly stratified society was constructed in the Andes region, inhabited by Aymara and Quechua. It was centred on the silver mining economy that emerged in the Potosí region and later, from the late nineteenth century onward, on tin mining a bit further north. The tropical *Oriente*, inhabited by indigenous peoples practising swidden agriculture in combination with hunting and gathering, remained largely peripheral until the quinoa and rubber booms of the nineteenth century triggered new incorporation efforts. Present-day Bolivia is characterized by a pattern of regional differentiation inherited from the mining economy with its satellite economies that supplied it with agricultural produce through the hacienda system, and a remote eastern periphery. Its historical development influenced the forms in which the indigenous population was incorporated into the dominant economy and the degrees to which it was able to preserve its own forms of organization (Ticona A., Rojas O., and Albó C. 1995; Rivera Cusicanqui 2003).

The Chaco war (1932–5) had profound consequences for the Bolivian polity and paved the way for the Bolivian Revolution of 1952. This disastrous adventure fuelled a change in the national political debate as the so-called 'Chaco generation' began to raise the Indian question, the land question, labour issues, and the dependency on the private mines owned by a few tin barons. The war was followed by a period of political instability during which representatives of the 'liberal' mining and landholding oligarchy alternated with governments headed by ex-combatants. During such governments Standard Oil of New Jersey, held responsible for the Chaco war, was nationalized and a state enterprise Yacimientos Petrolíferos Fiscales Bolivianos (YPFB) was created to manage the nationalized enterprise. The first labour laws saw the light and in the wake of a Primer Congreso Indigenal, which took place in 1945, decrees

were issued that prohibited serfdom and sought to promote rural education, though with little concrete effect. Meanwhile, new political parties,
most importantly the Movimiento Nacionalista Revolucionaria (MNR)
arose as well as labour unions among which the Federación Sindical de
Trabajadores Mineros de Bolivia (FSTMB) came to play a vanguard role.
Peasant unions began to emerge demanding the establishment of rural
schools and contesting the hacienda system. After the MNR gained the
1951 elections it was kept from assuming power by an army intervention
that eventually was defeated by the popular insurrection of April 1952. In
the view of the revolutionaries the 'nation'—middle class, workers, and
peasants—had defeated the 'anti-nation' represented by the feudal and
mining oligarchy and their imperialist allies.

2. The national revolutionary cycle

The coming to power of the MNR initiated the 'national-revolutionary
cycle' and a state capitalist development model that basically was kept
in place until 1985. The 1942 MNR revolutionary programme clearly
included welfare ideals in its final paragraph on the economic liberation
and sovereignty of the Bolivian people. It called for:

- A law that regulates peasant labour, taking regional peculiarities and
  the customs imposed by geographic circumstances into account, but
  guaranteeing the health and the satisfaction of the needs of the
  worker;
- Colonization projects that aim to turn every Bolivian, man or
  woman, into an owner of the land;
- The regulation of labour conditions of the organized workers
  and employees in international enterprises, creating a mechanism
  whereby salaries and wages are adjusted and to avoid social *malestar*
  (un-well-being);
- Obligatory social security and the elimination of the mechanisms
  that hinder the putting into effect of social laws and their benefits
  for the Bolivians;
- A statute of civil service that protects, assures, and regulates the
  functions of public servants, men and women;
- The death penalty for speculators, usurers, smugglers, falsifiers, those
  who bribe public servants and traders in vice;

- The identification of all Bolivians with the aspirations and needs of the peasantry: the programme proclaims that social justice is inseparable from the redemption of the Indian for the *economic liberation and sovereignty of the Bolivian people.*[2]

This constitutes a wish list that—except for the death penalty—quite befits a welfare state.

The 1952 Revolution brought four basic transformations:

- The universal franchise for all Bolivians, male and female, older than 21 if unmarried or older than 18 when married, independent of their income, occupation, or degree of education.

- The nationalization of the holdings of the three tin barons. These mines were brought under the administration of the Corporación Minera de Bolivia (COMIBOL) in which, during the first few years, the FSTMB played a key role. The FSTMB had also taken the initiative to create a trade-union umbrella organization, the Central Obrera Boliviana (COB), which became a key player in Bolivian politics and forced the MNR to accept 'co-government' during the first four years after the Revolution.

- In 1953 an agrarian reform was decreed under the pressure of peasant unrest and unionization from which the Confederación Nacional de Trabajadores Campesinos de Bolivia (CNTCB), initially linked to the COB, emerged. The agrarian reform put an end to the hacienda system that had dominated the Andes region, but failed to improve productivity. A lack of appropriate technical and financial support and the subdivision of holdings upon inheritance led to increasing fragmentation into *minifundia* and resource degradation. On the other hand, development policies adopted in the course of the 1950s would favour large-scale agriculture and extensive cattle breeding in the eastern lowlands, which effectively underwent a socially regressive land reform. By the 1980s the national agrarian structure had become extremely polarized again, with an impoverished indigenous peasantry in the Andes region and a lowland region dominated by huge enterprises crowding out the local indigenous population, which would start organizing politically in the 1980s.

- An education reform was initiated in 1955 and introduced free, obligatory, and universal education. The reform aimed at cultural

---

[2] The full text is reproduced in Arze Cuadros (2002: 605–43).

homogenization and imposed Spanish as the sole teaching language, which probably is one of the reasons for the relatively meagre results.

During the years leading up to the 1952 revolution and thereafter a Bolivian version of the welfare state emerged, inspired by the ideology of national developmentism and as part of a nation-building effort. As was the case in other Latin American states (Santos 1987; Oxhorn 2003) this welfare system remained precarious and patchy. Although it espoused a universalist ideology in fact it relied on a selective incorporation of specific groups or sectors of the population according to political convenience. What emerged in Bolivia in the wake of the 1952 Revolution has been described as a prebendalist, patrimonialist, or cartorial state; a state and a political regime that rely on doling out jobs in the state bureaucracy to the clientele of the governing sectors (Gamarra and Malloy 1995; Gamarra 2003; PNUD 2002; Tapia Mealla and Toranzo Roca 2000; World Bank 2000). During the first few years of 'co-government' between the MNR and the COB, the COMIBOL became an important employment-generating machine with a huge bureaucracy and well-subsidized company stores in the mining centres. As the MNR gradually moved to the right, however, the co-government arrangement broke down by 1956 and since then the relationship between governments and miners has been tense if not one of open confrontation. On the other hand, the peasantry was placated by the land reform and remained a loyal ally of the MNR governments as well as of the military governments that ruled the country after 1964. This alliance was formalized in a *pacto militar campesino* that lasted until the mid-1970s when the Banzer dictatorship killed between 80 and 200 peasants protesting its economic policies. The unravelling of the *pacto*, as we shall see, brought a reconciliation between workers and (indigenous) peasants, now united in the struggle against military dictatorships.

The outcome of the national-revolutionary model was that by the mid-1970s the state sector accounted for some 70 per cent of the national product with enterprises in the mining and oil and gas sector playing key roles. The state was the main employer and provider of goods and services. Salaries paid to the bureaucracy absorbed about 10 per cent of the national product. The number of state employees rose from 40,000 in 1951 to 90,000 in 1964 and about 170,000 in the late 1970s, about one-third of the economically active population; 55,000 were public employees (of which 30,000 were teachers), 30,000 worked in the nationalized enterprises, and 22,000 were on the payroll of the armed forces (Berthin Siles 1999: 367–9; World Bank 2000: 1).

In 1956 a unified social security system was created, which was to cover maternity, illness, professional risks, disability, old age, and burial, sort of 'from the cradle to the grave'. Since the state was the principal employer it contributed most of the funding in its capacity as employer, but failed to contribute the share it should fund as state. In the early 1970s the Banzer government sought to rationalize the system. A national fund was to be administered by a Caja Nacional de Seguro Social, while alongside, for different affiliated sectors, so-called complementary funds existed. Thus the customs service, the public service, the railways, teachers, the judicial branch, the police, the army, miners, universities, industrial workers, and other sectors had their specific funds to complement the meagre national fund disbursals. The result was a hodgepodge of mostly highly bureaucratized small social security funds that unevenly covered a minimal part of the population (Mercado Lora 1998), not to speak of the peasantry.

After twelve years of MNR rule and eighteen years of military governments the social achievements of the Revolution were rather modest. Life expectancy and literacy had improved, but per capita GDP may have declined in real terms (Morales 2003: 221; Klein 2003). The land reform had brought redistribution in the Andes region, but thirty years later landholding was highly fragmented and minimally productive and most of the indigenous peasantry desperately poor. In the *Oriente* a highly polarized rural structure had emerged, dominated by huge estates (Demeure V. 1999: 269–90). The nationalized mines were often exhausted and mismanaged while little had been invested (Jordán Pozo 1999: 219–39). No dynamic 'national bourgeoisie' had come into being. The *Oriente* agriculturalists and some medium-sized mining enterprises had emerged relying on extremely generous state subsidies (Rodriguez Ostria 1999: 291–304). Cocaine had become one of the major export products. The military regimes bequeathed the country a huge foreign debt.

In sum, the 1952–82 period was characterized by a politics structured largely around the axes of class and economic interest. In the context of a nation-building effort and state-centred national-developmentist economic policies a number of progressive economic and social policies were put into place. On the cultural dimension, the era was characterized by a denial of multiculturalism. The 1952 Revolution expressly abolished the term *indio*, which was regarded as demeaning, and referred to the rural population as 'peasantry'. Although the land reform recognized communal holding it basically sought to create individual family farms while other important programmes, such as education, were clearly assimilationist.

3. Democracy, free markets, and multiculturalism

After the turbulent 1978–82 period Bolivia finally returned to civilian government under a left-of-centre coalition, the Unidad Democrática y Popular (UDP).[3] Its attempt to revamp the national revolutionary model ended in dismal failure. The COB pressed for pent-up popular demands in the most 'maximalist' style while the opposition in parliament—the MNR faction of Victor Paz Estenssoro and the Acción Democrática Nacionalista (ADN) of ex-dictator General Banzer—gave the UDP government precious little room for manoeuvre. Inflation turned to hyperinflation while chaos was on the rise. In 1985, president Siles Zuazo decided to step down a year before ending his constitutional mandate.

The debacle set the stage for a turn to orthodox neoliberal adjustment policies. In this section I will first discuss Bolivian structural adjustment policies and the system of governance that allowed them to be carried through. In 1985 a 'first generation' of adjustment policies was introduced following the Washington Consensus recipe.[4] This shock therapy broke the backbone of the COB, which until then had been the major vehicle of popular protest. In political terms, the introduction of neoliberal adjustment policies basically relied on what has become known as 'pacted democracy', that is 'gentlemen's agreements' among the leaders of the principal parties concerning the division of the spoils. Although formally a representative democracy, this meant that the party system suffered a huge 'representation deficit'. By the late 1980s some new 'neo-populist' parties emerged, which appealed to the indigenous population and criticized the established party system as well as the neoliberal economic model. When between 1993 and 1997 a 'second generation' of reforms was introduced, multiculturalism became an important ingredient, partly in response to the neo-populist parties, which were soon co-opted into the

---

[3] The coalition was made up from a faction of the MNR joined by the Movimiento de Izquierda Revolucionaria (MIR), a left-wing party that had emerged in 1971, and the Bolivian Communist Party (PCB).

[4] It should be noted, though, that privatization of state enterprises did not figure prominently among the first generation reforms in Bolivia, basically as a result of the lingering influence of revolutionary nationalism. A Bolivian variant of privatization would be introduced after 1993, as part of the second-generation reforms.

pacted democracy system. As the neoliberal agenda pursued its course new forms of opposition in which indigenous movements played a prominent role emerged. Faced with this opposition the state increasingly turned to repressive measures, creating the conditions of emergence of the 'Bolivian crisis' that culminated in the ousting of president Sánchez de Lozada in October 2003.

Structural adjustment and governance

The 1985 elections resulted in a coalition between the MNR and ADN that elected Paz Estenssoro president.[5] A few weeks later he introduced a New Economic Policy, which achieved economic stabilization at tremendous social costs. The package included a reform of the monetary system, rationalization of the bureaucracy through mass dismissal, market liberalization, export promotion, and reform of the tax system. The tin market crash later that year accelerated the overhaul of COMIBOL and 23,000 miners were 'relocated', that is dismissed. Due to trade liberalization the market was swamped with cheap imports and many factories closed or downsized. Urban unemployment jumped from 6 per cent to 12 per cent. The dismissal of the miners and the restructuring of other sectors emasculated the COB.

As elsewhere, the turn to neoliberalism was accompanied by a shift in the social policy paradigm which now favours targeted assistance, presumably to increase efficiency by limiting the amount of leakage to middle- and upper-class groups. Under the pressure of multilateral agencies general subsidies and overly bureaucratic welfare policies are replaced by strictly needs-based direct assistance (Abel and Lewis 2002; Oxhorn 2003; Pérez Baltodano 1997; Sottoli 2000). To attenuate the worst effects of the adjustment measures, in 1986 Bolivia created a Social Emergency Fund (FSE)[6] to provide temporary employment in works of 'social impact'. Originally viewed as a temporary measure, in 1991 the FSE was transformed into a more permanent Social Investment Fund (FIS) to finance health and education infrastructure, as human capital building became a catchword in the new social policy paradigm of 'struggle against (extreme) poverty'. FIS fund targeting, however, became largely oriented by patronage criteria (Aguirre, Arze, and Montaño 1992; Prisma 2000; World Bank 2000: 53).

[5] If none of the candidates wins a straight majority, the Bolivian Congress elects the president.
[6] Bolivia was a pioneer in this field.

The turn to neoliberalism was sustained by what has become known as 'pacted democracy'. From 1985 onward a series of gentlemen's agreements were concluded among the main party leaders. Whitehead (2001*a*) has suggested that this system of inter-party bargaining and division of the spoils may present an alternative to what O'Donnell has called 'delegative democracy', which 'rests on the premise that whoever wins elections is thereby entitled to act as he or she sees fit, constrained only by the hard facts of existing power relations and by a constitutionally limited term of office'. Such weakly institutionalized democracies, characterized by a lack of accountability, have carried through the harsh adjustment 'packages' of the 1980s (O'Donnell 1999: 168). While Whitehead (2001*a*) argues that Bolivia's democratic institutions appear to function more effectively than those of various adjoining neo-democracies and that 'the broadly neoliberal framework of policy pursued since 1985 seems reasonably compatible with the persistence and even entrenchment of at least a "low intensity" form of market democracy' (Whitehead 2001*b*: 39), Bolivia's troubled recent past suggests otherwise. As I have argued elsewhere, rather than being superior to delegative democracy Bolivia's pacted democracy can be viewed as a functional equivalent that shares the features of weak institutionalization and lack of accountability as well as the inability to channel popular discontent with neoliberal policies, which was met with repression. Bolivian democracy became ever more of a *democradura* or what Seoane (2003) has called 'armed neoliberalism'. It was in this context that ethnically charged politics came to play an increasingly prominent role.

Neoliberalism and the politicization of ethnicity

As noted, in the wake of the Bolivian Revolution the term *indio* had officially been banned and a class perspective predominated, down-playing cultural or ethnic differences. In the context of the agrarian reform the organization of rural trade unions was strongly promoted. The local *sindicatos* became the basis of the pyramidal structure of the Confederación Nacional de Trabajadores Campesinos de Bolivia (CNTCB), strongly linked to the MNR governments and subsequently to the military governments under the formal *pacto military campesino*.[7] The unravelling of this alliance in the mid-1970s was accompanied by a resurgence of

[7] The CNTCB was formally part of the COB, but as the revolutionary governments veered to the right the COB became increasingly strongly opposed to these governments while the peasantry remained loyal.

307

'ethnic conscience'. 'Katarista' movements, named after the leaders of the late eighteenth-century indigenous revolt, gained increasing influence within the CNTCB. In 1973 the famous Manifiesto de Tiawanacu had been launched which, among other things, stated that 'We feel economically exploited and culturally and politically oppressed. In Bolivia there has not been an integration of cultures but superposition and domination, and we have been relegated to the lowest and most exploited rungs of this pyramid.'[8] Seeking a middle ground between radical indianism and its glorification of an idealized past and the emphasis on class struggle of the left, Katarismo underlined the necessity to look at Bolivia with 'two eyes'. It stressed the struggle of the Indian population against 'internal colonialism' but also viewed the *sindicato* (union) as the principal vehicle of struggle of the exploited *campesino*. It thus sought to synthesize the struggles of 'nation and class'. In 1979, a congress of 'peasant unification' sponsored by the COB resulted in the renaming of the CNTCB as Confederación Sindical Única de Trabajadores Campesinos de Bolivia (CSUTCB). Workers and peasants, who had become increasingly divided since 1952, now closed ranks in opposition to the military regimes. However, although Katarismo was important in the formation of the CSUTCB, its role in the political arena remained negligible. Some Katarist and Indianist parties emerged in the late 1970s but they never attracted more than 2 per cent of the vote. By the early 1980s Katarism was splintered by factional disputes, but it had prepared the ground for a greater acceptance of the 'pluri-multi'.

This development received further impetus when the indigenous peoples of the tropical lowlands arrived upon the scene. Since the late 1970s anthropologists and NGOs had promoted 'encounters' among the indigenous peoples of the region, leading in 1982 to the formation of the Confederación Indígena del Oriente Boliviano (CIDOB). Increasing pressure on local resources in the context of neoliberal policies as well as the continent-wide preparations for the commemoration of the 'encounter of cultures' provided the motives and the opportunity for the undertaking of a broadly publicized thirty-five-day March for Territory and Dignity to protest timber exploitation in what were considered indigenous territories. Then president Jaime Paz Zamora (1989–93) personally went to meet the marchers and subsequently signed a series of decrees recognizing indigenous territories in the eastern lowlands. In 1991 Bolivia ratified ILO Convention 169 on indigenous and tribal peoples in independent states.

---

[8] The full text can be found in Bonfil Batalla (1981: 216–23).

By that time ethnicity also had come to play a role in the party system. The system of pacted democracy that had emerged in 1985 relied on three 'traditional' parties; the MNR, which by then had adopted the neoliberal creed, the nominally social-democratic MIR, and ex-dictator Banzer's ADN. By the late 1980s, however, two new 'neo-populist' parties emerged which in different ways appealed to the indigenous and *cholo*[9] electorate. Conciencia de Patria (CONDEPA) was led by the popular radio and television host Carlos Palenque and had its main base in the La Paz highland region. Unidad Cívica Solidaridad (UCS) became the political vehicle of beer magnate Max Fernández and was less regionally confined. What the two parties had in common was that they attracted the protest vote of an impoverished electorate and that ethnic empathy played some role in appealing to this electorate.

Max Fernández's story is one of a 'darkish' shoeshine-boy who became a millionaire.[10] He accumulated a fortune, speculating and using credits in the times of hyperinflation to buy up shares in Bolivia's main beer brewery, the Cervecería Boliviana Nacional. Always emphasizing that he had known poverty he used part of his fortune to assist the poor in times when social policies were rolled back. Financing schools and clinics in medium-sized towns, where this had a relatively great impact for the less advantaged, and oiling his electoral campaigns with plenty of beer and invectives against the established parties, his party garnered up to 16 per cent of the vote in the 1997 elections. This, however, was a condolence-vote; in 1995 Max Fernández had died in a plane crash and his party, with little ideological content from the outset, would thenceforward join any government coalition to ward off the payment of a huge tax debt. Nonetheless, Fernández can be considered a precursor of the 'anti-systemics' for his 'moral' critique of the established parties and his *asistencialismo* (i.e. his commitment to clientalistic or corporatist support for the poor) in times of neoliberal austerity. And he was 'darkish'.

While Mayorga (2002) classifies Max Fernández as the more 'godfather-like' (*padriño*) type of politician, he classifies Carlos Palenque as the 'best-man' (*compadre*) type. While Fernández had a more diffuse appeal as a result of philanthropy, beer, and 'darkishness', Palenque's appeal was more restricted in regional terms and it built much more on ethnicity

---

[9] Mestizo and/or urbanized indigenous people in the highlands.

[10] What follows is largely based on the studies by Mayorga (2002), which provides biographies of Max Fernández and Carlos Palenque, and those contained in Mansilla and Zegada (1996). Romero Ballivián (2003) provides a summary of their careers in the latest edition of his studies on electoral processes and the electoral geography of Bolivia.

(only implied by Fernández's 'darkishness'), a rejection of neoliberalism, and antisystemic rhetoric. The 'best-man' style, at least discursively, implies a more horizontal relation. Palenque particularly appealed to the Aymara of the La Paz urban and rural highlands; a ground prepared by Katarism. His political career started when he interviewed a drug lord and his radio and tv station was closed in 1988, which caused intense protests. He had become enormously popular, particularly among Aymara women, with a talk show where people exposed their daily and domestic conflicts and problems, and were listened to and were helped in some way by Palenque and his team. In those talk shows he was seconded by Remedios Loza, dressing *chola* style—bowler hat and all—and fluent in Spanish, Aymara, and Quechua, while his wife Mónica Medina took charge of the 'social branch', distributing coffins for the dead, eyeglasses to the sightless, and wheelchairs to the crippled. On that basis, CONDEPA was founded in 1988 to give voice to the oppressed and defenceless through a discourse that stressed Andean values and the antagonism between *cholos* and *q'aras* (white, rich, dominant), denouncing neoliberalism and propagating a model of 'endogenous development'. In 1997, Palenque died of a heart attack. That year CONDEPA achieved about 17 per cent of the vote and entered Hugo Banzer's government coalition from which it soon was expelled as the party was falling apart due to factional struggles over Palenque's legacy.

In a context where miners' and urban trade unionism was shattered as a result of economic restructuring and growing informal (self-)employment these parties appealed to those excluded from the pacted democracy model. However, as Mayorga (2002: 86) argues, although these parties posed a challenge to the established party system they ended up contributing to its consolidation and the hegemony of democratic neoliberalism. They had the capacity to symbolically represent and incorporate new social identities into the democratic dynamic but Mayorga also cautiously points out that this capacity for symbolic incorporation contrasts with a weakness of institutional representation and efficacy in channelling social demands and transforming them into public policy proposals.

In sum, neoliberal adjustment policies, inspired by multilateral agencies and unrelated to multiculturalism policies, transformed the economic and social model of Bolivia and this particularly affected the sectors of the population subject to economic subordination and ethnic discrimination. At the same time, by eroding the bases for trade unionism adjustment policies undermined the conditions for class-based mobilization whereas the pacted democracy model restricted representation of the subordinated.

This provided the conditions of emergence for neo-populist parties, which in different ways tapped ethnic empathies but in the end failed to provide a genuine alternative and soon joined the spoils system of pacted democracy. Their appeal to ethnicity, however, paved the way for a reactive and opportunistic turn to multiculturalism among the traditional parties.

Recognition policies and second-generation reforms

By the early 1990s recognition of the multicultural and pluriethnic composition of the population had become fashionable in Bolivia, as elsewhere in Latin America. The Katarism of the rural trade unions, the new visibility of the indigenous peoples of the *Oriente*, and the emergence of two neo-populist parties that somehow tapped identity resources suggested that adopting a multiculturalist ploy might be electorally rewarding. In a reactive response, for instance, by the early 1990s the MNR embraced multiculturalism. Its new leader, Gonzalo Sánchez de Lozada, who had been the architect of the 1985 economic shock therapy, would sit down among indigenous peasants and state how much he liked their typical dishes, though his interlocutors would be a little uneasy about his heavy gringo accent,[11] stating things like 'I do not understand a word of what he says.' Taking into account a political marketing study Sánchez de Lozada invited one of the moderate and more intellectualist Katarista leaders, Víctor Hugo Cárdenas, to join him in the 1993 presidential race. Although initially this 'surprising and bold alliance between Aymaras and neoliberals' (Albó 1994) generated high expectations, the shine soon wore off. Upon assuming the vice-presidency Cárdenas had said that the principles of *ama quella, ama llulla, ama sua, ama llunku* (do not be lazy, do not lie, do not steal, do not be servile) would guide him but this was soon held against him as he was accused of being servile to the neoliberal model.[12]

Multiculturalism, however, was to be one of the outstanding features of the package of 'second-generation' reforms carried through by the

[11] Sánchez de Lozada was brought up and studied in the USA and never lost his accent.

[12] In his speech Cárdenas also stated that 'Indigenous development is national development. Each time the criticism that the indigenous not only want to establish states of their own and dismember the country and moreover, seek a "separate development", certainly utopian and regressive, is becoming more marginalized. We should recognize that, apart from some radicalized discourses, the indigenous peoples understand their own development as a component of national development, linked to the great objectives of our countries, incorporated in the dynamics of the market and, above all, based in the will to rely on their own effort to achieve that' (cited in Ibarra, n.d.). The latter remarks clearly indicate a drift away from his earlier Katarista discourse and its emphasis on looking at reality through the lenses of class and nation.

Sánchez de Lozada government (1993–7).[13] The most outstanding second-generation reforms were:

- Capitalization—a Bolivian variant of privatization whereby half of the shares in the most important national enterprises (electricity, telecommunications, airlines, railways, oil and gas exploitation, and transport, and a tin foundry) were handed over to mostly transnational enterprises in return for an equivalent investment in the sector. This reform was related to a reform of the pension system. The other half of the shares of the state enterprises was retained for the Bolivians and was to be managed by private Pension Fund Administrators that were to assure that every Bolivian reaching the age of 65 would receive a minimum pension, the BONOSOL (Mercado Lora 1998). While the privatization of the state enterprises turned out to be fraught with shady deals and often was regarded as a garage sale of the national patrimony, the allegedly low profitability of the privatized enterprises undermined the BONOSOL. With great difficulty a pension of about US$250 was paid out during the 1997 electoral campaign, but in 1998 the Banzer government scrapped the scheme and later replaced it with the BOLIVIDA of some US$60 per year.[14]

- The law of Popular Participation, which decentralized government and contained elements of multiculturalism. The previously insignificant sections of provinces were converted into municipalities. While municipal governments had been effective in at best some twenty larger cities, the country now counts over 300 municipalities that receive an important share of the national tax revenue. At the same time, Territorial Base Organizations, among them those of indigenous peoples, were recognized and given legal personality.[15] They were to play a role in overseeing municipal governments. Though initially this reform met with resistance of the CSUTCB, but not of the CIDOB, it soon was appropriated by local organizations to make inroads into local government, though not without difficulty or ambiguities (Assies 2003a; Grindle 2000). The coca growers of the Chapare region

[13] For a detailed and valuable analysis of Bolivian multiculturalism under Sánchez de Lozada see Van Cott (2000). Subsequent events, however, have called into question the optimistic tone of this account and pointed to the limitations of 'liberal indigenism' (Gustafson 2002) or what Hale (2002) has dubbed 'neoliberal multiculturalism'. Recently, Albó (2004) has also emphasized the superficiality of Sánchez de Lozada's conversion to multiculturalism.

[14] The subsequent, short-lived, second Sánchez de Lozada government reinstated the BONOSOL.

[15] This 'territorialization' was also intended to further sideline the already weakened 'corporatist' trade union structure.

in Cochabamba are an outstanding example of such appropriation, which provided them with a springboard that allowed for the shake-up of the party system in the 2002 presidential elections.

- Reforms in the agrarian and forestry legislation initially were market oriented in intention but were partly amended as a result of peasant and indigenous protests. As a result, the new legislation was a hybrid. On the one hand it introduced market elements applying to the private sector, while on the other hand peasant smallholdings and community lands continued to be protected. The new legislation also came to include the recognition of Originary Communitarian Lands (TCOs), thus including the territories that had been granted in the lowlands after the 1990 March. It was thought that the TCO concept would only apply to the tropical lowlands, but after a few years it was adopted by highland peoples to stake their territorial claims on the argument that the 'law applies to all'.[16] Although the reform has brought some tenuous benefits for the lowland peoples it hardly has benefited the highland population, which continues to suffer land fragmentation, resource degradation, and neglect (Artículo Primero 2003).

- An educational reform introduced bilingual education and thus abandoned the revolutionary policy of nation building through forcible hispanization.

The flurry of reforms was accompanied by a reform of the Constitution that recognized the multiethnic and pluricultural composition of the Bolivian population. It also paved the way for a reform of the electoral system, meant to strengthen the hold of the established parties at the local level or to make them more responsive to local needs. The reform created sixty-eight single seat districts for the election of part of the 130-seat Chamber of Deputies; a reform that opened the way for the political upheaval of the 2002 presidential elections (Albó 2002; Van Cott 2003*b*).

By the end of the Sánchez de Lozada administration the multilateral agencies regarded Bolivia as an outstanding pupil. The role of the state

---

[16] It should be noted that indigenous communities have adopted a double-edged strategy in the face of the new legal framework. On the one hand they seek the recognition of their property as TCO under the agrarian legislation, while on the other hand they seek recognition of their authority structures under the Popular Participation Law, and to make this recognition coincide with the recognition of TCOs. In this way they seek to reconstitute territories, not only as property, but rather as areas in which their authorities hold political sway and jurisdiction.

in the economy had been rolled back and the most important second-generation reforms were more or less in place. The economy was growing, though not spectacularly and with ups and downs, the incidence of poverty and extreme poverty was back to the 1986 level after having peaked around 1990, the human development index (HDI) showed signs of improving due to improvement in health and education standards, and democracy had been in place for some fifteen years in a notoriously unstable country. Such an assessment, however, happily overlooked that Bolivia was one of those cases where the macro-indicators look good, but the population does not fare well. Fanfani's (2001) 'felicitous' dictum that 'the rich got richer and the poor more numerous' also applies to Bolivia and the 2002 PNUD report characterizes Bolivian performance as a vicious circle of feeble economic growth, worsening income distribution and increasing poverty for important sectors of the population. Employment in the state sector dropped and this was not compensated by private sector performance. Growth of some non-traditional exports had its counterpart in the transnationalization of the internal market, crowding out the smaller local industries. Thus unemployment and informal self-employment increased while labour conditions in the more formal sector deteriorated as a result of flexibilization. State capitalism had successfully been dismantled, but it had been replaced by a rather savage brand of crony capitalism. The regulatory system that was to oversee the privatization process and regulate sectors likely to constitute natural monopolies was often inept and open to influence peddling (Grebe López 2001: 176), and it was more concerned with the investment climate and profitability than with consumer concerns. The 'representation deficit' of pacted democracy became increasingly notorious. A World Bank report euphemistically states that ever since 1985 states of siege have been declared to 'facilitate economic governance' (World Bank 2000: 51).

Thus, in response to the growing presence of indigenous movements and the emergence of ethnically charged politics, multiculturalism became an important feature of the second-generation reforms for pragmatic electoral reasons rather than out of conviction. It was a limited response. Whereas the educational reform introduced bilingual education, the Law of Popular Participation aimed for administrative decentralization in the first place while the recognition of indigenous authorities played a secondary and subordinated role (Calla 2000). In the cases of new agrarian and forestry legislation indigenous peoples' concerns were only taken into account due to mobilizations and pressure of the indigenous peasantry and effective implementation of such legislation where indigenous rights are concerned turned out to be extremely patchy and exceedingly slow as it often collided with the interests of business sectors (agriculture and mining) with strong links to the governing parties and committed to the Bolivian brand of neoliberalism. State sponsored multiculturalism may have generated some expectations but soon it became clear that it fell short where a redistribution of power and resources is concerned.

From discontent to social convulsions

Things became worse under the disastrous Banzer government (1997–2002). Corruption had never been absent in the country but it became rampant and the Banzer clan and its cronies were shamelessly involved.[17] Banzer relied on a 'megacoalition' of which the partners were endlessly involved in squabbles over the spoils. Although Banzer had criticized Sánchez de Lozada's neoliberal policies and his sell-out of the national patrimony, economic and social policies did not change but rather deteriorated (Assies and Salman 2003). After a brief 'honeymoon' with the coca-growers, relations imploded to 'ground zero' due to the militarization of eradication policies on behest of the American Embassy, while the simulated empathy with the plight of indigenous peoples of the Sánchez de Lozada government gave way to a manifest empathy with the large landholders of the *Oriente* and little concern for the highland peasantry (Assies 2002).

Meanwhile, the economy dipped in the wake of the Asian, Brazilian, and Argentine crises and unemployment reached double-digit levels. The year 2000 started with the protests against the opaque privatization of the water supply system in the Cochabamba region and the consequent price-hike. The Water War ended with the ousting of Aguas del Tunari, a company set up by the Bechtel concern and some partners, and a hurried modification of legislation on water rights that had been adopted some months earlier. Locally this was regarded as a first victory after fifteen years of defeats in the face of neoliberalism (Assies 2003*b*). At the same

[17] Curiously, after recounting the 'politicization' of the Customs, which became a domain of Banzer cronies (cf. Sivak 2001), and of the National Service for the Administration of Personnel in the 'last 18 months', a starry-eyed or simply cynical World Bank report (2000: 14) states that the 'current Government is strongly committed to succeeding with state reform where others have failed'.

Figure 11.1 Hugo Banzer and the remaining party leaders of his 'mega-coalition', Jaime Paz Zamora (MIR) and Johnny Fernández (UCS), celebrating Banzer's seventy-fourth birthday and claiming their shares of the cake or being disappointed with their small spoons to share the stew.

time peasant protests erupted in the highlands, starting a cycle of protests with increasingly ethnic overtones to demand land, tractors, credit, and a series of other things. These protests were led by Felipe Quispe, *el Mallku*,[18] who had become General Secretary of the CSUTCB in 1998. In November 2000 Quispe created his own 'political instrument', the Movimiento Indigenista Pachacuti (MIP), to participate in the 2002 presidential elections.[19] Violence also was on the rise in the Chapare region, where the Banzer government stubbornly carried out the 'war on drugs' to comply with the fundamentalism of the US Embassy. Although talk about the 'sacred leaf' is not absent from the coca-growers' discourse, it is far less ethnicized than Quispe's strident Indianism. Coca-growers' leader Evo Morales would be another presidential candidate in the 2002 elections, borrowing the Movimiento al Socialismo (MAS) label. To everyone's surprise, Morales

[18] 'The Condor', an Andean honorific title. Biographic profiles of Felipe Quispe and Evo Morales can be found in Albó (2003).

[19] If we look at Bolivia's electoral geography the coincidence between the old heartland of Katarism, the CONDEPA outreach, and later support for Felipe Quispe's MIP is striking. Romero Ballivián (2003: 311) suggests that this continuity is rooted in the protest against the behaviour of governing parties, against inconclusive modernization and frustration with the lack of opportunities among a relatively well-educated population. Since the late 1980s the vote for these parties has been positively correlated with school attendance and ethnic identification, particularly Aymara identification in the case of Katarism and the MIP. While Palenque played out the *cholo-q'ara* dichotomy, with a discourse of strident Aymara nationalism, for example stating that once he will be president he will create a Ministry for White Affairs, Quispe attracted support from the rural Aymara population of La Paz as well as the urban Aymara of La Paz and El Alto, where he won 17 per cent of the vote in 2002.

ended second in these elections with nearly 21 per cent of the vote, which made him a potential presidential candidate, while Quispe garnered about 6 per cent of the vote, more than any Katarist or Indianist party had ever achieved. Congress was flooded with indigenous Deputies and Senators, turning what had been the perk of 'professional' politicians donning suits and ties into a rather colourful tower of Babel. As it turned out, Sánchez de Lozada, who finished first in the elections, only slightly ahead of Morales, managed to broker a pact among the established parties, which brought him to the presidency for the second time. It would not be for long. In February 2003, the introduction of a new income tax, as advised by the multilateral agencies, caused a revolt during which about thirty people were killed and in October Sánchez de Lozada fled the country in the midst of a wave of protests against the intended sale of gas to the USA, by way of Chile; an intention that compounded the sell-out of national resources with anti-US and anti-Chile sentiments. By then the attempts to repress these protests had cost over sixty lives.

It is not the place here to discuss these protests and the political turmoil in Bolivia at length, which we have done elsewhere (Assies and Salman 2003; Assies 2004), but rather to point out that indigenous people played a prominent role in this process. I do not share Patzi Paco's (2003) rather exalted view that the conflicts were basically about colonialism and racial oppression or, as some press comments suggested, that they essentially were about Aymara nationalism. They rather were popular revolts against an economic model and a type of democracy that exclude a rather significant part of the population, the indigenous among them (Calla Ortega 2003b).[20] On the other hand, the dynamics of ethnic polarization that can be observed in Bolivia seem to corroborate Chua's (2004) thesis that exporting 'raw' free market democracy to ethnically divided societies can breed ethnic hatred. She argues that while free-marketeering disempowers the poor and economically empowers an ethnically visible

[20] The most recent Human Development Report on Bolivia (PNUD 2004) dedicates a full chapter to the much needed interculturalism for Bolivia. The Report distinguishes six codes of self-understanding of identity: (1) a code of polarized opposition, which clearly corresponds to the Palenque and Quispe type of anti-*q'ara* discourse; (2) a code of multiple defence, which shows similarities with the polarization code, but is mainly found among entrepreneurs, executives of transnational enterprises, and the like; (3) flexible adaptation is a strategy more typical of lowland indigenous people who adapt to circumstances and interlocutors; (4) a missionary code is found among religious groups; (5) a regionalist code reflects Centre–periphery frictions; and (6) *asistencialismo* corporatism can be wielded against transnational enterprises to force them to become 'socially sustainable'. Of course none of these codes is the patrimony of a specific segment of society or exists in a chemically pure form. It is an interesting and suggestive classification, however.

minority, democracy politically empowers the impoverished majority and that may unleash ethnic demagoguery, or worse.[21]

4. By way of conclusion

Let us return to the issues that orient the contributions to this volume. In this chapter I have sought to show that welfare state thinking has not been absent from Latin America and not even from Bolivia although, at best, it yielded a stunted and miserly version of a welfare state, wrecked by patronage, clientelism, and corporatism. In 1985 the national revolutionary development model was replaced by neoliberal structural adjustment policies that were implemented under a system of governance known as pacted democracy, inherently suffering from a representation deficit. In a country with a majority indigenous population, adjustment policies brought hardship for these majorities and exacerbated polarization between a rich minority and the rest. At the same time such policies corroded much of the trade union structures that earlier had been a vehicle of popular protest. The rise of neo-populist parties, particularly CONDEPA, was an indication of the discontent with the economic model and the limits of the prevailing mode of governance. Although this prompted an embrace of multiculturalism among the established parties, it did not bring about a change in overall economic policies. This multiculturalism was limited and superficial anyway and hardly involved a redistribution of resources in favour of indigenous peoples. Instead, in a context of increasingly blatant corruption in government circles, the economic model was upheld through increasingly violent repression of popular protests, culminating in the October 2003 events. Although ethnic factors and Aymara nationalist rhetoric became ever more prominent these protests were essentially popular revolts against an economic model and a mode of governance. The pattern of protest is typically one of fusion and fission from which no enduring coalitions have (yet?) emerged.

In her contribution to this volume Donna Lee Van Cott sketches five basic scenarios for the future of ethnopolitics and multiculturalism politics in Latin America. What can we say about future scenarios in Bolivia? First of all, I should point out that various pending issues have not been

---

[21] In a somewhat similar way Schierup (1997: 121) has argued that the contemporary *American Dilemma* 'is the incompatibility of elitist appeals for social cohesion and universalist allegiances with all of the powerful political and economic interests that both require and create growing segments of the population as ethnicized, enclavized and bereft of the rights of citizenship.'

discussed in this chapter and that the 'Bolivian condition' is extremely complex and regionally differentiated. The October 2003 'Gas War' and earlier conflicts have clearly called the neoliberal model into question and will certainly lead to modifications, like an enhanced role of the state and a turn to more humane policies. If not, a scenario of 'protracted conflict' and popular protest with ethnic overtones, as unfolded during the Banzer and second Sánchez de Lozada governments, is likely.

The October events, however, also opened the way for other scenarios. A reform of the Bolivian Constitution is on the books and this reform will have to deal with the extremely tricky and explosive issue of regional autonomy demands. In the foregoing we have touched upon the issue of Aymara nationalism but for reasons of space I have not discussed the elite-driven demands for regional autonomy of the Santa Cruz and Tarija departments, where most of the economic growth occurs and where the most important gas reserves are located. Santa Cruz regionalism, in particular, has in recent years become propped up by a virulently right-wing ethnicized ideology that emphasizes the mestizo character of its population and contrasts it with the highland population, accused of preying upon lowlands. A Constituent Assembly will certainly have to deal with such autonomy claims but given the configuration of power relations in much of the lowlands, with large landholders and cattle raisers playing a key role, greater autonomy for these regions may well result in an exacerbation of land conflicts and increased oppression of local indigenous peoples. Such autonomy claims, therefore, might result in a 'multinational state' but not a democratic utopia as envisioned by Van Cott.

Finally, the Bolivian party system is in tatters. For the time being, the MAS has emerged as the most important party and seeks to project itself as a democratic left-wing alternative. If something like that consolidates we might expect a scenario somewhere between, or combining, populist multiculturalism and radical ethno-nationalist development of multicul-turalist policies. The situation is extremely fluid, however, and I would not risk predicting the course of events.

Part III

Theoretical reflections

12

Multiculturalism and the welfare state: Theoretical reflections

David Miller

One way to describe the problem that this book is addressing is as a tension between two parts of the liberal ideal of equality. On the one hand, modern liberals are committed to the idea of equal citizenship, understood to include social and economic rights that are to be enjoyed equally by every member of the relevant political community. The institutions of the welfare state—public education, health care, income support, unemployment insurance, old age pensions, and so forth—are essential to guarantee those rights. On the other hand, under conditions of cultural diversity, liberals are also committed to equal treatment of citizens *qua* members of cultural groups. As many have argued, this may require multicultural policies that provide protection and support to cultural minorities, whether by granting them exemptions from generally prevailing laws, supplying them with additional resources, or granting them symbolic recognition in the public realm. A tension between these two commitments will arise if it turns out that the pursuit of multiculturalism in some way undermines equal citizenship, and in particular the social and economic rights that the welfare state is meant to guarantee. If this were to happen, liberals would be forced to reflect more deeply on what equality means to them, and to make some hard choices: to abandon multiculturalism for the sake of the welfare state, or vice versa.

But does the tension identified in the last paragraph really exist, or can multiculturalism and the welfare state be happy bedfellows? The essays

I should like to thank Keith Banting, Geoff Evans, and Will Kymlicka for their very helpful comments on an earlier draft of this chapter, and Sarah Butt for invaluable research assistance.

that make up this book were commissioned in response to a group of critics who claim to have identified such a tension (and who resolve it by giving priority to the welfare state and arguing against multiculturalism). In general the essays conclude that the critics' claims were exaggerated, and that a hard look at the evidence reveals no systematic tendency for states that pursue multicultural policies to retrench on welfare policies and expenditures. Before concluding that the problem is an illusory one, however, we need to look more closely at what the critics were claiming, and also draw some sharper distinctions, between different forms of multiculturalism, and between different types of welfare policies. Perhaps some part of the critics' case may survive empirical investigation, albeit not in the sweeping form in which it has sometimes been presented.

It is helpful here to begin by setting the critics of multiculturalism in political context. The authors cited by Banting and Kymlicka in their introductory chapter—Brian Barry, Todd Gitlin, Richard Rorty, Alan Wolfe, and Jyette Klausen—despite their differences can all be described as old-style social democrats, with a story to tell about the politics of the welfare state that takes roughly the following form. Within the Western democracies in the period following the Second World War, a majority consensus emerged in favour of the state's pursuit of economic and social equality, a consensus supported both by unionized workers and by leftist intellectuals. The capitalist economy was to be tamed by enhanced workers' rights, redistributive taxation, and the provision of essential services on a non-market basis, creating a form of social citizenship as theorized by T. H. Marshall and others. The consensus enabled the election of left-of-centre governments with the means at their disposal to carry out this taming, supported if necessary by inclusive political movements at grassroots level. Ethnic and racial minorities, especially blacks in America, could be expected to join the consensus and to benefit from it through the enforcement of equal rights in education and employment and through general economic redistribution.

This majority consensus was first disrupted by the rise of the New Left in the 1960s, whose radical demands not only placed new issues on the political agenda, but also divided the left coalition, setting workers against intellectuals, women against men, blacks against whites, and so forth. The authors in question see multiculturalism as an outgrowth of the identity politics first promoted by these 1960s radicals. Because the movement of the left has been fragmented, there is no longer any consistent pressure on parties and governments to make further moves in the direction of greater equality. Although social democratic parties have not disappeared, to achieve electoral success they have been forced to move to the centre, at best protecting the existing welfare state institutions and other instruments of equality, at worst succumbing to global economic forces and allowing those institutions to erode slowly over time. So for these supporters of older-style social democracy, the political outlook is somewhat bleak, and although the rise of multiculturalism is not necessarily seen as the main culprit, it is certainly regarded as contributing to the demise of a politics of equal citizenship. The reasons given explicitly or implicitly for this are those identified by Banting and Kymlicka: multiculturalism focuses political debate on cultural questions, often of a symbolic nature, and allows redistributive issues to slip off the agenda; it sets one group against another, and makes it difficult to form a broad-based coalition in favour of equality; and at best it delivers symbolic benefits to minority groups, whereas their real interests are in policies that would deliver them jobs, housing, health care, and other tangible benefits as part of a general redistribution in favour of the worse off.

A further aspect of the critics' thinking that deserves our attention is the importance they attach to the nation-state as the main instrument for achieving social democratic ideals. There are some differences about the emphasis to be placed on either side of that hyphenated term. Richard Rorty is most explicit about the need for what he calls 'national pride' as a motivating force for progressive policies. He argues that American reformers have always assumed that America at its best represented a special achievement, and that their task was to push reality closer to this national ideal (Rorty 1998: esp. First Lecture). Todd Gitlin uses the language of 'commonality' and 'common dreams' alongside that of citizenship, and Alan Wolfe and Jyette Klausen give the idea of 'the great community' a central place in the thinking of Tawney and Marshall, the two thinkers they believe best express the theoretical basis of social democracy (Gitlin 1995; Wolfe and Klausen 1997). Brian Barry is more cautious in his appeal to national identity (Barry 2001: ch. 3). He is critical of what he calls 'romantic nationalism' but recognizes at the same time that a purely legal notion of citizenship does not create a strong enough bond to sustain a politics of equality. He settles instead for 'civic nationality' as the common identity that citizens need to acquire, an identity that has cultural elements, but is flexible enough to allow its content to be renegotiated as new cultural groups join the state. For all these thinkers, however, the danger posed by multiculturalism is that it may promote rigid and exclusive sectional identities that are incompatible with the (thicker or thinner) overarching identity that citizens of a nation-state must share if it is to function successfully. Multiculturalism is criticized not only for its alleged direct effects on policy, but also for the way it shapes political identities, and therefore the relationships that will exist between citizens who belong to different cultural groups.

These claims about multiculturalism are somewhat intangible, and badly in need of empirical investigation of the kind undertaken in this book. The question we need to ask is whether the empirical testing that is carried out here really gets to the heart of the critics' case. Why might it not? Perhaps the variables that can be measured (for instance whether a state scores high or low on an index of multicultural policies) are not the variables that matter from the critics' point of view. Perhaps the causal effects of multiculturalism are longer term, and cannot be detected by studies that run over a couple of decades. Perhaps the causal effects are real, but are being blotted out by countervailing factors in the societies under study. Most of the authors who have contributed to this volume feel the intuitive force of the critics' argument, even while they present evidence that multiculturalism in practice appears not to have damaging effects on the welfare state. So besides looking at the evidence we need also to think about the various mechanisms that have been canvassed to explain why multiculturalism and the welfare state might be unhappy bedfellows, and ask whether they have really operated in the way that the critics suggest.

Multiculturalism is a vague term, and it may be useful to begin by trying to clarify it. Sometimes it is used in a purely descriptive sense, to refer to the fact of cultural diversity—to the coexistence within a political society of many distinct religious, ethnic, or racial groups whose members see their cultural differences as important parts of their identity. Although this usage is now common, it can lead to confusion and it might have been better to have used 'cultural diversity' or 'cultural difference' to refer to this phenomenon.[1] Then multiculturalism can be used in a normative sense, to refer to an ideology that attaches positive value to cultural diversity, calls for the equal recognition of different cultural groups, and calls upon the state to support such groups in various ways. This ideology

---

[1] This is not to say that multiculturalism in the descriptive sense is unimportant if we are looking for causal factors that may explain whether states do or do not adopt egalitarian social policies. These is some evidence that ethnic diversity in particular has a negative impact on such policies: see the discussion by Banting and Kymlicka in Chapter 1 above, and my own discussion in Miller (2004). Here, however, I shall focus on multiculturalism in the second and third senses distinguished in this paragraph—multiculturalism as ideology and multiculturalism as policy.

can take different forms—we can distinguish weaker or stronger versions of multiculturalism depending on how much significance is attached to group identity vis-à-vis national identity, for instance, or how radical the demands for cultural support become. Finally, multiculturalism can be used to refer to a set of policies that are designed to help cultural minorities, materially or symbolically, for example the policies identified by Banting et al. in Chapter 2 as 'multiculturalism policies'. It is important for two reasons to distinguish multiculturalism as ideology from multiculturalism as public policy. First, although the two phenomena are causally related to some extent, the relationship may not be a tight one: in particular, as some of the evidence from Holland and Germany presented in Chapters 6 and 7 suggests, a society may retreat ideologically from multiculturalism without abandoning multicultural policies.[2] Second, if we return to the critics discussed above, their primary target is multiculturalism as ideology. In their view a society in which people come to think of themselves primarily as belonging to separate identity groups, and who view their relationship to the state through that prism, is not a society that can sustain egalitarian politics. I don't mean that they have nothing to say about multicultural policies: Barry in particular attacks many of these policies as unjustifiable from the standpoint of liberal equality, and also as failing to provide cultural minorities with the resources that they really need.[3] But the critics are not inherently opposed to affirmative action, or bilingual education, or exemptions from dress codes. What mainly concerns them is the growth of a political culture in which these become the central issues of the day, displacing economic issues for instance, and in which they are debated from the perspective of each separate group, rather than from the perspective of an inclusive citizenship.

We also need to look more carefully at what is encompassed by the idea of the welfare state. It has long been recognized that, even confining our attention to the advanced liberal democracies, we find a range of different

---

[2] Another case that illustrates this point is Australia, one of only two countries with a 'Strong' rating for immigrant multiculturalism according to the analysis in Chapter 2. The high point of Australian multiculturalism as ideology was reached in the early 1980s, and the picture since then has been one of steady retreat from the idea among politicians and others engaged in public debate. Policies dating from that period such as programmes aimed at supporting newly arrived immigrants have not been abandoned, though in some cases their funding has been sharply cut. Such policies can continue partly through institutional inertia and the political pressure exerted by client groups, and partly because they serve integrationist as well as multicultural aims. The rise and fall of Australian multiculturalism is traced in Galligan and Roberts (2004: ch. 4).

[3] For a variety of critical responses to Barry's attack, see Held and Kelly (2002).

welfare regimes—different both in the kind of institutions they employ and in the distributive outcomes that result.[4] For the critics of multi-culturalism we are considering, the welfare state is important primarily as a redistributive mechanism that can help to offset the inequalities of life chances that a capitalist economy creates, and raise the position of the worst-off members of society to a level where they are able to function as equal citizens. Welfare states, however, serve other purposes besides redistribution in this sense. They can also be seen as social insurance mechanisms that protect citizens against hazards such as illness or unexpected loss of earnings.[5] Here they redistribute resources horizontally between the healthy and the sick, say, rather than vertically between the rich and the poor. Of course welfare state institutions can be redistributive in both senses at once: a national health service funded by progressive taxation not only transfers resources from the healthy to the sick, but also redistributes vertically to some extent.[6] The poor are made better off than they would be if they had to buy medical insurance on the market. For the question we are considering, however, it matters to what extent the welfare state functions as a redistributive mechanism in the vertical sense. For it is this kind of redistribution that appears to require social solidarity to support it. Self-interest alone will lead people to support welfare policies that insure them against unpredictable hazards of various kinds. Given sufficient uncertainty about the future, it makes sense to authorize the state to protect you against the risks of accident or illness and to pay taxes to cover those risks. But the same does not apply to benefits that predictably go to worse-off groups, such as housing subsidies, income supplements or long-term unemployment benefits. For better-off people—skilled workers and the middle class as well as the rich—to support these policies, they must see this as a matter of social justice. And, so it is claimed, this requires in turn that they should identify with the beneficiaries of the redistribution—an identification fostered by a sense of common national identity, and (allegedly) undermined by multiculturalism.

---

[4] The best-known analysis of this kind is probably Esping-Andersen (1990).

[5] Indeed the insurance aspect may be quite explicit, as it is, for instance, in the German welfare system, where health care, pensions, and unemployment benefits are funded by insurance linked to employment.

[6] The extent of this vertical redistribution is a matter of dispute among students of the welfare state. For a sceptical view, see Le Grand (1982), and also Goodin and Le Grand (1987). Later critical responses to Le Grand are helpfully synthesized in Powell (1995). See also Evandrou et al. (1993), which qualifies Le Grand's original study in certain respects. I have discussed the issue at greater length in Miller (2003).

So if we want to investigate the impact of multiculturalism on the welfare state, it is not enough just to look at, for example, overall levels of expenditure on health services, education, or social services. We also need to look in a more discriminating way at those elements of the welfare state that are genuinely redistributive, and at how far public attitudes are supportive of such redistribution. For if what the critics allege is true, we might expect something like the following to occur: the welfare state will not shrivel away overnight, but over time it will move closer to the insurance model, in the sense that it will serve mainly to protect people against risks and provide them with services that are more efficiently supplied by public means, but different groups will benefit from it roughly in proportion to the amount that they contribute. It will, therefore, no longer serve as a vehicle for social equality, except insofar as it provides a safety net that prevents people from becoming utterly destitute.

With this in mind, we can now look at the evidence about how the welfare state is faring in countries that have embraced multiculturalism to varying degrees. Let me begin with the data presented by Banting et al. in Chapter 2, which looks at overall social spending at as proportion of GDP, the redistributive impact of taxes and transfers on poverty and inequality, the extent of child poverty, and the final extent of income inequality once taxes and transfers are taken into account. Taking all the countries surveyed together first, and ignoring how they score on the various multiculturalism scales, what we find is broadly consistent with the somewhat pessimistic story about the welfare state sketched above. Overall social spending as a proportion of GDP has risen significantly, by 16.8 per cent on average, but the redistributive impact of taxes and transfers has barely risen at all, not enough to compensate for rising income inequality, caused presumably by changing conditions in the economic market. As a result child poverty (the percentage of children living in homes with less than 50 per cent of median income) has increased in all but three of the sixteen countries studied and post-tax income inequality has also increased in all but three, by 9 per cent on average (see Table 2.1 in that chapter for these figures). If we were to interpret these results as reflecting what most citizens in these societies want from their governments—admittedly a dangerous assumption, but I shall be looking at public attitudes in a moment—we would say that as liberal societies become more affluent, their members are happy to see more of the wealth they create channelled into public services of various kinds (health services particularly), but become increasingly less concerned about economic inequality. So although the welfare state in a broad sense does not wither away, there is no pressure to increase its redistributive impact to deal with rising levels of pre-tax income inequality. For social democrats who look to the welfare state as the primary instrument of egalitarian redistribution, this is bad news.

So the critics appear to be right to be concerned about the future of egalitarian politics, but are they right to point the finger of blame at multiculturalism? According to the figures presented in Chapter 2, there is certainly no general relationship between a country's decision to adopt strong multicultural policies and its ability to maintain a modest level of redistribution through taxes and transfers. Admittedly this claim is bolstered, as far as immigrant multiculturalism is concerned, by the performance of two countries, Australia and Canada, which started out with unusually low levels of social expenditure, and if these are taken out of the picture the trends point in the other direction. Nevertheless, it is reasonable to conclude here that the adoption of multicultural policies, taken by itself, cannot be held responsible for the diminishingly egalitarian outcome of the welfare state.

But what of the underlying ideology of multiculturalism and *its* impact on public attitudes towards welfare and equality? This is going to be hard to trace, but let's begin by looking at attitudes to welfare and equality first. Is there any significant weakening in the public's commitment to the values that the welfare state is meant to embody? The comparative evidence presented by Markus Crepaz in Chapter 3 uses only one item from the *World Values Survey*, which asks respondents to place themselves on a scale between 'people should take more responsibility to provide for themselves' and 'the government should take more responsibility to ensure that everybody is provided for'. Answers to this question reveal some surprisingly large shifts of opinion in different directions over a ten-year period in individual countries (no doubt reflecting local changes in the prevailing political climate), but the question itself does not distinguish between the many different ways in which governments might provide for people (jobs? health services? income supplements?), and so is not very helpful as a way of tracking attitudes towards redistribution. In the particular case of Britain, Geoffrey Evans cites figures recorded annually in the *British Social Attitudes* survey, which reveals a small but steady lessening of support for the proposition that 'government should spend more money on welfare benefits for the poor, even if it leads to higher taxes', a proposition that captures fairly accurately the central idea of what I have been calling the social democratic strategy of equality. This can be supplemented by some results from Peter Taylor-Gooby's article 'Commitment to the Welfare State' which uses data from the *International Social Survey Programme* comparing Western Germany, Britain, Italy, and Sweden (Taylor-Gooby 1998).[7] What this shows is that the percentages of people agreeing that government should definitely be responsible for providing 'health care for the sick' and 'a decent standard of living for the old' have remained fairly constant, but that there is weakening support for governmental responsibility for 'a decent standard of living for the unemployed', 'providing a job for everyone who wants one' and 'reducing income differences between the rich and the poor'. This goes some way to confirming my hypothesis that citizens are happy to continue supporting the insurance aspects of the welfare state—anyone may need health care, or find themselves in financial difficulties late in life—but have become less keen on policies that overtly redistribute resources in the direction of the worse off.

Attitudes to the welfare state, then, appear to be slowly shifting away from egalitarianism. What about public beliefs in, or attitudes towards, multiculturalism? Here the picture is also a complex one. First of all, there is clear evidence of increasing tolerance of racial, ethnic, and religious diversity, and along with this increasing acceptance that equality of opportunity must also mean equal treatment for members of minority groups. In Chapter 5, Geoffrey Evans gives data for Britain, which show growing acceptance of having people with minority backgrounds as your boss at work or as marrying into your family, and firm support for equal opportunities policies. The same questions were asked in ten European countries in the European Social Survey in 2003, producing results very much in line with those obtained for Britain,[8] so although we do not have comparable evidence over time for other European countries, it is reasonable to assume that tolerance levels will have risen in much the same way.

At the same time immigrants are expected to make adjustments to fit in with the cultural norms of their host country. Opinion on this is not so easy to pin down, because the question that is used to try to capture it is not in my view very revealing. Respondents are asked to choose between the view that immigrant groups should maintain their own customs and

[7] The article records responses over the time period 1985–96, but for Italy and Sweden the data are incomplete.

[8] As one might expect, there was a shallow North–South gradient, with Sweden emerging as the most tolerant of the societies sampled, and Greece as the least tolerant. See Jowell and the Central Co-ordinating Team (2003).

traditions and the view that they should 'take over the customs of the country' or 'adapt and blend into the larger society' (see Chapter 3 for these questions). But any thoughtful person would surely reject both of these positions, since a great deal depends on which 'customs and traditions' are at stake. If these involve an ethnic cuisine or a colourful festival like the Chinese New Year, most people would be more than happy for immigrant minorities to preserve their own customs. If on the other hand the relevant custom is female circumcision or participation in Triad gangs, then virtually everyone will think that immigrants must adapt to liberal norms that exclude these practices. So answers to this question do not tell us very much.

What is reasonably clear, however, is that immigrant minorities are expected to become loyal citizens of the country that receives them, and to play by the prevailing rules of the game. This may include in particular learning the national language. A relevant piece of evidence is that, when asked to choose between 'Immigrants should get the same level of welfare support as existing British citizens', 'Immigrants should get less welfare support than British citizens' and 'Immigrants should only get the same level of welfare support as British citizens if they demonstrate commitment to the country (e.g. learning language and history)', 18 per cent and 19 per cent respectively chose the first two options, but an overwhelming 58 per cent preferred the third (Duffy 2004a). We can conclude, therefore, that most citizens want neither straightforward assimilation, where immigrant minorities effectively disappear as they blend into the existing culture, nor 'parallel societies', where cultural groups coexist side-by-side without adapting to one another's norms and values, but integration, where this involves acquiring common citizenship and the national identity that goes along with it, as well as maintaining certain group-specific cultural traits.

If this is correct, where does this leave support for multicultural *policies*? What we should expect to find is support for such policies insofar as they serve the cause of integration, and opposition to them insofar as they are regarded as divisive, or as giving unfair advantages to minority groups. And this is precisely what the evidence we have appears to suggest. If we look at the policies that are presented in Chapter 3 as demonstrating popular support for multiculturalism, they are policies such as 'promote equality of opportunity in all areas of social life', 'encourage the creation of organizations that bring people from different races, religions and cultures together', and 'promote the teaching of mutual acceptance and respect in schools'. These would not, however, count as multicultural policies by the standard laid down by Banting et al. in Chapter 2 which defines them as policies 'that go beyond the traditional individual rights of citizenship to provide some additional form of public recognition or support or accommodation of ethnic groups, identities and practices'. I do not know of data that record public attitudes on each of the eight types of immigrant multicultural policies listed in that chapter, but two specific pieces of evidence are worth noting. First, there is not much support for the proposition that 'ethnic minorities should be given government assistance to preserve their customs and traditions', which seems to capture fairly precisely the central thrust of Chapter 2's understanding of multiculturalism, especially in those countries generally regarded as having taken the lead in developing multicultural policies. Twenty per cent or less of those surveyed in Australia, Canada, Great Britain, Netherlands, New Zealand, Norway, Sweden, and the USA endorsed this proposition (ISSP 1998).[9] (Rather surprisingly, the figure is much higher for other countries included in the ISSP survey, especially countries in Eastern Europe, but one explanation for this may be that respondents in these countries took the question to be referring primarily to long-established national minorities; German respondents, in particular, were asked about 'national minorities' rather than 'ethnic minorities'.) Second, the same is true of support for affirmative action, understood as policies that go beyond equal opportunity and give preferential treatment to ethnic minorities in hiring decisions and/or university applications. Most of the evidence here comes from the USA, where despite the relatively high proportion of the population that might be expected to benefit from such policies, opposition among the general public remains strong.[10] General questions about affirmative action for racial minorities tend to produce roughly equal percentages in favour and against.[11] But more specific questions that highlight preferential treatment reveal a different picture. When asked 'In order to give minorities more opportunity, do you believe race or ethnicity should be a factor when deciding who is hired, promoted, or admitted to college, or that hiring, promotions, and college admissions

---

[9] The question was repeated in 2003, but the cross-national data are not yet available. British data reported above in Chapter 5, Table 5.3 reveal very little change over this period.

[10] To my knowledge, no comparative European research has been conducted on this issue, although a French survey which asked about the policy of reserving a certain number of jobs for immigrants in different branches of work found 58 per cent in favour and 36 per cent against. This is perhaps a less sharp question than the one I have cited from the USA, which highlights the choice between preferential treatment and merit. See BVA Actualité (2005).

[11] See e.g. successive Gallup polls on the question 'Do you generally favor or oppose affirmative action programs for racial minorities?' summarized in Jones (2005).

should be based strictly on merit and qualifications other than race or ethnicity?', only 5 per cent of respondents said race and ethnicity should be a factor, while 92 per cent said merit alone should be taken into account. Even among blacks the corresponding figures were 12 per cent and 88 per cent.[12]

Of course, the fact that most citizens in liberal democracies are somewhat sceptical of multiculturalism both as ideology and as policy, while at the same time showing dwindling enthusiasm for the more overtly redistributive elements of the welfare state, does not show that the first set of attitudes is the cause of the second. To bridge the gap, we have to insert a piece of psychological speculation, albeit one that is plausible in itself, and supported by considerable evidence at small-group level. The speculation is that people are more willing to redistribute in favour of others when they see those others as like themselves in certain respects, and also when they regard them as 'playing fair'—as showing willingness to reciprocate when it is their turn to make a contribution. If we apply this to the case of ethnic minority immigrants, then we can predict that host country citizens will be reluctant to include them within the scope of welfare state policies if they perceive (a) that the immigrants are making no effort to adapt to the public culture of the country they have moved to (see the responses quoted earlier in the case of immigrants to Britain) and/or (b) if they perceive that immigrants are taking advantage of welfare benefits such as unemployment benefit without having contributed, or attempted to contribute, by working and paying taxes.[13] Such perceptions may very well not be accurate. Even if it turns out, for example, that immigrant groups are disproportionately represented among those drawing income support and other benefits, the explanation may have mainly to do with labour market policies that make it difficult for immigrants to find secure jobs. The problem, in other words, may have nothing directly to do with culture itself. Nonetheless once a perception is established that welfare services are being used unfairly by those who come from particular groups, defined in ethnic or religious terms, the predictable result is an

---

[12] Washington Post/Harvard Racial Attitudes Survey, quoted in Taylor (2002).

[13] For evidence of such a perception, we may refer to a recent MORI poll in Britain, in which asylum seekers and recent immigrants were the two groups most likely to be picked out as getting 'unfair priority over you when it comes to public services and state benefits'. See Duffy (2004b). The more general theme emerges in an informal study of popular attitudes by the Labour MP John Denham. He found that his constituents were strongly wedded to a 'fairness code' that is 'concerned with what rights you have earned, not just what your needs are today. The assessment of someone's needs should take into account the effort and contribution he or she has made in the past and will make in the future. Public services should be for people who are entitled to them, need them, and use them responsibly' (Denham 2004).

overall decline in support for redistributive welfare policies with universal scope.[14]

To guard against this danger, it is important that multicultural policies should not have the effect of widening the perceived gap between immigrant groups and the host community, or of conveying the impression that the former are under no obligation to adapt to the norms and practices of the society that has taken them in. They should visibly be combined with national citizenship policies whose aim is to integrate immigrant groups socially, foster their loyalty to the state, and encourage them to become involved in democratic politics. As the authors of Chapter 2 point out, this is precisely what has happened in those countries that score high on the index of multiculturalism, such as Canada, and more recently has begun to happen in countries such as the Netherlands and Britain, which previously had pursued a somewhat informal, low-key approach to nation building among immigrant groups. In these countries, citizenship education is now taken more seriously, and access to citizenship in the formal sense made subject to requirements such as demonstrating competence in the national language and familiarity with the culture of the host country.[15] Multicultural policies have not necessarily been abandoned (although as Chapter 5 reveals there has been some retrenchment in the Dutch case), but there has been an ideological 'retreat from multiculturalism' insofar as multiculturalism was thought to entail one-sided support for sectional group identities at the expense of an inclusive national identity. The reluctance of many politicians in these countries today to use the language of multiculturalism testifies to this perception.

---

[14] In the wake of the London bombings in July 2005, the tabloid press in Britain has run a series of 'benefit bombers' stories on its front pages, highlighting the use of welfare state services by Islamic terrorists and their supporters. For example:

For 19 years he lived off the fat of a land whose democracy and freedoms he despised. Now, having sown the seeds of carnage in the UK, where he enjoyed sanctuary from regimes much less tolerant of his Islamo-fascism, Sheik Omar Bakri Mohammed has taken his hurried leave even though, unfortunately, it is likely to be only temporary.

Due to an ankle injury in childhood the father of seven has never had to work here, but instead was able to claim, at one time or another, unemployment and child benefit, disability living allowance and housing benefit.

In the past two decades his handouts from the state have been somewhere in the region of £250,000–£300,000. The family live in a large council house in north London and earlier this year took delivery of a new £31,000 people carrier, paid for under the Motability scheme. (*Daily Mail* 2005)

[15] In Britain, citizenship ceremonies for immigrants were introduced for the first time in 2004, but initially the only requirement was to show competence in the English language; from 1 November 2005, however, would-be citizens have also been required to take a citizenship test in which they must demonstrate familiarity with the main political institutions of the UK, and certain other aspects of the British way of life.

In this context, it is worth underlining the sharp difference, so far as potential impact on the welfare state is concerned, between immigrants and national minorities, to use the conceptual framework laid out in Chapter 2 (I shall not discuss indigenous peoples here). As Nicola McEwen clearly demonstrates in her discussion of Canada, Belgium, and the UK, there is no evidence to suggest that minority nationalism in these countries has had an adverse effect on support for the welfare state, and some evidence that it may have had a positive effect. There are two points that need to be made here. First, where national minorities have been granted devolved forms of government—as in the three cases discussed by McEwen—subnational governments will have some responsibility for welfare policies within their own territories, and these will be supported by the inclusive political identities (as Québécois, Scots, etc.) that exist at this level. Second, insofar as social justice at the national level requires redistribution between the national majority and the minority nations (to compensate for lower levels of economic performance, for example), this will be accepted so long as members of national minorities have what I have elsewhere called 'nested' national identities, which allow them to identify both with the smaller unit (e.g. Quebec or Scotland) and with the larger (Canada or Britain) (see Miller 2000: ch. 8). Because the Scots, say, are seen as sharing a common cultural and historical background with the rest of the UK, and in that sense as plainly British, the perceptions of cultural difference that can make people reluctant to extend support to immigrant groups do not arise here.[16]

In cases where minority nationalism puts common identities under pressure, however, a different dynamic may emerge. The extreme cases are states that contain rival, rather than nested, nationalities—national groups who make conflicting claims to territorial sovereignty without sharing an overarching national identity, such as Jews and Palestinians in Israel, or Serbs, Croats, and Muslims in Bosnia. In these cases welfare state expenditures may be weighted significantly in favour of the majority community—in Israel, for example, the budget per head awarded to Arab local municipalities is significantly smaller than that awarded to Jewish local municipalities, and for this and other reasons far more Israeli Arab families than Israeli Jewish families are living below the poverty line (see Mossawa Center 2004).[17] In the case of a country such as Belgium

---

[16] Members of the immigrant groups may of course identify more strongly with their adopted nation than do those belonging to national minorities. The key question, however, is whether people belonging to the host nation identify with *them*.

[17] I am grateful to Avner de-Shalit for discussion of the Israeli case.

where national identities are still predominantly nested, the problems are far less severe, but as McEwen's chapter shows the solidaristic welfare policies that involve net transfers from Flanders to Wallonia have come under fire from Flemish politicians who would prefer to see social services and social security benefits provided on a regional basis (and by implication without involving redistribution between the two communities).

Inclusive national identities, then, are a resource that can be used to support egalitarian welfare policies; whether minority nationalism is a help or a hindrance depends on whether it reinforces or subverts these more inclusive loyalties. Having now examined the evidence, let me return finally to the thinkers I have been calling the critics of multiculturalism. How far does their critique hold water? I believe that they got three things, at least, right. First, they were right to argue that a redistributive welfare state which could attract majority support relied upon social solidarity across groups, only some of whose members could expect to be net beneficiaries from specific policies. Put differently, the welfare state depended upon a political coalition in pursuit of social justice and not merely self-interest, a coalition that appears to have formed in most advanced democracies in the middle years of the last century. Second, they were right to point out that this solidarity-based coalition had more recently been weakened if not dissolved, and that the rise of multiculturalism was part of this process. Political identities had become more specific and more divided, and where these identities were based in ethnicity or religion, a multicultural ideology had taken root. Third, they were right to point out the danger posed by multiculturalism to the nation-state, in circumstances where that institution was already being weakened by transnational and global forces. For anyone who saw the nation-state as the main vehicle for egalitarian politics, this was bad news.

In other words, the critics were right to raise the alarm. They were right to identify the danger posed by a certain brand of multiculturalism, even if they tended to exaggerate the specific contribution that multiculturalism had made to the decline of the social democratic left (other cultural shifts, for example in the realms of work and leisure, probably made a bigger difference). But they were wrong to suggest that the solution lay in abandoning multiculturalism per se, and returning to a simpler kind of egalitarian politics (if indeed they did suggest that: as I noted earlier, it turns out that the critics' objections are less to specific policies that favour cultural minorities, than to multiculturalism as an ideology that celebrates group identity and group difference at the expense of 'national pride', 'common dreams' etc.). If there is a solution, it lies in an intelligent form

337

of multiculturalism that extends special treatment to cultural minorities when, but only when, this serves to integrate them more closely into the wider community as equal citizens. What this means in particular cases—for example how far educational provision ought to be tailored to meet the needs of children from linguistic or religious minorities— needs careful analysis.[18] A policy that in one context may extend opportunities for minority groups—for instance separate schooling for religious minorities—may in another context contribute to the breakdown of common citizenship and the emergence of so-called 'parallel societies'. The same applies to institutions that guarantee political representation to minority groups.

To conclude: for those who are committed to the social democratic values that have motivated the critics of multiculturalism, the evidence presented in this book should be cause neither for gloom nor for complacency. There is no reason to believe that adopting multicultural policies will lead imminently to the collapse of the welfare state. But there is still a big question about how to maintain democratic support for redistributive policies, in circumstances where nation-states are increasingly constrained by global economic forces. We need to think hard about how integration policies can work *alongside* multicultural policies, so that citizens can respect one another's differences but still think of themselves as belonging to the same community with a responsibility to ensure equal rights for all. Recent terrorist outrages, and the evidence they have brought of individuals and groups who are deeply alienated from the societies in which they have chosen to live, show us how urgent such thinking has become.

[18] For further reflection on the normative issues at stake here, see Miller (2002).

13

Population diversity, multiculturalism, and the welfare state: Should welfare state theory be revised?

John Myles and Sébastien St-Arnaud

1. Introduction

The enormous expansion of welfare states from the 1950s to the 1970s and efforts at retrenchment since then have made welfare state politics a pivotal empirical 'window' for answering questions about the nature of the political process in the rich capitalist democracies. What is the role of political parties and the diversity of political ideologies they represent? How do differences in the political institutions that mediate the political process affect outcomes? What are the *social* foundations of more expansive welfare states? Are differences in the demographic or class structure of the population or the way these groups are mobilized and incorporated in the political process important?

These same decades were also a foundational period for establishing new social, legal, and political institutions for regulating and managing relations with historic *minorities* and for the selection and incorporation of *immigrants*. In the United States, the 1960s 'war on poverty' was coterminous with black insurgency and the civil rights movement. In Canada, Quebec's 'Quiet Revolution' brought official bilingualism followed by adoption of an official policy of multiculturalism. In Belgium, the Flemish nationalist movement gave rise to a process of federal devolution of powers between Flanders and Wallonia. In the field of immigration, selection criteria for new immigrants were opened up to non-Europeans in the traditional Anglo-American 'settler' societies. In England, France, and the Netherlands the end of empire brought waves of migrants from former colonies. High labour demand in continental Europe led to the establishment of 'guest worker' programmes for immigrants, mainly from Southern Europe.

Despite the temporal conjuncture of these two developments, references to the role of ethno-racial divisions and immigration have been largely absent in conventional narratives of welfare state development, in welfare state theories, and in comparative empirical analyses.[1] Standard overviews of comparative welfare state theory have been generally silent on the topic (Hicks and Esping-Andersen 2005; Myles and Quadagno 2002). The Anglo-American democracies are generally characterized as the weak sisters among modern welfare states and, the UK apart, they represent the most ethnically diverse nations among the affluent democracies. But, with the exception of the American case taken up below, the causal significance of this diversity in accounting for their underdevelopment as welfare states has not loomed large in the usual accounts.

Is it time to reconsider? Are the standard accounts (and debates) about the origins and development of welfare states in the affluent democracies in need of radical revision? Our answer to this question has two parts. First, our reading of this volume leads us to the general conclusion that the answer is no. Ethno-racial cleavages and MCPs, we will argue, have played a minor role in the development of contemporary welfare states in the affluent democracies, apart from a few well-documented exceptions. Welfare state 'theories' come in two varieties: *historical-causal* claims about the significance of specific social mechanisms within particular historical contexts and *probabilistic* claims that such social mechanisms are generalizable or systemic across a wide range of different settings and time periods. *Historical-causal* accounts of the development of the *American* welfare state provide the *locus classicus* from which more generic, probabilistic claims about the negative impacts of ethno-racial diversity and multicultural recognition on welfare states have been constructed. We conclude, however, this strategy is unpromising and that the evidence for *probabilistic* claims that high levels of

---

[1] An exception is Stephens's (1979) discussion of the role that ethnic and linguistic diversity played in impeding the development of strong cohesive labour movements, a necessary condition for the development of strong labour parties and more expansive welfare states.

population diversity and/or multicultural policies per se systematically weaken welfare states is simply too thin and contradictory to draw strong conclusions.

The second part of our answer concerns the future. Welfare state practices tend to be institutionally 'sticky', are subject to multiple competing forces, and tend to change through the accretion of many small reforms that take time to evolve. However, the emergence of significant ethnic diversity in Europe and the subsequent rise of radical right parties, that *combine* appeals for a neoliberal, anti-welfare state, agenda with xenophobic appeals targeted against immigrants, are relatively recent developments and parties of the radical right have had limited success until now. Hence, while it is asking a lot of our empirical analyses *of the past*, including the recent past, to provide conclusive evidence about the potential impact of these movements, the questions raised by this volume remain important. Will a politics that embraces multicultural recognition moderate or exacerbate ethno-racial cleavages? And will multicultural recognition (MCPs) mute or enhance support for an egalitarian welfare state agenda?

In thinking about this question, we need to move beyond the *generic* claims about the 'crowding out', 'corroding', or 'misplaced diagnoses' effects on welfare states that critics of MCPs have advanced (see Chapter 1). Unlike 'laws of nature', *social* mechanisms are best thought of as what James Coleman (1964: 516 ff.) once called 'sometime-true-theories', that account for the results or regularities that obtain in *some* specific cases. Rather than seeking to establish whether diversity inevitably undermines solidarity, our goal should be to determine under what conditions a politics of multicultural recognition is likely to find itself on a collision course with a politics of economic redistribution.

Without claiming to provide anything remotely like a full answer to the question, we do suggest a starting point. What is at stake is whether rising ethno-racial *diversity* also generates new ethno-racial political *cleavages* powerful enough to erode social solidarity and support for redistributive policies. The outcome, we argue, hinges critically on the ability of the host society to ensure full economic and political incorporation of immigrant minorities. Multicultural policies are one element of an immigration regime that may either *hasten* or *hinder* this process but they are not the only, or even the major, determinant of successful economic and political incorporation.

2. Racial diversity or racial exclusion? Can we generalize from the US experience?

Since much of the literature to date reflects American experience, where race clearly has been central to the development of social programmes, it is important to clarify what lessons we can learn from this case.

America's major ethno-racial division has figured prominently in historical-causal analyses of both the foundational New Deal legislation of the 1930s and the 'war on poverty' of the 1960s. The New Deal legislation of the 1930s was driven and constrained by an unusual coalition inside the Democratic Party that included both northern labour and a southern planter-merchant oligarchy struggling to preserve a pre-industrial plantation economy based on indentured black labour. As Jill Quadagno (1988) has shown, control over key Congressional committees allowed the southern wing of the Democratic Party to exclude southern blacks from the New Deal in the name of 'state rights'. Eligibility criteria and benefit levels for Old Age Assistance, Unemployment Insurance, and Aid to Dependent Children were left to the discretion of the states since programmes that created national standards would have undermined the southern economy. Agricultural workers were excluded from Old Age Insurance since even the meagre sum of $15 a month would provide more cash than a cropper family might see in a year.

This pattern persisted into subsequent stages of welfare state development. During the 1960s, both labour market policy (Weir 1992) and the development of new social programmes (Quadagno 1994) collided with and were deflected by the struggle for civil and political rights by African-Americans. Though the true counterfactual can never be known, it is not difficult to make the case that the struggle for *civil and political rights* had a crowding-out effect with respect to the achievement of new *social rights* in the United States during this formative period. The discussion of 'poverty' initiated by Michael Harrington's *The Other America* (1962) at the beginning of the 1960s was not primarily concerned with racial disparities but with other social groups (the elderly, Appalachia) who had missed out on the post-war economic boom. By the mid-sixties all this had changed as the civil rights movement and black urban insurgency came to the fore. As a result, the US war on poverty focused more on the incomplete character of *civil and political rights*—the right to vote and anti-discrimination legislation to break down barriers in the labour and housing markets—than on the creation or expansion of new *social rights*. Benefits for the elderly and the 'poor' were created (Medicare, Medicaid) or expanded (public pensions, social assistance) but working-age, working-class families gained little. Programmes such as unemployment insurance were left to stagnate and then to erode. Health insurance, sickness insurance, and family allowances for working-age Americans never became part of the agenda. As Archie Bunker, the racist anti-hero of the 1970s US situation comedy, *All in the Family*, complained, the 'government' was doing things to help blacks and women but nothing for him.

It is important to highlight, however, that the core struggle of these formative years was not mainly about affirmative action or other MCPs but over what Banting et al. (Chapter 2) refer to as non-discriminatory access by African-Americans to traditional political and civil rights. The focal point was equality before the law, not the politics of recognition or of compensation. If, as T. H. Marshall (1964) argued, the emergence of expansive social rights requires the full development of civil and political rights, the United States was simply not ready to build an institutionally comprehensive welfare state. The historical residues of what Myrdal et al. (1944) called the 'American dilemma' and Quadagno (1994) identifies as America's 'unfinished democracy', had to be confronted.

Precisely because of its 'exceptional' character, however, the story of America's racialization of welfare state politics has rarely been incorporated into more general theoretical narratives of welfare state development. No other advanced capitalist democracy began its modern history with an ethno-racial minority subject to the social institution of slavery or developed its post-slavery forms of economic and political exclusion. If there was a lesson to be learned from the US experience, it was a lesson about the politics of ethno-racial oppression and exclusion, not the politics of ethno-racial diversity and recognition. As a result, welfare state theorists have seen no reason to move from the American experience to probabilistic generalizations about the impact of diversity or MCPs in other countries.

But is this conventional reading of the US experience too narrow? Some analysts have suggested that the US experience reflects a more universal tension between diversity and the welfare state. We believe that such arguments suffer from three important flaws: the correlations are weak; the causal relationships are unclear; and there are important counter-examples where diversity can stimulate the welfare state.

For example, Alesina and Glaeser's (2004: 141) recent study attempts to generalize from US experience and concludes that the negative impact of ethno-racial diversity is a more general phenomenon. They report a strong negative cross-country correlation between racial *diversity* and social welfare spending across a wide range of affluent and less developed nations. Although the correlation stands up when the level of economic development is controlled, inspection of their scatterplot indicates that among the affluent countries the strength of the correlation between racial diversity and spending is mainly driven by the United States, an outlier on both measures.[2] Visual inspection of the scatterplot also indicates an equally weak case for the less developed countries, a negative association driven by Malta and Uruguay, two countries with low racial diversity and relatively high spending.

Similarly, Banting et al. (Chapter 2, Table 2.6, this volume) report a modest, but robust, negative cross-country correlation between growth in the foreign born population and change in social spending during the 1980s and 1990s. By 'robust' we mean the negative bivariate correlation stands up under a series of increasingly demanding statistical tests. The correlation is not self-explanatory—by itself it tells us nothing about the causal mechanisms involved. But the result remains important since we know there is a significant cross-national pattern in the evidence that must be accounted for. The authors help out by highlighting that the association hinges critically on the Netherlands and the USA, countries with two of the three highest foreign-born gains and the two slowest rates of spending growth. What of the USA? There can be little doubt that the ongoing association between 'welfare' and 'race' in the United States provided the political context for 'welfare reform' in the United States in the 1990s (Hero and Preuhs, this volume). It is also quite plausible that resentment against Mexican immigrants, especially illegals, amplified this trend. Hero and Preuhs's results show a very robust negative association between per cent Latino in a state and changes in welfare expenditures. In the Netherlands, social expenditures on income transfers to the working age population (i.e. net of health and pension expenditures) actually declined from 14.6 to 9.8 per cent of GDP between 1980 and 2000.[3] Did resentment against immigrants play a role? Possibly. The standard explanation (Kenworthy 2004), however, is that the decline was primarily driven by declining 'need' associated with the so-called 'Dutch miracle' that led to the sharp gains in employment during the 1990s. Reforms

[2] Among the affluent democracies only Australia, Canada, New Zealand, and the USA have racial diversity scores higher than the racially homogeneous countries of Europe (and Japan). Almost any social feature correlated with the Anglo-American countries will also be correlated with low social spending. The unanswered (historical-causal) question is whether high levels of ethno-racial diversity *explain* the Anglo-American pattern, especially in the three 'Anglo' settler societies, Australia, Canada, and New Zealand.

[3] Calculated by the authors from OECD social expenditure data (SOCEX).

during the 1990s focused mainly on (successful) projects to increase women's labour force participation and to reduce the soaring numbers of disability claimants. As Entzinger (this volume) concludes, the Dutch case provides sparse evidence for a *causal* link between welfare reform and the politics of migration and multiculturalism. The implication is that although the 'correlation' is robust, the imputation of causality may be less so.

Banting et al. (Chapter 2, this volume) also test for, but fail to find, a significant correlation between more and less developed multicultural policies and welfare spending. This result is consistent with at least two interpretations. The first is that multicultural policies really do have no effect on social spending. The second is that MCPs potentially have large effects but the effects differ and, depending on initial conditions, these effects may be in *opposite* directions.[4] The contrast between the Canadian and US experiences with MCPs is instructive in this respect (Banting 2005b). In Canada, welfare state expansion, rising rates of immigration from non-traditional source countries, the expansion of MCPs, and the emergence of a new *civic* nationalism from a traditional *ethnic* (i.e. British) national identity (Breton 1988) occurred more or less simultaneously in the 1960s and early 1970s. Canada adopted official bilingualism at the federal level in 1968 and followed with multicultural legislation in 1971. The same period brought new social programmes including national health insurance, two new old age pension schemes, as well as expanded social assistance and unemployment insurance programmes. One would be hard pressed to make a causal claim that a more expansive multiculturalism *stimulated* the development of a more expansive welfare state (or vice versa). Nevertheless, whereas the black–white cleavage often acted as a fetter on social policy expansion in the USA, it is arguably the case that the French–English divide accelerated social policy development in Canada. Until the end of the 1950s, the conservative governments that ruled Canada's French-speaking province more often than not constrained social policy development. In the subsequent period, however, Quebec politics, especially in its nationalist expressions, took on a distinctive social democratic hue (Guindon 1988) and more often than not

---

[4] The same issue arises in debates over the effects in studies of social spending and economic growth (Kenworthy 2004). On average the correlations between social spending and outcomes such as economic growth or employment are close to zero. But this may be because under some conditions, some forms of social spending impede economic growth and under other circumstances other forms of social spending enhance economic growth. Causality is likely to be conjunctural and time dependent.

served as a spur to social policy expansion and as a constraint on welfare state retrenchment (Béland and Myles 2005; Béland and Lecours 2006).

In short, the attempt to develop generalized probabilistic claims from US experience is unlikely to succeed. This does not mean, however, we should ignore or dismiss the issue of the impact of diversity and multiculturalism on the welfare state. Rather, we need to adopt a different approach, one that focuses on identifying the causal pathways that link population diversity, immigration, multiculturalism, and welfare state development. In the next section, we draw on Herbert Kitschelt's (1995) analysis of the rise of the new radical right (NRR) in Europe as an example of what these pathways might look like.

3. Charting causal pathways: The case of the rise of the new radical right in Europe

The major reason that standard welfare state theory has given short shrift to the impact of immigration, population diversity, and multiculturalism is undoubtedly historical. Quite simply, during the formative years of welfare state expansion from the 1950s to the 1970s, and especially in the large welfare states of Western Europe, there was no explicit linkage between the politics of immigration and multiculturalism, on the one hand, and the politics of welfare state expansion, on the other. Except for the case of the USA, one is hard pressed to think of any of the standard historical narratives of post-war welfare state development where such issues figure prominently. However, all this began to change with the rise of New Radical Right (NRR) in Western Europe, political parties that combine *nativism* in the area of citizenship rights and *laissez-faire* in social and economic policy.

Compared to the rather generic claims about the effects of ethno-racial diversity and multicultural policies on welfare states, Kitschelt's analysis specifies a detailed set of social and institutional pathways through which xenophobic reactions to rising immigration have become politically linked to anti-welfare state policy orientations in Western Europe. The analysis is complex and will only be cursorily summarized here. Kitschelt identifies the conditions conducive to both rising political 'demand' for such policies and the 'supply' of political parties to meet this demand.

The key claim is that shifts in political preferences associated with the transition to post-industrialism have created a strategic opening for new right-wing parties in Europe since the 1970s, parties that combine 'market-liberal', anti-statist, appeals with authoritarian, ethnocentric, and even racist messages. These political preferences remain largely unmet by traditional parties of the centre-right or the centre-left precisely because of their move to the 'centre'. The social foundations for the appeal to laissez-faire, according to Kitschelt (1995: 6), are to be found in economic sectors exposed to high levels of international competition where employees' main concern is with long-term industrial adaptation and hence they resist redistributive measures that potentially drain resources from new investment and private consumption. This preference for investments to enhance market flexibility is greatest in sectors such as manufacturing and financial services exposed to high levels of international competition. The rigidity of labour markets in Western welfare states also makes it difficult for younger, less skilled, workers to access the labour market and the welfare state benefits traditionally attached to employment. As a result, the 'socially excluded' turn to market liberalism in order to smash these institutions (Kitschelt 1995: 9). At the same time, Kitschelt argues, the work situation of less well-educated blue collar and lower salaried employees incline them toward particularistic, parochial definitions of citizenship and to oppose the pluralistic cosmopolitanism embedded in the ethos of multiculturalism. The New Radical Right of Western Europe, he concludes, has been successful by virtue of forging a new cross-class alliance between segments of the working class based on racist-xenophobic appeals and among shopkeepers and craftspeople on the basis of anti-tax appeals.

This political marriage between market liberalism and ethnic chauvinism is, of course, not the only possible outcome. The alternatives, as Kitschelt points out, include 'welfare chauvinism'—a strong defence of welfare rights but the exclusion of ethnic minorities from those rights. This was the strategy adopted by the (successful) ultra-nationalist Serbian Radical Party during the 1990s but for a variety of reasons, he argues, the future of welfare chauvinism in Western Europe is bleak.

For present purposes, the point is not whether Kitschelt's analysis and prognoses are ultimately correct. There is evidence, for example, that the laissez-faire emphasis of radical right parties in Western Europe has faded since the 1980s (Bastow 1997). And as Kitschelt emphasizes, the conditions favouring the emergence of this particular political configuration are historically contingent, not some quasi-automatic response to growing population diversity. The point, rather, is a theoretical one. Kitschelt identifies a *systemic* realignment in European political preferences, the reasons for the emergence of parties able to act as a *transmission belt* for these new coalitions into the public sphere, and, as importantly, the political and social conditions favouring or mitigating against the likely success of such movements. The claim is *not* that there has been a massive shift in public opinion (e.g. 'diminished solidarity') but rather a sufficient shift to produce new electoral constituencies that alter the electoral opportunity structure.

Given the *timing* of these developments and the limited success of new radical right parties until now, the fact that our empirical analyses of the past, including the recent past, fail to demonstrate large causal imprints of these movements on welfare state outcomes does not settle the issue for the future. As the literature on welfare state retrenchment highlights (Pierson 2001), welfare state practices tend to be institutionally 'sticky', are subject to multiple competing forces, and tend to change through the accretion of many small reforms that take time to evolve. It is hardly surprising therefore that faced with these developments, contemporary social democrats (the 'libertarian left' as Kitschelt calls them) should begin to worry about potential *future* trade-offs between ethnic diversity and multiculturalism, on the one hand, and, on the other, sustaining traditional commitments to economic redistribution. The success of US Republicans in forging a coalition between laissez-faire economic elites and *morally* conservative sectors of the American working class stands as a stark example of the fact that politics can make for strange bedfellows (Frank 2004).

4. Revising welfare state theory: Immigration regimes, multicultural policy and the power resources of minorities

We return to our original question: should welfare state theory be revised? We have argued that theoretical accounts of the growth and restructuring of the welfare state throughout the twentieth century do not need revision. As the case studies in this volume illustrate, outside the USA neither ethno-racial diversity nor MCPs appear to have played a decisive role in weakening welfare states until now. In the absence of a cumulative body of historical-causal accounts demonstrating that such a link is present, attempts to develop generalized, probabilistic, predictions about the impact of heterogeneity or MCPs on welfare states are unlikely to be persuasive. Even if they are 'statistically' successful in generating robust cross-national correlations, claims about the impact of ethno-racial diversity must contend with a large set of arguably more potent sources of welfare state retrenchment in the past quarter-century including slow economic growth, rising deficits, and national differences in the partisan composition of government (Korpi and Palme 2003).

However, the US experience along with continuing ethno-racial tensions and the emergence of new political formations in Europe provide good reason not to become analytically sanguine. If the effects of rising ethnic diversity on welfare politics have been modest until now, this may simply reflect that the social realignments highlighted by Kitschelt and the critics of multicultural policies have simply had insufficient time to mature. In thinking about the future, however, we have argued that it is important to identify *specific* causal mechanisms that might lead from growing ethnic diversity to welfare state retrenchment. And such analyses would obviously have to be incorporated into more general understandings of the challenges and forces affecting the welfare state.

The big questions in our view concern the extent to which: (*a*) growing ethno-racial *diversity* generates ethno-racial *cleavages*; and (*b*) these cleavages, in turn, provide an additional impetus for *generalized* welfare state retrenchment. The emergence of the first (new cleavages) is no guarantee that these cleavages will in turn become linked to a growing demand for more limited social rights and redistribution. Will anti-immigrant sentiment feed the fears associated with population ageing and bolster support for pension and health-care cutbacks? Will ethno-racial chauvinism impede the development of *new* welfare state initiatives in such areas as child and family policy or human capital formation? And what of the central question of this volume: how might national differences in multicultural policies affect this process?

Banting et al. make a heroic advance with respect to sorting out countries with more or less well-developed MCP policies. But perhaps scoring countries from high to low is not the way to go. Does the fact that New Zealand scores 5 and the Netherlands scores 4.5 on the immigrant MCP scale capture what we might think of as the potentially causally significant differences between these two countries? Esping-Andersen (1990) taught us about the limits of classifying welfare states on the basis of how much they spend while ignoring differences in how they spend and the models of state and society ('welfare regimes') that they embody. By analogy, it strikes us that multicultural policies that provide symbolic recognition and material resources to new ethnic minorities are only one element of a complex set of institutions and practices that differentiate national immigration regimes.

What will determine whether growing ethno-racial diversity in the new immigrant societies of Western Europe will generate a new ethno-racial political cleavage, similar to the black–white divide in the United States? The American experience strongly indicates that the outcome is contingent on the relative success of these nations at ensuring the full economic and political incorporation of these new minorities. 'Incorporation', as Raymond Breton (2005) makes clear, does not imply that ethnicity disappears as a basis of social organization and individual identity. Nor does the existence of vibrant ethnic communities indicate that incorporation is failing to occur. Rather incorporation entails involvement in institutions, the construction of social ties and, most important, 'equal access to the rewards that the economic and political systems generate and distribute' (Breton 2005: 188–9). Multicultural policies are one element of an immigration regime that may hasten or hinder this process but they are not the only, or even the major, determinant of economic and political incorporation.

Consider first the selection process, the ways in which states manage immigrant recruitment. Banting et al. point in this direction when they distinguish between nations that are 'countries of immigration' and those that are not. Countries of immigration—including the Anglo-American 'settler societies' and Israel—not only *admit* but also actively *recruit* immigrants, especially highly skilled *economic* immigrants and their families, as permanent residents and future citizens. These immigrant flows arrive literally 'by invitation' rather than as political or economic refugees, asylum seekers, or illegals. The post-war waves of immigrants to Britain, France, and the Netherlands, in contrast, represented a post-colonial legacy, accepted, often reluctantly, from a sense of national obligation rather than proactively recruited. In Northern Europe, immigrants were actively recruited in the post-war years but as guest workers, 'temporary' visitors to fill unskilled jobs rather than as skilled workers and future citizens.

Do these differences matter? Recruitment practices undoubtedly affect the subsequent pattern of *economic* incorporation of migrants irrespective of the presence of MCPs. Economic immigrants who are actively recruited for their labour market skills, not surprisingly, fare much better in the labour market than refugees or asylum seekers and are less likely to join the ranks of the 'socially excluded'. Whereas first generation migrants do experience significant 'transition costs', a now standard result in Canadian and US research is that the second generation does better in the labour market than their native born peers. Past success at incorporating 'differences' makes gloomy projections of apocalyptic failure in the future a difficult political message to sell. Successful economic incorporation of the many also offsets the imputed costs associated with the higher levels of support often required by refugees and asylum seekers. The enormous diversity in group outcomes in countries like Australia, Canada, and the USA makes it difficult to sustain a single dominant narrative about the social or economic costs associated with immigration per se.

Under what conditions are new ethno-racial divisions likely to provide the foundation for limiting the growth of or even cutting back existing welfare states? And what role might multicultural policies play in the process? A robust result from both cross-national and US research is that resistance to redistribution is closely related to the free-rider problem, the belief that the beneficiaries are 'undeserving' (Alesina and Angeletos 2005; Gilens 1999). People who attribute misfortune to the absence of personal effort rather than bad luck are more likely to oppose redistributive policies. Opposition to 'welfare' in the United States, for example, is closely associated with beliefs that 'blacks are lazy' (Gilens 1999) and, since the 1960s, 'welfare' has become widely constructed as a programme that primarily benefits blacks, i.e. viewed *as though* it were an MCP. At first glance, this result seems to support claims about the 'corroding effect' of any programme that becomes associated with a particular ethno-cultural minority. But as Gilens points out, such a reading is far too simplistic. Whites do oppose affirmative action programmes that establish race-based quotas in schools or in the labour market, rewards that appear to be 'undeserved'. But a strong majority simultaneously support racially *targeted* programmes (MCPs) aimed at helping minorities to help themselves. Sixty-six per cent of whites are in favour of 'educational programs to assist minorities in competing for college' and 69 per cent approve of 'job training for minorities to help them get ahead in industries where they are underrepresented' despite the fact these programmes 'aim to help blacks *in competition with whites*' (Gilens 1999: 172, emphasis in the original).

The point is that not all MCPs are born equal. Some may potentially erode support for the welfare state while others may enhance it. In this respect, MCPs are no different from welfare policies themselves. A long-standing premiss in the welfare state literature, for example, has been that 'means-tested' social programmes tend to limit support for welfare state expansion while 'universal' programmes encourage development. In a similar way, the challenge is to identify exactly *which* MCPs have the potential to erode welfare state support.

351

Comparison of Canada and the United States also highlights the importance of national differences in the degree of political incorporation and electoral power achieved by national and ethno-racial minorities. With a territorial base in the province of Quebec, Canada's francophone population has always played a pivotal role in national electoral politics and in social policy deliberations. American Blacks, in contrast, were historically excluded from full political and civil rights and despite the reforms of the 1960s their importance as a political constituency to be courted is relatively limited by comparison. Their share of the electorate is roughly half that of Canadian francophones, they are territorially dispersed in urban ghettos where electoral gerrymandering is prevalent, electoral turnout is low, and historic adhesion to the Democratic Party means there is little incentive for either party to compete intensively for their attention.

The role of *immigrant* minorities in electoral politics follows a similar pattern. Canada's immigration rate is much higher than the American and, due in part to Canada's multicultural policies, recent migrants to Canada become naturalized at twice the rate of their US counterparts (Bloemraad 2002) and have higher levels of political mobilization (Bloemraad 2005).[5] As a result, immigrant communities are critical constituencies to be courted at election time especially in Canada's largest urban centres (Toronto, Vancouver, Montreal). Together, the Quebec vote and the large urban immigrant vote have made political appeals that combine economic laissez-faire with ethno-cultural backlash, a losing electoral strategy in the Canadian context.[6]

As Breton (2005: 188–9) observes, ethnic social formations and, by extension, multicultural policies that facilitate such formation may either hinder or facilitate social incorporation. They may prevent the development of more encompassing solidarities and be used for the maintenance of inequalities in social status and separateness in social relations. By facilitating ethnic mobilization and collective action, however, multicultural policies may also provide the resources necessary to overcome obstacles to participation in the society's institutions. The degree of effective socio-political organization of an ethnic minority, he concludes

[5] Bloemraad (2002) estimates that 70 per cent of Canadian immigrants are naturalized citizens compared to 35 per cent in the USA.

[6] The Reform Party emerged in western Canada in the 1990s and subsequently merged with the established Progressive Conservative Party. Leadership of the new Conservative Party was assumed by Reform's Stephen Harper. At inception, Reform called for both more laissez-faire economic strategies and an end to 'privileging' both historic (i.e. francophone) and immigrant minorities. Electoral competition at the national level, however, has forced the party toward the political centre and to abandon Reform's Anglo-nativist cultural politics almost entirely.

(Breton 2005: 197), is *positively* related to incorporation, 'since such organization is an instrument with which to deal with the problems encountered'. In effect, successful ethnic incorporation and minority recognition are an *effect* of political strength rather than weakness.

There is more than a weak analogy between Breton's (2005) conclusions concerning the link between the political incorporation of ethnic minorities and those of power resource theory concerning the acquisition of political resources by workers in capitalist societies. As Korpi (1983, 1989) has argued, national variation in working-class 'incorporation' is a direct reflection of the success of working-class movements to institutionalize their power in unions and political parties. Korpi and Shalev (1980), for example, demonstrate that 'industrial conflict' as expressed in the volume and duration of strikes has historically been highest in nations where labour has been *weak* and lowest where labour has been *strong*, both as economic (unions) and political (labour parties) actors. As they conclude (Korpi and Shalev 1980: 324), industrial conflict and confrontation become redundant when the labour movement achieves access to political power and moves the conflicts of interest between labour and capital from the industrial to the political arena. As the US experience of the 1960s and the conflagrations in French immigrant suburbs in 2005 testify, it hardly requires a great stretch of the imagination to extend such an understanding to the relationship between low levels of economic and political incorporation and ethno-racial conflict in plural societies.

In short, the likelihood that increasing ethno-racial *diversity* will generate the sort of ethno-racial *cleavages* that can erode the welfare state is not determined by either the level of foreign-born population, or the level of MCPs per se. Rather, it depends primarily on the level of immigrant economic and political incorporation. This in turn depends on such factors as the immigrant selection process, whether MCPs conform with popular perception of 'just desert' and fair competition, and the electoral strength of minority groups themselves. In order to make sense of these dynamics, welfare state theorists need to go beyond simply adding heterogeneity or MCPs to regression analysis. Rather they need a more robust understanding of the preconditions and dynamics of immigrant incorporation.

5. Conclusion: Lessons for Europe?

Given current and anticipated fertility levels, Europe faces two possible futures: growing population diversity as a result of ongoing immigration or substantial population decline. Given the practical difficulties and economic challenges of constructing a 'Fortress Europe', growing diversity is the more likely outcome. Are there lessons to be learned from the settler societies where this process has been going on for over a century?

Social 'solidarity' in plural societies is contingent on redefining who 'we' are, a shift from a fictive ethnic identity to a civic national identity. The diverse experiences of the 'settler societies' provide no guarantees of success but do suggest more and less promising strategies. Successful economic integration, at least by the second generation, is undoubtedly a major ingredient. And successful economic integration is more likely with a proactive policy of recruiting immigrants with a high probability of success in the labour market, the young and the highly skilled, than strategies aimed at recruiting workers for low-productivity jobs at the bottom of the labour market.[7] The point is not to restrict the number of political and economic refugees admitted but rather to expand and diversify the flow to include migrants who are less likely to join the ranks of the 'socially excluded'.

But full *political* incorporation also matters. Rapid access to full political citizenship is important for symbolic reasons—redefining who 'we' are—and for reshaping the social terrain on which electoral competition takes place. Immigrants and minorities without electoral and other forms of political influence remain visitors without voice in the national household. As the political significance of immigrant minorities expands, the electoral space for parties of the new radical right contracts.

Successful transformation is likely to be slow in coming. Kymlicka's (1998) spirited advocacy of multicultural policies in plural societies rests on the claim that multicultural policies can help to accelerate the process of incorporation. Their effectiveness, however, hinges on the height of the economic and political barriers to be overcome.

---

[7] Such a strategy of course raises an additional ethical dilemma since it threatens to strip developing economies of their most skilled workers.

References

ABEL, C., and LEWIS, C. M. (eds.) (2002). *Exclusion and Engagement: Social Policy in Latin America.* London: ILAS.

ABU-LABAN, Y., and GABRIEL, C. (2002). *Selling Diversity: Immigration, Multiculturalism, Employment Equity, and Globalization.* Peterborough, Ont.: Broadview Press.

African-Canadian Legal Clinic (2004). 'Anti-Black Racism in Canada: A Report on the Canadian Government's Compliance with the International Convention on the Elimination of All Forms of Racial Discrimination' (**www.aclc.net/antiba_recommendcerd.html**).

Africville Genealogy Society (1992). *The Spirit of Africville.* Halifax: Formac Publishing.

Agencia de Noticias Plurinacional del Ecuador (2004). Resolutions of the La Asamblea Unitaria de Trabajadores y Pueblos del Ecuador, 9 February.

AGUIRRE, Á., ARZE, C., and MONTAÑO, G. (1992). 'Análisis integral del programa de ajuste estructural', in Á. Aguirre, C. Arze, H. Larrazábal, G. Montaño, and R. Moscoso, *La intencionalidad del ajuste en Bolivia.* La Paz: CEDLA.

ALAI (Agencia Latinamericana de Información) (2004). 'Bolivia: Asamblea Constituyente Democracia Participativa en Acción'. Via e-mail from **amazon amazonalliance.org**, 26 February.

ALBÓ, X. (1994). 'And from Kataristas to MNRistas? The Surprising and Bold Alliance between Aymaras and Neoliberals in Bolivia', in D. L. Van Cott (ed.), *Indigenous Peoples and Democracy in Latin America.* New York: St Martin's Press.

―― (2002). 'Bolivia: From Indian and Campesino Leaders to Councillors and Parliamentary Deputies', in R. Sieder (ed.), *Multiculturalism in Latin America: Indigenous Rights, Diversity and Democracy.* Houndmills: Palgrave MacMillan.

―― (2003). 'Andean Ethnicity Today: Four *Aymara* Narratives from Bolivia', in S. Ton and A. Zoomers (eds.), *Imaging the Andes: Shifting Margins of a Marginal World.* Amsterdam: Aksant.

―― (2004). '222 años después: la convulsionada Bolivia multiétnica'. *Artículo Primero*, 8(16): 39–67.

ALCÁNTARA SÁEZ, M., and FREIDENBERG, F. (2001). 'Los partidos políticos en América Latina'. *América Latina Hoy*, 27 (Apr.): 17–35.

ALESINA, A., and ANGELETOS, G.-M. (2005). 'Fairness and Redistribution: US vs. Europe'. *American Economic Review*, 95(4): 960–80.

References

ALESINA, A., BAQIR, R., and EASTERLY, W. (2001). 'Public Goods and Ethnic Divisions'. NBER Working Paper No. 6009. Cambridge, Mass.: NBER.

—— DELEESCHAUWER, A., EASTERLY, W., KURLAT, S., and WACZIARG, R. (2003). 'Fractionalization'. *Journal of Economic Growth*, 8(2): 155–94.

—— and GLAESER, E. (2004). *Fighting Poverty in the US and Europe: A World of Difference*. Oxford: Oxford University Press.

—— and LAFERRARA, E. (2005). 'Ethnic Diversity and Economic Performance'. *Journal of Economic Literature*, 43 (Sept.): 762–800.

ALLEN, D. (2001). Address to the Plenary Assembly, United Nations World Conference Against Racism, Durban, South Africa, 6 September. Reprinted as 'Lessons from Africville'. *Shunpiking* (**www.shunpiking.com/bhs/Lessons%20from%20Africville.htm**).

Amt für Multikulturelle Angelegenheiten (1990). *Bericht: Ein Jahr multikulturelle Arbeit* [Report: One year of multicultural work], Frankfurt.

ANDERSEN, J. (1992). 'Denmark: The Progress Party: Populist Neo-Liberalism and Welfare State Chauvinism', in P. Hainsworth (ed.), *The Extreme Right in Europe and the USA*. New York: St Martin's Press.

—— and BJØRKLUND, T. (1990). 'Structural Changes and New Cleavages: The Progress Parties in Denmark and Norway'. *Acta Sociologica*, 33(3): 195–217.

ANDOLINA, R. (1999). 'Colonial Legacies and Plurinational Imaginaries: Indigenous Movement Politics in Ecuador and Bolivia'. Ph.D. Dissertation, University of Minnesota.

—— (2003). 'The Sovereign and its Shadow: Constituent Assembly and Indigenous Movement in Ecuador'. *Journal of Latin American Studies*, 35(4): 721–50.

ANDREß, H.-J., HEIEN, T., and HOFÄCKER, D. (2001). *Wozu brauchen wir noch den Sozialstaat? Der deutsche Sozialstaat im Urteil seiner Bürger* [What do we need the welfare state for? The German welfare state as judged by its citizens]. Wiesbaden: Westdeutscher Verlag.

APPIAH, A. (1997). 'Multicultural Misunderstanding'. *New York Review of Books*, 44(15) (9 Oct.): 30–6.

Arbeiterwohlfahrt (1973). 'Zur Reform der Ausländerpolitik' [On the reform of aliens policy]. *Theorie und Praxis der sozialen Arbeit*, special issue.

ARCHER, K. (1985). 'The Failure of the New Democratic Party: Unions, Unionists, and Politics in Canada'. *Canadian Journal of Political Science*, 18: 353–66.

AROCHA, J. (1992). 'Los negros y la nueva constitución colombiana de 1991'. *América Negra*, 3(June): 39–54.

ARRIBA, A., and MORENO, L. (2004). 'Spain: Poverty, Social Exclusion and Safety Nets', in M. Ferrara (ed.), *Fighting Poverty and Social Exclusion in Southern Europe*. London: Routledge.

Artículo Primero (2003). *Artículo Primero, Año VII, no. 14: Reforma agraria 50 años: TCO y tierras campesinas*. Santa Cruz de la Sierra: CEJIS.

ARTS, W., ENTZINGER, H., and MUFFELS, R. (eds.) (2004). *Verzorgingsstaat vaar wel*. Assen: Van Gorcum.

ARZE CUADROS, E. (2002). *Bolivia, El programa del MNR y la Revolución Nacional: Del movimiento de Reformas Universitaria al ocaso del modelo neoliberal*. La Paz: Plural.

ASHER, K. (1998). 'Constructing Afro-Colombia: Ethnicity and Territory in the Pacific Lowlands'. Ph.D. dissertation, University of Florida.

Assembly of First Nations (1990). 'Redress for the Harms Inflicted upon First Nations by the Residential School Policy'. Resolution No. 25/90, Special Chiefs Assembly, Ottawa Ontario, 11 December (**www.afn.ca/resolutions/1990/sca/res25.htm**).

———— (1994). *Breaking the Silence: An Interpretive Study of Residential School Impact and Healing as Illustrated by the Stories of First Nation Individuals*. Ottawa: Assembly of First Nations.

ASSIES, W. (2002). 'From Rubber Estate to Simple Commodity Production: Agrarian Struggles in the Northern Bolivian Amazon'. *Journal of Peasant Studies*, 29(3/4): 83–130. (Special Issue on Latin American Peasants, ed. by T. Brass.)

———— (2003*a*). 'La descentralización a la boliviana y la "economía política" del reformismo', in W. Assies (ed.), *Gobiernos locales y reforma del Estado en América Latina*. Zamora, Mich.: El Colegio de Michoacán.

———— (2003*b*). 'David versus Goliath in Cochabamba: Water Rights, Neoliberalism, and the Revival of Social Protest in Bolivia'. *Latin American Perspectives*, 30(3): 14–36.

———— (2004). 'Bolivia: A Gasified Democracy'. *Revista Europea de Estudios Latino-americanos y del Caribe/European Review of Latin American and Caribbean Studies*, 76(April): 25–43.

———— and SALMAN, T. (2003). *Crisis in Bolivia: The Elections of 2002 and their Aftermath*, Research Paper 56. London: Institute of Latin American Studies, University of London.

———— VAN DER HAAR, G., and HOEKEMA, A. (eds.) (2001). *The Challenge of Diversity: Indigenous Peoples and Reform of the State in Latin America*. Amsterdam: Thela Thesis.

AUBRY, J. (1994). ' "Atrocities" Alleged in Mission Schools', *Vancouver Sun*, 8 Aug., p. A1.

BADE, K. J., and BOMMES, M. (2000). 'Migration und politische Kultur im Nicht-Einwanderungsland' [Migration and Political Culture in the Non-immigration Country], in K. J. Bade and R. Münz (eds.), *Migrationsreport 2000*. Bonn: Bundeszentrale für politische Bildung.

BANTING, K. G. (1987). *The Welfare State and Canadian Federalism* (2nd edn.). Kingston and Montreal: McGill-Queen's University Press.

———— (1995). 'The Welfare State as Statecraft: Territorial Politics and Canadian Social Policy', in S. Leibfried and P. Pierson (eds.), *European Social Policy: Between Fragmentation and Integration*. Washington, DC: The Brookings Institute.

BANTING, K. G. (1998). 'The Past Speaks to the Future: Lessons from the Post-war Social Union', in H. Lazar (ed.), *Canada: The State of the Federation 1997.* Kingston, Ont.: Institute of Intergovernmental Relations, Queen's University.

—— (1999). 'Social Citizenship and the Multicultural Welfare State', in A. C. Cairns, J. C. Courtney, P. MacKinnon, H. J. Michelmann, and D. E. Smith (eds.), *Citizenship, Diversity and Pluralism: Canadian and Comparative Perspectives.* Montreal: McGill-Queen's University Press.

—— (2005a). 'Canada: Nation-Building in a Federal Welfare State', in H. S. Obinger, H. S. Leibfried, and F. Castles (eds.), *Federalism and the Welfare State: New World and European Experiences.* Cambridge: Cambridge University Press.

—— (2005b). 'The Multicultural Welfare State: International Experience and North American Narratives'. *Social Policy and Administration,* 39(2): 98–115.

—— and KYMLICKA, W. (2003). 'Multiculturalism and Welfare', *Dissent* (Fall): 59–66.

—— (2004). 'Do Multiculturalism Policies Erode the Welfare State?' in P. Van Parijs (ed.), *Cultural Diversity versus Economic Solidarity.* Brussels: Deboeck University Press.

BARIÉ, C. G. (2003). *Pueblos Indígenas y derechos constitucionales en America Latina: un panorama* (2nd edn). Mexico: Comisión Nacional para el Desarrollo de los Pueblos Indígenas, Abya Yala.

BARKAN, E. (2000). *The Guilt of Nations: Restitution and Negotiating Historical Injustices.* New York: Norton.

BARNES, A. [pseud.]. (2004). Interview by M. James, 8 July, tape recording, Toronto, Ontario.

BARRY, B. (2001). *Culture and Equality: An Egalitarian Critique of Multiculturalism.* Cambridge: Polity Press; Cambridge, Mass.: Harvard University Press.

BASTOW, S. (1997). 'Front Nationale Economic Policy: From Neo-Liberalism to Protectionism'. *Modern and Contemporary France,* 5(1): 61–72.

BAUBOCK, R. (2003). 'Public Culture in Societies of Immigration', in B. Peters (ed.), *Migrant Categories, Groups and Collective Identities.* Avebury: Ashgate.

BAUMERT, J., and SCHÜMER, G. (2001). 'Familiäre Lebensverhältnisse, Bildungsbeteiligung und Kompetenzerwerb' ['Family Life Circumstances, Educational Participation and the Acquisition of Competences'] in Deutsches PISA-Konsortium (eds.). *PISA 2000: Basiskompetenzen von Schülerinnen und Schülern im internationalen Vergleich* [Basic Competences of Students in International Comparison]. Opladen: Leske & Budrich, 323–407.

BAZYLEVICH, M. (2002). Letter to the editor, *Star-Phoenix* (Saskatoon), 22 Mar., p. A17.

BECK, U. (1992). *Risk Society: Towards a New Modernity,* trans. M. Ritter. London: Sage.

BÉLAND, D., and LECOURS, A. (2005a). 'Nationalism and Social Policy in Canada and Quebec', in N. McEwen and L. Moreno (eds.), *The Territorial Politics of Welfare.* Abingdon: Routledge.

_____ (2005*b*). 'Nationalism, Public Policy, and Institutional Development: Social Security in Belgium'. *Journal of Public Policy*, 25(2): 265–85.

_____ (2006). 'Sub-state Nationalism and the Welfare State: Quebec and Canadian Federalism'. *Nations and Nationalism*, 12: 77–96.

_____ (forthcoming). *Contested Solidarities: Nationalism and the Politics of Social Policy in Belgium, Canada and the United Kingdom.*

_____ and MYLES, J. (2005). 'Stasis Amid Change: Canadian Pension Reform in an Age of Retrenchment', in G. Bonoli and T. Shinkawa (eds.), *Ageing and Pension Reform around the World.* Cheltenham: Edward Elgar.

BELSLEY, D. A., KUH, E., and WELSCH, R. E. (1980). *Regression Diagnostics: Identifying Influential Data and Sources of Collinearity.* New York: Wiley.

BELTZER, R., and BIEZEVELD, R. (2004). *De pensioenvoroziening als bindmiddel: Sociale cohesie en de organisatie van pensioen in Nederland.* Amsterdam: Aksant.

BENHABIB, S. (2002). *The Claims of Culture: Equality and Diversity in the Global Era.* Princeton: Princeton University Press.

BENNIE, L., BRAND, J., and MITCHELL, J. (1997). *How Scotland Votes.* Manchester: Manchester University Press.

Bericht der Beauftragten der Bundesregierung für Ausländerfragen über die Lage der Ausländer in der Bundesrepublik Deutschland [Report of the Federal Commissioner for Foreigners Questions on the Situation of Foreigners in the Federal Republic of Germany] (2000). Berlin/Bonn.

Bericht der Gemeinsamen Verfassungskommission [Report of the Joint Commission on the Constitution] (1993). Deutscher Bundestag, Drucksache 12/6000.

BERTHIN SILES, G. (1999). 'Evolución de las Instituciones Estatales', in F. Campero Prudencio (ed.), *Bolivia en el siglo XX: La formación de la Bolivia Contemporánea.* La Paz: Harvard Club de Bolivia.

BLAIR, T., MP, Prime Minister (2003). 'Now is the Time to Pull Together, Not Pull Apart'. Speech delivered at the Burrell Collection, Glasgow, 15 Apr.

BLOEMRAAD, I. (2002). 'The Naturalization Gap: An Institutional Approach to Citizenship Acquisition in Canada and the United States'. *International Migration Review*, 36(1): 194–229.

_____ (2005). 'The Limits of de Tocqueville: How Government Facilitates Organizational Capacity in Newcomer Communities'. *Journal of Ethnic and Migration Studies*, 31: 865–87.

_____ (2006). *Becoming a Citizen: Incorporating Immigrants and Refugees in the United States and Canada.* Berkeley, Calif.: University of California Press.

BOADWAY, R. (2004). 'Should the Canadian Federation be Rebalanced?' Working Paper No. 1. Kingston, Ont.: Institute of Intergovernmental Relations, Queen's University.

BOBO, L., and LICARI, F. C. (1989). 'Education and Political Tolerance'. *Public Opinion Quarterly*, 53: 285–308.

BOISMENU, G. (1993). 'When more is too much: Quebec and the Charlottetown Accord', in R. L. Watts and D. M. Brown (eds.), *Canada: The State of the Federation*

1993. Kingston, Ont.: Institute of Intergovernmental Relations, Queen's University.

BOLARIA, B. S., and LI, P. S. (1988). *Racial Oppression in Canada* (2nd edn.). Toronto: Garamond Press.

Boletín ICCI (2002). 'Evaluación política del movimiento indígena ecuatoriano'. *Boletín ICCI-Ary Rimay*, 4(34). On-line **icci.nativeweb.org**.

Bolivia (2003). *Bolivia: Características sociodemográficas de la población indígena*. La Paz: Instituto Nacional de Estadística, Ministerio de Hacienda, República de Bolivia.

BOLKESTEIN, F. (1991). Address to the Liberal International Conference at Luzern (Friday, 6 Sept.). The Hague: VVD.

BOMMES, M. (1999). *Migration und nationaler Wohlfahrtsstaat. Ein differenzierungstheoretischer Entwurf*. Opladen: Westdeutscher Verlag.

BONFIL BATALLA, G. (ed.) (1981). *Utopía y revolución: el pensamiento político contemporáneo de los indios en América Latina*. Mexico: Editorial Nueva Imagen.

BORNAIS, S. (2002). 'Readers: Africville Cash Won't Change Past', *Daily News* (Halifax), 10 July, p. 5.

—— (2004). 'Africville Was Compensated', *Daily News* (Halifax), 17 Mar., p. 2.

BOS, F. (2006). *De Nederlandse collectieve uitgaven in historisch perspectief*. The Hague: CPB.

BOURDIEU, P. (1977). *Outline of a Theory of Practice*, trans. R. Nice. Cambridge: Cambridge University Press.

—— (1986). 'The Forms of Capital', in J. G. Richardson (ed.), *Handbook of Theory and Research for the Sociology of Education*. New York: Greenwood Press.

—— and WACQUANT, L. J. D. (1992). *An Invitation to Reflexive Sociology*. Chicago: University of Chicago Press.

BRAITHWAITE, V., and LEVI, M. (eds.) (1998). *Trust and Governance*. New York: Russell Sage Foundation.

BRETON, R. (1988). 'From Ethnic to Civic Nationalism: English Canada and Quebec'. *Ethnic and Racial Studies*, 11: 85–102.

—— (2005). *Ethnic Relations in Canada: Institutional Dynamics*. Toronto: University of Toronto Press.

BROCHMANN, G., and HAMMAR, T. (eds.) (1999). *Mechanisms of Immigration Control: A Comparative Analysis of European Regulation Policies*. Oxford: Berg.

BRODIE, J. (2002). 'Citizenship and Solidarity: Reflections on the Canadian Way'. *Citizenship Studies*, 6: 377–94.

—— (2003). 'Globalization, In/Security, and the Paradoxes of the Social', in I. Bakker and S. Gill (eds.), *Power, Production and Social Reproduction: Human In/Security in the Global Political Economy*. Houndmills, UK: Palgrave Macmillan.

BROWN, G., Chancellor of the Exchequer (1999). Speech on *Britishness* delivered to the London School of Economics, 15 Apr.

BRUBAKER, R. (2001). 'The Return of Assimilation?' *Ethnic and Racial Studies*, 24(4): 531–48.

____ (2004). 'In the Name of the Nation: Reflections on Nationalism and Patriotism'. *Citizenship Studies*, 8(2): 115–27.

Bundesregierung (1969). *Jahresbericht der Bundesregierung 1968* [Annual report of the federal government 1968], Bonn.

Bundestag (1994). Debate on 30 June, Plenarprotokoll.

BURSTEIN, P. (1998). 'Bringing the Public back in'. *Social Forces*, 77: 27–62.

BVA Actualité (2005). 'L'opinion en question: les Français et la question de l'intégration des étrangers' (**www.bva.fr/new/index.asp#**).

CAIRNS, A. (1995). *Reconfigurations: Canadian Citizenship and Constitutional Change: Selected Essays*, ed. D. Williams. Toronto: McClelland & Stewart.

CALLA, R. (2000). 'Indigenous Peoples, the Law of Popular Participation and Changes in Government: Bolivia, 1994–1998', in W. Assies, G. van der Haar, and A. Hoekema (eds.), *The Challenge of Diversity: Indigenous Peoples and Reform of the State in Latin America*. Amsterdam: Thela Publishers.

CALLA ORTEGA, R. (2003*a*). 'Indígenas urbanos y rurales', in R. Calla Ortega, *Indígenas, política y reformas en Bolivia: hacia una etnología del estado en América Latina*. Guatemala: Ediciones ICAPI.

____ (2003*b*). *La caída de Sánchez de Lozada, la cuestión indígena y la historia reciente de Bolivia: algunos apuntes y temas para el debate*. La Paz: Plural.

Canada (1969). 'Income Security and Social Services'. Working Paper on the constitution, Ottawa, Ontario.

____ (1994). Ministry of Canadian Heritage News Release, 'Sheila Finestone Tables and Sends Letter on Redress to Ethnocultural Organizations', 14 Dec.

____ (2003). Office of Indian Residential Schools Resolution Canada, 'Negotiations Update' (**www.irsr-rqpa.gc.ca/English/information_sheets.html**).

____ (2004*a*). Indian and Northern Affairs Canada, 'Statement of Reconciliation: Learning from the Past' (**www.ainc-inac.gc.ca/gs/rec_e.html**).

____ (2004*b*). Parliament, House of Commons, Bill C-333, 1st Sess., 38th Parl., 53 Elizabeth II 2004, 'Chinese Canadian Recognition and Restitution Act' (**www.parl.gc.ca/PDF/38/1/parlbus/chambus/house/bills/private/c-333_1.pdf**).

Canadian Labour Congress (1984). *Proceedings of the Fifteenth Constitutional Convention of the Canadian Labour Congress*, Montreal, 28 May–1 June. Ottawa: Canadian Labour Congress.

Canadian Race Relations Foundation (2004). 'Activities' (**www.crr.ca/EN/Activities/eActHome.asp**).

CANOVAN, M. (1996). *Nationhood and Political Theory*. Cheltenham: Edward Elgar.

CAPUTO, C. (2001). 'Multiculturalism and Social Justice in the United States: An Attempt to Reconcile the Irreconcilable within a Pragmatic Liberal Framework'. *Race, Gender and Class*, 8(1): 161–82.

CARROLL, W. K., and RATNER, R. S. (1995). 'Old Unions and New Social Movements'. *Labour/Le Travail*, 35: 195–221.

CARROLL, W. K., and RATNER, R. S. (2001). 'Sustaining Oppositional Cultures in "Post-Socialist" Times: A Comparative Study of Three Social Movement Organizations'. *Sociology*, 35: 605–29.

CARUSO, F., MATHOT, F., MIGNOLET, M., MULQUIN, M. E., and VIESLET, L. (2002). 'Les Transferts entre les régions: réalités contemporaines et recul historique', in Institut Belge des Finances Publiques, *La Fin du déficit budgetaire: analyse de l'évolution récente des finances publiques belges*. Brussels: De Boeck University.

CASTLES, F. (1989). 'Social Protection by Other Means: Australia's Strategy for Coping with External Vulnerability', in F. Castles (ed.), *The Comparative History of Public Policy*. Cambridge: Polity Press.

—— (1998). *Comparative Public Policy: Patterns of Post-War Transformation*. Cheltenham: Edward Elgar.

—— (2004). *The Future of the Welfare State: Crisis Myths and Crisis Realities*. Oxford: Oxford University Press.

—— and MILLER, M. (2003). *The Age of Migration*. Houndmills: Palgrave Macmillan.

CATTOIR, P., and DOCQUIER, F. (1999). 'Sécurité sociale et solidarité interrégionale', in F. Docquier (ed.), *La Solidarité entre les regions: bilans et perspectives*. Brussels: De Boeck Université.

CBS (Statistics Netherlands) (2003). *Allochtonen in Nederland 2003*. Voorburg/Heerlen: CBS.

CHEN, X. (2003). 'The Birth of the Child-Victim Citizen', in J. Brodie and L. Trimble (eds.), *Reinventing Canada: Politics of the 21st Century*. Toronto: Prentice-Hall.

Chinese Canadian National Council (2004*a*). 'National Forum on Race and Homophobia' (**www.ccnc.ca/events/events.html#Forum**).

—— (2004*b*). 'Ride for Redress' (**www.ccnc.ca/RideForRedress**).

—— (2005). 'Canadians for Redress' (**www.ccnc.ca/redress/redress.html**).

CHOUDHRY, S. (2000). 'Distribution vs Recognition: The Case of Anti-Discrimination Laws'. *George Mason Law Review*, 9(1): 145–78.

CHRISTIE, R. N. (2001). Letter to the editor, *Edmonton Journal*, 4 September, p. A11.

CHUA, A. (2004). *World on Fire: How Exporting Free Market Democracy Breeds Ethnic Hatred and Global Instability*. New York: Anchor Books.

CHUNG, A. [pseud.] (2004). Interview by M. James, 9 July, tape recording, Toronto, Ontario.

CITRIN, J., REINGOLD, B., WALTERS, E., and GREEN, D. P. (1990). 'The "Official English" Movement and the Symbolic Politics of Language in the United States'. *Western Political Quarterly*, 43(Sept.): 535–59.

CLAES, R., and CLIFTON, D. (1998). 'Needs and Expectations for Redress of Victims of Abuse at Native Residential Schools'. Paper prepared for the Law Commission of Canada, Ottawa, October (**http://collection.collectionscanada.ca/100/200/301/lcc-cdc/needs_expectations_redres-e/pdf/sage-e.pdf**).

CLAIRMONT, D. H. (1992). 'Moving People: Relocation and Urban Renewal', in Africville Genealogy Society, *The Spirit of Africville*. Halifax: Formac Publishing.

_____ and MAGILL, D. W. (1999). *Africville: The Life and Death of a Canadian Black Community* (3rd edn.). Toronto: Canadian Scholars' Press.

CLAVERO, B. (2000). *Ama Llunku, Abya Yala: Constituyencia Indígena y Código Ladino por América*. Madrid: Centro de Estudios Políticos y Constitucionales.

_____ (n.d.) 'Tratados con Pueblos o Constituciones de Estados: Dilema para América'. Unpublished paper.

COHN-BENDIT, D., and SCHMID, T. (1992). *Heimat Babylon: Das Wagnis der multikulturellen Demokratie* [Heimat Babylon: The Adventure of Multicultural Democracy]. Hamburg: Hoffmann und Campe.

COLEMAN, J. S. (1964). *Introduction to Mathematical Sociology*. New York: Free Press.

COLEMAN, W. D. (1984). *The Independence Movement in Quebec 1945–1980*. Toronto: University of Toronto Press.

COLLIER, P. (2000). 'Ethnicity, Politics and Economic Performance'. *Economics and Politics*, 12(3): 225–46.

_____ (2001). 'Implications of Ethnic Diversity'. *Economic Policy*, 32(16): 127–66.

_____ and GUNNING, J. (1999). 'Explaining Africa's Economic Performance'. *Journal of Economic Literature*, 37(1): 64–111.

COLLINS, J. N. (2000). 'A Sense of Possibility: Ecuador's Indigenous Movement Takes Center Stage'. *NACLA Report on the Americas*, 33 (Mar.–Apr.): 40–9.

COOK, K. S. (ed.) (2001). *Trust in Society*. New York: Russell Sage Foundation.

CORNELIUS, P. K. (ed.) (2003). *The Global Competitiveness Report 2002–2003*. New York: Oxford University Press.

COX, K. (2001). 'N.S. Blacks Join Bid for Reparations', *Globe and Mail* (Toronto), 9 Aug., p. A6.

CREPAZ, M. (1998). 'Inclusion versus Exclusion: Political Institutions and Welfare Expenditures'. *Comparative Politics*, 31: 61–80.

_____ (forthcoming). *Trust without Borders: Immigration, the Welfare State and Identity in Modern Societies*. Ann Arbor, Mich.: The University of Michigan Press.

CRIC (Centre for Research and Information on Canada) (2004). 'Canadians Less Likely this Year to Say Governments Need More Money Yet Support for Equalization Program is Still Very Strong Across the Country'. Press Release on the publication of results from the *Portraits of Canada* survey (**www.cric.ca/en_re/portraits**).

CUNNINGHAM, M. (1999). 'Saying Sorry: The Politics of Apology'. *Political Quarterly*, 70 (July–Sept.): 285–93.

CUPERUS, R., DUFFEK, K., and KANDEL, J. (eds.) (2003). *The Challenge of Diversity: European Social Democracy Facing Migration, Integration and Multiculturalism*. Innsbruck: Studien Verlag.

CYLLORN, J. (2000). Letter to the editor, *Daily News* (Halifax), 31 Mar., p. 15.

DAGEVOS, J., GIJSBERTS, M., and VAN PRAAG, C. (2003). *Rapportage minderheden 2003*. The Hague: SCP.

Daily Mail (2005). '19 Years and Never Done a Day's Work', 10 Aug.

DANDOY, R., and BAUDEWYNS, P. (2005). 'The Preservation of Social Security as a National Function in the Belgian Federal State', in N. McEwen and L. Moreno (eds.), *The Territorial Politics of Welfare*. Abingdon: Routledge.

Datenreport 1997 (1997). *Daten und Fakten über die Bundesrepublik Deutschland* [Data and facts on the Federal Republic of Germany]. Edited by the Statistisches Bundesamt in cooperation with the Wissenschaftszentrum Berlin für Sozialforschung and the Zentrum für Umfragen, Methoden und Analysen, Mannheim. Bonn: Bundeszentrale für politische Bildung.

Datenreport 2004 (2004). *Zahlen und Fakten über die Bundesrepublik Deutschland*. Edited by the Statistisches Bundesamt in cooperation with the Wissenschaftszentrum Berlin für Sozialforschung and the Zentrum für Umfragen, Methoden und Analysen, Mannheim. Bonn: Bundeszentrale für politische Bildung.

DÁVALOS, P. (2003). 'Movimiento indígena ecuatoriano: la constitución de un actor politico' (**icci.nativeweb.org**).

DE BEER, P. (2004). 'Insluiting en uitsluiting: de keerzijden van de verzorgingsstaat', in H. Entzinger and J. van der Meer (eds.), *Grenzeloze solidariteit: Naar een migratiebestendige verzorgingsstaat*. Amsterdam: De Balie.

Declaración Internacional Cancún de los Pueblos Indígenas (2003). Reproduced in *SERVINDI Servicio de Información Indígena* 39, 2004 via e-mail. Received 5 Mar. 2004.

DE COCK, J. (2002). 'Federalism and the Belgian Health-care System', in K. G. Banting and S. Corbett (eds.), *Health Policy and Federalism*. Montreal and Kingston: McGill-Queen's University Press.

DE HART, B. (2004). 'Political Debates on Dual Nationality in the Netherlands (1990–2003)'. *IMIS-Beiträge*, 24: 149–62.

DE HEER, J.-C. (2004). 'The Concept of Integration in Converging Dutch Migration and Minorities Policies'. *IMIS-Beiträge*, 24: 177–88.

DEMEURE V., J. (1999). 'Agricultura; de la subsistencia a la competencia internacional', in F. Campero Prudencio (ed.), *Bolivia en el siglo XX: la formación de la Bolivia Contemporánea*. La Paz: Havard Club de Bolivia.

DENHAM, J. (2004). 'The Fairness Code'. *Prospect*, June, p. 29.

DICKEY, C. J. (2001). Letter to the editor, *Vancouver Sun*, 16 Jan., p. A15.

Die Grünen (1990). Die Grünen im Bundestag, *Die multikulturelle Gesellschaft, Argumente* [The multicultural society], Bonn.

DUFFY, B. (2004a). 'Can We Have Trust and Diversity?' (**www.Mori.com/polls/2003/community.shtml**).

—— (2004b). 'Free Rider Phobia'. *Prospect*, Feb., pp. 16–17.

EASTERLY, W. (2001a). 'Can Institutions Resolve Ethnic Conflict?' *Economic Development and Cultural Change*, 49(4): 687–706.

—— (2001b). *The Elusive Quest for Economic Development: Economists' Adventures and Misadventures in the Tropics*. Cambridge, Mass.: MIT Press.

—— and LEVINE, R. (1997). 'Africa's Growth Tragedy: Policies and Ethnic Divisions'. *Quarterly Journal of Economics*, 112: 1203–50.

Economist (2004). 'Bolivia's Troubles: From Here to 2007, Without Falling?' 24 Jan., pp. 33–4.

_____ (2005). 'Australians Old and New', 7 May, p. 13.

EDELMAN, M. (1977). *Political Language: Words that Succeed and Politics that Fail.* New York: Academic Press.

ENTZINGER, H. (2003). 'The Rise and Fall of Multiculturalism in the Netherlands', in C. Joppke and E. Morawska (eds.), *Toward Assimilation and Citizenship: Immigrants in Liberal Nation-States.* London: Palgrave.

_____ (2004). *Integration and Orientation Courses in a European Perspective.* Nürnberg: Bundesamt für Migration und Flüchtlinge.

_____ (forthcoming). 'Changing the Rules While the Game is on: From Multiculturalism to Assimilation in the Netherlands', in Y. M. Bodemann and G. Yurdakul (eds.), *Migration, Citizenship, Ethnos: Incorporation Regimes in Germany, Western Europe and North America.* New York: Palgrave MacMillan.

_____ and VAN DER MEER, J. (eds.) (2004). *Grenzeloze solidariteit: Naar een migratiebestendige verzorgingsstaat.* Amsterdam: De Balie.

ERIKSON, R. S. (1976). 'The Relationship between Public Opinion and State Policy: A New Look Based on Some Forgotten Data'. *American Journal of Political Science,* 20(1): 511–35.

_____ WRIGHT, G. C., and MCIVER, J. P. (1993*). Statehouse Democracy: Public Opinion and Policy in the American States.* Cambridge: Cambridge University Press.

ESPING-ANDERSEN, G. (1990). *The Three Worlds of Welfare Capitalism.* Cambridge: Polity/Cambridge University Press; Princeton: Princeton University Press.

_____ (1996). *Welfare States in Transition: National Adaptations in Global Economies.* London: Sage Publications.

Eurobarometer 53 (2000). (European Commission). Fieldwork: April–May. Made available by Zentralarchiv für Empirische Sozialforschung, University of Cologne, Cologne, Germany.

EVANDROU, M., FALKINGHAM, J., HILLS, J., and LE GRAND, J. (1993). 'Welfare Benefits in Kind and Income Distribution'. *Fiscal Studies,* 14: 57–76.

EVANS, G. (1999). 'Europe: A New Electoral Cleavage?' in G. Evans and P. Norris (eds.), *Critical Elections: British Parties and Voters in Long-term Perspective.* London: Sage.

EVANS, G. (2000). 'The Working Class and New Labour: A Parting of the Ways?' in R. Jowell, J. Curtice, A. Park, K. Thomson, C. Bromley, L. Jarvis, and N. Stratford (eds.), *British Social Attitudes, the 17th Report: Focusing on Diversity.* London: Sage.

_____ (2002*a*). 'In Search of Tolerance', in A. Park, J. Curtice, K. Thomson, L. Jarvis, and C. Bromley (eds.), *British Social Attitudes: The 19th Report.* London: Sage.

_____ (2002*b*). 'European Integration, Party Politics and Voting in the 2001 Election'. *British Elections & Parties Review,* 12: 95-110.

_____ and BUTT, S. (2005). 'Followers or Leaders? Political Parties and Attitudes towards the European Union'. *British Social Attitudes: The 22nd Report.* London: Sage.

EVANS, G., HEATH, A. F., and LALLJEE, M. G. (1996). 'Measuring Left–Right and Libertarian–Authoritarian Values in the British Electorate'. *British Journal of Sociology*, 47: 93–112.

FAIST, T. (1995). 'Ethnicization and the Racialization of Welfare-State Politics in Germany and the USA'. *Ethnic and Racial Studies*, 18(2): 219–50.

FANFANI, E. T. (2001). 'Metamorfosis del estado y la política: del poder central al poder local', in IIG, *Biblioteca de Ideas*, Colección de papers, Paper no. 10 (**www.iigov.org**).

FAVELL, A. (2001). *Philosophies of Integration: Immigration and the Idea of Citizenship in France and Britain*. New York: St Martin's Press.

FEARON, J., and LAITIN, D. (2003). 'Ethnicity, Insurgency and Civil War'. *American Political Science Review*, 97(1): 75–90.

FELLOWES, M. C., and ROWE, G. (2004). 'Politics and the New American Welfare State'. *American Journal of Political Science*, 48 (April): 362–73.

FENTIE, A. (1995). Letter to the editor, *Edmonton Journal*, 16 Jan., p. A7.

FERMIN, A. (2001). *The Justification of Mandatory Integration Programmes for New Immigrants*, ERCOMER Research Paper 2001/01. Utrecht: European Research Centre on Migration and Ethnic Relations.

FERRERA, M. (1996). 'The Southern Model of Welfare in Social Europe'. *Journal of European Social Policy*, 6(1): 17–37.

FIJALKOWSKI, J. (1991). 'Nationale Identität versus multikulturelle Gesellschaft: Entwicklungen der Problemlage und Alternativen der Orientierung in der politischen Kultur der Bundesrepublik in den 80er Jahren' [National identity versus multicultural society. The development of the situation and alternative orientations in the Federal Republic's political culture in the 1980s], in W. Süß (ed.), *Die Bundesrepublik in den achtziger Jahren. Innenpolitik, Politische Kultur, Außenpolitik*. Opladen: Leske und Budrich.

FILSINGER, D. (2002). 'Die Entwicklung der kommunalen Integrationspolitik und Integrationspraxis der neunziger Jahre' [The development of local integration policies and practice in the 1990s]. *iza*, 24(2): 13–20.

Finance Ministers (2003). 'Strengthening the Equalization Program: Perspective of the Finance Ministers of the Provinces and Territories', September (**www.gov.ns.ca/finance/Equalization.pdf**).

FISH, S., and BROOKS, R. (2004). 'Does Diversity Hurt Democracy?' *Journal of Democracy*, 15(1): 154–66.

FORDING, R. C. (1997). 'The Conditional Effect of Violence as a Political Tactic: Mass Insurgency, Welfare Generosity, and Electoral Context in the American States'. *American Journal of Political Science*, 41(1): 1–29.

FORMA, P. (1999). 'Welfare State Opinions among Citizens, MP Candidates and Elites', in S. Svallfors and P. Taylor-Gooby (eds.), *The End of the Welfare State?* London : Routledge.

FORTUYN, P. (2002). *De puinhopen van acht jaar paars*. Uithoorn: Karakter.

FOURNIER, K. (1995). Letter to the editor, *Toronto Star*, 14 Sept., p. A24.

FRANK, S. (1995). *Staatsräson, Moral und Interesse: Die Diskussion um die 'Multikulturelle Gesellschaft' 1980-1993* [Reason of State, Mores and Interests: The Debate about the 'Multicultural Society']. Freiburg: Lambertus.

FRANK, T. (2004). *What's the Matter with Kansas? How Conservatives Won the Heart of America*. New York: Henry Holt and Company.

FRASER, N. (1997). 'From Redistribution to Recognition? Dilemmas of Justice in a "Postsocialist" Age', in *Justice Interruptus: Critical Reflections on the 'Postsocialist' Condition*. New York: Routledge.

—— (1998). 'Social Justice in the Age of Identity Politics: Redistribution, Recognition and Participation', in *The Tanner Lectures on Human Values*, Vol. 19. Salt Lake City: University of Utah Press.

—— (2003). 'Social Justice in the Age of Identity Politics: Redistribution, Recognition, and Participation', in N. Fraser and A. Honneth, *Redistribution or Recognition? A Political-Philosophical Exchange*. London: Verso.

FREEMAN, G. (1986). 'Migration and the Political Economy of the Welfare State'. *Annals of the American Academy of Political and Social Science*, 485: 51–63.

GAGNON, A.-G. (1993). 'Quebec-Canada: Constitutional Developments', in A.-G. Gagnon (ed.), *Quebec, State and Society* (2nd edn.). Scarborough, Ont.: Nelson Canada.

—— and LACHAPELLE, G. (1996). 'Quebec Confronts Canada: Two Competing Societal Projects Searching for Legitimacy'. *Publius, The Journal of Federalism*, 26(3): 177–91.

GALLIGAN, B., and ROBERTS, W. (2004). *Australian Citizenship*. Melbourne: Melbourne University Press.

GALSTON, W. (2001). 'Who's a Liberal?' *Public Interest*, 144 (Summer).

GAMARRA, E. (2003). 'Political Parties since 1964: The Construction of Bolivia's Multiparty System', in M. S. Grindle and P. Domingo (eds.), *Proclaiming Revolution: Bolivia in Comparative Perspective*. Cambridge, Mass.: David Rockefeller Center series on Latin American Studies, Harvard University.

GAMARRA, E., and MALLOY, J. M. (1995). 'The Patrimonial Dynamics of Party Politics in Bolivia', in S. Mainwaring and T. R. Scully (eds.), *Building Democratic Institutions: Party Systems in Latin America*. Stanford, Calif.: Stanford University Press.

GEIßLER, H. (ed.) (1983). *Ausländer in Deutschland: Für eine gemeinsame Zukunft* [Foreigners in Germany: For a Joint Future], vol. ii. Munich: Günter Olzog Verlag.

—— (1990). *Zugluft: Politik in stürmischer Zeit* [Politics in Stormy Times]. Munich: C. Bertelsmann.

GELISSEN, J. (2002). *Worlds of Welfare, Worlds of Consent?* Leiden: Brill.

GIDDENS, A. (1971). *Capitalism and Modern Social Theory: An Analysis of the Writings of Marx, Durkheim and Max Weber*. Cambridge, Mass.: Cambridge University Press.

References

GILENS, M. (1999). *Why Americans Hate Welfare: Race, Media, and the Politics of Antipoverty Policy*. Chicago, Ill.: University of Chicago Press.

—— (2003). 'How the Poor Became Black: The Racialization of American Poverty in the Mass Media', in J. Soss, S. Schram, and R. Fording (eds.), *Race and the Politics of Welfare Reform*. Ann Arbor, Mich.: University of Michigan Press.

GITLIN, T. (1995). *The Twilight of Common Dreams: Why America is Wracked by Culture Wars*. New York, NY: Metropolitan Books.

GLAZER, N. (1997). *We Are All Multiculturalists Now*. Cambridge, Mass.: Harvard University Press.

—— (1998). 'The American Welfare State: Exceptional no Longer?' in H. Cavanna (ed.), *Challenges to the Welfare State: Internal and External Dynamics for Change*. Cheltenham, UK: Edward Elgar.

Globe and Mail (2003*a*). 'On-line Poll Results' (**www.globeandmail.com**).

—— (2003*b*). 'Canadians Going to Japan for Germ-Warfare Case', 16 May, p. A6.

GOERZEN, M. (2004). 'The Japanese-Canadian War Experience Part I' (**www.theforeigner-japan.com/index.htm?http://www.theforeigner-japan.com/archives/200405/feature.htm**).

GOGOLIN, I., NEUMANN, U., AND REUTER, L. (eds.) (2001). *Schulbildung für Kinder aus Minderheiten in Deutschland 1989–1999* [School Education for Minority Children in Germany, 1989–1999]. Münster, etc.: Waxmann.

GONZALEZ, M. L. (1994). 'How Many Indigenous People?' in G. Psacharopoulos and H. A. Patrinos (eds.), *Indigenous People and Poverty in Latin America: An Empirical Analysis*. Washington, DC: The World Bank.

GOODHART, D. (2004). 'Too Diverse?' *Prospect Magazine*, Feb.

GOODIN, R. E., and LE GRAND, J. (1987). *Not Only the Poor: The Middle Classes and the Welfare State*. London: Allen and Unwin.

GRAFTON, Q., KNOWLES, S., and OWEN, D. (2002). 'Social Divergence and Productivity: Making a Connection', in A. Sharpe, F. St-Hilaire, and K. Banting (eds.), *The Review of Economic Performance and Social Progress: Towards a Social Understanding of Productivity*. Montreal: Institute for Research on Public Policy.

GRAY, V., and HANSEN, R. L. (2004). *Politics in the American States: A Comparative Analysis* (8th edn.). Washington, DC: Congressional Quarterly Press.

GREBE LÓPEZ, H. (2001). 'The Private Sector and Democratization', in J. Crabtree and L. Whitehead (eds.), *Towards Democratic Viability: The Bolivian Experience*. Houndmills: Palgrave.

GRINDLE, M. S. (2000). *Audacious Reforms: Institutional Invention and Democracy in Latin America*. Baltimore: The Johns Hopkins University Press.

GUEST, D. (1997). *The Emergence of Social Security in Canada* (3rd edn.). Vancouver: UBC Press.

GUGGENBERGER, B., PREUß, U. K., and ULLMANN, W. (eds.) (1991). *Eine Verfassung für Deutschland. Manifest—Text—Plädoyers* [A Constitution for Germany: Manifesto—Text—Pleadings]. Munich: Hanser.

GUIBERNAU, M. (1999). *Nations without States*. Cambridge: Polity Press.

GUINDON, H. (1988). *Quebec Society: Tradition, Modernity and Nationhood*. Toronto: University of Toronto Press.

GUSTAFSON, B. (2002). 'Paradoxes of Liberal Indigenism: Indigenous Movements, State Processes, and Intercultural Reform in Bolivia', in D. Maybury-Lewis (ed.), *The Politics of Ethnicity: Indigenous Peoples in Latin American States*. Cambridge, Mass.: Harvard University Press.

HAHN, M. J. (1993). 'Die rechtliche Stellung der Minderheiten in Deutschland' [The Legal Position of the Minorities in Germany], in J. A. Frowein et al. (eds.), *Das Minderheitenrecht europäischer Staaten*, part 1. Berlin, etc.: Springer.

HALE, C. R. (2002). 'Does Multiculturalism Menace? Governance, Cultural Rights, and the Politics of Identity in Guatemala'. *Journal of Latin American Studies*, 34 (Aug.): 485–524.

HANSEN, R. (forthcoming). 'Diversity, Integration and the Turn from Multiculturalism in the UK', in K. Banting, T. Courchene, and L. Seidle (eds.), *Belonging? Diversity, Recognition and Shared Citizenship in Canada*. Montreal: Institute for Research on Public Policy.

HARDIN, R. (2002). *Trust and Trustworthiness*. New York: Russell Sage Foundation.

HARRINGTON, M. (1962). *The Other America: Poverty in the United States*. New York: Macmillan.

HÄUSSERMANN, H., and SIEBEL, W. (2001). *Soziale Integration und ethnische Schichtung. Zusammenhänge zwischen räumlicher und sozialer Integration* [Social integration and ethnic stratification: Connections between spacial and social integration]. *Gutachten im Auftrag der Unabhängigen Kommission 'Zuwanderung'*, Berlin/Oldenburg.

HEATH, A. F., JOWELL, R., CURTICE, J., and EVANS, G. A. (1990). 'The Rise of a New Political Agenda?' *European Sociological Review*, 6: 31–49.

HEATH, A., and ROTHON, C. (2003). 'Trends in Racial Prejudice', in A. Park, J. Curtice, K. Thomson, L. Jarvis, and C. Bromley (eds.), *British Social Attitudes: The 20th Report: Continuity and Change Over Two Decades*. London: Sage.

HEITMEYER, W. (1998). 'Versagt die "Integrationsmaschine" Stadt? Zum Problem der ethnisch-kulturellen Segregation und ihrer Konfliktfolgen' [Is the Integration Machine City Failing? On the Problem of Ethnic-Cultural Segregation and Resulting Conflicts], in W. Heitmeyer, R. Dollase, and O. Backes (eds.), *Die Krise der Städte*. Frankfurt on Main: Suhrkamp.

—— MÜLLER, J., and SCHRÖDER, H. (1997). *Verlockender Fundamentalismus: Türkische Jugendliche in Deutschland* [Tempting Fundamentalism: Turkish Youths in Germany]. Frankfurt on Main: Suhrkamp.

HELD, D., and KELLY, P. (eds.) (2002). *Multiculturalism Reconsidered*. Cambridge: Polity Press.

HERO, R. E. (1998). *Faces of Inequality: Social Diversity and American Politics*. New York: Oxford University Press.

HERO, R. E., and TOLBERT, C. (1996). 'A Racial/Ethnic Diversity Interpretation of Politics and Policy in the States of the US'. *American Journal of Political Science*, 40: 851–71.

HERSHBERG, E. (2003). 'Latin America at the Crossroads: An Introductory Essay'. *NACLA Report on the Americas*, 37(3): 20–3.

HICKS, A. (1999). *Social Democracy and Welfare Capitalism: A Century of Income Security Policies*. Ithaca, NY: Cornell University Press.

—— and ESPING-ANDERSEN, G. (2005). 'Comparative and Historical Studies of Social Policy and the Welfare State', in T. Janoski, R. R. Alford, A. Hicks, and M. Schwartz (eds.), *The Handbook of Political Sociology: States, Civil Societies, and Globalization*. Cambridge: Cambridge University Press.

—— and MISRA, M. (1993). 'Political Resources and Growth of Welfare in Affluent Capitalist Democracies, 1960–1982'. *American Journal of Sociology*, 99(3): 668–710.

—— and SWANK, D. (1992). 'Political Institutions and Welfare Spending in Industrialized Countries, 1960–82'. *American Political Science Review*, 86(3): 658–74.

HOBSBAWM, E. J. (1984). 'Labour and Human Rights', in *Worlds of Labour: Further Studies in the History of Labour*. London: Weidenfeld & Nicolson.

HOBSON, P. A. R. (2002). 'What Do We Already Know about the Appropriate Design for a Fiscal Equalization Program in Canada and How Well Are We Doing?' Working Paper No. 26. Kingston, Ont.: Institute of Intergovernmental Relations, Queen's University.

HOFFMANN, L. (2002). 'Ausländerbeiräte in der Krise' [Foreigners' advisory councils in crisis]. *Zeitschrift für Ausländerrecht und Ausländerpolitik*, 21(2): 63–70.

HÖRMEL, U., and SCHERR, A. (2004). *Bildung für die Einwanderungsgesellschaft* [Education for the Immigration Society]. Policy Paper for the Bertelsmann Foundation (**www.bertelsmann-stiftung.de**).

HOUGHTON, J., with BELL, B. (2004). 'Indigenous Movements and Globalization in Latin America'. *Native Americas,* Spring: 11–19.

HOWARD, C. (1999). 'The American Welfare State, or States?' *Political Research Quarterly*, 52(2): 421–42.

HTUN, M. (2004). 'From "Racial Democracy" to Affirmative Action: Changing State Policy on Race in Brazil'. *Latin American Research Review*, 39(1): 59–89.

HUBER, E. (1996). 'Options for Social Policy in Latin America: Neoliberal versus Social Democratic Models', in G. Esping-Andersen (ed.), *Welfare State in Transition: National Adaptations in Global Economy*. London: Sage Publications.

—— RAGIN, C., and STEPHENS, J. (1993). 'Social Democracy, Christian Democracy, Constitutional Structure and the Welfare State'. *American Journal of Sociology*, 99(3): 711–49.

—— and SOLT, F. (2004). 'Successes and Failures of Neoliberalism'. *Latin American Research Review*, 39(3): 150–64.

_____ and STEPHENS, J. D. (2000). 'The Political Economy of Pension Reform: Latin America in Comparative Perspective'. Occasional Paper no. 7, UNRISD, Geneva, May.

_____ (2001). _Development and Crisis of the Welfare State: Parties and Policies in Global Markets._ Chicago: University of Chicago Press.

HUNTINGTON, S. P. (2004). _Who Are We? The Challenges to America's National Identity._ New York: Simon and Schuster.

HVINDEN, B. (2006). _Is Increased Cross-Border Mobility Incompatible with Redistribution Welfare States? The North European Case_ (Bremen: Centre for Social Policy Research, University of Bremen, Working Paper #2/2006).

HYMAN, H. H., and WRIGHT, C. R. (1979). _Education's Lasting Influence on Values._ Chicago: University of Chicago Press.

IBARRA, H. (n.d.). 'Tendencias y cambios en las relaciones indígenas Estado en los Andes', in _Pueblos indígenas de América Latina: retos para el nuevo milenio_, OXFAM, Ford Foundation (cd-rom).

INGLEHART, R. et al. (2003). 'World Values Surveys and European Values Surveys, 1981–1984, 1990–1993, and 1995–1997' [computer file]. ICPSR02790-v1. Ann Arbor, Mich.: Institute for Social Research [producer], 1999 and Inter-university Consortium for Political and Social Research [distributor], 2003.

_____ (2004a). 'World Values Surveys and European Values Surveys, 1981–1984, 1990–1993, 1995–1997, and 1999–2001' [computer file]. Ann Arbor, Mich.: Institute for Social Research [producer], 1999 and Inter-university Consortium for Political and Social Research [distributor], 2004.

_____ (2004b). 'World Values Surveys and European Values Surveys, 1999–2001' [computer file]. Ann Arbor, Mich.: Institute for Social Research [producer], 1999 and Inter-university Consortium for Political and Social Research [distributor], 2004.

Integrationspolitisches Memorandum der Bundesarbeitsgemeinschaft Freier Wohlfahrtspflege (c.2001).

Inter-American Dialogue (2002). _Race Report._ Washington: Inter-American Dialogue.

IRELAND, P. (2004). _Becoming Europe: Immigration, Integration, and the Welfare State._ Pittsburgh: University of Pittsburgh Press.

ISSP (International Social Survey Programme) (1998). _1995 National Identity Codebook._ Cologne: Zentralarchiv für Empirische Sozialforschung, University of Cologne.

IVARSFLATEN, I. (2005). 'Threatened by Diversity: Why Restrictive Asylum and Immigration Policies Appeal to Western Europeans'. _Journal of Elections, Public Opinion & Parties_, 1: 21–45.

JAMES, E. (1987). 'The Public/Private Division of Responsibility for Education in International Comparison'. _Economics of Education Review_, 6(1): 1–14.

_____ (1993). 'Why Do Different Countries Choose a Different Public/Private Mix of Education Services?' _Journal of Human Resources_, 28(3): 531–92.

JAMES, M. (1999). 'Redress Politics and Canadian Citizenship', in T. McIntosh and H. Lazar (eds.), *The State of the Federation 1998/99: How Canadians Connect*. Montreal: McGill-Queen's University Press.

—— (2004). 'Recognition, Redistribution, and Redress: The Case of the 'Chinese Head Tax'. *Canadian Journal of Political Science*, 37(4): 1–20.

—— (forthcoming). 'The Permanent-Emergency Compensation State: A "Postsocialist" Tale of Political Dystopia', in M. Orsini and M. Smith (eds.), *Critical Policy Studies: Contemporary Canadian Approaches*. Vancouver: University of British Columbia Press.

JAMES, P., and LUSTZIG, M. (2002). 'Say Goodbye to the Dream of One Canada: The Costly Failure to Purchase National Unity', in H. Telford and H. Lazar (eds.), *Canada: The State of the Federation, 2001: Canadian Political Cultures in Transition*. Montreal-Kingston: McGill-Queen's University Press.

JEFFERY, C. (2005). 'Devolution and Social Citizenship: Which Society, Whose Citizenship?' in S. L. Greer (ed.), *Territory, Democracy, and Justice*. Basingstoke: Palgrave.

JENSON, J., and PHILLIPS, S. D. (2001). 'Redesigning the Canadian Citizenship Regime: Remaking the Institutions of Representation', in C. Crouch, K. Eder, and D. Tambini (eds.), *Citizenship, Markets, and the State*. Oxford: Oxford University Press.

JOHNSON, A. F. (1997). 'Strengthening Society III: Social Security', in A. F. Johnson and A. Stritch (eds.), *Canadian Public Policy: Globalization and Political Parties*. Toronto: Copp Clark.

JOHNSON, M. (2001). 'The Impact of Social Diversity and Racial Attitudes on Social Welfare Policy'. *State Politics and Policy Quarterly*, 1(1): 27–49.

—— (2003). 'Racial Context, Public Attitudes, and Welfare Effort in the American States', in J. Soss, S. Schram, and R. Fording (eds.), *Race and the Politics of Welfare Reform*. Ann Arbor, Mich.: University of Michigan Press.

JONES, J. M. (2005). 'Race, Ideology and Support for Affirmative Action' (**www.gallup.com**).

JONES, M. (1999). Letter to the editor, *The Daily Bulletin* (Kimberley, BC), 13 Dec., p. 4.

JOPPKE, C. (2004). 'The Retreat of Multiculturalism in the Liberal State: Theory and Policy'. *British Journal of Sociology*, 55(2): 237–57.

—— (forthcoming). 'Convergent Trends in Immigrant Immigration in Western Europe', in K. Banting, T. Courchene, and L. Seidle (eds.), *Belonging? Diversity, Recognition and Shared Citizenship in Canada*. Montreal: Institute for Research on Public Policy.

—— and MORAWSKA, E. (2003). 'Integrating Immigrants in Liberal Nation-States: Policies and Practices', in C. Joppke and E. Morawska (eds.), *Toward Assimilation and Citizenship: Immigrants in Liberal Nation-States*. London: Palgrave/Macmillan.

JORDÁN POZO, R. (1999). 'Minería; Siglo XX: la era del estaño', in F. Campero Prudencio (ed.), *Bolivia en el siglo XX: la formación de la Bolivia Contemporánea*. La Paz: Havard Club de Bolivia.

JOWELL, R., and the Central Co-ordinating Team (2003). *European Social Survey 2002/2003: Technical Report*. London: Centre for Comparative Social Surveys, City University.

JUNGER-TAS, J. (2002). 'Etnische minderheden, maatschappelijke integratie en criminaliteit', in J. Lucassen and A. de Ruijter (eds.), *Nederland multicultureel en pluriform?* Amsterdam: Aksant.

KANG, M. L. [pseud.] (2004). Interview by M. James, 9 July, tape recording, Toronto, Ontario.

KASCHUBA, W. (1995). 'Kulturalismus: Kultur statt Gesellschaft?' [Culturalism: Culture instead of Society?]. *Geschichte und Gesellschaft*, 21(1): 80–95.

KATE, M.-A. (2005). 'The Provision of Protection to Asylum-Seekers in Destination Countries'. Working Paper No. 114, New Issues in Refugee Research, Evaluation and Policy Analysis Unit, UNHCR.

KATZENSTEIN, P. J. (1987). *Policy and Politics in West Germany: The Growth of a Semisovereign State*. Philadelphia: Temple University Press.

KATZNELSON, I. (1981). *City Trenches: Urban Politics and the Patterning of Class in the United States*. New York: Pantheon Books.

KEATING, M. (2001). *Nations against the State* (2nd edn.). New York: Macmillan Press.

—— (2002). 'Devolution and Public Policy in the United Kingdom: Divergence or Convergence?' in J. Adams and P. Robinson (eds.), *Devolution in Practice: Public Policy Differences within the UK*. London: IPPR.

—— STEVENSON, L., CAIRNEY, P., and MACLEAN, K. (2004). 'Does Devolution Make a Difference? Legislative Output and Policy Divergence in Scotland'. *Journal of Legislative Studies*, 9(3): 110–39.

KEEBLE, E. (2005). 'Immigration, Civil Liberties, and National/Homeland Security'. *International Journal*, 60(2): 359–74.

KEISER, L. R., MUESER, P. R., and CHOI, S.-W. (2004). 'Race, Bureaucratic Discretion and Implementation of Welfare Reform'. *American Journal of Political Science*, 48 (Apr.): 314–27.

KENWORTHY, L. (2004). *Egalitarian Capitalism*. New York: Russell Sage Foundation.

KIMBER, S. (1992). 'The Africville Experience: Lessons for the Future', in Africville Genealogy Society, *The Spirit of Africville*. Halifax: Formac Publishing.

KIRBY, C. (1987). Letter to the editor, *The Ottawa Citizen*, 18 Aug., p. A9.

KITSCHELT, H. (1995). *The Radical Right in Western Europe: A Comparative Analysis*. Ann Arbor, Mich.: University of Michigan Press.

KLEIN, H. S. (2003). 'Social Change in Bolivia since 1952', in M. S. Grindle and P. Domingo (eds.), *Proclaiming Revolution: Bolivia in Comparative Perspective*. Cambridge, Mass.: Harvard University Press.

References

KLINKNER, P. A., and SMITH, R. M. (1999). *The Unsteady March: The Rise and Decline of Racial Equality in America*. Chicago: University of Chicago Press.

KOBAYASHI, A. (1992). 'The Japanese-Canadian Redress Settlement and its Implications for "Race Relations" '. *Canadian Ethnic Studies*, 24: 1–19.

KOOPMANS, RUUD (2005). 'Tradeoffs between Equality and Difference: The Failure of Dutch Multiculturalism in Cross-National Perpective'. Paper for the Conference on Immigrant Political Incorporation, Radcliffe Institute for Advanced Study, 22–3 April.

KORPI, W. (1983). *The Democratic Class Struggle*. London: Routledge & Kegan Paul.

—— (1989). 'Power, Politics, and State Autonomy in the Development of Social Citizenship: Social Rights During Sickness in Eighteen OECD Countries Since 1930'. *American Sociological Review*, 54: 309–28.

—— and PALME, J. (2003). 'New Politics and Class Politics in the Context of Austerity and Globalization: Welfare State Regress in 18 Countries, 1975–1995'. *American Political Science Review*, 97: 425–46.

—— and SHALEV, M. (1980). 'Strikes, Power and Politics in the Western Nations: 1900–1976'. *Political Power and Social Theory*, 1: 301–34.

KRÜGER-POTRATZ, M. (2004). 'Migration als Herausforderung für Bildungspolitik' [Migration as a Challenge for Education Policy], in R. Leiprecht (ed.), *Schule in der pluriformen Einwanderungsgesellschaft*. Königstein/Taunus: Wochenschauverlag.

KRUSE, I., ORREN, H. E., and ANGENENDT, S. (2003). 'The Failure of Immigration Reform in Germany'. *German Politics*, 12(3): 129–45.

KUKATHAS, C. (2003). *The Liberal Archipelago: A Theory of Diversity and Freedom*. Oxford: Oxford University Press.

Kultusministerkonferenz (1996). *Empfehlung der Kultusministerkonferenz 'Interkulturelle Bildung und Erziehung in der Schule'*. Beschluss vom 25.10.1996, **www.buendnis-toleranz.de** ['Intercultural Education in Schools'—Resolution of the Standing Conference of the Ministers of Education and Cultural Affairs of 25/10/1996].

KYMLICKA, W. (1995). *Multicultural Citizenship*. Oxford: Oxford University Press.

—— (1998). *Finding our Way: Rethinking Ethnocultural Relations in Canada*. Oxford: Oxford University Press.

—— (2001). *Politics in the Vernacular: Nationalism, Multiculturalism, and Citizenship*. Oxford: Oxford University Press.

—— (2002). *Contemporary Political Philosophy: An Introduction*. Oxford: Oxford University Press.

—— (2003). 'Canadian Multiculturalism in Comparative and Historical Perspective'. *Constitutional Forum*, 13(1): 1–8.

—— (2004). *Culturally Responsive Policies*. Report prepared for the 2004 United Nations Human Development Report (**http://hdr.undp.org/publications/background_papers/2004/HDR2004_Will_Kymlicka.pdf**).

374

____ (forthcoming *a*). 'A Multicultural Welfare State?' in Gray Craig, David Gordon, and Tania Burchardt (eds), *Social Justice and Public Policy: Seeking Fairness in Diverse Societies*. Bristol: Policy Press.

____ (forthcoming *b*). *Multiculturalism On The Move: Navigating the New International Politics of Diversity*. Oxford: Oxford University Press.

Labour Party (Scottish Council) (1958). *Let Scotland Prosper: Labour's Plans for Scotland's Progress*. Document prepared by working party of representatives of NEC, SCLP, and the Scottish Group of Parliamentary Labour Party.

LA FERRARA, E. (2002). 'Self-Help Groups and Income Generation in the Informal Settlements of Nairobi'. *Journal of African Economics*, 11(1): 61–89.

____ (2003). 'Ethnicity and Reciprocity: A Model of Credit Transactions in Ghana'. *American Economic Review*, 93(5): 1730–51.

LAITIN, D., and POSNER, D. (2001). 'The Implications of Constructivism for Constructing Ethnic Fractionalization Indices'. *Newletter of the Comparative Politics Section of the American Political Science Association*, 12: 13–17.

Landeshauptstadt München (2002). *Münchner Bürgerbefragung 2000: Soziale Entwicklung und Lebenssituation der Münchner Bürgerinnen und Bürger* [Munich citizens survey. Social development and life situation of Munich's citizens], Munich (**www.muenchen.de/Rathaus/plan/Stadtentwicklung/grundlagen**).

LAURIN-FRENETTE, N. (1978). *Production de l'état et formes de la nation*. Montreal: Nouvelle Optique.

LAZAR, H., ST-HILAIRE, F., and TREMBLAY, J.-F. (2004). 'Vertical Fiscal Imbalance, Myth or Reality', in H. Lazar and F. St-Hilaire (eds.), *Money, Politics and Health Care*. Montreal: The Institute for Research on Public Policy.

LEGGEWIE, C. (1993). *Multi Kulti: Spielregeln für die Vielvölkerrepublik* [Multi Kulti. Rules for the multinational republic] (3rd edn.). Berlin: Rotbuch Verlag.

LE GRAND, J. (1982). *The Strategy of Equality: Redistribution and the Social Services*. London: Allen and Unwin.

LEÓN, J. T. (2001). 'El contexto y el sistema politico en el movimiento indígena ecuatoriano'. Paper prepared for the conference, 'Beyond the Lost Decade: Indigenous Movements and the Transformation of Development and Democracy in Latin America', Princeton University, 2–3 Mar.

LETTS, D. (2002). 'Time for an Apology' (**www.rabble.ca/rabble_interview.shtml?x=17164**).

LEVITSKY, S., and CAMERON, M. A. (2001). 'Democracy without Parties? Political Parties and Regime Collapse in Fujimori's Peru'. Paper prepared for presentation at the Congress of the Latin American Studies Association in Washington, DC, 6–8 Sept.

LEVY, J. (2000). *The Multiculturalism of Fear*. Oxford: Oxford University Press.

LIAN, B., and ONEAL, J. (1997). 'Cultural Diversity and Economic Development: A Cross-National Study of 98 Countries, 1960–1985'. *Economic Development and Cultural Change*, 46: 61–77.

LIEBERMAN, R. C. (2003). 'Race and the Limits of Solidarity: American Welfare State Development in Comparative Perspective', in J. Soss, S. Schram, and R. Fording (eds.), *Race and the Politics of Welfare Reform*. Ann Arbor, Mich.: University of Michigan Press.

LIJPHART, A. (1975). *The Politics of Accommodation: Pluralism and Democracy in the Netherlands*. Berkeley, Calif.: University of California Press.

LINEBERRY, R. L., and SHARKANSKY, I. (1978). *Urban Politics and Public Policy*. New York: Harper and Row.

LIPSET, S. M. (1981). *Political Man* (2nd edn.). Garden City, NY: Doubleday.

—— and MARKS, G. (2000). *It Didn't Happen Here: Why Socialism Failed in the United States*. New York: Norton.

LU, C. (2005). 'Delivering the Goods and the Good: Repairing Moral Wrongs', in D. Dyzenhaus and M. Moran (eds.), *Calling Power to Account: Law, Reparations, and the Chinese Canadian Head Tax Case*. Toronto: University of Toronto Press.

LUCASSEN, L., and KÖBBEN, A. J. F. (1992). *Het partiële gelijk: Controverses over het onderwijs in de eigen taal en cultuur en de rol daarbij van beleid en wetenschap, 1951–1991*. Lisse: Swets & Zeitlinger.

LUCERO, J. A. (2001). 'Crisis and Contention in Ecuador'. *Journal of Democracy*, 12(2): 59–73.

LUCIUK, L. (1988). *A Time for Atonement: Canada's First National Internment Operations and the Ukrainian Canadians, 1914–1920*. Kingston: The Limestone Press.

LUTTMER, E. (2001). 'Group Loyalty and the Taste for Redistribution'. *Journal of Political Economy*, 109(3): 500–28.

MACDONALD, M. (2004). Debates and Proceedings, *Nova Scotia Hansard*, 1st Sess., 10 May, p. 3404 (**www.gov.ns.ca/legislature/hansard/han59-1/ house_04may10.htm**).

MACDONALD, R. (2000). Letter to the editor, *Edmonton Journal*, 30 Dec., p. A15.

MCDONOUGH, A. (2004). Parliament of Canada, Debates and Proceedings, *Edited Hansard*, 37th Parl., 3d Sess., 30 Mar., p. 1410. (**www.parl.gc.ca/37/3/ parlbus/chambus/house/debates/032_2004-03-30/han032_1410- e.htm**).

MCEWEN, N. (2002). 'State Welfare Nationalism: The Territorial Impact of Welfare State Retrenchment in Scotland'. *Regional and Federal Studies*, 10(1): 66–90.

—— (2006). *Nationalism and the State: Welfare and Identity in Scotland and Quebec*. Brussels: Peter Lang.

MACPHERSON, W. (1999). *The Stephen Lawrence Inquiry: Report of an inquiry by Sir William Macpherson of Cluny*, Cmnd 4262-I. London: The Stationery Office.

MACPIO (2001). *Pueblos indígenas y originarias de Bolivia: diagnóstico nacional*. La Paz: Ministerio de Asuntos Campesinos Pueblos Indígenas y Originarias.

MCROBERTS, K. (1993). *Quebec: Social Change and Political Crisis*. Toronto: McClelland & Stewart.

—— (1997). *Misconceiving Canada: The Struggle for National Unity*. Toronto: Oxford University Press.

376

MAHLER, V., and JESUIT, D. (2005). 'Fiscal Redistribution in the Developed Countries: New Insights from the Luxemboug Income Study'. Working Paper No. 392, Luxembourg Income Study (updated version) (**www.lisproject.org/publications/wpapersh.htm**).

MAIER, C. S. (1993). 'A Surfeit of Memory? Reflections on History, Melancholy, and Denial'. *History and Memory*, 5 (Fall/Winter): 136–52.

MALIK, KENAN (2005). 'Born in Bradford'. *Prospect* (Oct.): 54–6.

MANSILLA, H. C. F., and ZEGADA, M. T. (1996). *Política, cultura y etnicidad en Bolivia*. La Paz, Cochabamba: CEBEM, CESU.

MARGALIT, A., and HALBERTAL, M. (1994). 'Liberalism and the Right to Culture'. *Social Research*, 61(3): 491–510.

MARSHALL, B. (1995). Letter to the editor, *Vancouver Sun*, 1 Nov., p. A13.

MARSHALL, T. H. (1950). 'Citizenship and Social Class', in T. H. Marshall and T. Bottomore, *Citizenship and Social Class*. London: reprinted by Pluto Press (1992).

—— (1964). *Class, Citizenship and Social Development*. Chicago: University of Chicago Press.

—— and BOTTOMORE, T. (1992). *Citizenship and Social Class*. London: Pluto Press.

MAYORGA, F. (2002). *Neopopulismo y democracia: compadres y padrinos en la política boliviana (1988–1999)*. La Paz, Cochabamba: Plural, CESU-UMSS.

MERCADO LORA, M. (1998). 'La reforma del sistema de pensiones de la seguridad social', in J. C. Chávez Corrales (ed.), *Las reformas estructurales en Bolivia*. La Paz: Fundación Milenio.

MEYER, T. (2002). *Identitätspolitik. Vom Missbrauch kultureller Unterschiede* [Identity Politics: On the Abuse of Cultural Differences]. Frankfurt on Main: Suhrkamp.

MICKSCH, J. (ed.) (1983). *Multikulturelles Zusammenleben: Theologische Erfahrungen* [Multicultural Co-existence: Theological Experiences]. Frankfurt on Main: Verlag Otto Lembeck.

MIGUEL, E. (2004). 'Tribe or Nation? Nation-Building and Public Goods in Kenya and Tanzania'. *World Politics*, 56(3): 327–62.

—— and GUGARTY, M. K. (2005). 'Ethnic Diversity, Social Sanctions, and Public Goods in Kenya'. *Journal of Public Economics*, 89: 2325–68.

MIKI, A. (1996). 'Japanese Canadian Redress Strategy'. Paper presented at Chiefs' Special Assembly on Residential Schools, British Columbia Union of Indian Chiefs, Vancouver, 25–6 Mar.

—— (2003). *The Japanese Canadian Redress Legacy*. Winnipeg: National Association of Japanese Canadians.

—— (2004). *Redress: Inside the Japanese Canadian Call for Justice*. Vancouver: Raincoast Books.

MIKI, R., and KOBAYASHI, C. (eds.) (1991). *Justice in our Time: The Japanese Canadian Redress Settlement*. Vancouver: Talon Books.

MILAVSKY, T. [pseud.] (2004). Interview by M. James, 4 June, transcript, Winnipeg, Manitoba.

References

MILLER, D. (1995). *On Nationality*. Oxford: Oxford University Press.

—— (2000). *Citizenship and National Identity*. Cambridge: Polity Press.

—— (2002). 'Group Rights, Human Rights and Citizenship'. *European Journal of Philosophy*, 10: 178–95.

—— (2003).'What's Left of the Welfare State?' *Social Philosophy and Policy*, 20: 92–112.

—— (2004). 'Social Justice in Multicultural Societies', in P. Van Parijs (ed.), *Cultural Diversity versus Economic Solidarity*. Brussels: Deboeck University Press.

MILLER, J. R. (1996). *Shingwauk's Vision: A History of Native Residential Schools*. Toronto: University of Toronto Press.

Minority Rights Group (1997). *World Directory of Minorities*. London: Minority Right Group International.

MITCHELL, J., and BENNIE, L. (1996). 'Thatcherism and the Scottish Question', in *British Elections and Parties Yearbook 1995*. London: Frank Cass.

MONROE, A. D. (1979). 'Consistency between Public Preferences and National Policy'. *American Politics Quarterly*, 7(1): 3–19.

MONTALVO, J. and REYNAL-QUEROL, M. (2005). 'Ethnic Diversity and Economic Development'. *Journal of Development Economics*, 76(2): 293–323.

MOODY, K. (1988). *An Injury to All: The Decline of American Unionism*. London: Verso.

MORALES, J. A. (2003). 'The National Revolution and its Legacy', in M. S. Grindle and P. Domingo (eds.), *Proclaiming Revolution: Bolivia in Comparative Perspective*. Cambridge, Mass.: Harvard University Press.

MORENO, L. (2003). 'Europeanization, Mesogovernments and Safety Nets'. *European Journal of Political Research*, 42(2): 185–99.

—— and MCEWEN, N. (2005). 'Exploring the Territorial Politics of Welfare', in N. McEwen and L. Moreno (eds.), *The Territorial Politics of Welfare*. Abingdon: Routledge.

MORLEY, S. A., MACHADO, R., and PETTINATO, S. (1999). *Indexes of Structural Reform in Latin America*. Serie Reformas Económicas 12 (Jan.), ECLAC.

Mossawa Center (2004). 'Poverty Report 2003 Reflects the Discriminatory Policies against the Arab Community' Press Release (**www.mossawacenter.org/en/pressreleases/2004/11/041126.html**).

MYLES, J., and QUADAGNO, J. (2002). 'Political Theories of the Welfare State'. *Social Service Review*, 76: 34–57.

MYRDAL, G., ROSE, A. M., and STERNER, R. M. E. (1944). *An American Dilemma: The Negro Problem and Modern Democracy*. New York: Harper.

National Association of Japanese Canadians (1991). Presentation to the Special Joint Committee on a Renewed Canada, *Minutes of Proceedings and Evidence*, No. 16, 4 Nov.

National Clearinghouse for Bilingual Education (1999). *State Survey of Legislative Requirements for Educating Limited English Proficient Students* (**www.ncela.gwu.edu/pubs/reports/state-legislation/noframe.htm**).

NETTLE, D. (2000). 'Linguistic Fragmentation and the Wealth of Nations'. *Economic Development and Cultural Change*, 49: 335–48.

NIE, N. H., JUNN, J., and STEHLIK-BARRY, K. (1996). *Education and Democratic Citizenship in America*. Chicago: University of Chicago Press.

NIELSEN, R. (2001). 'Trudeau, Québec, and Imagined Grievances'. *Policy Options/Options politiques* (Jan.–Feb.): 88–90.

NITZSCHKE, V. (ed.) (1982). *Multikulturelle Gesellschaft: Multikulturelle Erziehung?* [Multicultural Society: Multicultural Education?]. Stuttgart: J. B. Metzler.

NOËL, A. (1999). *Etude générale sur l'Entente*. Report Commissioned by the Government of Quebec.

NORMAN, W. (1995). 'The Ideology of Shared Values: A Myopic Vision of Unity in the Multi-nation State', in J. H. Carens (ed.), *Is Quebec Nationalism Just? Perspectives from Anglophone Canada*. Montreal: McGill-Queen's University Press.

NRW (2000). *Zuwanderung und Integration in NRW* [Immigration and Integration in NRW]. Bericht der Interministeriellen Arbeitsgruppe 'Zuwanderung' der Landesregierung. Edited by the Ministerium für Arbeit und Soziales, Qualifikation und Technologie des Landes Nordrhein-Westfalen, Düsseldorf.

—— (2004). *Zuwanderung und Integration in Nordrhein-Westfalen. 3. Bericht der Landesregierung*. Ministerium für Gesundheit, Soziales, Frauen und Familie des Landes Nordrhein-Westfalen, Düsseldorf.

—— (2006). *Nordrhein-Westfalen: Land der neuen Integrationschancen—Aktionsplan Integration*, Düsseldorf.

O'BEIRNE, J. (1997). Letter to the editor, *Calgary Herald*, 3 Apr., p. A16.

OBERNDÖRFER, D. (1994). ' "Völkisches" Denken' ['Völkisch' thinking], *Die Zeit*, 10 June.

OBINGER, H., LEIBFRIED, S., AND CASTLES, F. (eds.) (2005). *Federalism and the Welfare State: New World and European Experiences*. Cambridge: Cambridge University Press.

O'DONNELL, G. (1999). 'Delegative Democracy', in G. O'Donnell, *Counterpoints: Selected Essays on Authoritarianism and Democratization*. Notre Dame: University of Notre Dame Press.

OECD (Organization for Economic Cooperation and Development) (1993). *Trends in International Migration* (Sopemi Reports).

—— (2003). *Trends in International Migration* (Sopemi Reports).

—— (2005). *Trends in International Migration, Annual Report* (**www.oecd.org/ dataoecd/24/29/34643131.DOC**).

Office of National Statistics (2004*a*). *Social Trends 3*. London: Palgrave.

—— (2004*b*). *Economics Trends Annual Supplement 29*. London: Palgrave.

Ökumenischer Vorbereitungsausschuss für den Tag des ausländischen Mitbürgers (1980). *Thesen zum Gespräch* [Discussion points]. Frankfurt on Main, 24 Sept.

OMATSU, M. (1992). *Bittersweet Passage: Redress and the Japanese Canadian Experience*. Toronto: Between the Lines.

References

ORLOFF, A. (1988). 'The Political Origins of America's Belated Welfare State', in M. Weir, A. Orloff, and T. Skocpol (eds.), *The Politics of Social Policy in the United States*. Princeton: Princeton University Press.

OXHORN, P. (2003). 'Social Inequality, Civil Society, and the Limits of Citizenship in Latin America', in S. E. Eckstein and T. P. Wickham-Crowley (eds.), *What Justice? Whose Justice?: Fighting for Fairness in Latin America*. Berkeley: University of California Press.

PALLETT, G. (1998). Letter to the editor, *Edmonton Journal*, 18 Nov., p. A21.

PALMER, B. D. (1983). *Working-Class Experience: The Rise and Reconstitution of Canadian Labour, 1800-1980*. Toronto: Butterworth.

PATERSON, L. (1994). *The Autonomy of Modern Scotland*. Edinburgh: Edinburgh University Press.

PATZI PACO, F. (2003). 'Rebelión indígena contra la colonidad y la transnacionalización de la economía: triunfos y vicisitudes del movimiento indígena desde 2000 a 2003', in F. Hylton, F. Patzi, S. Serulnikov, and S. Thomson, *Ya es otro tiempo el presente: cuatro momentos de insurgencia indígena*. La Paz: Muela del Diablo.

PAUNOVIC, I. (2000). *Growth and Reforms in Latin America and the Caribbean in the 1990s*. Serie Reformas Económicas 70 (May), ECLAC.

PEARCE, N. (2004). 'Diversity versus Solidarity: A New Progressive Dilemma'. *Renewal: A Journal of Labour Politics*, 12(3).

PELINKA, A., and ROSENBERGER, S. (2003). *Österreichische Politik: Grundlagen, Strukturen, Trends* [Austrian Politics: Fundamentals, Structures, Trends]. Vienna: WUV.

PELS, D. (2003). *De geest van Pim: Het gedachtegoed van een politieke dandy*. Amsterdam: Anthos.

PÉREZ BALTODANO, A. (ed.) (1997). *Globalización, ciudadanía y política social en América Latina: tensiones y contradicciones*. Caracas: Nueva Sociedad.

PETERSON, P. (1995). *The Price of Federalism*. Washington, DC: Brookings Institution.

PHALET, K., and TER WAL, J. (eds.) (2004). *Moslim in Nederland*. The Hague: SCP/Ercomer.

—— VAN LOTRINGEN, C., and ENTZINGER, H. (2000). *Islam in de multiculturele samenleving: Opvattingen van jongeren in Rotterdam*. Utrecht: ERCOMER.

PHILLIPS, A. (1995). *The Politics of Presence*. Oxford: Oxford University Press.

—— (1999). *Which Equalities Matter?* Cambridge: Polity Press.

—— (2003). 'Recognition and the Struggle for Political Voice', in B. Hobson (ed.), *Recognition Struggles and Social Movements: Contested Identities, Agency, and Power*. Cambridge: Cambridge University Press.

PIERSON, P. (2001). 'Coping with Permanent Austerity: Welfare State Restructuring in Affluent Democracies', in P. Pierson (ed.), *The New Politics of the Welfare State*. Oxford: Oxford University Press.

—— (ed.) (2001). *The New Politics of the Welfare State*. Oxford: Oxford University Press.

PIVEN, F. (1995). 'Is it Global Economics or Neo-laissez-faire?' *New Left Review*, 213: 107–14.

PLOTNICK, R., and WINTERS, R. (1985). 'A Politico-Economic Theory of Income Redistribution'. *American Political Science Review*, 79: 458–73.

PNUD (2002). *Informe de desarrollo humano en Bolivia, 2002*. La Paz: Programa de las Naciones Unidas para el Desarrollo.

—— (2004). *Interculturalismo y globalización: La Bolivia posible—Informe Nacional de Desarrollo Humano 2004*. La Paz: Programa de las Naciones Unidas para el Desarrollo.

POIRIER, J., and VANSTEENKISTE, S. (2000). 'Le Débat sur la fédéralisation de la sécurité sociale en Belgique: le miroir du vouloir-vivre ensemble?' *Revue belge de securité sociale*, 2: 331–79.

POSNER, D. (2005). 'Ethnic Diversity and Local Goods Provision: Evidence from Kampala, Uganda'. Paper prepared for presentation to the World Bank conference on 'New Frontiers of Social Policy: Development in a Globalizing World', Arusha, Tanzania, December.

POSTERO, N. (2003). 'The Conditions of Democracy: Governmentality and Indigenous Citizenship in Neoliberal Bolivia'. Unpublished paper.

POWELL, M. (1995). 'The Strategy of Equality Revisited'. *Journal of Social Policy*, 24: 163–85.

PREUHS, R. R. (2005). 'Descriptive Representation, Legislative Leadership, and Direct Democracy: Latino Influence on English Only Laws in the States, 1984–2002'. *State Politics and Policy Quarterly*, 5(3): 203–24.

Prisma (2000). *Las políticas sobre la pobreza en Bolivia: dimensión, políticas y resultados (1985–1999)*. La Paz: Instituto Prisma, Plural.

PUTNAM, R. D. (1993). *Making Democracy Work: Civic Traditions in Modern Italy*. Princeton: Princeton University Press.

—— (2004). 'Who Bonds? Who Bridges? Findings from the Social Capital Benchmark Survey'. Presentation to the annual meetings of the American Political Science Association, Chicago, September.

QUADAGNO, J. (1988). *The Transformation of Old Age Security: Class and Politics in the American Welfare State*. Chicago: University of Chicago Press.

—— (1994). *The Color of Welfare*. New York: Oxford University Press.

RADTKE, F.-O. (1991a). 'Die Politik des Multikulturalismus' [The Politics of Multiculturalism]. *Kommune*, (2): 42–4.

—— (1991b). 'Lob der Gleich-Gültigkeit: Die Konstruktion des Fremden im Diskurs des Multikulturalismus' [In praise of Indifference: The Construction of the Alien in the Multicultural Discourse], in U. Bielefeld (ed.), *Das Eigene und das Fremde*. Hamburg: Junius.

—— (2003). 'Multiculturalism in Germany: Local Management of Immigrants' Social Inclusion'. *International Journal on Multicultural Societies*, 5(1): 55–76.

RATH, J. (1991). *Minorisering: de sociale constructie van 'etnische minderheden'*. Amsterdam: Sua.

RAUDENBUSH, S. W., and BRYK, A. S. (2002). *Hierarchical Linear Models: Applications and Data Analysis Methods*. London: Sage Publications.

REICH, H. H. (2000). 'Die Gegner des Herkunftssprachen-Unterrichts und ihre Argumente' [The Opponents of the Teaching of the Languages of Origin and their Arguments]. *Deutsch lernen*, 2: 112–26.

RHODES, M. (1996). 'Globalization, the State and the Restructuring of Regional Economies', in P. Gummet (ed.), *Globalization and Public Policy*. Cheltenham: Edward Elgar.

RICE, J., and PRINCE, M. (1993). 'Lowering the Safety Net and Weakening the Bonds of Nationhood: Social Policy in the Mulroney Years', in S. D. Philips (ed.), *How Ottawa Spends 1993-94: A More Democratic Canada?* Ottawa: Carleton University Press.

RIVERA CUSICANQUI, S. (2003). *Oprimidos pero no vencidos: luchas del campesinado aymara y qhechwa 1900–1980*. La Paz: Yachaywasi (1st edn. in 1984).

ROBERTS, K. M. (1998). *Deepening Democracy? The Modern Left and Social Movements in Chile and Peru*. Stanford, Calif.: Stanford University Press.

RODDEN, J. (2003). 'Reviving Leviathan: Fiscal Federalism and the Growth of Government'. *International Organization*, 57(4): 695–729.

RODRÍGUEZ OSTRIA, G. (1999). 'Industria; producción, mercancías y empresarios', in F. Campero Prudencio (ed.), *Bolivia en el siglo XX: la formación de la Bolivia Contemporánea*. La Paz: Havard Club de Bolivia.

ROKKAN, S., and URWIN, D. W. (1982). 'Centres and Peripheries in Western Europe', in S. Rokkan and D. W. Urwin, *The Politics of Territorial Identity: Studies in European Regionalism*. London: Sage Publications.

ROMERO BALLIVIÁN, S. (2003). *Geografía electoral de Bolivia* (3rd edn.). La Paz: Fundemos.

ROODENBURG, H. J., EUWALS, R., and TER REELE, H. J. M. (2003). *Immigration and the Dutch Economy*. The Hague: CPB.

RORTY, R. (1998). *Achieving our Country: Leftist Thought in Twentieth Century America*. Cambridge, Mass.: Harvard University Press.

—— (2000). 'Is "Cultural Recognition" a Useful Concept for Leftist Politics?' *Critical Horizons*, 1: 7–20.

RUIZ HERNÁNDEZ, M., and BURGUETE CAL Y MAYOR, A. (2001). 'Indigenous Peoples without Political Parties: The Dilemmas of Indigenous Representation in Latin America', in K. Wessendorf (ed.), *Challenging Politics: Indigenous Peoples' Experiences with Political Parties and Elections*. Copenhagen: IWGIA.

RÜTTEN, A. (1998). 'Integrationspolitik der Landesregierung Nordrhein-Westfalen' [The Integration Policy of the State Government of North Rhine Westfalia], in Forschungsinstitut der Friedrich-Ebert-Stiftung, Abt. Arbeit und Sozialpolitik (ed.) [Electronic ed.]. *Ghettos oder ethnische Kolonie? Entwicklungschancen von Stadtteilen mit hohem Zuwandereranteil*, (Gesprächskreis Arbeit und Soziales; 85, Bonn).

SALTER, F. K. (ed.) (2004). *Welfare, Ethnicity and Altruism: New Findings and Evolutionary Theory*. London: Frank Cass.

SANEY, I. (2002). 'On Reparations', *Shunpiking* (**www.shunpiking.com/bhs/On%20Reparations.htm**).

SANTOS, W. G. (1987). *Cidadanía e justiça: a política social na ordem brasileira* (2nd edn.). Rio de Janeiro: Campus.

SCHAIN, M. (1999). 'Minorities and Immigrant Integration in France', in C. Joppke and S. Lukes (eds.), *Multicultural Questions*. Oxford: Oxford University Press.

SCHEFFER, P. (2000). 'Het multiculturele drama', *NRC Handelsblad*, 29 Jan.

_____ (2003). 'The Land of Arrival', in R. Cuperus, K. A. Duffek, and J. Kandel (eds.), *The Challenge of Diversity: European Social Democracy Facing Migration, Integration and Multiculturalism*. Innsbruck: StudienVerlag (English translation of Scheffer 2000).

SCHIERUP, C. U. (1997). 'Multiculturalism and Universalism in the United States and EU-Europe', in H.-R. Wicker (ed.), *Rethinking Nationalism and Ethnicity: The Struggle for Meaning and Order in Europe*. Oxford: Berg.

_____ HANSEN, P., and CASTLES, S. (2006). *Migration, Citizenship, and the European Welfare State: A European Dilemma*. Oxford: Oxford University Press.

SCHILDKRAUT, D. J. (2001). 'Official English and the States: Influence on Declaring English the Official Language in the United States'. *Political Research Quarterly*, 54 (June): 445–57.

SCHILY, O. (2002a). 'Ich möchte keine zweisprachigen Ortsschilder haben' [I do not want to have bilingual city signs], *Süddeutsche Zeitung*, 27 June.

_____ (2002b). 'Soziale Integration in der deutschen Gesellschaft als politische Aufgabe' [Social integration in German society as a political task]. *Zeitschrift für Ausländerrecht und Ausländerpolitik*, ZAR-Dokumentation, 22(10): 371–5.

SCHNAPPER, D. (1998). *The Community of Citizens*. New Brunswick, NJ: Transaction Publishers.

SCHÖNWÄLDER, K. (1991). 'Zu viele Ausländer in Deutschland? Zur Entwicklung ausländerfeindlicher Einstellungen in der Bundesrepublik' [Too Many Foreigners in Germany? On the Development of Xenophobic Attitudes in the Federal Republic]. *Vorgänge*, 112: 1–11.

_____ (1995). 'No Constitutionally Guaranteed Respect for Minorities in Germany'. *New Community*, 21: 421–4.

SCHÖNWÄLDER, K. (1996a). 'The Constitutional Protection of Minorities in Germany: Weimar Revisited'. *Slavonic and East European Review*, 74: 38–65.

_____ (1996b). 'Migration, Refugees and Ethnic Plurality as Issues of Public and Political Debates in (West) Germany', in M. Fulbrook and D. Cesarani (eds.), *Citizenship, Nationality and Migration in Europe*. London: Routledge.

_____ (1997). 'Schutz ethnischer Minderheiten' [The Protection of Ethnic Minorities], in P. Nitschke and N. Konegen (eds.), *Revision des Grundgesetzes?* Opladen: Leske und Budrich.

SCHÖNWÄLDER, K. (2001). *Einwanderung und ethnische Pluralität. Politische Entscheidungen und öffentliche Debatten in Großbritannien und der Bundesrepublik von den 1950er bis zu den 1970er Jahren* [Immigration and Ethnic Plurality. Political Decisions and Public Debates in Great Britain and the Federal Republic from the 1950s to the 1970s]. Essen: Klartext.

—— (2004) 'Kleine Schritte, verpasste Gelegenheiten, neue Konflikte: Zuwanderungsgesetz und Migrationspolitik' [Small Steps, Missed Opportunities, New Conflicts: Immigration Law and Migration Policy]. *Blätter für deutsche und internationale Politik*, 49(10): 1205–14.

SCHRAM, S., and SOSS, J. (1998). 'Making Something out of Nothing: Welfare Reform and a New Race to the Bottom'. *Publius, the Journal of Federalism*, 28(3): 67–88.

SCHULTE, A. (1990). 'Multikulturelle Gesellschaft: Chance, Ideologie oder Bedrohung?' [Multicultural Society: Opportunity, Ideology, or Threat?]. *Aus Politik und Zeitgeschichte* B 23–4: 3–15.

SCHULTZ, G. M. (2003). 'A New Day for Bolivia'. *NACLA Report on the Americas*, 37(3): 8–10.

SCP (Social and Cultural Planning Office) (2004). *In het zicht van de toekomst: Sociaal en Cultureel Rapport 2004*. The Hague: SCP.

SEOANE, J. (ed.) (2003). *Movimientos sociales y conflicto en América Latina*. Buenos Aires: CLACSO.

Shack Jang Mack et al. v. A.G. Canada (2002). 165 O.A.C. 17.

SHERIF, M., HARVEY, O. J., WHITE, B. J., HOOD, W. R., and SHERIF, C. W. (1961). *Intergroup Conflict and Cooperation: The Robber's Cave Experiment*. Norman: University of Oklahoma Book Exchange.

Shunpiking (2002). 'Annual Black History Supplement 2002' (**www.shunpiking.com/bhs/bhsindex.htm**).

SIEDER, R. (ed.) (2002). *Multiculturalism in Latin America: Indigenous Rights, Diversity and Democracy*. London: Palgrave/MacMillan.

SIMEON, R. (1972). *Federal-Provincial Diplomacy: The Making of Recent Policy in Canada*. Toronto: University of Toronto Press.

SIMMONDS, G. B. (2001). Letter to the editor, *Daily News* (Halifax), 26 Aug., p. 16.

SIVAK, M. (2001). *El dictador elegido: biografía no autorizada de Hugo Banzer Suárez*. La Paz: Plural.

SKOCPOL, THEDA (1992). *Protecting Mothers and Soldiers: The Political Origins of Social Policy in the United States*. Cambridge, Mass.: Harvard University Press.

SMITH, M. (2005). 'Resisting and Reinforcing Neoliberalism: Lesbian and Gay Organizing at the Federal and Local Levels in Canada'. *Policy & Politics*, 33 (Jan.): 75–93.

SMITH, T. (2004). *France in Crisis: Welfare, Inequality and Globalization since 1980*. Cambridge: Cambridge University Press.

SNIDERMAN, P., PERI, P., DE FIGUEREDI, R., and PIAZZA, T. (2001). *The Outsider: Prejudice and Politics in Modern Italy*. Princeton, NJ: Princeton University Press.

―――― BRODY, R. A., and TETLOCK, P. E. (1991), *Reasoning and Choice: Explorations in Political Psychology*. Cambridge: Cambridge University Press.

SOROKA, S., BANTING, K., and JOHNSTON, R. (2006). 'Immigration and Redistribution in the Global Era', in M. Wallerstein and S. Bowles (eds.), *Globalization and Social Redistribution*. Princeton and New York: Princeton University Press and the Russell Sage Foundation.

―――― JOHNSTON, R., and BANTING, K. (2006). 'Ethnicity, Trust, and the Welfare State', in F. Kay and R. Johnston (eds.), *Social Capital, Diversity and the Welfare State*. Vancouver, BC: University of British Columbia Press.

SOSS, J., SCHRAM, S., and FORDING, R. (eds.) (2003). *Race and the Politics of Welfare Reform*. Ann Arbor, Mich.: University of Michigan Press.

―――― ―――― VARTANIAN, T., and O'BRIEN, E. (2001). 'Setting the Terms of Relief: Explaining State Policy Choices in the Devolution Revolution'. *American Journal of Political Science*, 45(2): 378–95.

SOTTOLI, S. (2000). 'La política social en América Latina bajo el signo de la economía de mercado y la democracia'. *Revista Europea de Estudios Latinoamericanos y del Caribe/European Review of Latin American and Caribbean Studies*, 68: 3–22.

SPD (2002). *Regierungsprogramm 2002–2006* [Government Programme 2002–6] (**http://regierungsprogramm.spd.de**).

SPD-Bundestagsfraktion (2001). Querschnittsarbeitsgruppe Integration und Zuwanderung, *Die neue Politik der Zuwanderung: Steuerung, Integration, innerer Friede. Die Eckpunkte der SPD-Bundestagsfraktion* [The New Policy of Immigration: Control, Integration, Internal Peace. The Key Points of the Parliamentary Faction of the SPD], Berlin.

SPINNER, J. (1994). *The Boundaries of Citizenship: Race, Ethnicity and Nationality in the Liberal State*. Baltimore: Johns Hopkins University Press.

STEPHENS, J. (1979). *The Transition from Capitalism to Socialism*. Urbana: University of Illinois Press.

STRAßBURGER, G. (2001). *Evaluation von Integrationsprozessen in Frankfurt am Main* [Evaluation of Integration Processes in Frankfurt on Main]. Bamberg: efms.

STREECK, W. (1997). 'German Capitalism: Does it Exist? Can it Survive?' *New Political Economy*, 2(2): 237–56.

STRONG-BOAG, V. (1994). 'Contested Space: The Politics of Canadian Memory'. *Journal of the Canadian Historical Association*, 5: 3–17.

SULLIVAN, J. L., and TRANSUE, J. E. (1999). 'The Psychological Underpinnings of Democracy: A Selective Review of Research on Political Tolerance, Interpersonal Trust, and Social Capital'. *Annual Review of Psychology*, 50: 625–50.

SVALLFORS, S. (1997). 'Worlds of Welfare and Attitudes to Redistribution: A Comparison of Eight Western Nations'. *European Sociological Review*, 13(3): 283–304.

SWANK, D. (2002). *Global Capital, Political Institutions, and Political Change in Developed Welfare States*. Cambridge: Cambridge University Press.

SWENDEN, W. (2002). 'Asymmetric Federalism and Coalition-making in Belgium'. *Publius, the Journal of Federalism*, 32(3): 67–88.

SZÉKELY, M., LUSTIG, N., CUMPA, M., and MEJÍA, J. A. (2000). *Do We Know How Much Poverty There Is?* Washington: Inter-American Development Bank.

TAMIR, Y. (1993). *Liberal Nationalism*. Princeton: Princeton University Press.

TAPIA MEALLA, L., and TORANZO ROCA, C. (2000). *Retos y dilemas de la representación política*. La Paz: PNUD (Cuaderno de Futuro 8).

TATALOVICH, R. (1995). *Nativism Reborn? The Official English Language Movement and the American States*. Lexington, Ky.: The University of Kentucky Press.

TAVUCHIS, N. (1991). *Mea Culpa: A Sociology of Apology and Reconciliation*. Stanford, Calif.: Stanford University Press.

TAYLOR, C. (1994). 'The Politics of Recognition', in A. Gutmann (ed.), *Multiculturalism and the Politics of Recognition*. Princeton, NJ: Princeton University Press.

TAYLOR, S. (2002). 'Do African-Americans Really Want Racial Preferences', *National Journal*, 20 Dec.

TAYLOR-GOOBY, P. (1998). 'Commitment to the Welfare State', in R. Jowell et al. (eds.), *British—and European—Social Attitudes: The 15th Report*. Aldershot: Ashgate.

—— (2005). 'Is the Future American? Or, Can Left Politics Preserve European Welfare States from Erosion through Growing "Racial" Diversity?' *Journal of Social Policy*, 34(4): 661–72.

TICONA A., E., ROJAS O., G., and ALBO C., X. (1995). *Votos y Wiphalas: campesinos y pueblos originarios en democracia*. La Paz: Fundación Milenio, CIPCA.

TORPEY, J. (2001). ' "Making Whole What Has Been Smashed": Reflections on Reparations'. *Journal of Modern History*, 73 (June): 333–59.

—— (2003). 'Introduction: Politics and the Past', in J. Torpey (ed.), *Politics and the Past: On Repairing Historical Injustices*. Lanham, Md.: Rowman and Littlefield.

—— (forthcoming). 'Victims and Citizens: The Discourse of Reparation(s) at the Dawn of the New Millennium', in S. Parmentier (ed.), *Reparation for Victims of Gross and Systematic Human Righs Violations*. Antwerp: Intersentia.

TUMLIN, K., ZIMMERMAN, W., and OST, J. (1999). *State Snapshots of Public Benefits for Immigrants: Occasional Paper Number 24, Supplemental Report*. Washington, DC: The Urban Institute.

UDAPE (2003). *Bolivia: Evaluación de la Economía—Primer semestre 2003*. La Paz: Unidad de Análisis de Políticas Sociales y Económicas.

UITERMARK, J., and DUYVENDAK, J. W. (2004). 'De weg naar sociale insluiting. Over segregatie, spreiding en sociaal kapitaal', in RMO (Council for Social Development), *Over insluiting en vermijding: Twee essays over segregratie en integratie*. The Hague: RMO.

Ukrainian Canadian Civil Liberties Association (2004). 'Conservative Party of Canada Supports Redress' (**www.uccla.ca/pressreleases/internment/press68.html**).

ULLRICH, C. G. (2000*a*). *Solidarität im Sozialversicherungsstaat: Die Akzeptanz des Solidarprinzips in der gesetzlichen Krankenkasse* [Solidarity in the Social Insurance State: The Acceptance of the Principle of Solidarity in the Obligatory Health Insurance]. Frankfurt on Main: Campus.

―― (2000*b*) 'Die soziale Akzeptanz des Wohlfahrtsstaates: Ergebnisse, Kritik und Perspektiven einer Forschungsrichtung' [The Acceptance of the Welfare State: Results, Criticism and Perspectives of a Strand of Research]. *Soziale Welt*, 51: 131–52.

VAILLANCOURT, F., and RAULT, S. (2003). 'The Regional Dimensions of Federal Inter-governmental and Interpersonal Transfers in Canada, 1981–2001', in C. Jeffery and D. Heald (eds.), *Money Matters: Territorial Finance in Decentralized States*. Special issue of *Regional and Federal Studies*, 13(4): 130–52.

VAILLANCOURT, Y. (1988). *L'Évolution des Politiques Sociales au Québec, 1940–1960*. Montreal: Les Presses de l'Université de Montréal.

VALLS, A. (1999). 'The Libertarian Case for Affirmative Action'. *Social Theory and Practice*, 25: 299–323.

VAN COTT, D. L. (2000). *The Friendly Liquidation of the Past: The Politics of Diversity in Latin America*. Pittsburgh: University of Pittsburgh Press.

―― (2001). 'Explaining Ethnic Autonomy Régimes in Latin America'. *Studies in Comparative International Development*, 35(4): 30–58.

―― (2002). 'Constitutional Reform in the Andes: Redefining Indigenous-State Relations', in R. Sieder (ed.), *Multiculturalism in Latin America: Indigenous Rights, Diversity and Democracy*. London: Palgrave Press.

―― (2003*a*). 'Andean Indigenous Movements and Constitutional Transformation: Venezuela in Comparative Perspective'. *Latin American Perspectives*, 30(1): 49–70.

―― (2003*b*). 'From Exclusion to Inclusion: Bolivia's 2002 Elections'. *Journal of Latin American Studies*, 35: 751–75.

―― (2005). *From Movements to Parties: The Evolution of Ethnic Politics in Latin America*. Cambridge: Cambridge University Press.

Vancouver Sun (1998). 'Residential Schools: A Sad History of Abuse', 8 Jan., p. A3.

VAN PARIJS, P. (2004). 'Cultural Diversity against Economic Soliarity', in P. Van Parijs (ed.), *Cultural Diversity versus Economic Solidarity*. Brussels: Deboeck University Press.

VEENMAN, J. (ed.) (2002). *De toekomst in meervoud: Perspectief op multicultureel Nederland*. Assen: Van Gorcum.

VENNE, M. (1996). 'Le déroulement de la campagne', in D. Monière and J. H. Guay (eds.), *La Bataille du Québec, troisième épisode: 30 jours qui ébranlèrent le Canada*. Montreal: Fides.

VERNON, R. (2003). 'Against Restitution'. *Political Studies*, 51: 542–57.

WALTON, M. (2004). 'Neoliberalism in Latin America: Good, Bad, or Incomplete?' *Latin American Research Review*, 39(3): 165–83.

WANSINK, H. (2004). *De erfenis van Fortuyn: De Nederlandse democratie na de opstand van de kiezers*. Amsterdam: Meulenhoff.

WEIR, M. (1992). *Politics and Jobs: The Boundaries of Employment Policy in the United States*. Princeton: Princeton University Press.

WELLER, M. (ed.) (2004). *The Rights of Minorities: A Commentary on the European Framework Convention for the Protection of National Minorities*. Oxford: Oxford University Press.

WHITEHEAD, L. (2001*a*). 'The Viability of Democracy', in J. Crabtree and L. Whitehead (eds.), *Towards Democratic Viability: The Bolivian Experience*. Houndmills: Palgrave.

—— (2001*b*). 'The Emergence of Democracy in Bolivia', in J. Crabtree and L. Whitehead (eds.), *Towards Democratic Viability: The Bolivian Experience*. Houndmills: Palgrave.

WHITELEY, P. (1981). 'Public Opinion and the Demand for Social Welfare in Britain'. *Journal of Social Policy*, 10(4): 453–70.

WHITE PAPER (2002). *Secure Border, Safe Haven: Integration with Diversity in Modern Britain*. London: Government Printing Office.

WILENSKY, H. (1975). *The Welfare State and Equality: Structural and Ideological Roots of Public Expenditures*. Berkeley, Calif.: University of California Press.

—— (1981). 'Democratic Corporatism, Consensus and Social Policy: Reflections on Changing Values and "Crisis" of the Welfare State', in H. Wilensky, *Welfare State in Crisis*. Paris: OECD.

—— (2002). *Rich Democracies: Political Economy, Public Policy, and Performance*. Berkeley, Calif.: University of California Press.

—— and LEBEAUX, C. N. (1965). *Industrial Society and Social Welfare*. New York: The Free Press.

WILLIAMS, M. (1998). *Voice, Trust and Memory: Marginalized Groups and the Failings of Liberal Representation*. Princeton: Princeton University Press.

WILSON, W. J. (1980). *The Declining Significance of Race*. Chicago: University of Chicago Press.

WINCOTT, D. (2005). 'Reshaping Public Space? Devolution and Policy Change in British Early Childhood Education and Care', in M. Keating and N. McEwen (eds.), *Devolution and Public Policy*. Special issue of *Regional and Federal Studies*, 14(4): 453–70.

WLEZIEN, C. (2004). 'Patterns of Representation: Dynamics of Public Preferences and Policy'. *Journal of Politics*, 66: 1–24.

WOLFE, A., and KLAUSEN, J. (1997). 'Identity Politics and the Welfare State'. *Social Philosophy and Policy*, 14(2): 231–55.

—— —— (2000). 'Other Peoples'. *Prospect* (Dec.): 28–33.

WOLFINGER, R. E. (1974). *The Politics of Progress*. Englewood Cliffs, NJ: Prentice-Hall.

WOODS, K. (2002). 'Health Policy and the NHS in the UK 1997–2002', in J. Adams and P. Robinson (eds.), *Devolution in Practice: Public Policy Differences within the UK*. London: IPPR.

World Bank (2000). *Bolivia: From Patronage to a Professional State; Bolivia Institutional and Governance Review*, Vol. i, Main Report (Report No. 20115-BO). Washington: World Bank.

YOUNG, C. (2000). 'Deciphering Disorder in Africa: Is Identity the Key?' *World Politics*, 54(4): 532–57.

YOUNG, I. M. (1995). 'Together in Difference: Transforming the Logic of Group Political Conflict', in W. Kymlicka (ed.), *The Rights of Minority Cultures*. Oxford: Oxford University Press.

Name Index

Abel, C. 306
African-Canadian Legal Clinic 230
Africville Genealogy Society 226, 236
Agencia de Noticias Plurinacional del
    Ecuador 289
Aguirre, A. 306
Albó C., X. 291, 300, 312 n13, 313,
    316 n18
Alcántára Sáez, M. 290
Alesina, A. 25, 26, 27, 28, 30, 81, 93, 343,
    351
Allen, D. 236
Andersen, J. 43
Andolina, R. 285, 292
Andreß, H.-J. 219
Angeletos, G.-M. 351
Angenendt, S. 205
Appiah, A. 13
Archer, K. 239
Arocha, J. 273 n2
Arriba, A. 256
Arts, W. 194
Arze, C. 306
Arze Cuadros, E. 302
Asher, K. 273 n2
Assies, W. 37, 278 n5, 288, 312, 314,
    317
Aubry, J. 244

Bade, K.J. 211
Balkenende, J. P. 185
Banting, K.G. 32, 43, 65 n14, 77, 79,
    80 n20, 80 n21, 94–95, 100 n1, 104–105,
    109, 110 n8, 152, 154, 178, 187, 190, 195,
    197, 202 n, 205, 222, 223, 229, 234, 235,
    253, 255, 256, 257, 259, 262, 275, 276,
    279, 284, 289, 324, 325, 326 n1, 329, 344,
    345, 350
Baqir, R. 25
Barié, C.J. 277
Barkan, E. 224, 225, 243
Barnes, A. [pseud.] 230, 237, 242

Barry, B. 6, 8 n5, 10 n9, 11, 12, 13, 15–16,
    17, 20, 21 n15, 39, 63 n12, 71, 85–88,
    93–94, 97–98, 104, 149, 152, 222 n1, 253,
    324, 325–326, 327
Baubock, R. 41
Baudewyns, P. 264, 265, 266
Baumert, J. 215
Bazylevich, M. 240
Beck, U. 233
Béland, D. 255, 264, 265, 266, 346
Belltzer, R. 194
Belsley, D.A. 109
Benhabib, S. 9
Bennie, L. 267
Berthin Siles, G. 304
Biezefeld, R. 194
Bjørklund, T. 43
Blair, T. 269
Bloemraad, I. 40 n25, 352
Blunkett, D. 157
Boadway, R. 262
Bobo, L. 157, 175–176
Boismenu, G. 262 n4
Boletin ICCI 288 n12
Bolkestein, F. 182
Bommes, M. 178, 211
Bonfil Batalla, G. 308 n8
Bornais, S. 242
Bos, F. 191, 192
Bottomore, T. 252
Bourdieu, P. 228, 234, 243
Braithwaite, V. 109
Brand, J. 267
Breton, R. 345, 350, 352, 353
Brochmann, G. 178
Brodie, J. 233
Brody, R.A. 176
Brooks, R. 30
Brown, G. 269
Brubaker, R. 6, 41, 53
Bryk, A.S. 112
Burguete Cal y Mayor, A. 289

Subject Index

The letter f indicates a figure, n a note and t a table